Oil Paintings in Public Ownership in Devon

The *Oil Paintings in Public Ownership* series of catalogues is an extraordinary work in progress. Published by The Public Catalogue Foundation, it is the result of the determined efforts of a small team of administrative staff, researchers and photographers spread across the United Kingdom.

Our national collection of oil paintings in public ownership is probably one of the finest anywhere in the world. It is held not just by our museums and galleries but is also to be found in hospitals, universities and other civic buildings throughout the United Kingdom. A large proportion of these paintings are not on display and many have never before been reproduced.

This series of books for the first time allows the public to see an entire photographic record of these works – a collection likely to number some 200,000 in total. In doing so, these volumes provide a unique insight into our nation's artistic and cultural history.

As Patron of The Public Catalogue Foundation, my visits to collections across the country have highlighted to me not only the desire of curators to publicise their paintings, but also the limited resources at their disposal. The Foundation's work goes a long way towards helping to create access to these collections, while at the same time giving the British public the opportunity to see and enjoy *all* the paintings that they own.

I wish The Public Catalogue Foundation every success in its continuing endeavours.

Camilla

Oil Paintings in Public Ownership

in

Devon

Master Patron
The Lord-Lieutenant of Devon

Coordinator: Caroline Nicholson
Photographer: Ian Wilkinson

The Public Catalogue Foundation

Patron
HRH The Duchess of Cornwall

Christie's is proud to be the sponsor of The Public Catalogue Foundation in its pursuit to improve public access to paintings held in public collections in the UK.

Christie's is a name and place that speaks of extraordinary art. Founded in 1766 by James Christie, the company is now the world's leading art business. Many of the finest works of art in UK public collections have safely passed through Christie's, as the company has had the privilege of handling the safe cultural passage of some of the greatest paintings and objects ever created. Christie's today remains a popular showcase for the unique and the beautiful.
In addition to acquisition through auction sales, Christie's regularly negotiates private sales to the nation, often in lieu of tax, and remains committed to leading the auction world in the area of Heritage sales.

CHRISTIE'S

Contents

Image opposite HRH The Duchess of Cornwall's statement: Frost, Terry, 1915–2003, *Lemon and White, Spring '63*, 1963,
Royal Albert Memorial Museum, (p. 132)
Image opposite title page: Lawrence, Thomas, 1769–1830 & Robertson, Christina, active 1823–1850, *Lady Louisa Barbara Rolle
(1796–1885)*, Great Torrington Almshouse, Town Lands and Poors Charities, (p. 225)

i   Appledore Library, Bideford Library, Devon Record Office, Larkbeare House, Exmouth Library, Honiton Library and Moretonhampstead Library are managed by Devon County Council.

ii   Ashburton & Buckfastleigh Community Hospital, Axminster Hospital, Dartmouth and Kingswear Hospital, Dawlish Community Hospital, Honiton Hospital, Moretonhampstead Hospital, Ottery St Mary Hospital, Seaton Hospital, Sidmouth Victoria Hospital and Totnes Hospital are managed by Devon Primary Care Trust.

iii   Axminster Guildhall is owned by Axminster Town Council.

iv   Penrose Almshouses are managed by the Barnstaple Municipal Trust.

v   Burton Art Gallery and Museum is managed by Torridge District Council.

vi   Dartmouth Guildhall is managed by Dartmouth Town Council.

vii   Exeter Guildhall is managed by Exeter City Council.

viii   Royal Albert Memorial Museum is managed by Exeter City Council.

ix   Royal Devon and Exeter Hospital is managed by the NHS Foundation Trust.

x   Wonford House Hospital is managed by the Devon Partnership NHS Trust.

xi   Tavistock Town Hall is managed by Tavistock Town Council.

xii   Tiverton Town Hall is managed by Mid Devon District Council.

xiii   Totnes Guildhall is managed by Totnes Town Council.

Foreword

For those whose childhoods span the '40s and early '50s and for whom entertainment in the pre-T.V. age was Papa's 12" Ravel 78s on the radiogram or a surreptitious expedition to the see-saws on the public playground – the circus was the Big Adventure. Coconut shies and Punch and Judy, elephants and clowns and trapeze artists. And Roundabouts.

Roundabouts meant horses. At home, it was ponies: live and truculent, edging forward as, with one foot in the stirrup and one still on the ground, you tried to mount; that blew out their bellies as you tightened the girth and shrank them as you grabbed the pommel to get on and the loose-girthed saddle sagged and slid round and down.

None of that at the circus. A proper twelve-hand horse that stood still as you mounted, a saddle that never slipped, reins to be dropped with impunity. No pulling of the head nor the ominous sag forwards onto its front knees with the intent to roll on the leaf bed with you still astride. Higher than the crowd, taller than your sisters, galloping effortlessly in a race you'd always win. And when all that palled with the years, the Dodgems. No Bumping or Boring. What was Boring? Bumped you happily were, but Bored? Never!

Devon is a place of memories for me. Ice creams and small wooden jigsaw puzzles; tales of Drake and scones and cream teas. Bideford and Barnstaple. Donkeys, sand and windbreaks. All of these memories there to be reawakened by a wander amongst the flashing fairground bulbs and tinny organ music, and the gaudily painted revolving platforms of that disappeared fairground adventure, still to be found at the Dingles Fairground Heritage Centre at Lifton.

For all the happiness of those post-war Devon holidays, there was much that was missed too. The Royal Albert in Exeter is worth a visit if only to enjoy its building. Yet the collection that graces it is fully worthy of that City. The enormous collection of portraits by Thomas Hudson in the Guildhall at Barnstable is a remarkable memorial to a Devon Master. It includes a portrait of John Gay, creator of The Beggar's Opera, whose success 'made the Rich, gay; and Gay, rich'.

To the south, don't ignore the Town Hall at Great Torrington. It used to include a magnificent Batoni of John Rolle Walter, though sadly (and expensively) he recently decamped to Exeter. There remain though, some excellent Hudsons and two fine, dazzling portraits by Lawrence of Lord and Lady Rolle in their coronation robes. That of Lady Louise is both grand and charming at the same time. Her sense of enjoyment at being painted remains palpable.

My affection for Devon I owe to my mother, for the holidays she arranged there. This catalogue though, is indebted elsewhere. The Lord Lieutenant of Devon, Eric Dancer, kindly and generously became our Master Patron. Assisted by Judy Grainger, whose diplomatic skills and persistence can only be marvelled at, he raised the funds that have made this volume possible. The County and the Foundation owe the Lieutenancy a considerable debt of gratitude.

As, too, all owe to those listed in this volume as its Financial Supporters, in particular Marjorie and Geoffrey Jones, Gavin Dollard and Devon County Council.

No volume ever happens, though, without the diligence and dedication of its County Coordinator, nor the techinical skill and the elegance of eye of the county photographer. Caroline Nicholson's expertise as our Coordinator is manifest throughout this catalogue – as are Ian Wilkinson's skills as our photographer. To them both, to the team of editors led by Daniel Whibley, to Sophie Kullmann, and to my assistant, Ruth Chadwick, go the Foundation's wholehearted thanks. As well as mine.

Fred Hohler, Founder

The Public Catalogue Foundation: People Involved

Financial Supporters

The Public Catalogue Foundation would like to express its profound appreciation to the following organisations and individuals who have made the publication of this catalogue possible.

The Lord-Lieutenant of Devon

Donations of £5,000 or more

Marjorie and Geoffrey Jones
    Charitable Trust

Donations of £1,000 or more

Devon County Council
G. J. D. Dollard

Other Donations

AVM Don Attlee
Lord Clinton's Charitable Trust
Lady Margaret Fortescue and The
    Countess of Arran
Major Terence Knox
Members of the Devon Lieutenancy

Dr P. J. and Mrs S. A. Norrey
Mrs Mark Parkhouse
Rear Admiral Chris Snow
Air Chief Marshal Sir Peter Squire
The Tucker Charitable Trust
Sir David Williams

Catalogue Scope and Organisation

Medium and Support

The principal focus of this series is oil paintings. However, tempera and acrylic are also included as well as mixed media, where oil is the predominant constituent. Paintings on all forms of support (e.g. canvas, panel, etc.) are included as long as the support is portable. The principal exclusions are miniatures, hatchments or other purely heraldic paintings and wall paintings *in situ*.

Public Ownership

Public ownership has been taken to mean any paintings that are directly owned by the public purse, made accessible to the public by means of public subsidy or generally perceived to be in public ownership. The term 'public' refers to both central government and local government. Paintings held by national museums, local authority museums, English Heritage and independent museums, where there is at least some form of public subsidy, are included. Paintings held in civic buildings such as local government offices, town halls, guildhalls, public libraries, universities, hospitals, crematoria, fire stations and police stations are also included.

Geographical Boundaries of Catalogues

The geographical boundary of each county is the 'ceremonial county' boundary. This county definition includes all unitary authorities. Counties that have a particularly large number of paintings are divided between two or more catalogues on a geographical basis.

Criteria for Inclusion

As long as paintings meet the requirements above, all paintings are included irrespective of their condition and perceived quality. However, painting reproductions can only be included with the agreement of the participating collections and, where appropriate, the relevant copyright owner. It is rare that a collection forbids the inclusion of its paintings. Where this is the case and it is possible to obtain a list of paintings, this list is given in the Paintings Without Reproductions section. Where copyright consent is refused, the paintings are also listed in the Paintings Without Reproductions section. All paintings in collections' stacks and stores are included, as well as those on display. Paintings which have been lent to other institutions, whether for short-term exhibition or long-term loan, are listed under the owner collection. In addition, paintings on long-term loan are also included under the borrowing institution when they are likely to remain there for at least another five years from the date of publication of this catalogue. Information relating to owners and borrowers is listed in the Further Information section.

Layout

Collections are grouped together under their home town. These locations are listed in alphabetical order. In some cases collections that are spread over a number of locations are included under a single owner collection. A number of collections, principally the larger ones, are preceded by curatorial forewords. Within each collection paintings are listed in order of artist surname. Where there is more than one painting by the same artist, the paintings are listed chronologically, according to their execution date.

The few paintings that are not accompanied by photographs are listed in the Paintings Without Reproductions section.

There is additional reference material in the Further Information section at the back of the catalogue. This gives the full names of artists, titles and media if it has not been possible to include these in full in the main section. It also provides acquisition credit lines and information about loans in and out, as well as copyright and photographic credits for each painting. Finally, there is an index of artists' surnames.

Key to Painting Information

Adam, Patrick William 1854–1929
Interior, Rutland Lodge: Vista through Open Doors 1920
oil on canvas 67.3 × 45.7
LEEAG.PA.1925.0671.LACF

Almost all paintings are reproduced in the catalogue. Where this is not the case they are listed in the Paintings Without Reproductions section. Where paintings are missing or have been stolen, the best possible photograph on record has been reproduced. In some cases this may be black and white. Paintings that have been stolen are highlighted with a red border. Some paintings are shown with conservation tissue attached to parts of the painting surface.

Artist name This is shown with the surname first. Where the artist is listed on the Getty Union List of Artist Names (ULAN), ULAN's preferred presentation of the name is given. In a number of cases the name may not be a firm attribution and this is made clear. Where the artist name is not known, a school may be given instead. Where the school is not known, the painter name is listed as *unknown artist*. If the artist name is too long for the space, as much of the name is given as possible followed by (…). This indicates the full name is given at the rear of the catalogue in the Further Information section.

Painting title A painting title followed by *(?)* indicates that the title is in doubt. Where the alternative title to the painting is considered to be better known than the original, the alternative title is given in parentheses. Where the collection has not given a painting a title, the publisher does so instead and marks this with an asterisk. If the title is too long for the space, as much of the title is given as possible followed by *(…)* and the full title is given in the Further Information section.

Execution date In some cases the precise year of execution may not be known for certain. Instead an approximate date will be given or no date at all.

Artist dates Where known, the years of birth and death of the artist are given. In some cases one or both dates may not be known with certainty, and this is marked. No date indicates that even an approximate date is not known. Where only the period in which the artist was active is known, these dates are given and preceded with the word *active*.

Medium and support Where the precise material used in the support is known, this is given.

Dimensions All measurements refer to the unframed painting and are given in cm with up to one decimal point. In all cases the height is shown before the width. An (E) indicates where a painting has not been measured and its size has been calculated by sight only. If the painting is circular, the single dimension is the diameter. If the painting is oval, the dimensions are height and width.

Collection inventory number In the case of paintings owned by museums, this number will always be the accession number. In all other cases it will be a unique inventory number of the owner institution. (P) indicates that a painting is a private loan. Details can be found in the Further Information section. Accession numbers preceded by 'PCF' indicate that the collection did not have an accession number at the time of catalogue production and therefore the number given has been temporarily allocated by The Public Catalogue Foundation. The ❋ symbol indicates that the reproduction is based on a Bridgeman Art Library transparency (go to www.bridgemanart.com) or that Bridgeman administers the copyright for that artist.

Facing page: Minton, John, 1917–1957, *Boy in a Landscape (Eric Verrico)* (detail), 1948, Royal Albert Memorial Museum, (p. 148)

THE PAINTINGS

Appledore Library

Clark, E. L
Seascape 1976
acrylic on board 40 x 67
PCF2

Mead, Geraldine active 2000
Portrait of a Vicar of Appledore
oil on board 76 x 59
PCF3

unknown artist
Garden Gate
acrylic on board 35 x 44
PCF1

North Devon Maritime Museum

The North Devon Museum Trust maintains a small collection of paintings in oils and acrylics housed at the North Devon Maritime Museum in Appledore, North Devon. The collection currently comprises 27 works, all with local or maritime connections, some of which are on public display, the remainder being kept in storage. They vary widely in technique, quality and date, from nineteenth-century local views and ship portraits to modern panels for museum displays.

The paintings' subjects include ship portraits, shipwrecks, historical incidents, local individuals and local views. Among the 13 ship portraits are works by eminent Victorian marine artists, Chinese School ship painters, local 'naïve' ship painters, and late twentieth-century artists. Three paintings of shipwrecks are roughly contemporary with the incidents depicted and two are later reconstructions. The collection includes two portraits by unidentified artists, one of a mariner and another of a gentleman. Two of the local scenes are nineteenth century, and two are modern reconstructions of historic scenes. The remaining paintings are largely generic scenes of ships and boats.

Mark Myers, North Devon Maritime Museum Trust Management Committee

Braund, P.
A Topsail Schooner
oil on canvas 33 x 47
2002.65

Chinese School
The Ship 'Glamorganshire'
oil on canvas card 41 x 58
2002.64

Cockell, Herb
The Five Masted Barque 'France'
oil on black velvet 42 x 49
2002.78

Cockell, Herb
The Four Masted Barque 'Rewa'
oil on black velvet 42 x 49
2002.79

Day, Archibald McCullum c.1852–1923
The Four Masted Ship 'Falls of Dee', 1896
oil on canvas 45 x 60
2002.59

Harris, L. (?)
The 'Pace di Fiume' Ashore at Westward Ho!
oil on canvas 18 x 23.5
2008.24

Heard, Joseph 1799–1859
The Brig 'Star' of Bideford, Devon 1853
oil on canvas 51 x 74
2002.75

Heard, Joseph (attributed to) 1799–1859
The Barque 'Hugenot' in a Gale
oil on canvas 54 x 76
2002.61

Jamieson, A.
The Four Masted Barque 'Colonial Empire' 1912
oil on canvas 50 x 66
2002.85

T. M.
The Topsail Schooner 'Kate'
oil on canvas 36 x 53
2002.66

Myers, Mark Richard b.1945
A Medieval Ship, Boat and Coaster in the Taw 1977
acrylic on hardboard 52 x 89
2002.77

Myers, Mark Richard b.1945
The 'Prudence' Prize at Barnstaple Quay, 1590 1977
acrylic on hardboard 122 x 165
2002.76

Myers, Mark Richard b.1945
The Relief of the 'Investigator' 1853 1977
acrylic on canvas 46 x 46
2001.55

Myers, Mark Richard b.1945
The 'Volunteer' Service to the 'Daniel', 1829 1978
acrylic on canvas 46 x 46
2001.56

Quance, G. M.
The Ketch 'Minnie Flossie' 1906
oil on canvas 59 x 83
2002.63

Ross, George active 1904–1912
The Four Masted Barque 'Loch Torridon' 1910
oil on canvas 61 x 91
2002.62

Ross, George active 1904–1912
The Schooner 'Madeleine' Ashore 1911
oil on canvas 53 x 38
2002.82

Ross, George active 1904–1912
A Yacht Race off the Isle of Wight 1912
oil on canvas 86 x 100
2002.81

Ross, George active 1904–1912
The Ketch 'Johnny Toole'
oil on canvas 58.5 x 76.5
1997.161

Semple, Joseph 1830–1877
The Barque 'Edmund Preston' 1864
oil on canvas 51 x 79
2002.6

Smith, Ivor
A Tribute to Bravery 1982
oil on hardboard 61 x 76
1997.109

unknown artist
A Sailing Boat in a Fresh Breeze
oil on card 18 x 23.5
2002.86

unknown artist
A View of Bideford, Devon, from the East
oil on paper 32 x 53
2002.84

unknown artist
Braunton Burrows Lighthouse, Devon
oil on canvas 18 x 36
1997.172

unknown artist
Portrait of a Gentleman (probably Mr Alexander Beara)
oil on canvas 61 x 46
2002.83

unknown artist
Portrait of a Mariner (associated with Philip R. Dart, mariner of Bideford)
oil on canvas 71 x 57
2000.8

unknown artist
The Ketch 'Margaret'
oil on board 30.5 x 40.5
PCF1

unknown artist
The Smack 'BE1'
oil on panel 31 x 51
1998.231

Ashburton & Buckfastleigh Community Hospital

Crowley, A. M. (Miss)
Bridge at Nantes, France
oil on board 50 x 75.5
PCF1

Axminster Guildhall

Gill, William active 1826–1871
View of Axminster, Devon*
oil on canvas 107 x 180
PCF1

Axminster Heritage

Hudson, Esdaile active 2004–2005
An Artist's Impression of Thomas Whitty (1716–1792) 2004
oil on canvas 38.5 x 29
PCF1

Lynch, Kate Mary b.1949
Carpet Weaving, Axminster Carpets, Axminster, Devon
oil on paper 29 x 23.5
PCF3

Lynch, Kate Mary b.1949
The Twister Attending His Bobbins of Plying Yarn, Buckfast Spinning Mill, Buckfastleigh, Devon
oil on paper 29 x 23.5
PCF2

Axminster Hospital

Clark, B.
Nyman's Gardens, West Sussex 2000
oil on board 29 x 39.5
PCF8

Cole, Susan
Flowers
oil on board 29.8 x 24.7
PCF9

B. H.
Roses
oil on canvas 40 x 30
PCF4

B. H.
Poppies
oil on board 29.3 x 40
PCF11

Humphries, Amelia
The Spinney
oil on board 38.5 x 49
PCF13

Martens
Still Life with a Magnifying Glass 1986
acrylic on board 29.2 x 39.5
PCF2

Morris, M. E. (Mrs)
Toller Fratrum Farmhouse, Dorset
oil on canvas 44.8 x 59.7
PCF1

Morris, Peter
View to the Obelisk
oil on board 34.5 x 19.5
PCF6

Pickard, Daphne Eileen b.1921
Axminster Market, Devon
oil on board 33.5 x 49.5
PCF16

Ridgeway, C. J.
Riverside Cottages 1978
oil on board 44.5 x 75
PCF10

Stalman, Joy active 1996–1998
Francesca's Camellias 1996
oil on board 40.5 x 54.5
PCF7

Stalman, Joy active 1996–1998
Dorset Hills 1998
oil on board 33 x 57
PCF12

unknown artist
Dr Jacinth Morton 1962
oil on board 47.7 x 37.9
PCF15

unknown artist
Harvest
oil on board 51 x 45
PCF14

unknown artist
Woodland
acrylic on board 34.5 x 24.5
PCF5

White, Margaret
Garden Corner 1999
oil on board 29.5 x 39.5
PCF3

Facing page: Gheeraerts the younger, Marcus (attributed to), 1561/1562–1635/1636, *Portrait of a Lady* (probably Mary Hungate), c.1620, Royal Albert Memorial Museum (p. 133)

Axminster Museum

Gill, William active 1826–1871
East Devon Farm
oil on board 44.7 x 59.5
1994.763

Gill, William active 1826–1871
Still Life with Flowers
oil on canvas 6.2 x 7.5
1994.764

Barnstaple Town Council

In 1739, Henry Rolle donated 29 paintings believed to be by Thomas Hudson to the borough. The Collection holds 32 works now recorded as 'studio of', 'style of' and 'attributed to' the artist. These were housed in the Guildhall, built during Henry VII's reign. Later they were moved to the present Guildhall.

It is unclear in what capacity Rolle and Hudson knew each other, but undoubtedly they were acquaintances. Little is known about Henry Rolle. He was elected to the position of Member of Parliament for Devon from 1730 to 1741 and then for Barnstaple from 1741 to 1747 – at that time Barnstaple still returned two MPs.

Thomas Hudson (1701–1779) was born in Devon, possibly in Bideford. He was a pupil of Jonathan Richardson. Embracing the art of portraiture as his profession, he succeeded Richardson as the most fashionable portraitist of that timeand, between 1745 and 1755, he operated the most successful studios in London. Thus, the portraits donated to the borough in 1739 are examples of a fledgling artist trying to make his mark.

Hudson painted countless portraits of the upper classes, 'people of quality' – a big difference from the tradesmen and merchants who made up Barnstaple borough. He fully deserved his eminence and plaudits, though the uninteresting character of costume and posture then in vogue has prevented full admiration of his endeavours. His style reveals a taste for refinement and elegance, and his portraits have often been noted for the excellence of their painted white satin and other portions of drapery, though this is perhaps due to the proficiency of Joseph Van Haecken, who was largely engaged to add the drapery while Hudson concentrated on the minutiae.

In 1740 Hudson, who was a frequent visitor to Bideford, came across the youthful Joshua Reynolds. The latter was shortly afterwards apprenticed by his parents to Hudson, whose studio he entered as assistant and pupil. Hudson's tuition could hardly have failed to be of lasting benefit to Reynolds, but the superior genius and brilliance of the latter soon showed itself, and after two years he resigned, or was dismissed, by Hudson through some discord. With the rise of Reynolds to prominence and prosperity, Hudson's supremacy came to an end and he eventually retired contentedly, remaining on good terms with Reynolds.

Other works in the Collection include portraits, like that of *Lionel T. Bencraft, Mayor of Barnstaple (1883)*. Bencraft served as Town Clerk and later became Mayor. Similarly, the Collection includes a picture of John Penrose, an oval bust in the style of Cornelius Janssens van Ceulen (1593–1661). Penrose, a wealthy wool merchant and Mayor in 1620, stipulated that the bulk of his wealth should be used to establish the almshouses constructed in 1627. *Frederick Hodgson, Esq.*, painted by Sir William Beechey (1753–1839) was presented to the Collection by Reverend Christopher Haggard, Hodgson's nephew. Hodgson was an MP and wealthy brewer who later died in Paris in 1854. There is a painting of *Richard Bremridge, Mayor of Barnstaple (1829 & 1859)* by an unknown artist of the English School, c.1850, who, in 1853, was unseated following an enquiry for buying votes in the election of 1852. Of all the votes counted more than a third had been corruptly acquired. In the 1864 election Bremridge stood again – and won – he was sworn in as a new Member of Parliament on 18th April 1864.

Also in the Collection is a portrait of *John Gay (1685–1732), Poet and Dramatist* the writer of *The Beggar's Opera* (1728) after John Vanderbank (c.1694–1739). Gay was educated at the town's grammar school. He was apprenticed to a silk mercer in London but being weary, according to Samuel Johnson, 'of either the restraint or the servility of his occupation', he soon returned to Barnstaple, where he spent some time with his uncle, the Reverend John Hanmer, before returning to London. Gay's most famous play was a disguised satire on society, for he made it plain that in describing the moral code of the characters of *The Beggar's Opera* he had in mind the corruptions of the governing class. He was buried in Poets' Corner, Westminster Abbey.

William Frederick Rock (1802–1890), businessman and dedicated philanthropist, painted by his friend and Devon native John Edgar Williams, hangs in the Main Chamber. Rock was the son of Henry Rock, a tradesman, and his wife Prudence. After working in banks in Bideford and London, Rock went to work with printer and inventor Thomas de la Rue where he amassed enough money to establish his own print business with John Payne. Successful, Rock became a wealthy man, but with no family he gave generously to Barnstaple. He was the founder of the Literary and Scientific Institution in 1845, later the North Devon Athenaeum in 1888, and financed the acquisition of land for Rock Park, where an obelisk still stands commemorating this most altruistic gesture. Rock is still regarded as one of the town's greatest sons, his munificence enshrined in the town's history as a true Victorian benefactor.

Williams' portrait of *Mrs Payne (1811–1890)* stands out as the only painting of a woman in the Collection. Born Prudence Rock, William Rock's sister, she married John Payne. Throughout their lives both Prudence and William generously endowed good causes in Barnstaple with contributions.

Barnstaple's own *Francis Carruthers Gould (1844–1925)* is immortalised by his son Alexander. Gould was a caricaturist and political satirist, the first of his kind on a national newspaper. Although in early youth he showed great love of illustration, he began his professional life in a bank, later joining the London Stock Exchange where he constantly doodled the members and illustrated significant events in the financial world; many of these sketches were reproduced as lithographs and published for private circulation. In 1887, he became a contributor to the Pall Mall Gazette, later transferring his allegiance to the Westminster Gazette.

The painting of *The Honourable Mark George Kerr Rolle (1835–1907), High Steward (1861–1907)*, by Henry Richard Graves (1818–1882) is worth noting. Rolle was a diminutive individual and when Graves presented the completed painting to his sitter he was so incensed that Graves had to alter it to make his subject significantly taller. Indeed, this anomaly is very obvious when a keen eye observes Rolle's legs, which are disproportionate to the rest of his appearance and the backdrop.

The Collection also includes some Brian Dick Lauder Thomas cartoons of designs for the Chapel of the Order of the British Empire, St Paul's Cathedral. Some paintings are on loan to the Museum of Barnstaple and North Devon and North Devon District Council, including two works by Joseph Kennedy: *The River Taw from Rock Park, Devon* and *Old Guildhall, Barnstaple, Devon*, and John Lynn's spectacular maritime scenes of yachts cresting the ocean waves.

Martyn Barrow, Administration Assistant

Adcock, Mollie
Portrait of a Bearded Cleric
oil on board 61 x 49
PCF24

Beechey, William 1753–1839
Frederick Hodgson, Esq.
oil on canvas 142 x 109
PCF33

British (English) School
Richard Bremridge, Mayor of Barnstaple (1829 & 1859) c.1850
oil on canvas 127 x 102
PCF31

British (English) School 19th C
Gilbert Inner Wallas, MA
oil on canvas 75 x 62
PCF56

British (English) School 19th C
Lionel T. Bencraft, Mayor of Barnstaple (1883)
oil on canvas 62 x 50
PCF52

British (English) School 19th C
Portrait of a Young Soldier Officer Wearing a Uniforn
oil on canvas 61 x 46
PCF27

British (English) School 19th C
Stephen Bencraft
oil on canvas 62 x 50
PCF28

Gould, Alexander Carruthers 1870–1948
Francis Carruthers Gould (1844–1925), at His Desk 1899
oil on canvas 38 x 50
PCF5

Graves, Henry Richard 1818–1882
The Honourable Mark George Kerr Rolle (1835–1907), High Steward (1861–1908) 1871
oil on canvas 236 x 145
PCF41

Hudson, Thomas (attributed to) 1701–1779
Benjamin Incledon, Recorder (1758–1796)
oil on canvas 123.5 x 99
PCF54

Hudson, Thomas (attributed to) 1701–1779
Reverend Robert Luck, Master of the Grammar School (1698–1740)
oil on canvas 75 x 62
PCF19

Hudson, Thomas (studio of) 1701–1779
Alexander Webber, Mayor of Barnstaple (1737)
oil on canvas 75 x 62
PCF43

Hudson, Thomas (studio of) 1701–1779
Charles Marshall, Mayor of Barnstaple (1748)
oil on canvas 75 x 62
PCF44

Hudson, Thomas (studio of) 1701–1779
*Charles Velly, Mayor of Barnstaple (1734 &
1749)*
oil on canvas 75 x 62
PCF46

Hudson, Thomas (studio of) 1701–1779
Charles Wright, Mayor of Barnstaple (1744)
oil on canvas 75 x 62
PCF61

Hudson, Thomas (studio of) 1701–1779
George Score, Mayor of Barnstaple (1730)
oil on canvas 75 x 62
PCF57

Hudson, Thomas (studio of) 1701–1779
George Wickey, Mayor of Barnstaple (1739)
oil on canvas 75 x 62
PCF47

Hudson, Thomas (studio of) 1701–1779
*Gregory Anthony, Town Clerk of Barnstaple
(1733–1747)*
oil on canvas 75 x 62
PCF26

Hudson, Thomas (studio of) 1701–1779
*Henry Beavis, Mayor of Barnstaple (1738 &
1751)*
oil on canvas 75 x 62
PCF45

Hudson, Thomas (studio of) 1701–1779
*Henry Drake (1745–1806), Town Clerk of
Barnstaple*
oil on canvas 75 x 62
PCF34

Hudson, Thomas (studio of) 1701–1779
Henry Wickey, Councillor
oil on canvas 75 x 62
PCF42

Hudson, Thomas (studio of) 1701–1779
John Baker, Mayor of Barnstaple (1715 &
1729)
oil on canvas 75 x 62
PCF53

Hudson, Thomas (studio of) 1701–1779
John Fraine, Mayor of Barnstaple (1740 &
1752)
oil on canvas 75 x 62
PCF60

Hudson, Thomas (studio of) 1701–1779
John Gaydon (1685–1732), Mayor of
Barnstaple (1726)
oil on canvas 75 x 62
PCF36

Hudson, Thomas (studio of) 1701–1779
John Swayne, Councillor
oil on canvas 75 x 62
PCF51

Hudson, Thomas (studio of) 1701–1779
Mark Slee, Mayor of Barnstaple (1747)
oil on canvas laid on panel 75 x 62
PCF49

Hudson, Thomas (studio of) 1701–1779
Marshall Swayne, Mayor of Barnstaple (1746)
oil on canvas 75 x 62
PCF39

Hudson, Thomas (studio of) 1701–1779
Matthew Rock, Mayor of Barnstaple (1741 &
1753)
oil on canvas 75 x 62
PCF40

Hudson, Thomas (studio of) 1701–1779
Nicholas Glass, Mayor of Barnstaple (1787 &
1804)
oil on canvas 75 x 62
PCF62

Hudson, Thomas (studio of) 1701–1779
Paul Tucker, Mayor of Barnstaple (1736)
oil on canvas 75 x 62
PCF59

Hudson, Thomas (studio of) 1701–1779
Reverend Thomas Steed, Vicar of Barnstaple
oil on canvas 74.5 x 61.5
PCF22

Hudson, Thomas (studio of) 1701–1779
Richard Chapple, Mayor of Barnstaple (1742, 1762 & 1781)
oil on canvas 75 x 62
PCF50

Hudson, Thomas (studio of) 1701–1779
Richard Knight, Mayor of Barnstaple (1735, 1750 & 1761)
oil on canvas 75 x 62
PCF37

Hudson, Thomas (studio of) 1701–1779
Richard Mervyn, Deputy Recorder and Mayor of Barnstaple
oil on canvas 75 x 62
PCF35

Hudson, Thomas (studio of) 1701–1779
Richard Newell, Mayor of Barnstaple (1728)
oil on canvas 75 x 62
PCF48

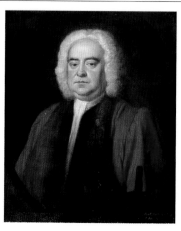

Hudson, Thomas (studio of) 1701–1779
Robert Incledon, Deputy Recorder and Mayor of Barnstaple (1712)
oil on canvas 75 x 62
PCF63

Hudson, Thomas (studio of) 1701–1779
Robert King, Mayor of Barnstaple (1745)
oil on canvas 75 x 62
PCF38

Hudson, Thomas (studio of) 1701–1779
Samuel Berry, Mayor of Barnstaple (1731)
oil on canvas 75 x 62
PCF32

Hudson, Thomas (studio of) 1701–1779
Thomas Harris, Mayor of Barnstaple (1733)
oil on canvas 75 x 62
PCF58

Facing page: Opie, John, 1761–1807, *Dr Thomas Glass (1709–1786), Physician (1741–1775)*, Royal Devon and Exeter Hospital (p. 169)

Hudson, Thomas (studio of) 1701–1779
William Lantrow, Councillor
oil on canvas 75 x 62
PCF55

Hudson, Thomas (style of) 1701–1779
Reverend Samuel Thompson, Vicar of Barnstaple
oil on canvas 75 x 62
PCF30

Janssens van Ceulen, Cornelis (style of) 1593–1661
John Penrose (1778–1859)
oil on canvas 73 x 59
PCF17

Janssens van Ceulen, Cornelis (style of) 1593–1661
John Penrose (1778–1859)
oil on canvas 64 x 53
PCF25

Kennedy, Joseph c.1838–1893
Old Guildhall, Barnstaple, Devon 1886
oil on canvas 66 x 77
PCF1

Kennedy, Joseph c.1838–1893
Old Northgate and the Bluecoat School, Barnstaple, Devon 1886
oil on board 66 x 77
PCF6

Kennedy, Joseph c.1838–1893
The Strand, Barnstaple, Devon
oil on canvas 64 x 80
PCF2

Reid, F. Michael P.
St Cuthbert Mayne, Born Shirwell, Barnstaple, Martyred 1577
oil on board 49 x 39
PCF7

Richardson, Jonathan the elder (style of) 1664/1665–1745
John Gay (1685–1732), Poet and Author
oil on canvas 124.5 x 89
PCF23

Rutherford, R. G.
Long Bridge, Barnstaple, Devon 1986
oil on canvas 44.7 x 65
PCF3

Thomas, Brian Dick Lauder 1912–1989
A View in the Roman Campagna
oil on canvas 39.5 x 49.5
PCF4

Thomas, Brian Dick Lauder 1912–1989
Ascension of Christ, Cartoon for the New Shrine of the Order of the British Empire in St Paul's Cathedral
oil on board 148 x 120
PCF11

Thomas, Brian Dick Lauder 1912–1989
Clouded Yellow Butterfly
oil on board 18 x 46
PCF12

Thomas, Brian Dick Lauder 1912–1989
Dr F. L. Thomas, Mayor of Barnstaple (1922)
oil on canvas 40.6 x 50.6
PCF9

Thomas, Brian Dick Lauder 1912–1989
Meadow Brown Butterfly
oil on board 18 x 46
PCF14

Thomas, Brian Dick Lauder 1912–1989
Mrs F. L. Thomas (Margaret), Mayoress
oil on canvas 30.5 x 19.5
PCF10

Thomas, Brian Dick Lauder 1912–1989
Red Admiral Butterfly
oil on board 18 x 46
PCF13

Thomas, Brian Dick Lauder 1912–1989
The Entombment, Cartoon for the New Shrine of the Order of the British Empire in St Paul's Cathedral
oil on board 148.1 x 125.1
PCF8

unknown artist
Spring Plowing 1977
oil on canvas 44.9 x 60.2
PCF15

unknown artist
A Three-Masted Vessel in a Swell
oil on canvas 108 x 151
PCF64

unknown artist
Bruce Oliver, Mayor of Barnstaple (1931)
oil on panel 58.3 x 43.8
PCF16

unknown artist
Reverend Henry Nicholls, Mayor of Barnstaple (1826)
oil on panel 24.6 x 18.9
PCF29

Vanderbank, John (after) 1694–1739
John Gay (1685–1732), Poet and Dramatist
oil on canvas 75 x 62
PCF20

Williams, John Edgar c.1821–1891
Mrs Payne (1811–1890) 1885
oil on canvas 110 x 85
PCF21

Williams, John Edgar c.1821–1891
Wiliam Frederick Rock (1802–1890) 1885
oil on canvas 110 x 85
PCF18

Museum of Barnstaple and North Devon

The paintings in the collections of the Museum of Barnstaple and North Devon include two historic collections. The North Devon Athenaeum previously occupied the Museum building, and on its departure in 1988 the bulk of its Museum Collections (as distinct from archives and books) remained at the Museum. The paintings remaining at the Museum are mostly of local interest, and include a number of portraits, including the Athenaeum's founder, *William Frederick Rock, Aged 35* and his friend *John Roberts Chanter (1816–1895), Originator and First Honorary Secretary of the Barnstaple Literary and Scientific Institute (1845–1861)*, both painted by unknown artists. Between them they gave Barnstaple Rock Park (for healthy bodies) as well as the Athenaeum (for healthy minds).

The second historic collection was transferred to the Council from the old Borough Museum in St Anne's Chapel at local government reorganisation in 1974. This collection includes some delightful eighteenth-century portraits. Both collections include examples of the work of Joseph Kennedy, master of the Barnstaple School of Art for many years, and an interesting man who allegedly killed himself by jumping from a window in an alcoholic haze. Many of Kennedy's paintings were based on earlier prints and depict views of structures, including *The Old Guildhall, Barnstaple, Devon* and *Barnstaple North Gate, Devon* (attributed to Joseph Kennedy), which had already been demolished earlier in the nineteenth century. He seems to have painted many copies at different sizes, possibly with the help of his students, and presumably for the growing tourist market.

Since the establishment of the Council's Museum in 1990, collecting has focused almost exclusively on local topographic views. The most important collection was acquired from the estate of Brian Chugg (1926–2003), again a previous head of the School of Art who went on to teach at North Devon College. Chugg grew up in Braunton, North Devon, and his work includes material based on his childhood exploration of the Second World War defences created for the training of US troops on Braunton Burrows as well as interesting realistic and abstract work derived from the landforms of the North Devon Coast. The collection also contains sketches and notebooks held both at the Museum and at the North Devon Records Office.

Most recent work has been acquired from gifts, but there are two interesting exceptions. *Appledore Shore with Boats, Devon* by Thomas Adolphus Falcon was acquired with the assistance of the Art Fund, and completes a series of decorative panels from Sharlands House, Braunton, the remainder of which (depicting Braunton) are held at Braunton and District Museum. The painting *Phillip Gosse Finding a Chrysaora Cyclonota in a Pool Below the Tunnels at Ilfracombe, Devon, 14 September 1852* by Peter Stiles was commissioned as part of a project all about Darwin, George Eliot, Victorian seaweed collecting and the development of the resort of Ilfracombe as part of the Darwin 150 project called 'Vivarium', which was funded by the Museums, Libraries and Archives Council South West New Expressions programme in 2009.

Alison Mills, Museums Development Officer

Beattie, A. active 1840–1856
The Valley of the Taw, Devon 1853
oil on panel 28.9 x 50
1991.1555

Briggs, Henry Perronet 1791/1793–1844
Frederick R. Lee, (1798–1879), RA
oil on canvas 75 x 62.5
1991.1479

G. C. active 20th C
Country Scene with a River and a Bridge
oil on paper 19.5 x 34.4
1991.1182

Chugg, Brian 1926–2003
*Coast Guard Lookout, Used as Target 1943,
Baggy Point, Devon (Area F, US Army ATC)
(painted on the spot)* 1949
oil on board 31 x 35.5
2005.1.5

Chugg, Brian 1926–2003
*Reinforced Concrete, Strong Point 1943, Baggy
Point, Devon* 1949
oil on board 31 x 35.5
2005.1.4

Chugg, Brian 1926–2003
Hovering Rock No.1 1950s
oil on board 126.8 x 76.3
2007.1.2

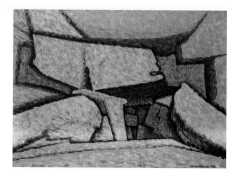

Chugg, Brian 1926–2003
Continental Shelf 1952
oil on board 61 x 122
2007.1.11

Chugg, Brian 1926–2003
*Saunton Rock and Atomic Cloud (Nuclear
Dissolution)* 1957
oil on board 122.3 x 121.8
2007.1.1

Chugg, Brian 1926–2003
Raised Beach 1958
oil on board 40.7 x 57
2007.1.9

Chugg, Brian 1926–2003
Rampart 1958
oil on board 39.2 x 56
2007.1.12

Chugg, Brian 1926–2003
Saunton Cliff, Devon 1958
oil on board 63.5 x 37.9
2007.1.6

Chugg, Brian 1926–2003
Atlantic Coast 1959
oil on board 40.5 x 57.1
2007.1.7

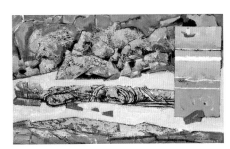

Chugg, Brian 1926–2003
Giant's Cave No.2 1959
oil on board 50.8 x 72.3
2007.1.4

Chugg, Brian 1926–2003
The Gulf Dream 1959
oil on board 50.6 x 86.4
2007.1.3

Chugg, Brian 1926–2003
Atlantic No.4 1961
oil on board 37 x 62
2007.1.15

Chugg, Brian 1926–2003
Form Experiment No.4 1961
oil on board 61 x 86.1
2007.1.5

Chugg, Brian 1926–2003
Rock Form No.1 1961
oil on board 50.8 x 72.2
2007.1.8

Chugg, Brian 1926–2003
Developing Rock No.3 1962
oil on board 49.7 x 49.4
2007.1.14

Chugg, Brian 1926–2003
Evolving Rock No.4 1962
oil on board 50.6 x 50.6
2007.1.13

Chugg, Brian 1926–2003
Devonian Outcrop No.6 1964
oil on board 84.7 x 59.7
2007.1.16

Chugg, Brian 1926–2003
Composite of Beach Defences I
oil on board 30.7 x 152.7
2005.1.9

Chugg, Brian 1926–2003
Composite of Beach Defences II
oil on board 30.7 x 152.7
2005.1.8

Chugg, Brian 1926–2003
Rocks at Saunton, Devon
oil on board 76 x 126.8
2007.1.10

Falcon, Thomas Adolphus 1872–1944
Appledore Shore with Boats, Devon
oil on panel 161.2 x 82.3
2007.149

Foster, J. J.
Henry Rock (1774–1846), Father of William Frederick Rock 1843
oil on canvas 74.7 x 61.9
1991.1493

Gould, Francis Carruthers 1844–1925
John Penrose (d.1624) (copy after an earlier painting in the Penrose Alsmshouses)
oil on canvas 53 x 40
1991.1487

Hopwood
Isaac Clark, Esq. 1824
oil on panel 25.2 x 20.4
1991.1579

Jack, Richard 1866–1952
Lady Barclay Black of Yelland Manor 1927
oil on canvas 125.7 x 99.5
1993.68

Kennedy, Joseph c.1838–1893
Barnstaple and the River Taw, Devon 1867
oil on canvas 59.8 x 89.7
1991.1472

Kennedy, Joseph c.1838–1893
North Gate and Rolle Quay, Barnstaple 1882
oil on panel 29.5 x 47
1991.1469

Kennedy, Joseph c.1838–1893
The 'Star Inn' 1884
oil on panel 26.5 x 38.4
E0928.2 (P)

Kennedy, Joseph c.1838–1893
River Taw from Rock Park, Devon 1886
oil on canvas 52.1 x 87.5
1991.712

Kennedy, Joseph c.1838–1893
*The Construction of the Railway Bridge at
Pottington, Devon* 1886
oil on canvas 52.4 x 82.7
1991.715

Kennedy, Joseph c.1838–1893
Mill
oil on board 25 x 33.6
1993.36

Kennedy, Joseph c.1838–1893
Raleigh Mill from the River Yeo
oil on board 25 x 34
1991.1484

Kennedy, Joseph c.1838–1893
The Old Guildhall, Barnstaple, Devon
oil on panel 23.5 x 30.5
E0928.1 (P)

Kennedy, Joseph c.1838–1893
Town Mill with Ship
oil on board 36.5 x 51.9
1991.1471

Kennedy, Joseph (attributed to) c.1838–1893
Barnstaple North Gate, Devon (detail)
oil on panel 36 x 35.4
1991.1468

Lee, Frederick Richard 1798–1879
View from the River, Barnstaple, Devon 1824
oil on panel 14.5 x 26.6
2005.7

Lee, Frederick Richard 1798–1879
River Taw and the Railway, Bishop's Tawton, near Barnstaple, Devon 1868
oil on canvas 110 x 182
PCF1

Lee, Frederick Richard 1798–1879
West Lyn, Lynton, Devon
oil on board 25.4 x 35.3
1991.799

Lely, Peter 1618–1680
Portrait of a Lady with a Bouquet c.1660
oil on canvas 73.5 x 60.5
1991.1478

Nasmyth, Patrick (attributed to) 1787–1831
Lime Kilns
oil on panel 23.3 x 30.9
2010.29.9

Perrett, J.
The Old Mill, Lynmouth, Devon
oil on panel 27.6 x 40.9
PCF6 (P)

Shaddick, G.
The Castle, Barnstaple, Devon
oil on board 40.5 x 50.5
1992.977

Facing page: Ramsay, Allan (attributed to), 1713–1784, *Portrait of an African* (probably Ignatius Sancho, 1729–1780), c.1757–1760, Royal Albert Memorial Museum (p. 153)

Shaw, George 1843–1915
Doone Valley, Devon 1905
oil on canvas 25 x 71
1991.1486

Stiles, Peter b.1959
Phillip Gosse Finding a Chrysaora Cyclonota in a Pool Below the Tunnels at Ilfracombe, Devon, 14 September 1852 2009
oil on canvas 75.5 x 60
PCF11

unknown artist
Barnstaple from Sticklepath, Devon c.1740
oil on canvas 68.2 x 132
1991.1379

unknown artist
West Hill Farm, Braunton, Devon c.1900
oil on canvas 49 x 59
1991.311

unknown artist
Barnstaple Leat, Devon
oil on board 30 x 24.5
PCF13

unknown artist
Hugh Fortescue (1783–1861), 2nd Earl Fortescue
oil on canvas 75 x 62.3
1991.1482

unknown artist
Hugh Fortescue (1818–1905), 3rd Earl Fortescue
oil on canvas 75 x 62.3
1991.1483

unknown artist
John Abbott of Culley, Frithelstock (1639–1727), Sculptor
oil on canvas 72 x 60 (E)
E1267

unknown artist
John Roberts Chanter (1816–1895), Originator and First Honorary Secretary of the Barnstaple Literary and Scientific Institute (1845–1861)
oil on canvas 75 x 62.3
1991.1481

unknown artist
Mr Rendle
oil on canvas 23.3 x 18.3
1991.763

unknown artist
Mrs Prudence Hartree Rock (1770–1846)
oil on canvas 75.2 x 62
1991.1492

unknown artist
*Mrs Prudence Payne (1810–1890), Sister of
William Frederick Rock*
oil on canvas 74.2 x 61.7
1991.1491

unknown artist
Mrs Rendle
oil on canvas 23.3 x 18.3
1991.764

unknown artist
*Penrose Almshouses, Litchdon Street,
Barnstaple, Devon*
oil on canvas 34.5 x 52
1992.145

unknown artist
'Poltimore Arms', Boutport Street, Barnstaple
oil on board 23 x 31.6
1991.1525

unknown artist
Portrait of a Man with Beard in Profile
oil on canvas 31.5 x 26.7
PCF10

unknown artist
*Reverend Jonathan Hanmer (1606–1687), MA,
St John's College Cambridge, One of Two
Thousand Clergy Ejected from the Church (...)*
oil on canvas 73 x 61
E3515

unknown artist
*Reverend Jonathan Hanmer (1606–1687), MA,
St John's College, Cambridge*
oil on canvas 74 x 61.1
E3515

unknown artist
River with a House and Church
oil on canvas 25.5 x 35.7
1991.2227

unknown artist
The 'Exeter Inn'
oil on board 117 x 87.5
PCF9

unknown artist
The Rhenish Tower, Lynmouth, Devon
oil on panel 21.2 x 33.1
1991.14

unknown artist
Three Tuns
oil on tin 127 x 91.5
PCF7

unknown artist
Three Tuns
oil on tin 127 x 91.5
PCF8

unknown artist
View of Barnstaple from Fort Hill, Devon
oil on canvas 88 x 119
2003.31

unknown artist
William Avery (1812–1893), Mayor (1846, 1851, 1875 & 1878–1880)
oil on canvas 75.3 x 62.3
1991.148

unknown artist
William Frederick Rock (1802–1890), Aged 35
oil on canvas 75 x 62.5
1991.1494

Vanderbank, John 1694–1739
John Gay (1685–1732)
oil on canvas 92 x 70.5
1991.1465

Warren, M. F. J.
The Old Smithy, North Molton, Devon
(reputed to be associated with the fictional
character Tom Faggus, in the book, 'Lorna (...)
oil on board 29.5 x 39.5
1995.14

Williams, John Edgar c.1821–1891
William Frederick Rock (1802–1890) 1863
oil on canvas 74.6 x 61.8
1991.1495

North Devon Athenaeum

Founded in 1888 by William Frederick Rock, the North Devon Athenaeum was a free library and museum – which also acted as a record office – for Barnstaple and North Devon. The North Devon Athenaeum has its roots in the Barnstaple Literary and Scientific Institute, which was founded in 1845 and largely funded by William Frederick Rock. Rock had made his money in London, working with Thomas de la Rue, making stationery and novelty items. The Literary and Scientific Institute was Barnstaple's first library and museum. Members had to pay various amounts, depending on which type of membership they had and whether they paid yearly or quarterly. There were also up to 100 free places available each year for those who could not afford to be members; one of these members was the 'Postman Poet', Edward Capern. Being a member also meant you could take advantage of the various classes held, including maths, French and art. The art classes were the most popular and their members included the architect and educationalist William Richard Lethaby and the art potter C. H. Brannam. The classes were eventually taken over by the Town Council who created an Art School. The North Devon Athenaeum holds a small number of paintings by one of the School's principals, Joseph Kennedy, one of which is in oils.

When Rock founded the North Devon Athenaeum, the holdings of the Literary and Scientific Institute were transferred to the new institution and housed in a new building which had been converted from a private house. As a result, the North Devon Athenaeum's collections have been built up over a long period of time. As with other collections owned by the North Devon Athenaeum, the paintings have been given by various people over the years and many of Barnstaple's notable residents have donated items from their collections. The Collection has several portraits of these residents, including William Frederick Rock, his sister, Prudence, and John Gay – most of these portraits are now on loan to the Museum of Barnstaple and North Devon. Most paintings have a local connection: they may feature a local place or person, or may have been painted by a local artist or someone who had a strong connection to the area. Perhaps the most iconic image owned by the Collection is that of Barnstaple itself. Believed to have been painted sometime around 1740 by an unknown artist, *Barnstaple from Sticklepath, Devon* depicts Barnstaple and the neighbouring parish of Pilton from across the River Taw. The painting is on loan to the Museum of Barnstaple and North Devon, who now own the building originally occupied by the North Devon Athenaeum and whose paintings also feature in this catalogue.

In 1988, the North Devon Athenaeum moved to the newly-built North Devon Library and Record Office, joining with the North Devon Record Office and the North Devon Local Studies Library to become one third of the North Devon Local Studies Centre. The majority of the museum items – including most of the painting collection – remained behind in the old building and are now on loan to the Museum of Barnstaple and North Devon. The North Devon Athenaeum now focuses on aiding local and family historians with their research and this is reflected in the collections the Athenaeum now holds. These include large collections of photographs, images, original documents, newspapers and books relating to the North Devon area as well as the rest of Devon and neighbouring counties.

The North Devon Athenaeum is a small registered charity which is primarily funded by a trust set up by its founder, William Frederick Rock.

Naomi Ayre, Librarian

Kennedy, Joseph c.1838–1893
The Fish Shambles, St Nicholas' Chapel and 'The Old Star' Inn, Barnstaple, Devon
oil on panel 26.5 x 36.5
1991.1473

Lee, Frederick Richard 1798–1879
Bideford, Devon
oil on panel 19.3 x 26.8
PCF3

Lee, Frederick Richard 1798–1879
Devon Cottages
oil on board 25.3 x 35.5
PF092

Slade, R. W.
The Square, Braunton, North Devon 1945
oil on board 41 x 58.2
PF.101

unknown artist
William Frederick Rock (1802–1890)
oil on canvas 74.3 x 62
PCF1

North Devon Council

Golds, Christopher Charles b.1936
Brig Rounding a Cape 1980
oil on canvas 70.5 x 100.7
PCF1

Penrose Almshouses

Hasler, F.
Penrose Almshouses, Barnstaple, Devon
oil on board 25 x 35
PCF3

Janssens van Ceulen, Cornelis 1593–1661
John Penrose, Aged 26 1601
oil on panel 58 x 43.2
PCF1

unknown artist
Mr Gilbert Paige c.1650
oil on canvas 73.5 x 61
PCF2

Bideford Library

Bowyer, Alan J. active 1956–1969
Miss M. E. Abbott, Founder and Headmistress of West Bank School, Bideford (1896–1938) 1956
oil on canvas 60 x 47
PCF2

Mead, Geraldine
Sand Dunes
oil on board 25 x 34
PCF3

Mead, Geraldine
The Quay at Bideford, Devon
oil on board 24.5 x 34
PCF3

Mead, Geraldine
Under Construction, Kenwith Viaduct, Devon
oil on board 29 x 39
PCF6

Pearce, Jon
The Frozen Torridge, Devon 1963
oil on board 35 x 50
PCF5

Facing page: Cotton, Alan, b.1938, *Hartland Point I, Devon*, 1977, University of Exeter, Fine Art Collection (p. 190)

Williams, John Edgar c.1821–1891
*Edward Capern (1819–1895), Bideford
Postman Poet*
oil on canvas 75 x 61.5
PCF1

Bideford Town Council

British (English) School
*John Strange (1590–1646), Former Mayor of
Bideford (1643–1646)* c.1600
oil on canvas 107 x 80
PCF10

British (English) School 19th C
*John Willcock (b.1736), Mayor of Bideford
(1783 & 1800)* 1822
oil on canvas 60 x 49
PCF9

British (English) School 19th C
Charles Carter (1771–1862)
oil on canvas 75 x 62
PCF1

British (English) School 19th C
Josias Wren, Mayor of Bideford (1842)
oil on canvas 61.5 x 51
PCF8

Dosser, Marguerite b.1942
La Maison du Haut, Landivisau, France 2006
oil on canvas 80 x 80
PCF6

Dyer, Edmund active c.1820–1875
Sir Richard Grenville (1542–1591)
oil on canvas 106 x 72
PCF2

Hoare, William (school of) 1706–1792
Portrait of a Gentleman
oil on canvas 74.5 x 62
PCF11

King, Charles b.1912
*William Ewart Ellis (1884–1958), Mayor of
Bideford (1934–1935)* 1952
oil on canvas 60 x 49
PCF5

Opie, John (school of) 1761–1807
John Chanter, Mayor of Bideford (1815–1816)
oil on canvas 74 x 60
PCF7

Romney, George (follower of) 1734–1802
George Stucley Buck (1754–1791) c.1750
oil on canvas 75 x 62
PCF13

Sandercock, M.
Bideford Quay, Devon
oil on canvas 28.5 x 59
PCF12

Sutton, Fran
*Fred Pitfield Bailey (1915–1987), Mayor of
Bideford (1979)* 1982
oil on canvas 60 x 49
PCF4

Burton Art Gallery and Museum

The Burton Art Gallery and Museum was established in 1951 by Thomas Burton, a local businessman, and Hubert Coop, the successful watercolour artist. Throughout Coop's life he amassed a fine collection of paintings, both watercolours and oils, and also a range of porcelain and antiques, including some noteworthy Napoleonic ship models. As Coop felt that there was a special appreciation of the arts in Bideford, he left his collection to the town, under the proviso that it would be 'properly housed'. He was eventually instrumental in assisting Thomas Burton (Mayor, Alderman, Freeman of the Borough and philanthropist) to build the Burton Art Gallery and Museum in memory of Burton's daughter, Mary, who died in 1949. The original Coop collection forms the basis of the Burton's permanent Collection.

In a letter to the *Bideford Gazette* in October 1949, Coop wrote:

It's a happy chance that two old townsmen have come together to make a last effort to leave the town richer than they found it. The gallery should be a peaceful haven where one may take a quiet look at beautiful things; a gallery for the enjoyment, education and good of all, old and young, inhabitants and visitors – everyone; and as far as one can tell, of lasting credit to the living and those to come.

The permanent Collection has continued to expand and now consists of over 2,500 objects of art and heritage, many of which are directly related or connected to the local area. The most recent acquisition is a collection of over 500 ceramics, predominantly North Devon Slipware, collected by the artist R. J. Lloyd.

Hubert Coop, a fine artist himself, collected works by other painters of his own era. These include works by E. Aubrey Hunt, George Clausen, Arthur A. Friedenson, Sir John Lavery, and John Littlejohns, all of which form the foundation of the oil painting collection. The Collection has increased through purchases by the Friends of the Gallery and gifts from the public, and now contains works by some of the local artists who have exhibited here in the past.

The permanent Collection includes works by a number of notable artists. Sir John Lavery (1856–1941), who was born in Belfast, studied in Glasgow and subsequently in Paris, where he was influenced by Whistler and the Impressionists. He was a member of the Glasgow School before settling in London in 1895. Lavery had an immensely successful career as a fashionable portrait artist.

American-born E. Aubrey Hunt (1856–1922) travelled widely in France and North Africa, and died in England. Hunt was a friend of Hubert Coop. His portrait, painted by Sir John Lavery, was given to Hubert Coop by Hunt's wife.

Sir George Clausen (1852–1944), R.A. was an English painter of Danish parentage. In the late 1870s he visited Holland and Paris, where he came under the influence of Bastien-Lepage. Later, he reverted to the habit of composing in the studio from open-air studies and developed a modified Impressionist technique.

The Collection also includes a large selection of works by Hubert Coop (1872–1953), R.B.A., himself. Born at Olney in Buckinghamshire, the son of the Reverend Thomas Coop, Hubert Coop was educated at Birmingham and Wolverhampton, and was elected to the Royal Society of British Artists at the tender age of 22. His paintings, both in oil and watercolour, tend to fall into two groups: those painted quickly out of doors, and those painted in the studio in more detail.

Coop came to Bideford in the late 1920s and stayed 'because he enjoyed the subjects he found on the estuary, the river valleys and the neighbourhood, and his paintings inevitably captured the clear beauty and colour he saw there.' (*Bideford Gazette*, 1953). He exhibited at the Royal Academy, and also in Liverpool, Glasgow and Manchester. In Bideford he helped to promote the development of the visual arts, and became Vice-President of what is now the Westward Ho! and Bideford Art Society.

The Burton Art Gallery and Museum hosts a range of temporary exhibitions of visual arts and crafts. Many historical objects from the Collection are displayed permanently, and selected works from the oil painting Collection are exhibited annually as part of the ongoing exhibition programme.

Warren Collum, Collections/Exhibitions Officer

Beresford-Williams, Mary b.1931
Summer on the Dart
oil on canvas 75 x 100
199.5802

Braund, Allin 1915–2004
Copse Path, April 1940 1940
acrylic on canvas 74 x 49
PCF16

Braund, Allin 1915–2004
Pebble and Seaweed 1987
acrylic on board 73.8 x 59.2
2001.5884

Braund, Allin 1915–2004
Kelp
oil on board 46 x 36.5
1991.110

Braund, Allin 1915–2004
Seascape with a White Bird
acrylic on board 59.7 x 74.5
2001.5883

Carpenter, Margaret Sarah 1793–1872
Study of a Girl in a Red Cloak
oil on canvas 56 x 48
1992.46

Charles, James 1851–1906
The Home Field
oil on board 18.5 x 25.5
1992.52

Chugg, Brian 1926–2003
Marine Organism 1964
oil on board 60 x 82
2006.6448

Clausen, George 1852–1944
A Little Brook in Essex
oil on canvas 50 x 39.5
1991.73

Coop, Hubert 1872–1953
Chalk at Dover, Kent
oil on canvas 75 x 62
1991.74

Coop, Hubert 1872–1953
Hanging Cloud, Silver and Anglesey, and Beyond
oil on canvas 55 x 42
1991.75

Cooper, Thomas Sidney 1803–1902
Three Cows
oil on canvas 28.4 x 51
1992.370

Correggio (after) c.1489–1534
Meditation (based on the painting 'The
Penitent Magdalene')
enamel on porcelain 13 x 18.5
1992.203

Dutch School 18th C
*Still Life with Fruit (in the style of the 17th
century)*
oil on canvas 75.2 x 95.4
1992.530

Ellis, Edwin 1842–1895
Running for Shelter
oil on canvas 37 x 70
1991.53

Ellis, Edwin 1842–1895
Study of a Lobster
oil on canvas 27 x 44
1992.51

Ellis, Edwin 1842–1895
The Old Breakwater Walderswick, Suffolk
oil on canvas 43 x 121.5
1992.109

Fisher, Mark 1841–1923
Algerian Landscape
oil on canvas 46.1 x 73
1991.38

Fisher, Mark 1841–1923
Essex Marshes
oil on canvas 44.4 x 65
1992.54

Fisher, Mark 1841–1923
Essex Meadows
oil on canvas 35 x 52.5
1992.39

Fisher, Mark 1841–1923
Great Elms
oil on canvas 76 x 104.5
1991.43

Fisher, Mark 1841–1923
Spring in Orchard
oil on canvas 36.5 x 51
1992.37

Fisher, Mark 1841–1923
Still Life with Flowers
oil on canvas 40.2 x 48.8
1991.58

Fisher, Mark 1841–1923
Vasouy near Honfleur, France
oil on canvas 47 x 42.2
1992.62

Friedenson, Arthur A. 1872–1955
Belstone near Okehampton, Devon
oil on panel 20.1 x 25
1991.70

Friedenson, Arthur A. 1872–1955
Evening over the Isles of Purbesck, Dorset
oil on panel 32.5 x 41
1991.65

Friedenson, Arthur A. 1872–1955
Landscape, Corfe Castle, Dorset
oil on panel 30 x 38
1991.72

Friedenson, Arthur A. 1872–1955
On the River at Wareham, Dorset
oil on canvas 30 x 39
1991.204

Furse, Patrick John Dolignon 1918–2005
Lady in a Hat 1996
oil on canvas 51 x 40
2010.001

Girling, William H. 1913–1991
Still Life 1
oil on board 48.5 x 64
1992.214

Hall, Oliver 1869–1957
Entrance to Egdean Wood, West Sussex
oil on board 32 x 44.3
1992.56

Hayward, Alfred Frederick William 1856–
1939
Bucks Mills, Devon 1881
oil on canvas 75.1 x 49.9
1996.5675

Heard, Hugh Percy 1866–1940
Sea and Landscape
oil on canvas 49.5 x 75.4
PCF5

Heard, Hugh Percy 1866–1940
Stormy Sea
oil on canvas 71 x 98.5
1992.235

Hunt, Edgar 1876–1953
Tangier, Morocco 1894
oil on canvas board 100 x 133.8
2007.6517

Hunt, Edward Aubrey 1855–1922
A Tidal River
oil on canvas 99 x 126
1992.217

Hunt, Edward Aubrey 1855–1922
An Old Dutch Town
oil on canvas 42.7 x 60.5
1991.198

Hunt, Edward Aubrey 1855–1922
Broadly That's It
oil on canvas 42 x 54.5
1992.44

Hunt, Edward Aubrey 1855–1922
Cattle in a Field
oil on canvas 59.5 x 72
2007.6518

Hunt, Edward Aubrey 1855–1922
Cows and a Village
oil on canvas 68.7 x 88.7
1992.85

Hunt, Edward Aubrey 1855–1922
Desert Camels near Tangiers, Morocco
oil on canvas 63 x 84
1992.66

Hunt, Edward Aubrey 1855–1922
*Mrs Howard Stormont and Her Pikinese
'Prince Pri'*
oil on canvas 123 x 100
1992.59

Hunt, Edward Aubrey 1855–1922
Off the Moroccan Coast
oil on canvas 105.5 x 136
1991.67

Hunt, Edward Aubrey 1855–1922
On the Marne above Nogent, France
oil on canvas 65.2 x 86.5
1992.82

Hunt, Edward Aubrey 1855–1922
River Scene
oil on canvas 20 x 25
1991.50

Hunt, Edward Aubrey 1855–1922
Sallee Rover
oil on canvas 63 x 84
1992.68

Hunt, Edward Aubrey 1855–1922
Silver Sky and Shining Sands
oil on canvas 79.5 x 119
1991.78

Hunt, Edward Aubrey 1855–1922
Study of Cattle by a Clump of Willows
oil on canvas 42.5 x 54
1992.81

Facing page: Williams-Lyouns, Herbert Francis, 1863–1933, *Watercress Seller*, Kingsbridge Town Council (p. 235)

Hunt, Edward Aubrey 1855–1922
Study of Cattle in the Shade of a Large Willow Tree
oil on canvas 43.1 x 54
1992.88

Hunt, Edward Aubrey 1855–1922
The Drinking Place
oil on canvas 42 x 55
1991.55

Hunt, Edward Aubrey 1855–1922
The White Pony
oil on panel 18.7 x 27.5
1991.125

Hunter, Colin 1841–1904
Kelp Gatherers 1881
oil on canvas 50 x 90
1991.63

Hunter, Colin 1841–1904
Summer Fishing, Skye 1881
oil on canvas 47 x 90
1991.71

James, Clifford Boucher d.1913
The Wail of the Banshee, Waving Her Hands and Chanting a Sweet Song of Life
oil on canvas 101 x 151.5
1992.240

Jones, Patrick b.1948
Pilaster 2003
acrylic on canvas 221 x 33
2006.6456

Knight, John William Buxton 1842/1843–1908
Building the Rick
oil on canvas 60 x 90.3
1992.45

Knight, John William Buxton 1842/1843–1908
Loading the Haywain
oil on canvas 59.5 x 90
1992.41

Lavery, John 1856–1941
E. Aubrey Hunt (1855–1922) 1894
oil on canvas board 44.5 x 35.5
1991.69

Littlejohns, John b.1874
Bruges, Belgium
oil on canvas 72.5 x 59.1
1992.541

Lloyd, Reginald James b.1926
Estuary
oil on board 90.5 x 101
1992.239

Mead, Geraldine active 2000
Still Life in Silver and Grey
oil on board 39 x 49.5
2000.5833

Milne, William Watt 1865–1949
A Corner of the Farmyard 1906
oil on canvas 25 x 34.7
1992.99

Milne, William Watt 1865–1949
Corner of the Farmyard
oil on canvas 79 x 69.5
1992.79

Mumford, Howard
Elizabeth Athrens, Died Aged 98 1995
oil on board 47.8 x 37.4
1995.5662

Opie, John 1761–1807
Doctor Burton
oil on canvas 73 x 61
1991.47

Ousey, Buckley 1850–1889
*The Tail End of a Blow, Bull Bay,
Anglesey* 1888
oil on canvas 32 x 65
1991.49

Owen, William 1769–1825
The Rest by the Wayside
oil on canvas 158 x 125
1991.107

Peacock, Ralph 1868–1946
Master Wilson
oil on canvas 147.5 x 57
1992.128

Peacock, Ralph 1868–1946
Miss Wilson
oil on canvas 137 x 73
1992.127

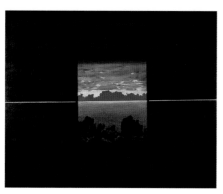

Pipkin, James Edward b.1945
The Sunset Line
oil on canvas 152 x 186
1994.5659

Prance, Bertram 1889–1958
Winter Scene
oil on panel 22.2 x 30.8
1991.211

Reid, Peter
A Letter to Peter Reid
acrylic on canvas 106 x 90
1992.216

Reid, Peter
Appledore Shipyard, Devon
oil on canvas 84.5 x 73.5
2008.6525

Reynolds, Joshua 1723–1792
Mrs John Clevland of Tapley
oil on canvas 71 x 59
1991.205 (P)

Sadler, Walter Dendy 1854–1923
The Attorney
oil on canvas 38 x 30
1992.64

Sadler, Walter Dendy 1854–1923
There's Joy in Remembrance (Portrait of a Lady at Her Desk)
oil on canvas 56.5 x 41
1992.40

Shayer, William 1788–1879
The Stable
oil on canvas 90 x 90
1991.117

Shayer, William 1788–1879
Travellers by a Gypsy Encampment
oil on canvas 61.5 x 75.5
1991.259

Sims, Charles 1873–1928
April
oil on canvas 70 x 90
1991.57

Trefusis, Hilda 1891–1980
Self Portrait 1910
oil on canvas 38.5 x 25
1996.5673

unknown artist
A View of Bideford from Upcott Hill, Devon c.1845
oil on canvas 70 x 100
1991.201

unknown artist
Bertha Burton
oil on canvas 75 x 58.8
1995.5665

unknown artist
Edward Capern (1819–1894), Postman Poet
oil on canvas 90 x 70
2001.5951

unknown artist
Thomas Burton
oil on canvas 75.1 x 59.8
1995.5666

Wilson, Richard 1712/1713–1782
*Lake Nemi Showing Castel Gandolfo and the
Barberini Palace, Italy*
oil on canvas 72 x 96
1992.61

Bovey Tracey
Heritage Trust

Elphick, David b.1942
Bovey Signal Box, Devon 2004
oil on canvas 43 x 59
PCF1

Malpass, I.
Kelly Cottage, Bovey Tracey, Devon
oil on board 15 x 20
PCF6

Yendall, Arthur active c.1935–1965
The Bovey Pottery, Devon c.1935
oil on board 39.5 x 49
PCF3

Yendall, Arthur active c.1935–1965
Bovey Station, Devon c.1946
oil on board 40 x 50
PCF4

Yendall, Arthur active c.1935–1965
'Church Steps', Bovey Tracey, Devon
oil on board 20 x 32
PCF5

Yendall, Arthur active c.1935–1965
Waiting for the Train at Bovey Station, Devon
oil on board 37 x 44
PCF2

Braunton and District Museum

Adams, Arthur b.1930
Knowle, Devon
oil on canvas 45.5 x 67
2010.5

Cabot
Under Sail (possibly 'Bessie Clarke') 1986
oil on board 19.1 x 24.4
1994_3

Dye, Lewis G. d. late 1960s
Braunton, Devon: An English Village
oil on board 42 x 58
1993_577

Dye, Lewis G. d. late 1960s
Buckland Farm Cottages
oil on board 40.2 x 50.2
1993_578

Dye, Lewis G. d. late 1960s
North Devon Coast Scene
oil on board 40.7 x 50.8
1993_575

Dye, Lewis G. d. late 1960s
Rocks of Saunton, Devon
oil on board 42 x 58
1993_574

Dye, Lewis G. d. late 1960s
Winter, North Street, Braunton, Devon
oil on board 42 x 58
1993_576

Falcon, Thomas Adolphus 1872–1944
Braunton, Devon, View from East Hill 1913
oil on panel 143 x 164
2010.1

Falcon, Thomas Adolphus 1872–1944
North Devon Coast View 1913
oil on panel 163.8 x 68.2
2010.3

Falcon, Thomas Adolphus 1872–1944
View across Braunton with Estuary and Great Field in the Distance 1913
oil on panel 128.5 x 147
2010.2

unknown artist
Mariners' Close, South Street, Braunton, Devon
oil on board 24.5 x 39.5
2000_59

Wilson, L.
View of Braunton, Devon, with Two Bridges 1910
oil on canvas 31.9 x 74.6
2000.215

Facing page: Pratt, Albert, *The Gee Gees, Girl Riding on a Merry-Go-Round* (shutter from Saunt's Hoopla), The Fairground Heritage Trust (p. 252)

Buckfastleigh Town Hall

Mann, Warwick Henry 1838–1910
John Hamlyn (1816–1878) 1874
oil on canvas 122 x 88.7
PCF2

unknown artist 19th C
William Hamlyn (b.1852)
oil on canvas 95.5 x 72.5
PCF3

Vigard, W. active 1886–1889
Joseph Hamlyn (1809–1888) 1886
oil on canvas 75 x 62.5
PCF1

Budleigh Salterton Town Council

Dennys, Joyce 1893–1991
Above Steamer Steps
oil on board 58 x 89
PCF3

Dennys, Joyce 1893–1991
Beach Party, the Old Capstan
oil on board 45 x 58
PCF5

Dennys, Joyce 1893–1991
Eating Ice Creams on Budleigh Seafront, Devon
oil on board 59.5 x 74.5
PCF1

Dennys, Joyce 1893–1991
Fore Street Hill, Budleigh Salterton, Devon
oil on board 49.5 x 64.5
PCF6

Dennys, Joyce 1893–1991
The Coffee Morning, 'Markers' Restaurant
oil on board 44.5 x 67.3
PCF4

Dennys, Joyce 1893–1991
The Longboat Café
oil on board 54.5 x 74.5
PCF2

Fairlynch
Museum

Carpenter, George Ellis 1891–1971
Rainy Day
oil on board 39 x 49
2007.26

Cotton, Alan b.1938
Otter Valley, Devon, Evening Light 1986
oil on canvas 45.7 x 61.2
2001.12.1

Dennys, Joyce 1893–1991
*Family on the Beach at Budleigh Salterton,
Devon*
oil on board 39.5 x 62.2
1999.98

Dennys, Joyce 1893–1991
Flower Painting
oil on board 49.2 x 39.9
1994.99

Dennys, Joyce 1893–1991
On the Parade
oil on board 59.5 x 90
loan06

Dennys, Joyce 1893–1991
Still Life with Flowers
oil on board 65 x 50
loan21 (P)

Goodhall, Peter b.1957
*A Revenue Cutter Apprehends the Smuggler
Jack Rattenbury off Budleigh Salterton*
oil on panel 60 x 120
PCF3

Goodhall, Peter b.1957
*The Dutch Privateer 'Zeuse' Brought as a Prize
into Exmouth by the 'Defiance' after a Two
Hour Action in the Bay, June 1782*
oil on canvas 61.5 x 123
PCF2

Crediton Area History and Museum Society

unknown artist
*Marjorie Jago, Music Teacher at Queen
Elizabeth School, Crediton, Devon and Choir
Mistress at the Parish Church*
acrylic on hardboard 49.5 x 39.5
PCF2

unknown artist
Pauls and Whites, Crediton Mill, Devon
tempera on paper 76 x 123.5
PCF1

Britannia Royal Naval College

Britannia Royal Naval College (BRNC) opened in 1905 and replaced two wooden hulks, HMS *Britannia* and HMS *Hindostan*, moored on the River Dart, as the site of naval officer training. There is little evidence to suggest that the old ships had much in the way of artwork, but when the new College was opened there was a conscious effort to adorn the walls with paintings that would inspire the young cadets. The College opened in the same year as the centenary of the Battle of Trafalgar and several scholars have suggested that BRNC was, in part, the memorial to Nelson that a grateful nation might have built to commemorate its greatest naval hero. Nelsonian artefacts, which together with the early paintings of famous sea battles and Admirals formed the core of the original collection, were consciously displayed throughout the College as further inspiration to the cadets.

Since 1905 the art collection has grown considerably, through gifts, bequests, loans and, more recently, commissions, and transfers from other naval establishments that have closed, such as the former Royal Naval Colleges at Greenwich and Manadon. Recent commissions have included the action painting *San Carlos, Falkland Islands, May 1982* by Derek George Montague Gardner, and portraits of the three Commanders-in-Chief in office during the Falklands conflict. These three portraits, all Admirals of the Fleet, are *Admiral of the Fleet Lord Fieldhouse (1928–1992), Commander-in-Chief Fleet* and *Admiral Sir Henry Leach (b.1923), First Sea Lord*, both by Nicholas St John Rosse, and *Admiral of the Fleet Terence Thornton Lewin, Baron Lewin (1920–1999), Chief of the Defence Staff*, by Michael Noakes. They all hang in the magnificent Senior Gun Room along with other notable naval leaders from the past. They serve both to inspire those upon whom they look down and illustrate more recent aspects of naval history.

One painting of particular interest is a full-length portrait of Nelson by Leonardo Guzzardi. It is similar to one in the ownership of the National Maritime Museum and another that was hung in the Admiralty Board Room. For many years it was thought to be a copy but has been identified as genuine in recent years, although only about 40 per cent is original as it was badly damaged when the College was bombed in 1942, suffering 918 perforations.

The College is fortunate to have William Lionel Wyllie's *The Battle of Trafalgar, 21 October 1805*. This painting was renowned in the Navy but for many years the whereabouts of the original was unknown until it was discovered in 1964 after it had been hanging in a derelict house for many years. Fortunately, the Captain of the College purchased it so now it can be fully appreciated by the young officers under training. Another magnificent painting, *View of Bruges Harbour* by Hendrick van Minderhout, signed and dated 1666, is clearly the oldest painting in the Collection. It was presented in 1925 by HRH Princess Louise, Duchess of Argyll (the sixth child of Queen Victoria) and is just one of a number of gifts made to the College by members of the Royal family.

The closure of the Royal Naval College at Greenwich saw a number of paintings transferred to Dartmouth, the most important of which is the Birley Collection. It is believed to be the largest collection of portraits by Oswald Hornby Joseph Birley on view to the public. They came to Dartmouth on the understanding that they were to be displayed together and they all hang in what is now known as the Birley Gallery. The Collection comprises 19 portraits, depicting King George VI and 18 Admirals of the 1939–1945 war. The King's portrait was commissioned in 1939 to mark the inauguration of the Painted Hall at Greenwich as the premier Officers' Mess in the Royal Navy. The 18 Admirals were all Flag Officers during World War Two and an appeal was launched to raise the funds to commission Sir Oswald Birley to carry out the painting of the portraits.

The closure of the Colleges at Manadon and Greenwich served to highlight the fact that these art collections do not always have a secure future. To ensure the future of the collection at Dartmouth, the Britannia Museum Trust was formed in 2007 and all the College-owned paintings were transferred to it. The Commanding Officer, Commodore Tim Harris, was instrumental in the formation of the Trust and with properly constituted collection and disposal policies the Dartmouth Collection is now secure in an uncertain future.

In an attempt to encourage artistic talent within the Royal Navy, a Contemporary Naval Artists Collection was initiated. The Commanding Officer asked a number of retired and serving officers if they would donate a painting to the College. These were displayed in the Contemporary Naval Artists Gallery and some fine works were given by some talented amateur artists, serving to highlight that a career in the Royal Navy is not incompatible with painting as a hobby. To compliment this, the College has staged a number of temporary art exhibitions to encourage young talent and these have always been well received.

The BRNC Collection serves as an inspiration to those young officers under training at the College. The paintings are used to illustrate and compliment their education in naval history and to instil a sense of ethos, which in turn helps to emphasise the centuries-old heritage of the navy that they have recently joined. This can be summarised in the first two paragraphs of the Britannia Museum's mission statement:

'The Britannia Museum's principal aim is to promote public understanding of Britain's naval and maritime heritage, as a key element in the development of British history, culture, international relations and national identity.

It also serves to instil a sense of identity and ethos in the young officers of the Royal Navy in the twenty-first century through the preservation and promotion of the heritage and history of Britannia Royal Naval College.'

Dr Richard Porter, Curator and Dr Jane Harrold, Deputy Curator

Abbott, Lemuel Francis 1760–1803
Captain Thomas Masterman Hardy (1769–1839)
oil on canvas 75 x 62
A106

Armitage, Edward 1817–1896
The Death of Nelson 1848
oil on canvas 163 x 230
A702

Bambridge, Arthur Leopold 1861–1923
Alfred Ernest Albert (1844–1900), Duke of Saxe-Coburg and Gotha, Duke of Edinburgh
oil on canvas 157 x 93
PCF1

Birley, Oswald Hornby Joseph 1880–1952
George VI (1895–1952) 1944
oil on canvas 125 x 100
PCF48

Birley, Oswald Hornby Joseph 1880–1952
Admiral of the Fleet Sir Max Horton (1883–1951), GCB 1945
oil on canvas 75 x 62
PCF34

Birley, Oswald Hornby Joseph 1880–1952
Admiral Sir Algernon Willis (1889–1976) 1945
oil on canvas 76 x 63
PCF44

Birley, Oswald Hornby Joseph 1880–1952
Admiral Sir Henry Harwood (1888–1950), KCB 1945
oil on canvas 78 x 70
PCF43

Birley, Oswald Hornby Joseph 1880–1952
Admiral Sir Percy Noble (1880–1955) 1946
oil on canvas 80 x 63
PCF37

Birley, Oswald Hornby Joseph 1880–1952
Admiral of the Fleet Earl Viscount Mountbatten of Burma (1900–1979), KC 1947
oil on canvas 110 x 79
PCF45

Birley, Oswald Hornby Joseph 1880–1952
*Admiral of the Fleet Lord Tovey (1885–1971),
GCB* 1947
oil on canvas 113 x 83
PCF33

Birley, Oswald Hornby Joseph 1880–1952
*Admiral of the Fleet Sir Charles Forbes
(1880–1960), GCB* 1947
oil on canvas 75 x 62.5
PCF32

Birley, Oswald Hornby Joseph 1880–1952
*Admiral of the Fleet Sir James Somerville
(1882–1949), GCB* 1947
oil on canvas 125 x 90
PCF47

Birley, Oswald Hornby Joseph 1880–1952
*Admiral of the Fleet The Earl of
Mountbatten* 1947
oil on canvas 123 x 100
A111

Birley, Oswald Hornby Joseph 1880–1952
*Admiral of the Fleet Viscount Cunningham
(1883–1963)* 1947
oil on canvas 125 x 88
PCF49

Birley, Oswald Hornby Joseph 1880–1952
*Admiral Sir Bertram Ramsay (1883–1945),
KCB* 1947
oil on canvas 110 x 83
PCF41

Birley, Oswald Hornby Joseph 1880–1952
*Admiral Sir John Cunningham (1885–1962),
GCB* 1947
oil on canvas 76 x 63
PCF42

Birley, Oswald Hornby Joseph 1880–1952
Lord Fraser (1888–1981) 1947
oil on canvas 108 x 83
PCF36

Birley, Oswald Hornby Joseph 1880–1952
Sir Bernard Rawlings (1889–1962) 1947
oil on canvas 76 x 63
PCF40

Birley, Oswald Hornby Joseph 1880–1952
*Admiral of the Fleet Sir Neville Syfret
(1889–1972), KCB* 1948
oil on canvas 75 x 62
PCF35

Birley, Oswald Hornby Joseph 1880–1952
Sir Phillip Vian (1894–1968) 1948
oil on canvas 80 x 65
PCF39

Birley, Oswald Hornby Joseph 1880–1952
*Admiral of the Fleet Dudley-Pound (1877–
1943)*
oil on canvas 100 x 77.5
PCF46

Birley, Oswald Hornby Joseph 1880–1952
Admiral Sir Arthur J. Power (1889–1960)
oil on canvas 76 x 63
PCF38

Boel, Maurice 1913–1998
Abstraction 1972
oil on board 110 x 190 (E)
PCF78

Bolwell, Norman William 1938–2009
Battle Group South Atlantic 1982
oil on board 44.5 x 64
PCF7

Brie, Anthony de 1854–1921
*Admiral George Legge (c.1647–1691), Lord
Dartmouth* (after Joseph Vivien)
oil on canvas 124 x 98.7
A101

British (English) School
*HMS 'Britannia' and HMS 'Trafalgar' at
Portland* c.1862
oil on canvas 134 x 215
A301

Brooks, Frank 1854–1937
*His Royal Highness The Duke of Windsor
(1894–1972)* c.1926
oil on canvas 69 x 48
A003

Bumford, Frederick W. active 1979–1986
HMS 'Thunderer' Devastation Class, 1877 1979
oil on canvas 49.5 x 75.5
PCF15

Bumford, Frederick W. active 1979–1986
HMS 'Thunderer' Orion Class, 1912 1979
oil on canvas 50 x 75
PCF16

Bumford, Frederick W. active 1979–1986
HMS 'Thunderer' Culloden Class, 1781 1980
oil on canvas 59.7 x 80.2
PCF106

Bumford, Frederick W. active 1979–1986
HMS 'Thunderer' Lion Class, 1939 1986
oil on canvas 49.5 x 90
PCF14

Burke, Terry b.1927
Dartmouth, Devon
oil on board 29.8 x 75.2
PCF115

Carmichael, John Wilson 1799–1868
The Battle of Copenhagen, 16 August–5 September 1807
oil on tin 54 x 70 (E)
PCF62

Clarke, Sarah d.c.2001
Britannia Royal Naval College
acrylic on paper 33.5 x 29.9
PCF07

Clegg, Ernest active 1951
HMS 'Cardiff' (polyptych, panel 1 of 6)
oil on board 44 x 68.5
A706_1

Clegg, Ernest active 1951
SMS 'Seydlitz' (polyptych, panel 2 of 6)
oil on board 44 x 69.5
A706_2

Facing page: Hudson, Thomas, 1701–1779, *Christiana Maria Rolle (1710–1780)*, Great Torrington Almshouse, Town Lands and Poors Charities (p. 225)

65

Clegg, Ernest active 1951
SMS 'Derfflinger' (polyptych, panel 4 of 6)
oil on board 44 x 69.5
A706_4

Clegg, Ernest active 1951
SMS 'Hindenburg' (polyptych, panel 5 of 6)
oil on board 44 x 69.5
A706_5

Clegg, Ernest active 1951
SMS 'Von der Tann' (polyptych, panel 6 of 6)
oil on board 44 x 69.5
A706_6

Cobb, Charles David b.1921
Operation Loyalty
oil on canvas 50 x 75
PCF28

Collins, William Wiehe 1862–1951
The Channel Squadron, 1898 1899
oil on canvas 126 x 181.7
A501

Condy, Nicholas Matthew 1816–1851
HMS 'Pike'
oil on board 13 x 17.8
A402

Cope, Arthur Stockdale 1857–1940
Edward VII (1841–1910)
oil on canvas 88 x 68
A001

Cope, Arthur Stockdale 1857–1940
George V (1865–1936)
oil on canvas 88 x 68
A002

Cundall, Charles Ernest 1890–1971
Dunkirk
oil on canvas 118 x 179.5
A604 ⬙

De Lacy, Charles John 1856–1936
HMS 'Vindictive' Storming Zeebrugge Mole 1918
oil on board 37 x 57
PCF6

Dodd, Robert (attributed to) 1748–1815
HMS 'Victory' at Spithead, 1791 (The British fleet under Lord Hood: The Russian Armament, 1791)
oil on canvas 62 x 86
A300

Drew, Pamela 1910–1989
Prince Philip Presents the Queen's Colour to the Britannia Royal Naval College, Dartmouth, Devon 1 July 1958 1958
oil on metal 63 x 93
A201

Eves, Reginald Grenville 1876–1941
The Admiral of the Fleet John Rushworth Jellicoe (1859–1935), OM, 1st Earl Jellicoe
oil on canvas 58.8 x 48.4
PCF85

Fearnley, Alan b.1942
HMS 'Bacchante' Conducting PWD Firings against Shelduck X2538 off Gibraltar on 25 October 1978 1979
oil on canvas 59.5 x 90
PCF52

Fildes, Denis 1889–1974
Elizabeth II (b.1926) 1960
oil on canvas 172 x 127
A005

Fildes, Denis 1889–1974
The Duke of Edinburgh (b.1921) 1962
oil on canvas 140 x 104
A006

Fisher, Roger Roland Sutton 1919–1992
HMS 'Manchester' on Armilla Patrol
oil on board 29.5 x 50.8
PCF68

Fleck, J.
The First Battle Cruiser Squadron 1919
oil on canvas 36 x 61
PCF4

Fleck, J.
First Battle Cruiser Squadron Returning from Jutland, June 1916
oil on canvas 36 x 61
PCF5

Gardner, Derek George Montague 1914–2007
San Carlos, Falkland Islands, May 1982 1983
oil on canvas 54.5 x 100
PCF26

George, Colin
Moorland Fire
oil on paper 23.7 x 33
PCF95

Goodwin, Albert 1845–1932
The Invincible Armada 1904
oil on canvas 105 x 145
A600

Goodwin, Albert 1845–1932
The Phantom Ship
oil on canvas 105 x 145 (E)
A800

Green, George Pycock Everett c.1811–1893
The Deposition of Christ (after Peter Paul Rubens) c.1845
oil on canvas 124 x 91
A900

Gribble, Bernard Finnigan 1872–1962
Nelson's First Prize
oil on canvas 106.3 x 150
A701

Gribble, Bernard Finnigan 1872–1962
The Doomed Raider
oil on canvas 134.5 x 170.4
A705

Guzzardi, Leonardo active 1798–1800
Horatio Nelson (1758–1805), 1st Viscount Nelson 1799
oil on canvas 216 x 129
A104

Hailstone, Bernard 1910–1987
Charles, Prince of Wales (b.1948) 1977
oil on canvas 91 x 71
A007

Hailstone, Bernard 1910–1987
Prince Andrew (b.1960) 1980
oil on canvas 90.5 x 75.5
A009

Hailstone, Bernard 1910–1987
Princess Anne (b.1950)
oil on canvas 91 x 70
A008

Halliday, Edward Irvine 1902–1984
*Her Royal Highness Princess Elizabeth (b.1926)
and the Duke of Edinburgh (b.1921)* 1949
oil on canvas 91 x 73
PCF102

Herkomer, Herman 1863–1935
*Admiral of the Fleet Sir Edward Seymour
(1840–1929)* 1900
oil on canvas 90.1 x 74.5
PCF60

Higson, Max
Chipmunks over Dartmouth, Devon 1987
oil on canvas 29.8 x 39.7
PCF94

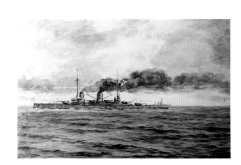

Johnson, Desmond b.1922
SMS 'Moltke' (after Ernest Clegg) 1983
oil on board 44 x 69.5
A706_3

Johnson, Desmond b.1922
Sailing in Dartmouth Harbour
oil on board 28 x 42
PCF96

Lady Abercromby
Admiral Lord Duncan (after Joshua
Reynolds) 1909
oil & pastel on paper 124.7 x 99.9
A103

Langmaid, Rowland 1897–1956
Battle Fleet 1926
oil on canvas 100 x 190 (E)
PCF71

Leigh-Pemberton, John 1911–1997
George VI (1895–1952) (copy after Oswald Hornby Joseph Birley)
oil on canvas 124 x 99.8
A004 (P)

Long, Leonard Hugh b.1911
Creswell Naval College, Jervis Bay, Australia
oil on canvas 44 x 64
A200

Luny, Thomas 1759–1837
The Battle of Trafalgar, 21 October 1805
oil on canvas 59 x 84.5
A602

Mason, Frank Henry 1876–1965
HMS 'Superb'
oil on canvas 95 x 185 (E)
PCF72

McDowell, William 1888–1950
HMS 'Liverpool'
acrylic on board 60.5 x 53.5
PCF112

Mendoza, June b.1945
Admiral of the Fleet Sir Michael Le Fanu (1913–1970) 1978
oil on canvas 100 x 75
A113

Mendoza, June b.1945
Admiral of the Fleet the Earl Mountbatten of Burma (1900–1979) 1982
oil on canvas 101 x 75
A112

Menzies, William A. active 1886–1928
Lord Nelson (1758–1805), after Copenhagen (copy after John Hoppner)
oil on canvas 125.5 x 100
A105

Minderhout, Hendrik van 1632–1696
View of Bruges Harbour 1666
oil on canvas 168 x 310
A801

Mitchell, A. L.
Admiral Sir William Parker (1781–1866), GCB
oil on canvas 126.2 x 100
PCF59

Mitchell, F.
The Red Fleet, 1781
oil on canvas 70 x 101.2
PCF114

Neate, Andrew
Britannia Royal Naval College 1960
oil on board 52 x 75
PCF50

Nibbs, Richard Henry 1816–1893
HMS 'Bombay' 1860
oil on canvas 117 x 183 (E)
PCF70

Noakes, Michael b.1933
*Admiral of the Fleet Terence Thornton Lewin,
Baron Lewin (1920–1999), Chief of the Defence
Staff*
oil on canvas 99.3 x 75.2
PCF91

Noble, John Rushton b.1927
Destroyer Screen c.1950
oil on canvas 62.3 x 75
A707

Phillips, Rex b.1931
Helicopter 1988
oil on canvas 69 x 92
PCF29

Phillips, Rex b.1931
Jellicoe Crosses the 'T', Jutland 31 May 1916
oil on canvas 59.3 x 90
PCF93

Pocock, Nicholas (after) 1740–1821
The Capture of 'L'Étoile'
oil on panel 68.2 x 94.8
A704

Poole, Burnell 1884–1933
Sixth Battle Squadron, Grand Fleet Rear Admiral Hugh Rodman, United States Navy Commanding 1922–1923
oil on canvas 103 x 154
A503

Powell, Charles Martin 1775–1824
HMS 'Enchantress' in the River Dart c.1804
oil on canvas 89 x 168
A401

Riley, James Lewis b.1925
Mountbatten at Singapore
acrylic on canvas 49.5 x 59.5
PCF110

Robins, Henry 1820–1892
HMS 'Britannia' and 'Hindostan' c.1880–1890
oil on canvas 56 x 71
A300

Rosse, Nicholas St John b.1945
Admiral of the Fleet Lord Fieldhouse (1928–1992), Commander-in-Chief Fleet
oil on board 98 x 73
PCF90

Rosse, Nicholas St John b.1945
Admiral Sir Henry Leach (b.1923), First Sea Lord
oil on canvas 90 x 69.6
PCF92

Saumarez, Marion 1885–1978
Admiral James Saumarez (1757–1836), 1st Baron de Saumarez (copy after Thomas Phillips)
oil on canvas 235 x 144 (E)
PCF61

Swan, Robert John 1888–1980
Admiral of the Fleet Andrew Browne Cunningham (1873–1968), PC, GCB, OM, 1st Viscount Cunningham of Hyndhope
oil on canvas 105.5 x 80
A109

Facing page: Dyer, Edmund, active c.1820–1875, *Sir Richard Grenville (1542–1591)*, Bideford Town Council (p. 39)

AN° DÑI · 1571
ÆTATIS · SVÆ
29

Sir Richard Grenville killed
in a sea-fight near the Azores.
1591

Swan, Robert John 1888–1980
*Admiral of the Fleet Andrew Browne
Cunningham, 1st Viscount Cunningham of
Hyndhope*
oil on canvas 109.5 x 94
A110

Swan, Robert John 1888–1980
*Admiral of the Fleet Lord Fisher of Kilverstone
(1841–1920) (copy after Hubert von
Herkomer)*
oil on canvas 125.2 x 94.4
A107

Taylor, Robert b.1946
HMS 'Kelly' 1978
oil on canvas 75 x 121 (E)
PCF75

unknown artist
*Admiral Edward Russell (1653–1727) (copy
after an earlier painting by unknown artist)*
oil on canvas 124.9 x 97
A102

unknown artist
*Admiral of the Fleet George Anson (1697–
1762), 1st Baron Anson*
oil on canvas 67 x 44
PCF88

unknown artist
Admiral Sir David Milne (1763–1845), GCB
oil on board 76 x 62
PCF25

unknown artist
Portsmouth Harbour
oil on canvas 77 x 97
A803

unknown artist
Seascape
oil on panel 30 x 35 (E)
PCF63

unknown artist
Seascape
oil on panel 30 x 40 (E)
PCF64

unknown artist
Seascape
oil on panel 30 x 40 (E)
PCF65

unknown artist
The Last of the 'Revenge' (triptych, left wing)
oil on canvas 79.5 x 56
A700.1

unknown artist
The Last of the 'Revenge' (triptych, centre panel)
oil on canvas 109.8 x 138.8
A700.2

unknown artist
The Last of the 'Revenge' (triptych, right wing)
oil on canvas 79.5 x 56
A700.3

Velde II, Willem van de (school of) 1633–1707
Large Seascape
oil on canvas 152 x 179
A802

Vincent
HMS 'Sheffield' 1982
oil on board 60.5 x 75.5
PCF111

Watherston, Evelyn Mary 1880–1952
William Howard (c.1510–1573), 1st Baron Howard of Effingham (copy after Daniel Mytens)
oil on canvas 127.5 x 101.8
A100

Webster, John b.1932
Entering Dartmouth Harbour
oil on board 39.2 x 49.7
PCF69

Webster, John b.1932
HMS 'Westminster' off Greenwich
oil on canvas 50 x 75
PCF20

Wilcox, Leslie Arthur 1904–1982
Admiral of the Fleet Earl Jellicoe (1858–1935)
(copy after Reginald Grenville Eves)
oil on canvas 118 x 94
A108

Wilkinson, Norman 1878–1972
HMS 'Lion', Battlecruiser
oil on canvas 120 x 120
A504

Wilkinson, Norman 1878–1972
The Normandy Landings, 1944
oil on canvas 60 x 81
A605

Wood, Frank Watson 1862–1953
HMS 'Renown' with HMS 'Terrible' in
Company Leaving Portsmouth Harbour 1906
oil on canvas 76 x 128
A502

Wood, Tim G. c.1929–1998
Dartmouth Castle, Devon
oil on board 60 x 44.5
PCF116

Wyllie, William Lionel 1851–1931
The Battle of Trafalgar, 21 October 1805 1905
oil on canvas 148 x 272
A601

Wyllie, William Lionel 1851–1931
The Destruction of the German Raider
'Leopard' by His Majesty's Ships 'Achilles' and
'Dundee', 16 March 1917
oil on canvas 79 x 87.5
PCF113

Dartmouth and Kingswear Hospital

Beulke, Reinhardt 1926–2008
Devil's Marbles, Australia
oil on board 36.5 x 50.7
PCF3

Donaldson, John b.1945
Dartmouth Harbour Scene, Devon
oil on canvas 48.8 x 59
PCF1

Tiffen, S.
Riders in a Wood 1985
oil on canvas 60 x 89.7
PCF2

Dartmouth Guildhall

The portraits of some of the former Mayors of Dartmouth, and one Mayoress, are located in the Council Chamber. The majority are oil on canvas. Some are signed and dated and have plaques with an inscription stating the sitter's name and years of office. The portraits have no doubt been commissioned and, over the years, have been displayed in previous Guildhalls before they came to the current building in Victoria Road.

Chris M. Horan, Town Clerk

Campbell, T. H.
Sir Thomas Wilton, Mayor of Dartmouth
(1900–1901 & 1914–1919) 1920
oil on canvas 110 x 92
PCF4

Girard, Michel b.1939
A French Fishing Port
oil on canvas 20 x 26
PCF5

Harris, George Frederick 1856–1926
Sir Henry Paul Seale (1806–1897), Bt, Mayor
of Dartmouth 1885
oil on canvas 126 x 100
PCF11

unknown artist
Arthur Howe Holdsworth (1780–1860),
Governor of Dartmouth Castle (1807–1857)
oil on canvas 236 x 146
PCF12

unknown artist
Elizabeth Kennicott, Mayoress of Dartmouth
(1683)
oil on canvas 74 x 61
PCF10

unknown artist
Francis Charles Simpson, Mayor of Dartmouth
(1882–1891)
oil on canvas 150 x 120
PCF2

unknown artist
George Kennicott, Mayor of Dartmouth (1683)
oil on canvas 91 x 72
PCF7

unknown artist
Hercules Hoyles, BA Oxon, Clerk of
Dartmouth (1695)
oil on canvas 74 x 60
PCF9

unknown artist
Reverend John Flavel (c.1630–1691), BA Oxon,
Rector of Dartmouth (1656–1662)
oil on canvas 58 x 43
PCF1

unknown artist
Robert Cranford, Mayor of Dartmouth
(1871–1872)
oil on paper 52 x 38
PCF6

unknown artist
Samuel Were Prideaux (1803–1874)
oil on canvas 75 x 63
PCF3

unknown artist
William Smith, Mayor of Dartmouth
(1891–1893)
oil on canvas 150 x 120
PCF15

Way, William Hopkins 1812–1891
Charles Chalker, First Postmaster of
Dartmouth (1870) 1884
oil on canvas 95 x 70
PCF14

Wimbush, John L. c.1854–1914
Charles Peek, Mayor of Dartmouth (1911–1914
& 1919–1921) 1912
oil on canvas 182 x 124
PCF13

Wray, G.
John Morgan Puddicombe, Mayor of
Dartmouth (1873–1876) 1873
oil on canvas 120 x 90
PCF8

Dartmouth Museum

The 26 paintings that have been acquired by Dartmouth Museum over the last 50 years are of varying standards, both aesthetically and technically. They range from crude paintings on leather and robust views of the town by unknown artists to luminous maritime paintings by Thomas Luny and naive works by Hubert E. Beavis and Gustav Butler. The Museum also houses The Henley Collection, amongst which the sensual *Portrait of a Girl* and theatrical, melancholy *The Jester*, both by John L. Wimbush, are the most interesting. The Henley Collection is catalogued and treated as if part of the main Dartmouth Museum collection with the approval of the Museums, Libraries and Archives Council.

The street scene and surrounding landscape views of Dartmouth provide an invaluable record of a town that has undergone many stages of development as the river and the creek mud have been gradually reclaimed.

The great wealth brought to the town by the Triangular Trade (Dartmouth, Newfoundland and Portugal) enabled the leading families and merchants to build, improve and embellish their dwellings. The architectural and social details recorded here give us snapshots of a town and harbour long since lost. Amongst what are, for the most part, works of limited interest beyond social record, a few deserve a closer look.

Higher Street Looking South, 'The Old Shambles', Dartmouth, Devon by C. B. (Miss) Hunt has acquired a new significance since the recent disastrous fire in 2010 destroyed everything except the facade of the Tudor House. Work has begun to stabilise and to finally restore the area, but it will never look like this painting again. It is interesting, too, to see the Cherub Inn before its restoration.

Dartmouth Harbour from Castle Walk, Devon by Edward Tucker is an enchanting piece. Trees, lush and leafy, frame a view of Warfleet Creek and Half-Tide Rock, looking towards Coombe Mud (the land not yet reclaimed to form Coronation Park). The painting is a romantic vision of Mount Boone overlooking the North side of the town and of St Saviour's Church. Extravagant, blue, mystic hills rise above Dittisham and in the foreground a pool of light dignifies three working folk in Gallant's Bower.

Two maritime paintings attributed to Thomas Luny are *HMS 'Dartmouth'* and *Mouth of the Dart with a Merchant Ship Entering.* They are luminous, splashy, unrealistic – and deeply attractive. In *Merchant Ship* we see a dark foreground with a silhouetted rowing boat, in contrast to the sunlit stern of a ship, all set against a flaming sky. In *HMS 'Dartmouth'*, the ship rides a theatrical, bumpy sea. Both are jewels.

Bayard's Cove, Devon by William Hopkins Way is a lively painting, seemingly in two parts: the foreground full of action – low-tide at Bayard's Cove, with crab boat, watching woman and child and the sea-wall bustling with life; the background, by contrast, is impressionistic, in loose jewel colours.

Looking towards improbable mountains at the mouth of the river, in *Dartmouth from King's Quay, Devon* (after Clarkson Stanfield), we see St Petrox Church with spire (later removed when the lighthouse was built). Looking over the pool, before it was drained, the bridge leads from the back of the Butterwalk and the Museum to the New Ground.

Townstal Hill, Dartmouth by T. G. Wood is a lovely exercise in light and shade, delivered in a loose, impressionistic style, using palette knife and brush. It depicts the bridge that once spanned the road above Vicarage Hill, linking The Keep with its gardens.

The small modern section in the collection – *Dawn Exercise, Motor Torpedo Boat, HMT 'Himalaya'* and *Hurricane Fighting Dornier* – are executed in a naïve style and with a thin, modern palette. The two Harold Ing paintings are observational, detailed and use pastel colours in a clinical style.

Sadly, most of the remaining paintings are dirty and in a bad state of repair. It is doubtful whether they are of sufficient quality to merit the cost of conservation.

Angela White, Museum Designer

A. H.
'Annie', Yarmouth, Isle of Wight
oil on canvas 50.9 x 25.5
1996.773

Assar, W.
Dartmouth from King's Quay, Devon (after Clarkson Stansfield) c.1877
oil on board 32.1 x 45
1997.326

Beavis, Hubert E. b.1925
Motor Torpedo Boat MTB 777 1981
oil on board 27.3 x 44.2
2009.028

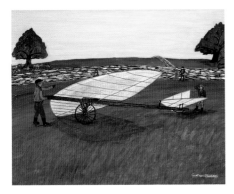

Butler, Gustav
The 'Dittisham Flyer', Lilienthal's Aerostat in Fields c.1890–1903
oil on board 26.5 x 34.2
1997.611

Holwill, Fred Cyril 1887–1980
Morning Departure, 'Mayflower II 'Leaving Dartmouth, 19 April 1957
oil on board 29.8 x 44.7
1997.579

Hunt, C. B. (Miss)
Higher Street Looking South, 'The Old Shambles', Dartmouth, Devon c.1839
oil on board 30 x 45
1996.005

Ing, Harold Vivian 1900–1973
Lightship under Repair, HMS 'Venus' in the Background 1955
oil on canvas 65 x 73 (E)
1997.562

Ing, Harold Vivian 1900–1973
Tall Ships in Dartmouth Harbour, Devon, Prior to a Race 1956
oil on canvas 62.4 x 75
1997.526

Luny, Thomas 1759–1837
HMS 'Dartmouth'
oil on canvas 24.2 x 33.8
1996.001

Luny, Thomas 1759–1837
*Mouth of the Dart with a Merchant Ship
Entering*
oil on canvas 24.2 x 34.1
1996.003

Mackay, K. (Miss)
*New Ground Bridge and Plumleigh Conduit,
Dartmouth, Devon* 1884
oil on canvas 29.1 x 51.6
1996.004

Mackay, K. (Miss) (copy of)
*New Ground Bridge and Plumleigh Conduit,
Dartmouth, Devon*
oil on canvas 29.2 x 39.5
1990.24 (P)

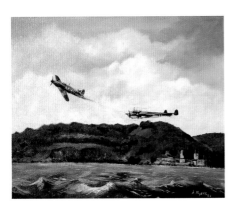

Myers, A.
*Hurricane Fighting Dornier over Dartmouth
Harbour, Devon in 1940* 1982
oil on board 49.6 x 59.5
1996.371

Payne, Charles
*'Dawn Exercise', Blackpool Sands, near
Dartmouth, Devon, April 1944* 1994
oil on canvas 89.6 x 69.6
1997.664.001

Tucker, Edward c.1825–1909
*Dartmouth Harbour from Castle Walk,
Devon* 1835
oil on board 65.7 x 101
1997.338

unknown artist
Dartmouth Castle, Devon
oil on canvas 28.5 x 39.4
1990.209 (P)

unknown artist
Ellen Langley, Aged 5
oil on board 55.2 x 44.6
1997.341

unknown artist
*HMT 'Himalaya', Hong Kong, China, 1922,
January*
oil on canvas 30.6 x 55
PCF2

Facing page: Furse, Patrick John Dolignon, 1918–2005, *Lady in a Hat*, 1996, Burton Art Gallery and Museum (p. 44)

unknown artist
Mountain Landscape
oil on leather 4.8 x 10
1996.104.2

unknown artist
Portrait of a Gentleman
oil on canvas 40 x 36.2
1990.274 (P)

unknown artist
Portrait of a Gentleman
oil on canvas 57 x 41.9
PCF6

unknown artist
Ship
oil on leather 5.2 x 10.6
1996.104.1

Way, William Hopkins 1812–1891
Bayard's Cove, Devon
oil on canvas 42 x 59.1
1997.327

Wimbush, John L. c.1854–1914
Portrait of a Girl
oil on canvas 27.3 x 20.5
1990.271 (P)

Wimbush, John L. c.1854–1914
The Jester
oil on canvas 49.2 x 37
1990.273 (P)

Wood, Tim G. c.1929–1998
Townstal Hill, Dartmouth 1965
oil on canvas 81.5 x 61
1997.543

Dawlish
Community
Hospital

Stacey, Andrew b.1951
Dawlish Warren Seascape, Devon (triptych, left wing) 1996
oil on canvas 141 x 141
PCF3

Stacey, Andrew b.1951
Dawlish Warren Seascape, Devon (triptych, centre panel) 1996
oil on canvas 141 x 141
PCF2

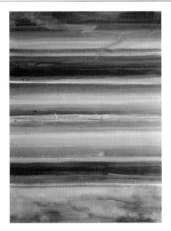

Stacey, Andrew b.1951
Dawlish Warren Seascape, Devon (triptych, right wing) 1996
oil on canvas 141 x 141
PCF1

Stacey, Andrew b.1951
Seascape 1
oil on board 59.5 x 44.7
PCF5

Stacey, Andrew b.1951
Seascape 2
oil on board 59.5 x 44.7
PCF4

Stacey, Andrew b.1951
Dawlish Seascape, Devon
oil on board 49.5 x 59
PCF6

Stacey, Andrew b.1951
Dawlish Seascape, Devon
oil on board 59 x 49.5
PCF7

Stacey, Andrew b.1951
Dawlish Seascape, Devon
oil on board 75 x 49.5
PCF8

Stacey, Andrew b.1951
Dawlish Seascape, Devon
oil on board 75 x 49.5
PCF9

Stacey, Andrew b.1951
Dawlish Seascape, Devon
oil on board 59 x 45
PCF11

Stacey, Andrew b.1951
Dawlish Seascape, Devon
oil on board 75 x 49.5
PCF12

Dawlish Museum Society

Chapman, L.
Eventide with Fishing Boats 1925
oil on board 42 x 24
1998_21_1

Chapman, L.
Eventide with Fishing Boats 1925
oil on board 42 x 24
1998_21_2

Elliott, Les
Cows on a Hill above Dawlish, Devon 2004
oil on plywood 66 x 99
PCF15

Elliott, Les
Dawlish Black Swan 2004
oil on plywood 99 x 59
PCF10

Elliott, Les
Jubilee Bridge at Dawlish, Devon 2004
oil on plywood 99 x 66
PCF14

Elliott, Les
The Brook at Dawlish, Devon 2004
oil on plywood 99 x 88
PCF11

Elliott, Les
The Mill at Dawlish, Devon 2004
oil on plywood 99 x 76
PCF12

Godfrey, Elsa 1900–1991
Southwood Farm, Dawlish, Devon 1969
oil on board 39 x 49
PCF3

Godfrey, Elsa 1900–1991
The Coast at Dawlish, Devon 1976
oil on canvas 21.5 x 70
PCF6

Hutchings, E. A.
*The Atmospheric Railway, Starcross,
Devon* 1947
oil on panel 196 x 259
PCF9

Hutchings, E. A.
The Cow's Hole
oil on panel 142 x 108
PCF8

Hutchings, E. A.
The Lawn at Dawlish, Devon
oil on panel 141 x 98.5
PCF7

Sanders, L. M.
Landscape with a Church
oil on board 17.5 x 35
PCF2

Sanders, L. M.
Landscape with a Farm
oil on board 17.5 x 35
PCF1

unknown artist
Cold: Dawlish Fountain Frozen in Winter, Devon
oil on board 31 x 22.5
PCF4

unknown artist
St Mark's Church, Dawlish, Devon
oil on board 30 x 44
PCF5

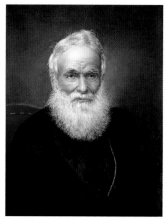

unknown artist
William Cousins, Esq. (1780–1871) of Langdon House, Dawlish
oil on canvas 59 x 45
2009_1231

Bicton College

Bicton owes its name to a sixth-century Saxon Chief, Beocca, who first colonised the area; the word was then coupled with the Saxon word 'tun' meaning 'fortified hamlet'.

The present Georgian house was constructed around 1730, and Napoleonic prisoners of war built the magnificent lake that still graces the front of the house. Sir Winston Churchill visited, and George VI, who was a personal friend of the Clinton family (previous owners of the house), spent part of his honeymoon there.

After World War Two, Bicton House was set up as a Farm Institute to train ex-servicemen and women in agriculture as part of a rehabilitation programme. Academic staff welcomed students of Bicton's first six-month course in 1947.

1993 brought the most significant event in the College's history since its foundation. Bicton College was taken out of the control of Devon County Council following the Further and Higher Education Act of 1992 and became a Further Education Corporation and an Exempt Charity with a new smaller Board of Governors.

The range of academic programmes currently offered covers: Agriculture, Animal Care, Arboriculture, Business Studies, Countryside Management, Engineering and Mechanisation, Equine Studies, Floristry, Horticulture, Outdoor Leisure, Sports Studies and Veterinary Nursing.

The College does not have an Art Department; however, accredited art courses began in 2005 within the School of Contemporary Floristry. Watercolours, working with mixed media, encaustic painting and latterly fibre arts (felt-making) have been taught, with a number of students progressing to higher education in art or textiles. An Art Summer School was held in 2007 for the first time and in 2010 the first exhibition of work produced in (residential student) art classes was held. The College grounds, arboretum, schools of horticulture and floristry are inspirational for a diverse range of artists – from botanical to abstract. In 2007, a Final Year Exhibition (Foundation Degree) of Environmental Arts and Crafts took place.

Current oil and acrylic paintings owned by the college include: a George Deakins, *Village Scene*, presented to the College by students in 1967; a Debeuf, *Woodland in Sunset*, which is believed to be a scene of Woodbury Common; two large oil paintings of cattle and sheep on loan from the artist, Shan Miller, that grace the upper grand staircase; and a student contemporary work in acrylic that hangs in the Principal's outer office. Other commissioned acrylic paintings hanging in the Library and Refectory are the work of the current tutor, Gill Burbidge. Influenced by the work of Reg Cartwright, these colourful, textural canvases were created with young people in mind and a 'healthy eating' theme. By the same artist, the oil painting *Devon Summer* hangs in the staff dining room.

In addition to the above, the College owns a John Piper print *Wyndham Cathedral*, 1972, an Arts and Crafts refectory table and the Grand Entrance is adorned with E. B. Stephens' sculpture of Lord Rolle (1834).

We are delighted to be included in The Public Catalogue Foundation's project and to bring Bicton College, its ancient, rich and diverse heritage, historic house, environment and academies to a wider public appreciation.

Gill Burbidge, Lecturer, Art and Design

Burbidge, Gill b.1946
Bicton House, Devon 2005
acrylic on canvas 120 x 140
PCF21

Burbidge, Gill b.1946
Aunty Mary's Hat 2006
mixed media & acrylic on canvas 60.3 x 76
PCF11

Burbidge, Gill b.1946
Young People's Refectory Series 2006
acrylic on canvas 101.5 x 76.5
PCF4

Burbidge, Gill b.1946
Young People's Refectory Series 2006
acrylic on canvas 101.5 x 76.5
PCF5

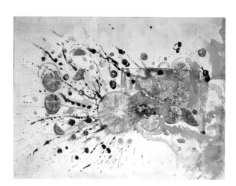

Burbidge, Gill b.1946
Young People's Refectory Series 2006
acrylic on canvas 76.5 x 101.5
PCF6

Burbidge, Gill b.1946
Young People's Refectory Series 2006
acrylic on canvas 101.5 x 76.5
PCF7

Burbidge, Gill b.1946
Young People's Refectory Series 2006
acrylic on canvas 101.5 x 76.5
PCF8

Burbidge, Gill b.1946
Young People's Refectory Series 2006
acrylic on canvas 76.5 x 101.5
PCF9

Burbidge, Gill b.1946
Young People's Refectory Series 2006
acrylic on canvas 101.5 x 76.5
PCF10

Burbidge, Gill b.1946
Young People's Refectory Series 2006
mixed media & acrylic on canvas 60.3 x 76
PCF12

Burbidge, Gill b.1946
Young People's Refectory Series 2006
acrylic on canvas 101.5 x 76.5
PCF13

Burbidge, Gill b.1946
Young People's Refectory Series 2006
acrylic on canvas 101.5 x 76.5
PCF14

Facing page: Hayward, Alfred Frederick William, 1856–1939, *Bucks Mills, Devon*, 1881, Burton Art Gallery and Museum (p. 45)

Burbidge, Gill b.1946
Young People's Refectory Series 2006
acrylic on canvas 76.5 x 101.5
PCF15

Burbidge, Gill b.1946
Young People's Refectory Series 2006
acrylic on canvas 101.5 x 76.5
PCF16

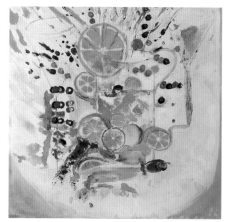

Burbidge, Gill b.1946
Young People's Refectory Series 2006
acrylic on canvas 101.5 x 76.5
PCF17

Burbidge, Gill b.1946
Devon Summer
oil on canvas 120 x 80
PCF20

Deakins, George 1911–1981
Village Scene
oil on board 44.2 x 62
PCF1

Debeuf, A.
Woodland in Sunset
oil on canvas 56.2 x 77.5
PCF2

Dyson, Collette
Sunset 2009
acrylic on canvas 101.5 x 75.5
PCF3

Miller, Shannon Frances b.1963
Friesian Calves
oil on board 60 x 242.5
PCF18 (P)

Miller, Shannon Frances b.1963
Sheep
oil on board 120.5 x 243
PCF19 (P)

Dean and Chapter, Exeter Cathedral

Davies, Janet M. b.1939
The Very Reverend Marcus Knight (1903–1988), Dean of Exeter (1960–1972) 1976
oil on board 80.2 x 62
PCF2

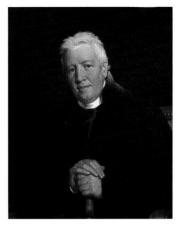

Halls, John James 1776–1853
The Very Reverend John Garnett, D. D., Dean of Exeter (1810–1813) 1853
oil on canvas 75 x 62.5
PCF5

Knapton, George 1698–1778
Sir Philip Sidney (after Isaac Oliver) 1739
oil on canvas 125 x 99.2
PCF9

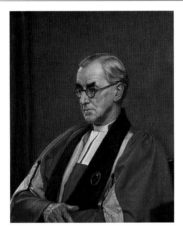

Knight, Harold 1874–1961
Spencer Cecil Carpenter (1877–1959), Dean of Exeter (1950–1960)
oil on canvas 75 x 62.2
PCF3

Raphael (after) 1483–1520
Madonna and Child, Madonna del Granduca
oil on canvas 96 x 75
PCF6

unknown artist
Unknown Dean c.1700
oil on canvas 73.8 x 60.8
PCF4

unknown artist
George III (1738–1820)
oil on canvas 280 x 146
PCF11

unknown artist
The Very Reverend Alured Clarke, Dean of Exeter (1740–1741)
oil on canvas 126 x 101
PCF1

unknown artist
The Very Reverend Dr Whittington Landon,
Dean of Exeter (1813–1838)
oil on canvas 140.6 x 110.2
PCF8

unknown artist
William of Orange
oil on canvas 280 x 146
PCF10

Devon & Somerset Fire & Rescue Service

Ford, Fred
The Burning of the Theatre Royal, Exeter, 3
September 1887
oil on canvas 90 x 120
PCF3

Lynham, J. 1864–1942
Somerset Fire Brigade at Hestercombe 1989
oil on hardboard 76.5 x 123
PCF1

Olsson, Albert Julius 1864–1942
Sea and Rocks, Moonlight
oil on canvas 61 x 81.5
51/1987/53

Spear, Ruskin 1911–1990
Mr William Herbert Barratt, Chief Fire Officer,
Somerset Fire Brigade (1948–1959) 1960
oil on board 72 x 59.6
PCF3

Devon County Council

Devon has strong traditions of artistic excellence and community engagement with the arts. Many artists are producing work of high quality in the county today and there is a constant flow of creative projects. This activity takes place in rural areas as much as urban, and sometimes in remote locations where the natural environment can be a powerful stimulus to the artistic imagination.

Devon County Council is proud of its commitment to cultural activities and has been a stalwart supporter of the arts through changing administrations over many years. With this record, it is perhaps rather surprising that the Council itself has not developed a larger collection of paintings. Most of the art works on display in the Council's premises are on loan or produced in other media. For example, in the corridors and offices of County Hall, the Council's headquarters in Exeter, there are photographic prints of Devon scenes by James Ravilious as well as temporary exhibitions of work by other photographers or printmakers, and often paintings by young learners at Devon schools or young people at the regional secure unit in Exeter.

This catalogue provides separate sections for those works held by the Devon Record Office and for the Art Collection managed by Devon Learning Resources. Beyond these, the Council has a few paintings at County Hall and at nearby Larkbeare House, which was used until recently as judges' lodgings. Each Chairman of the County Council features in a large set of individual portraits displayed at these two buildings. Although the more recent images are photographic, the set also includes some paintings from earlier years. Larkbeare is also home to *Devon Seascape* and the landscape *Dartmoor, Devon*, by F. T. Widgery, both of them works on a large scale that fits the artist's local reputation.

Other paintings owned by the County Council are located at a community college and in libraries around the county. As well as portraits they include landscapes, such as the works in Exmouth Library from the collections of the Westcountry Studies Library. Among the portraits is one at Bideford Library of Edward Capern who was born in Tiverton and buried at Heanton Punchardon. Capern worked for several years delivering mail between Bideford and Buckland Brewer, an experience he describes in his verse which was published and popular in the Victorian period. There are other portraits of the 'postman poet' at the Burton Art Gallery and Museum.

David Whitfield, County Arts Officer

Buhler, Robert A. 1916–1989
Sir George C. Hayter-Hames, Kt, Chairman of Devon County Council (1955–1965)
oil on canvas 90.6 x 70.5
PCF6 🐝

Dring, William D. 1904–1990
John Adam Day (1901–1966), Chairman of Devon County Council (1965–1966) 1966
oil on canvas 75.5 x 62.5
PCF5 🐝

Dring, William D. 1904–1990
Eric Palmer, Chairman of Devon County Council (1971–1974) 1973
oil on canvas 75.5 x 62.5
PCF1 🐝

Dring, William D. 1904–1990
Charles Arthur Ansell, Chairman of Devon County Council (1973–1977)
oil on canvas 75 x 62.5
PCF2 🐝

Dring, William D. 1904–1990
Gerald Whitmarsh, Chairman of Devon County Council (1966–1971)
oil on canvas 75 x 62.5
PCF7 🐝

Gurney, Hugh b.1932
Landscape at Odam Bridge, Devon 1982
acrylic on board 60 x 94
PCF9

Gurney, Hugh b.1932
The River Mole near Meethe, Devon 1991
acrylic on board 58 x 90
PCF10

Neale, Maud Hall 1869–1960
Sir John F. Shelley, Bt, Chairman of Devon County Council (1946–1955)
oil on canvas 71 x 58
PCF4

Tollet-Loeb, Jacqueline b.1931
Calvados Townscape, France
oil on canvas 44.5 x 37
PCF8

Weatherley, Dudley Graham 1912–2004
*Warnicombe Bridge, the Grand Western
Canal, Devon*
oil on canvas 72.5 x 101
PCF3 (P)

Devon Record Office

To appreciate why a miscellaneous collection of paintings (and also prints, engravings, and framed maps) has come to be held in a county record office, it is necessary to understand how the present Devon Record Office came into being. The story begins in 1854, with the founding of the Exeter School of Art, under the presidency of Sir Stafford Northcote (later to become the 1st Earl of Iddesleigh). On the death of the Prince Consort in 1861, Northcote proposed that a museum combined with an art and science centre should be founded in his memory, and the Royal Albert Museum was opened in 1869. This was to comprise 'a School of Art, a Free Library, and a Reading Room, in addition to a Depository of Natural History and Antiquities'. It was also partly due to Northcote's prompting that what was later to become the University of Exeter was established towards the end of the century.

Until the opening of the new library building in Castle Street in October 1930, books, documents, paintings, artefacts, and natural history specimens were held at the Museum's premises, as was usual in the nineteenth century. The minutes of the Exeter City Library Committee and the Museum, Library and Fine Arts Committee show little evidence of demarcation between the different parts of the Collection. That works of art came to be held in the library building, alongside the books, is therefore not as surprising as might be thought, though why certain items are where they are is more of a mystery. It is possible that some pictures were thought to be of more historical than artistic interest, but this is not recorded. On 13th October 1908 a letter was received from the executors of the late Mr W. H. H. Brooking Rowe of Plymouth enclosing extracts from his will, in which he had bequeathed to the City, among other things, manuscripts, papers, and brass rubbings, along with the provision to employ someone to catalogue them. This was the beginning of systematic record collection in Devon.

The new library, which included a muniment room for the City Archives and a manuscript room for other records, suffered minor damage in an air raid on 24th April 1942 (after which library staff carried out temporary repairs), before receiving a direct hit on the night of 3rd May. The following was reported to the Library Committee on 13th July: 'the bindery equipment, all the Library records, stationery and every printed book which was in the building on the night of the raid has been totally destroyed, together with some Mss. records and ancient deeds belonging to, or deposited at, the Library, and which were being prepared for evacuation'. Fortunately, most of the documents (and presumably any paintings which were in the building) had already been evacuated and were saved. In December 1945 it was noted that the Mayor of Torquay had given to the Mayor of Exeter 'a view of the Cathedral and the destroyed High Street which had been exhibited in connection with the Torquay Thanksgiving Week', and the Mayor suggested that a place should be found for it at the library. It is not known what kind of picture this was, or whether it is still in the Collection.

After the war, professional archivists were employed at the City Library for the first time, and the Exeter City Record Office was established in part of the old library building when the new library was built in the late 1960s. Meanwhile, the Devon Record Office had been founded just along the road at the Castle in 1952. In the 1974 reorganisation of local government, the Exeter City office became part of the county service, and the two offices merged fully in 1977. From then until the move to Great Moor House in 2005 the Devon Record Office's headquarters were in the old City Library building. Non-archival material, which had been in the building since the 1960s or earlier, was left there and assimilated into the record office's holdings. This continuity of location, and in earlier times community of governance, accounts for the mixture of books, manuscripts, documents, and paintings held together in one place. Attempts to rationalise holdings have been made from time to time, but in the end it seemed better to leave everything where it was.

There is an interesting postscript to the story of the paintings. On 8th August 1974 the Devon Record Office (East Devon Area), as it then was, received from Mrs Woollatt of Budleigh Salterton 18 paintings by her late husband, Leighton Hall Woollatt; a further watercolour followed in July 1975. There are in all 11 oil paintings and eight watercolours; two of the oils date from 1940 and show bomb damage to Clyst St George Church, and the remainder are dated 1942 and show the results of the Exeter air raids. Until they were moved out of the city centre, these paintings were held very near to the sites which they represented, apart from a brief visit to Normandy for an exhibition in 1994. They are valued as much as historical records as they are as works of art, and they form a direct link with key events in Exeter's past.

John Draisey, County Archivist

Brice, Henry c.1831–1903
Sir John Bowring (1792–1872)
oil on canvas 60.5 x 51
PCF33

Brockedon, William 1787–1854
Miss Louisa Champernowne (b.1809)
oil on canvas 76 x 64
PCF27

Chatterton, Henrietta Georgiana Maria Lascelles Iremonger 1806–1867
Ernest Lane and His Sister
oil on canvas 61 x 52
PCF1

Kieling, M.
J. Watkins, Aged 77 3/4, Author of the History of Devon 1918
oil on canvas 76 x 63
PCF29

Logsdail, William 1859–1944
Agnes Elizabeth, only Daughter of William Reginald and Mother of Charles Frederick Lindley Wood, Viscount Halifax 1920
oil on canvas 72.5 x 49.5
PCF13

Swan, E. active 1937–1944
Portrait of a Judge 1938
oil on canvas 91 x 71
PCF26

unknown artist
Billy Wotton, the Last Exeter Water-Catcher
oil on canvas 30 x 22
PCF9

unknown artist
Captain Thomas Tanner, HEICS, Mayor of Exeter (1858)
oil on panel 21.5 x 17
PCF24

unknown artist
Mr John Score (b.c.1680), Woolmerchant of Exe Island, Exeter
oil on canvas 76 x 63
PCF11

unknown artist
*Mr Smith, Headmaster of St John's Hospital
School*
oil on board 60 x 49
PCF30

unknown artist
Portrait of a Bearded Gentleman
oil on panel 48.5 x 38
PCF34

unknown artist
Portrait of a Gentleman
oil on canvas 128 x 102
PCF3

unknown artist
Portrait of a Gentleman
oil on canvas 76 x 63
PCF23

unknown artist
Portrait of a Gentleman
oil on canvas 76 x 63
PCF31

unknown artist
Portrait of a Gentleman Holding a Letter
oil on board 76 x 63
PCF22

unknown artist
Portrait of a Gentleman Wearing a Red Coat
oil on canvas 82.5 x 65
PCF28

unknown artist
*Portrait of a Gentleman Wearing a Tartan
Waistcoat*
oil on panel 61 x 50
PCF35

unknown artist
Portrait of a Girl and Her Dog
oil on canvas 127 x 102
PCF5

Facing page: British (English) School, *Alexander Pope (1688–1744)*, Royal Albert Memorial Museum (p. 117)

unknown artist
Portrait of a Lady in a Lace Bonnet
oil on canvas 76 x 63
PCF12

unknown artist
Portrait of a Lady Wearing a Pearl Necklace
oil on canvas 127 x 102
PCF4

unknown artist
Portrait of a Seated Lady
oil on canvas 127 x 102
PCF7

unknown artist
Portrait of a Young Girl with a Basket of Flowers
oil on canvas 128 x 102
PCF2

unknown artist
Portrait of a Young Man with a Cane
oil on canvas 127 x 102
PCF6

Williams, M. F. A.
Portrait of a Lady Wearing a Headband
oil on canvas 53 x 46
PCF32

Woollatt, Leighton Hall 1905–1974
Parish Church of Clyst St George, Devon, North East View 1940
oil on canvas 64 x 76
PCF25

Woollatt, Leighton Hall 1905–1974
Parish Church of Clyst St George, Devon, Looking East through the Tower 1940
oil on canvas 61 x 51
PCF14

Woollatt, Leighton Hall 1905–1974
Behind Sidwell Street, Exeter, Devon 1942
oil on canvas 51 x 61
PCF20

Woollatt, Leighton Hall 1905–1974
Church of St Lawrence, High Street, Exeter, Devon 1942
oil on canvas 46 x 56
PCF19

Woollatt, Leighton Hall 1905–1974
Exeter Cathedral, Devon, from Catherine Street 1942
oil on canvas 62 x 76
PCF15

Woollatt, Leighton Hall 1905–1974
Interior, Lower Market, Exeter, Devon 1942
oil on canvas 51 x 61
PCF17

Woollatt, Leighton Hall 1905–1974
Looking from Castle Street across High Street, Exeter, Devon 1942
oil on canvas 51 x 61
PCF18

Woollatt, Leighton Hall 1905–1974
Post Eleven Speaking 1942
oil on canvas 56.5 x 77
PCF21

Woollatt, Leighton Hall 1905–1974
Remains of the General Post Office, High Street, Exeter, Devon 1942
oil on canvas 41 x 51
PCF8

Woollatt, Leighton Hall 1905–1974
South Chancel, Exeter Cathedral, Devon 1942
oil on canvas 51 x 40.5
PCF36

Woollatt, Leighton Hall 1905–1974
Sun Street, Exeter, Devon 1942
oil on canvas 56 x 76
PCF16

Exeter Guildhall

Exeter's historic and ancient Guildhall houses many hidden treasures of local, regional and even national importance and I feel honoured to be the custodian of such a wonderful Collection.

The Main Hall acts as a fitting setting to seven large portraits of individuals who have had some bearing on the 800 year history of the Guildhall and City Mayoralty. These include two portraits by Sir Peter Lely. Princess Henrietta, daughter of Charles I, is the only member of the Royal Family to have been born in the City. The full-length portrait was presented to the City in 1672 by Charles II, and still looks down on the Council meetings held in the Hall, acting as a lasting reminder of the City's loyalty to the Crown during the English Civil War. The other Lely portrait is also full-length and depicts General Monck, 1st Duke of Albemarle, who, after an early run-in with the law in Exeter, became High Steward of the City in 1662.

Other significant portraits include *John Rolle Walter (1712–1779), MP for Exeter (1754–1776),* by the circle of Thomas Gainsborough; *Sir Charles Pratt (1714–1794), Lord Chief Justice of the Common Pleas,* and *George II (1683–1760),* both by Thomas Hudson.

Many of these works have undergone recent conservation so that their significance to the City, as well as their importance as works of art, can be enjoyed by future generations. This delicate and careful work brought out many significant details in the paintings, details that had for many years been hidden by a build-up of dirt, but whose colours have now been restored to their original vibrancy.

The inclusion of these paintings in this catalogue will help spread the word of their existence and hopefully encourage many more visitors to take advantage of the free public access to them.

John Street, Head of Corporate Customer Services

Bird, Isaac Faulkner 1803–1884
View from the Castle Wall Looking towards Southernhay, Exeter, Devon 1880
oil on canvas 49 x 73
PCF13

Gainsborough, Thomas (circle of) 1727–1788
John Rolle Walter, Esq. (1712–1779), MP for Exeter (1754–1776)
oil on canvas 152.5 x 127 (E)
PCF8

Hudson, Thomas 1701–1779
Sir Charles Pratt (1714–1794), Lord Chief Justice of the Common Pleas 1764
oil on canvas 254 x 152.5 (E)
PCF7

Hudson, Thomas 1701–1779
George II (1683–1760)
oil on canvas 279.5 x 137 (E)
PCF5

Hudson, Thomas 1701–1779
John Tuckfield, Esq., MP for Exeter (1745–1776)
oil on canvas 279.5 x 152.5 (E)
PCF3

Hudson, Thomas (attributed to) 1701–1779
Thomas Heath, Mayor and Sheriff of Exeter
oil on canvas 122 x 96.5 (E)
PCF10

Leakey, James 1775–1865
Henry Blackall, Esq. (1770–1845), Thrice Mayor of Exeter
oil on canvas 279.5 x 152.5 (E)
PCF4

Lely, Peter 1618–1680
General Monck (1608–1670), 1st Duke of Albermarle, KG
oil on canvas 254 x 127 (E)
PCF1

Lely, Peter 1618–1680
Princess Henrietta (1644–1670), Daughter of Charles I
oil on canvas 254 x 137 (E)
PCF2

Mogford, Thomas 1800–1868
H. W. Hooper, Mayor of Exeter (1843), Sheriff of Exeter (1849), Builder of the Exeter Market
oil on canvas 91.5 x 71
PCF12

Mogford, Thomas 1800–1868
William Page Kingdom
oil on canvas 91.5 x 71
PCF11

Northcote, James (attributed to) 1746–1831
The Duke of Wellington (1769–1852), Mounted on a Grey Charger 1829
oil on canvas 305 x 180 (E)
PCF9

Pine, Robert Edge c.1720/1730–1788
*Benjamin Heath (d.1766), LLD, Town Clerk of
Exeter for Fourteen Years*
oil on canvas 279.5 x 142 (E)
PCF6

Salisbury, Frank O. 1874–1962
Lady J. Kirk Owen, Mayoress (1914–1915)
oil on canvas 75 x 62.3
PCF14

Salisbury, Frank O. 1874–1962
Sir James Owen
oil on canvas 75.3 x 62.3
PCF15

Exeter Royal Academy for Deaf Education

Burlton
*R. E. Olding, OBE, Headmaster of the Royal
West of England Residential School for the
Deaf (1965–1985)* 1989
oil on canvas 67.2 x 54.2
PCF3

Burlton
*H. P. Jones, Headmaster of the Royal West of
England Residential School for the Deaf
(1985–1996)* 1989
oil on canvas 67.2 x 54.2
PCF2

unknown artist
*H. P. Bingham, Headmaster of the Royal West
of England Residential School for the Deaf
(1827–1834)*
oil on canvas 74.7 x 61.8
PCF4

Whinney, Maurice 1911–1997?
*Sir Paul H. W. Studholme, Treasurer of the
Royal West of England Residential School for
the Deaf (1973–1990), President of the (...)*
oil on canvas 85.2 x 59.5
PCF1

Larkbeare House

Copnall, Frank Thomas 1870–1949
*Sir Henry Hepburn, Kt, Chairman of Devon
County Council (1916)*
oil on canvas 90.3 x 70
PCF14

Crealock, John 1871–1959
Portrait of a Judge 1926
oil on canvas 110.4 x 85.3
PCF5

Jenkins, George Henry 1843–1914
Cart Travelling across Dartmoor, Devon
oil on canvas 44.6 x 75.2
PCF3

Jenkins, George Henry 1843–1914
Dartmoor, Devon
oil on canvas 45 x 75
PCF4

Neale, George Hall 1863–1940
*Sir Henry Yarde Buller Lopes (1859–1938),
Chairman of Devon County Council (1916–
1937)*
oil on canvas 75 x 62
PCF10

Neale, Maud Hall 1869–1960
*Sir John Daw, Kt, Chairman of Devon County
Council (1938–1946)*
oil on canvas 74.7 x 62
PCF15

Shaw, George 1843–1915
Dartmoor, Devon 1899
oil on canvas 85 x 181.6
PCF6

unknown artist
*Albert Edmund Parker (1843–1905), 3rd Earl
of Morley, Chairman of Devon County Council
(1901–1904)*
oil on canvas 75.5 x 62.5
PCF12

unknown artist
Charles Henry Rolle Hepburn-Stuart-Forbes-Trefusis (1834–1904), 20th Baron Clinton, Chairman of Devon County Council (...)
oil on canvas 75.5 x 62.5
PCF11

unknown artist
Hugh Fortescue (1854–1932), 4th Earl Fortesque, Chairman of Devon County Council (1904–1916)
oil on panel 76.7 x 62
PCF13

Widgery, Frederick John 1861–1942
Devon Seascape
oil on canvas 103.2 x 179.6
PCF1

Widgery, Frederick John 1861–1942
Dartmoor, Devon
oil on canvas 102.6 x 181
PCF2

Facing page: Eastlake, Charles Lock, 1793–1865, *Contemplation*, c.1836, Royal Albert Memorial Museum (p. 130)

Royal Albert Memorial Museum

The Great Exhibition of 1851 and the South Kensington museums which followed, owed much to the personal initiative of Prince Albert, the Prince Consort, and Sir Stafford Northcote Pynes of Exeter. It was no surprise then that the City of Exeter should adopt the same principles, uniting a museum, free library, school of art and school of science in the same building.

Soon after the death of Albert in December 1861, an appeal was launched. A site for the proposed institution was gifted by Richard Somers Gard MP – the front section of the present building in Queen Street. The remainder of the site was purchased for £2,000. In 1864, John Hayward's design was selected from among the 24 submitted. Hayward was an Exeter architect with a local reputation for work on public buildings, including All Hallows Church on Bartholomew Street, St Luke's College and the New Gaol. His Italian-influenced Gothic design used red-coloured stone from Chudleigh in Devon as well as Bath stone and Aberdeen granite. On the 30th October 1865, the foundation stone was laid by Gard and the project was completed four years later on the 19th August 1869 at a total cost of £14,741. In 1899, a new wing was officially opened by the Duke and Duchess of York (later King George V and Queen Mary) and the institution was granted 'Royal' status.

In addition to fine art, the Royal Albert Memorial Museum holds important collections of natural history, world cultures, archaeology, decorative art and local history. Today, the art collection comprises some 8,000 works, including paintings, drawings, prints and sculpture. In the early years, this was a disparate group, assembled from donations and bequests. Among the many donors, there were three particularly prominent individuals: the businessman and philanthropist Kent Kingdon (1810–1889), the horticulturalist Sir Harry Veitch (1840–1924), and the publisher John Lane (1854–1925).

Following the success of the Loan Exhibition of Works by Early Devon Painters, held in 1932, more emphasis was placed on the acquisition of works by Devon-born artists. As a result, the collection is now particularly strong in pictures by eighteenth- and nineteenth-century artists with connections to Exeter and Devon, such as Francis Towne, John White Abbott, James Northcote, Thomas Patch, Francis Hayman, Thomas Hudson and John Gendall. More recently, the remit has broadened to include works connected to the region through provenance and by artists trained or resident in the locale.

Undoubtedly one of our best known paintings is William Powell Frith's *The Fair Toxophilites (English Archers, Nineteenth Century)*, 1872. Frith's daughters, Alice, Fanny and Louisa modelled for the work which, through reproduction, has become one of the most famous images of affluent Victorian leisure. However, our most reproduced painting by far is the eighteenth-century *Portrait of an African*. Once believed to have been of the African abolitionist, Olaudah Equiano, the painting is now thought to depict Ignatius Sancho, an eighteenth-century composer, actor and writer and the first Black Briton to vote in a British election. This powerful and enigmatic portrait is one of the few painted during the age of slavery to depict an African of individual status.

Edward John Poynter's *Diadumene* is one of the classical genre scenes the artist produced throughout the 1880s. The title refers to a celebrated statue showing a man tying a fillet around his head. Poynter's painting of a woman engaged in the same action was based on another statue entitled *Venus* which had been discovered in 1874. The painting also reflects the artist's detailed knowledge of Italian mosaics. By contrast, Frank Holl's *Song of the Shirt*, c.1874, reflects the bleaker side of life. Holl focused upon the hardships of the poor in Victorian England and the title is taken from a poem by Thomas Hood, which relates the plight of a needlewoman employed on pitiful wages:

> With fingers weary and worn,
> With eyelids heavy and red,
> A woman sat, in unwomanly rags
> Plying her needle and thread –
> Stitch! Stitch! Stitch!
> In poverty, hunger and dirt
> And still with a voice of a dolorous pitch
> She sang the 'Song of the Shirt'.

Francis Danby is another artist who would have been familiar with Victorian life in the West Country, as he worked in Bristol as a young man and lived in Exmouth from 1847 until his death in 1861. His *Dead Calm – Sunset at the Bight of Exmouth* looks across the Exe estuary to Starcross. For a few months after his arrival in Devon he would have seen smoke belching from the tower depicted in the centre as well as trains running, smokeless along the far bank. The Exeter to Newton Abbot Section of Brunel's Atmospheric Railway had operated briefly in 1846 but was abandoned in favour of conventional steam engines in 1848.

At the beginning of the twentieth century, Applehayes Farm at Clayhidon on the Devon-Somerset border belonged to Harold Harrison. A retired rancher from Argentina, Harrison became friends with members of the Camden Town Group while a mature student at the Slade School of Art. From 1910 these artists visited the farm, among them Spencer Gore, Charles Ginner and Robert Polhill Bevan. The Museum holds a small but important collection of paintings by the Group, extended, in 2004, by the purchase at auction of Lucien Pissarro's *Apple Blossom, Riversbridge Farm, Blackpool, Devon*, 1921

In 2008, after a long fund-raising campaign, the Museum acquired a rare portrait, by Pompeo Batoni, of John Rolle Walter, MP for Exeter between 1754 and 1776. Batoni, who lived in Rome, was the greatest Italian portrait painter of the eighteenth century and the favourite of wealthy British travellers on the Grand Tour. The purchase is evidence of the vital assistance given by organisations such as the Art Fund, Museums, Libraries and Archives Council/Victoria and Albert Museum Purchase Grant Fund, Heritage Lottery Fund and the Friends of the Museum.

The Royal Albert Memorial Museum holds several hundred representations of the Devon landscape and is particularly strong in late eighteenth- and nineteenth-century works. In recent years, our acquisitions policy has sought to extend this strength into the modern era. We were therefore grateful in 2010 to be allocated an important work by David

Bomberg under the Government's Acceptance in Lieu scheme. In the latter part of his career, Bomberg painted some of the most powerful landscapes in twentieth-century British art and *Bideford, Devon* must be counted among them. When Bomberg came to Devon on holiday with his wife in 1946 he was continuing a tradition started by Turner, Girtin and the Picturesque Movement some 150 years before – a tradition which has lasted to this day.

Caroline Worthington, Assistant Curator of Fine Art (2000) and John Madin, Curator of Art (2010)

Abbott, John White 1763–1851
The High Street, Exeter, Devon, in 1797 1797
oil on panel 27.3 x 32.9
164/1883

Abbott, John White 1763–1851
The Old Lime-Kilns near Topsham on the Exe, Devon 1808
oil on canvas 100.4 x 149.7
77/1937/1

Abbott, John White 1763–1851
Portrait of the Artist's Daughter, Elizabeth, Aged 18 1816
oil on canvas laid on panel 38 x 32
130/1993

Abbott, John White 1763–1851
Landscape with Figures and Cattle at a Stream 1820
oil on canvas 81.5 x 61.2
81/1933

Abbott, John White 1763–1851
The Stepping Stones 1824
oil on canvas 124.5 x 91.6
52/1929/1

Abbott, John White 1763–1851
Jaques and the Wounded Stag 1838
oil on canvas 97 x 123.7
52/1929/2

Abbott, John White 1763–1851
Landscape with Abraham and Isaac
oil on canvas 85.5 x 114.6
52/1929/3

Adams, John Clayton 1840–1906
The Golden Vale (Junction of the Wye and Irfran near Builth Wells, Powys) 1895
oil on canvas 99.8 x 152.5
142/1978x

Baird, Nathaniel Hughes John 1865–1936
A Devonshire Stream
oil on canvas 46 x 61.2
93/1973

Baird, Nathaniel Hughes John 1865–1936
Evening Sunlight
oil on canvas 32 x 41
94/1973

Baird, Nathaniel Hughes John 1865–1936
The Bison Hunters
oil on canvas 94 x 94
91/1978x

Ball, Wilfred Williams (attributed to) 1853–1917
Large Falcons of the Palearctic 1879
oil on canvas 102.2 x 147.5
206/2003

Barker, Thomas (attributed to) 1769–1847
Scotsman in a Cottage Interior c.1820
oil on canvas 91.4 x 71
120/1969

Barker, Thomas (attributed to) 1769–1847
Scotswoman with Cabbages, in Cottage Interior c.1820
oil on canvas 91.7 x 71
119/1969

Barret the elder, George 1728/1732–1784
Llyn Nantlle c.1777
oil on canvas 99.3 x 151.4
359/1971

Batoni, Pompeo 1708–1787
*John Rolle Walter (1712–1779), MP for Exeter
(1754–1776)* 1753
oil on canvas 98.1 x 73.3
411/2008

Bayes, Walter (attributed to) 1869–1956
*Victoria Station, London, Troops Leaving for
the Front* c.1915
oil on canvas 150 x 202
136/1975

Beale, Mary (attributed to) 1633–1699
Portrait of a Lady (called 'Mrs Walkey of
Alphington') c.1678
oil on canvas 122.1 x 95.1
46/1925/709

Beeson, Jane 1930–2006
Still Life with Pots 1961
oil on board 61 x 115.6
112/2002

Bennett, Frank Moss 1874–1952
Conscience 1909
oil on canvas 91.7 x 138.1
95/1978x

Bennett, William Mineard 1778–1858
Self Portrait 1815
oil on canvas 75.9 x 62.9
51/1938

Bennett, William Mineard 1778–1858
Self Portrait 1832
oil on canvas 72.8 x 59.2
348/1979

Berchem, Nicolaes (attributed to) 1620–
1683
Landscape with Cattle and Sheep at a Fountain
oil on canvas 73.5 x 63.5
210/1892

Bevan, Robert Polhill 1865–1925
A Devonshire Valley, Number 1 c.1913
oil on canvas 20 x 24
262/1968

Bird, Isaac Faulkner 1803–1884
Henry Matthews (1793–1842), Druggist of Exeter 1823
oil on canvas 73.7 x 64.8
37/1923/1

Bird, Isaac Faulkner 1803–1884
View from the Castle Wall, Looking towards Southernhay, Exeter, Devon 1880
oil on canvas 50 x 73.7
829/1913

Birkmyer, James Bruce 1834–1899
When the Tide Is Low, Maer Rocks, Exmouth, Devon
oil on canvas 45.6 x 91.2
3/19/1891

Birkmyer, James Bruce (attributed to) 1834–1899
Landscape with a Gate and Buildings
oil on canvas 13.5 x 23.1
103/2000/13

Brice, Henry c.1831–1903
Sir John Bowring (1792–1872) c.1860
oil on canvas 75.7 x 63
714/1902

British (English) School
Joan Tuckfield (1506–1573) c.1560
oil on panel 75.8 x 59.8
136/1998

British (English) School
William Hurst (d.1568) 1568 (?)
oil on panel 76.4 x 63.6
163/1998

British (English) School
Lawrence Atwill (or Atwell) (c.1511–1588) 1588
oil on panel 74 x 61.5
139/1998

British (English) School
Mrs Browne c.1600
oil on canvas 68.5 x 54.7
37/1946/2

British (English) School
John Hoker (or Hooker) (c.1527–1601) 1601
oil on panel 80.2 x 65.8
141/1998

British (English) School
Lady Browne c.1605–1610
oil on panel 107.5 x 83.2
37/1946/1

British (English) School
Nicholas Spicer (1581–1647) 1611
oil on panel 101.2 x 74.1
166/1998

British (English) School
John Perriam (1540–after 1616) 1616
oil on canvas 91 x 64.7
138/1998

British (English) School
Walter Borough (1554–1632) 1628
oil on panel 84.5 x 64.5
254/2008

British (English) School
Elizabeth Flaye (1587–1673) c.1640
oil on canvas 101.1 x 88.2
140/1998

British (English) School
Thomas Jefford (d.1703) c.1688
oil on canvas 109.2 x 86.7
255/2008

British (English) School 17th C
Portrait of a Gentleman in a Landscape
oil on panel 113.4 x 93.2
37/1946/4

British (English) School 17th C
Portrait of a Lady
oil on canvas 75 x 63.5
144/1978x

British (English) School 17th C
Portrait of a Lady and Her Dog
oil on canvas 74.7 x 61.4
K216

British (English) School 17th C
Portrait of a Lady in a Landscape
oil on canvas 75 x 62.5
29/1970

British (English) School
John Gay (1685–1732) c.1730
oil on canvas 76.4 x 63.5
46/1925/7

British (English) School
*A Gentleman of the Needham Family of
Melton Mowbray* c.1740–1750
oil on canvas 76.4 x 64
35/1974

British (English) School
Samuel Taunton (b.1749), as a Child c.1750
oil on paper 37.3 x 28.7
885/1910

British (English) School
*Thomas Taunton (1744–1828), as a
Child* c.1750
oil on paper 37.8 x 29
884/1910

British (English) School
*Henry Langford Brown (b.1721), of
Combsatchfield and Kingskerswell* 1756
oil on canvas 127 x 101.5
64/1957/3

British (English) School
John Campion (1742–1822) c.1790
oil on canvas 61 x 50.7
227/1996

British (English) School 18th C
Alexander Pope (1688–1744)
oil on canvas 76.5 x 63.8
46/1925/13

British (English) School 18th C
Commander Robert Bastin (1786–1854), RN
oil on canvas 75.2 x 63.6
28/1917

British (English) School 18th C
Landscape near Pope's House on the Thames at Twickenham (?)
oil on canvas 36 x 42.4
56/1948

British (English) School 18th C
Landscape, Woodland Glade
oil on canvas 77.7 x 64.8
25/1934

British (English) School 18th C
Portrait of a Gentleman
oil on canvas 86.5 x 71.5
256/2008

British (English) School 18th C
Portrait of a Lady
oil on canvas 76.2 x 66.2
266/2008

British (English) School 18th C
Portrait of a Lady
oil on canvas 67.9 x 57.7
882/1910

British (English) School 18th C
Portrait of a Lady of the Brown Family
oil on canvas 76.3 x 63
64/1957/10

British (English) School 18th C
Portrait of a Naval Officer
oil on canvas 75 x 63.8
265/2008

British (English) School 18th C
Study of a Monk
oil on canvas 60.6 x 53.7
883/1910

Facing page: Wootton, John, c.1682–1764, *Landscape with Angelica and Medoro*, Royal Albert Memorial Museum (p. 165)

British (English) School 18th C
The Flight into Egypt
oil on panel 37.4 x 31.7
93/1936/3

British (English) School 18th C
William Kennaway, Senior (1718–1793)
oil on canvas 76.4 x 63.5
34/1976

British (English) School
Judge John Heath (1736–1816) c.1800
oil on canvas 84.2 x 65.7
145/1978x

British (English) School
The Fight on the Bridge 1810
oil on card bonded to canvas 43.6 x 60.8
88/1947

British (English) School
Carter, the Mail Coach Driver c.1810
oil on panel 26.6 x 20.3
69/1933

British (English) School
*Tommy Osborne (d.1823), Itinerant Bookseller
of Exeter* c.1812
oil on panel 25.7 x 17.5
60/1921

British (English) School
*Charles Lewis, Secretary of the West of England
Fire and Life Insurance Company (1810–
1850)* c.1820–1830
oil on canvas 74.5 x 64
220/2003

British (English) School
*William Matthews (d.1839), Woollen
Merchant of Exeter* c.1820–1830
oil on canvas 76.9 x 62.5
37/1923/2

British (English) School
*Clementina Hooper, née Burnside
(b.1803)* c.1823
oil on canvas 76.1 x 63.5
389/1971

British (English) School
Captain Cooke (1765–1841), Chief of the Exeter Javelin Men c.1826
oil on panel 27.7 x 22.7
112/1951

British (English) School
J. B. and Mary Davey c.1828
oil on panel 33.7 x 29.9
118/1998

British (English) School
Mrs Hanford Waters c.1830
oil on canvas 60.9 x 50.7
23/1946/2

British (English) School
Portrait of a Young Man (possibly Thomas Latimer, 1803–1888, JP) c.1840–1850
oil on canvas 76 x 63.4
19/1923/2

British (English) School
Richard Somers Gard (1797–1868) c.1845
oil on canvas 76.2 x 64
207/1911

British (English) School
Mr Thomas Camble of the West of England Fire Brigade, Exeter c.1865
oil on panel 60.3 x 47
57/1999

British (English) School
The Guildhall on Election Night, 1880 c.1880
oil on canvas 94.1 x 137.7
333/1997

British (English) School 19th C
Benjamin Floud
oil on canvas 77.1 x 63.4
257/1972/2

British (English) School 19th C
Churchyard
oil on paper laid onto board 22.1 x 32.3
686/1997/1

British (English) School 19th C
History
oil on canvas 60 x 50.4
264/2008

British (English) School 19th C
John Hoker (or Hooker) (c.1527–1601)
oil on panel 35.6 x 27.7
450/1980

British (English) School 19th C
John Veitch (1752–1839)
oil on canvas 76.4 x 63.2
59/1934

British (English) School 19th C
Lake Scene
oil on board 18.2 x 25.4
686/1997/2

British (English) School 19th C
Landscape
oil on canvas 73.8 x 61.3
118/2003

British (English) School 19th C
Lighthouse and Ships
oil on panel 30 x 40.5
75/1917/3

British (English) School 19th C
Old Heavitree Church, Exeter, Devon
oil on canvas 27.7 x 29.3
828/1913

British (English) School 19th C
Old Houses, Exeter, Devon (demolished for St
Edmund's Church, c.1870)
oil on canvas 42.7 x 52.1
69/1929/2

British (English) School 19th C
Plymouth, Devon
oil on canvas 49.5 x 66.7
46/1925/2

British (English) School 19th C
Plymouth Harbour, Devon, with Shipping
oil on canvas 49.3 x 66.9
46/1925/1

British (English) School 19th C
Portrait of a Gentleman
oil on canvas 112.5 x 86
253/2008

British (English) School 19th C
Portrait of a Gentleman
oil on canvas 74.5 x 64.8
263/2008

British (English) School 19th C
Portrait of a Gentleman (possibly Solomon Floud)
oil on canvas 76.3 x 63.5
257/1972/1

British (English) School 19th C
Portrait of a Lady
oil on canvas 47.9 x 37
304/1997

British (English) School 19th C
St Lawrence Church, High St, Exeter, Devon
oil on canvas 49 x 64.5
2x/1982

British (English) School 19th C
Still Life with Roses
oil on canvas 55.6 x 76
262/2008

British (English) School 19th C
Study of the Interior of a Church (possibly in Heavitree, Exeter, Devon)
oil on canvas 50.9 x 61
300/1997

British (English) School 19th C
The College of Vicars' Choral, Exeter, Devon
oil on canvas 42.7 x 52.2
69/1929/1

British (English) School
Floor Boards 1991
acrylic on canvas 51.3 x 41.2
323/1997

British School 19th C
Unknown Warrior (possibly Robert the Bruce, 1274–1329)
oil on panel 36 x 30
283/1997

Brooking, Charles (attributed to) 1723–1759
Ship on Fire
oil on canvas 72 x 92.2
29/1869

Brown, John Alfred Arnesby 1866–1955
Autumn Morning
oil on canvas 42.7 x 57
109/1920

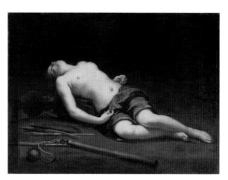

Cagnacci, Guido 1601–1681
The Young Martyr (possibly St Martina)
oil on canvas 111.6 x 144.1
90/1931/1

Carter, Sydney 1874–1945
Reverend Sabine Baring-Gould (1834–1924) c.1920
oil on canvas 111.6 x 86.8
L114

Carter, Sydney 1874–1945
Richard Carter, Father of the Artist
oil on canvas 91.2 x 70.9
611/1997

Caunter, Henry (attributed to) active c.1846–c.1850
Abraham Cann (1794–1864), the Last Champion in Devon-Style Wrestling c.1846
oil on canvas 75.8 x 63.7
12/1959

Cawse, John (attributed to) 1779–1862
James Northcote (1746–1831), painting Sir Walter Scott (1771–1832) c.1825–1830
oil on canvas 71.7 x 54.4
96/1949

Christen, Rodolphe 1859–1906
A Man Preparing Microscope Slides 1901
oil on canvas 27.9 x 39.8
98/1978x

Clack, Richard Augustus 1801–1880
*Thomas Gray (1788–1848), the Railway
Pioneer* 1848
oil on panel 38.1 x 28.3
155/1881

Clack, Richard Augustus 1801–1880
Self Portrait 1851
oil on canvas 76.8 x 63.7
97/1978x

Clack, Richard Augustus 1801–1880
*William Wills Hooper (1807–1872), Mayor of
Exeter (1850–1851 & 1851–1852)* c.1853
oil on canvas 143.2 x 112.9
68/1923/1

Clack, Richard Augustus 1801–1880
*The Reverend Frederick Bell, Chaplain of His
Majesty's Forces in Exeter for Many
Years* 1870
oil on canvas 81.1 x 67.3
48/1930/1

Clack, Richard Augustus 1801–1880
Henry Langford Brown (1802–1857)
oil on canvas 74.2 x 61.6
64/1957/6

Clack, Richard Augustus 1801–1880
*Self Portrait by Sir Joshua Reynolds in the robes
of a DCL Oxford* (copy of Joshua Reynolds)
oil on canvas 74.6 x 64
38/1869

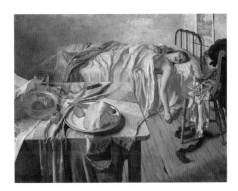

Codrington, Isabel 1874–1943
Morning
oil on canvas 87 x 112.5
26/1934

Collins, Cecil 1908–1989
By the Waters of Babylon 1932
oil on canvas 20 x 30
53/2001/7

Condy, Nicholas 1793–1857
Cleaning the Fish
oil on panel 39.2 x 30
73/1951

Condy, Nicholas 1793–1857
Nicholas Matthew Condy (1816–1851)
oil on panel 25.3 x 20.1
134/1964

Condy, Nicholas 1793–1857
Old Man Smoking
oil on canvas 30.4 x 25.7
K241

Condy, Nicholas Matthew 1816–1851
Harbour Scene
oil on panel 30.5 x 25.5
84/1935

Condy, Nicholas Matthew 1816–1851
*HMS 'Warspite' 50 Guns Conveying Lord
Ashburton on a Special Mission to the United
States, Beating Down the Channel*
oil on panel 44.8 x 61.4
50/1950

Condy, Nicholas Matthew 1816–1851
*The Spinnaker Sail (Cutter with a Spinnaker
Set)*
oil on panel 24.9 x 32.5
103/1935

Coombes, George
*Thomas Osborne (d.1823), Itinerant Bookseller
of Exeter* c.1812
oil on panel 24.3 x 17.9
46/1929/2

Coombes, George
*Thomas Osborne (d.1823), the
Bookseller* c.1812
oil on panel 29.3 x 18.5
46/1929

Corri, F. J.
West Front of Exeter Cathedral, Devon c.1860
oil on canvas 68.5 x 82.9
69/1934

Facing page: Gandy, James, 1619–1689, *Deborah Hopton (c.1627–1702), and Her Son*, 1649, Royal Albert Memorial
Museum (p. 132)

AE 1649
AE 31

Deane Deborah Hopton

Deborah Hopton, daught.
of *Serjeant* Hatton, of Thame.
-Ditton. Wife of S.ʳ Edward
Hopton of Can—frome
Knight Banneret. &c.

Cortona, Pietro da (follower of) 1596–1669
The Discovery of Moses in the Bulrushes
oil on canvas 59.1 x 55.8
146/1978x

Cosway, Richard 1742–1821
Master Carew (probably Sir Henry Carew, 1779–1830) c.1790
oil on canvas 125.8 x 97.9
39/1941/10

Cosway, Richard (attributed to) 1742–1821
Portrait of the Artist (Self Portrait with Mahl Stick and Brush) c.1785
oil on canvas 68.9 x 58.5
137/1935

Cotton, Alan b.1938
Hartland Quay, North Devon 1976
oil on canvas 111.7 x 152.5
25/1978

Cox, W. H. (attributed to)
The First Paddle Steamer to Navigate the Exe up to Exeter 1832
oil on canvas 35.8 x 46.3
44/1929

Cranch, John 1751–1821
The Village Cooper 1791
oil on panel 15.4 x 16.4
85/1950

Cranch, John 1751–1821
The Carrier's Cart 1796
oil on panel 31 x 44
125/1937/2

Cranch, John 1751–1821
The Miser c.1830
oil on canvas 18.2 x 25.7
295/1968

Cranch, John 1751–1821
The Village Baker
oil on panel 13.8 x 15.6
57/1949/2

Cranch, John 1751–1821
The Village Butcher
oil on panel 13.8 x 15.6
57/1949/1

Critz, John de the elder (after) 1551/1552–1642
Sir Thomas White (1495–1567) 1566
oil on panel 79.3 x 64.7
137/1998

Crome, John Berney 1794–1842
Tell's Chapel, Lake of Lucerne, Switzerland
oil on canvas 51.3 x 40.9
24/1915

Crosse, Richard 1742–1810
Self Portrait 1765
oil on canvas 109.1 x 101.2
89/1962

Dabos, Laurent (attributed to) 1761–1835
Napoléon Bonaparte (1769–1821)
oil on canvas 50.3
87/1869

Danby, Francis 1793–1861
Dead Calm, Sunset at the Bight of Exmouth 1855
oil on canvas 77.4 x 107
306/1976

Dawson, Henry 1811–1878
Dartmouth from St Petrox Churchyard, Devon 1852
oil on canvas 85 x 122.4
108/2004

De Passe, Willem 1598–c.1637 **(after) & Van De Passe, Magdalena** 1600–1638 **(after)**
John Rainolds (1549–1607), DD
oil on canvas 75.9 x 63.5
21/1920

Dicksee, Thomas Francis 1819–1895
Study of a Lady's Head
oil on canvas 49.5 x 42.7
72/1933/1

Dingle, Thomas 1818–after 1900
Winter 1874
oil on canvas 40.7 x 30.7
K223

Downman, John (attributed to) 1750–1824
*Dr Hugh Downman (1740–1809), Physician
and Author, Exeter, Devonshire* 1796
oil on canvas 30.2 x 25
46/1925/4

Drummond, Malcolm 1880–1945
The Park Bench c.1910
oil on canvas 61.3 x 41
100/1969

Drummond, Samuel 1765–1844
*Admiral Edward Pellew (1757–1833), 1st
Viscount Exmouth* c.1816
oil on canvas 127.2 x 102.1
145/1876

Dutch School
Flower Piece 1713
oil on canvas 58.7 x 49.7
216/1970

Eastlake, Charles Lock 1793–1865
Contemplation c.1836
oil on canvas 91.9 x 71.6
140/1933

Eastlake, Charles Lock 1793–1865
Cypresses at L'Ariccia, Italy
oil on canvas 40 x 28.6
67/1955

Elford, William c.1749–1837
*Landscape, Sheepstor, near Burrator Reservoir,
Devon* 1818
oil on canvas 30.4 x 37.8
65/1934

Etty, William 1787–1849
*Andromeda, Perseus Coming to Her
Rescue* c.1840
oil on canvas 85.1 x 62.5
250/1972

Fischer, Karl 1862–1940
The Church of St Mary Steps, Exeter,
Devon c.1886
oil on canvas 61 x 152.5
15/1928

Fisher, Mark 1841–1923
River Landscape
oil on canvas 47.8 x 66.5
29/1940/1

Fisher, Mark 1841–1923
The Bridge
oil on canvas bonded to panel 20.6 x 26.5
29/1940/2

Fishwick, Clifford 1923–1997
Secret Cove 1966
oil on canvas 122.2 x 152.3
303/1968

Forbes, Stanhope Alexander 1857–1947
The 22 January 1901 (Reading the News of the
Queen's Death in a Cornish Cottage) 1901
oil on canvas 96.4 x 124
103/1978x

Foweraker, Albert Moulton 1873–1942
Afterglow, the Alhambra and Sierra Nevada,
Granada, Spain
oil on canvas 112.6 x 137.3
899/1910

French School 18th C or **Italian (Venetian)**
School
Perseus and Andromeda
oil on canvas 95.7 x 77.4
377/1971

Friedman, J.
The Castle 1918
oil on board 25 x 34.8
700/1997

Frith, William Powell 1819–1909
The Fair Toxophilites (English Archers,
Nineteenth Century) 1872
oil on canvas 98.2 x 81.7
305/1976

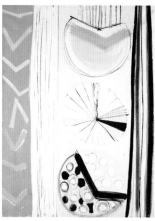

Frost, Terry 1915–2003
Lemon and White, Spring '63 1963
acrylic on canvas 122.2 x 92.2
75/1969/2

Gainsborough, Thomas 1727–1788
William Jackson (1730–1803) c.1762–1765
oil on canvas 127.1 x 102
41/1950

Gandy, James 1619–1689
Deborah Hopton (c.1627–1702), and Her Son 1649
oil on canvas 181.6 x 122.6
18/1945

Gandy, William c.1655–1729
Matthew Pear (1694–1765), Sword-Bearer of Exeter, and His Brother Philip Pear (b.1696) c.1700
oil on canvas 86 x 83.5
1893/6/11

Gandy, William c.1655–1729
Sir Henry Langford (d.1725), Bt 1710
oil on canvas 125.3 x 100.7
64/1957/4

Gandy, William c.1655–1729
Philippa Brown, née Musgrave (c.1699–1735), Wife of Thomas Brown 1720
oil on canvas 127.6 x 101.6
64/1957/8

Gandy, William c.1655–1729
Thomas Brown (1691–1728), Son of Susannah Brown of Combsatchfield 1720
oil on canvas 128.9 x 102.9
64/1957/1A

Gandy, William c.1655–1729
Thomas Brown (1691–1728), Son of Susannah Brown of Combsatchfield c.1720
oil on canvas 74.9 x 61.9
64/1957/2

Gandy, William (attributed to) c.1655–1729
Benjamin Oliver (1601–1672) c.1670
oil on canvas 111.3 x 90.8
164/1998

Garstin, Norman 1847–1926
Oudenarde, Belgium
oil on panel 22.5 x 30
208/1981/2

Garstin, Norman 1847–1926
The Pardon of Saint Barbe, Brittany, France
oil on panel 20.8 x 15.3
208/1981/4

Gheeraerts, Marcus the younger (attributed to) 1561/1562–1635/1636
Portrait of a Lady (probably Mary Hungate) c.1620
oil on canvas 163.2 x 126.8
37/1946/3

Gendall, John 1790–1865
Lydford Bridge on the Avon, Brent, Devon 1854
oil on canvas 102.1 x 84.3
K228

Gendall, John 1790–1865
Bridge near South Brent, Devon (Didsworthy Bridge?)
oil on canvas 82.4
1894/1/2

Gendall, John 1790–1865
Children Spinning Tops
oil on canvas 43.4 x 53.4
73/1938

Gendall, John 1790–1865
Landscape, River Scene
oil on canvas 54.5 x 64.5
148/1978x

Gendall, John 1790–1865
River and Bridge
oil on canvas 46.4 x 63.8
90/1940

Gendall, John 1790–1865
View on the Avon
oil on canvas 65.2 x 81.8
K243

Gendall, John 1790–1865
View on the Dart
oil on canvas 65.5 x 80
49/1935/2

Giannicola di Paolo (after) c.1460–1544
The Annunciation
oil on canvas 61 x 103.4
26/1919

Gilman, Harold 1876–1919
Girl Combing Her Hair c.1911
oil on canvas 61.5 x 46.5
122/1968

Ginner, Charles 1878–1952
Clayhidon, Devon 1913
oil on canvas 38.4 x 63.9
129/1983

Gore, Spencer 1878–1914
Panshanger Park, Hertfordshire 1909
oil on canvas 50.9 x 61.1
263/1968

Gould, Alexander Carruthers 1870–1948
Sir Francis Carruthers Gould (1844–1925) 1900
oil on canvas 51.3 x 66.4
46/1925/45

Gowing, Lawrence 1918–1991
Judith at Sixteen 1945
oil on canvas 41.2 x 61.2
256/1968

Grant, Duncan 1885–1978
Reclining Nude c.1930
oil on paper bonded to card and panel 55.1 x 75.9
39/1969

Hainsselin, Henry 1815–1886
Friesland Boer Skating
oil on copper 23.1 x 15.8
1894/3/4

Hallett, William H. 1810–1858
View of Exmouth from the Beacon Walls,
Devon c.1850
oil on canvas 86.8 x 120.3
101/1952

Halnon, Frederick James (attributed
to) 1881–1958
Portrait of a Boy in a Boating Cap
oil on canvas 68 x 56
33/2004

Hart, F. active 19th C
Study of a Dodo
oil on canvas 63.2 x 110
4/1865

Hart, Solomon Alexander 1806–1881
Self Portrait
oil on canvas 60 x 48
46/1925/10

Hawker, Thomas (attributed
to) c.1640–c.1725
Dr William Musgrave (1655–1721) c.1710
oil on canvas 76 x 63.4
64/1957/9

Haydon, Benjamin Robert 1786–1846
Self Portrait as the Spirit of the Vine c.1812
oil on canvas mounted on panel 28.1 x 24.3
29/1952

Haydon, Benjamin Robert 1786–1846
The Mock Election 1827
oil on canvas 43.3 x 53.5
6/1943/1

Haydon, Benjamin Robert 1786–1846
Chairing the Member 1828
oil on panel 42.4 x 51.5
6/1943/2

Haydon, Benjamin Robert 1786–1846
Henrietta Nelson Noble c.1830–1835
oil on canvas 76.7 x 63.6
78/1921

Haydon, Benjamin Robert 1786–1846
Curtius Leaping into the Gulf 1842
oil on canvas 304.8 x 213.3
138/1933

Hayman, Francis 1708–1776
Portrait of a Lady (probably the wife of the artist) c.1734
oil on canvas 63 x 44
241/2007

Hayman, Francis 1708–1776
Self Portrait of the Artist in His Studio c.1734
oil on canvas 41.2 x 32.5
5/1963/7

Hayman, Francis 1708–1776
Grosvenor Bedford and His Family c.1747
oil on canvas 63.8 x 76.2
71/1939

Hayman, Francis 1708–1776
Portrait of the Artist at His Easel c.1750
oil on canvas 60.7 x 43.5
99/1953

Hayman, Francis 1708–1776
The Muses Paying Homage to Frederick, Prince of Wales and Princess Augusta (The Artists Presenting a plan for an (...) c.1750–1751
oil on canvas 69.2 x 81.8
392/1974

Hayman, Francis 1708–1776
Don Quixote Knighted by the Innkeeper c.1755
oil on canvas 51.7 x 61.1
5/1963/1

Hayman, Francis 1708–1776
Don Quixote Attacking the Barber to Capture the Basin c.1765–1770
oil on canvas 52.9 x 62.3
5/1963/3

Hayman, Francis 1708–1776
Don Quixote Brought Home by the Peasant after the Tilt with the Toledo Merchant c.1765–1770
oil on canvas 52.6 x 62.9
5/1963/2

Facing page: Ballantyne, John, 1815–1897, *Miss Bertha Salter, Singer from North Devon*, 1890, University of Exeter, Fine Art
Collection (p. 185)

Hayman, Francis 1708–1776
Don Quixote Disputing with the Mad Cardenio c.1765–1770
oil on canvas 52.4 x 62.5
5/1963/4

Hayman, Francis 1708–1776
Don Quixote's Battle with the Wine Skins c.1765–1770
oil on canvas 52.5 x 63
5/1963/5

Hayman, Francis 1708–1776
The Barber Reclaiming His Basin from Don Quixote c.1765–1770
oil on canvas 52.8 x 63.2
5/1963/6

Hayman, Francis (attributed to) 1708–1776
The Wagg Family of Windsor c.1740
oil on canvas 64.2 x 76.9
13/1951

Hayman, John
East View of the East Gate, Exeter, Devon 1786
oil on canvas 66.3 x 87.5
64/2004/2

Hayman, John
West View of East Gate, Exeter, Devon 1786
oil on canvas 66.3 x 87.5
64/2004/1

Hayter, Stanley William 1901–1988
Rippled Water 1957
oil on canvas 91.5 x 72.5
261/1968

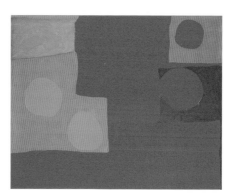

Heron, Patrick 1920–1999
Two Vermilions, Green and Purple in Red 1965
acrylic on canvas 122.9 x 152.9
75/1969/1

Holder, Edward Henry 1847–1922
A Cottage Home in Surrey 1891
oil on canvas 51 x 76.2
50/1921

Holl, Frank 1845–1888
The Song of the Shirt c.1874
oil on canvas 48.3 x 66.2
127/1975

Hoppner, John 1758–1810
Henry Langford (1758–1800) c.1790–1800
oil on canvas 74.5 x 61.5
64/1957/5

Howard-Jones, Ray 1903–1996
Bird in a Landscape c.1940
oil on canvas 62.8 x 75
179/1992

Hudson, Thomas 1701–1779
Frances Brown, née Tucker (d.1769) c.1740–
1750
oil on canvas 76 x 63.5
64/1957/7

Hudson, Thomas 1701–1779
*Anne van Keppel (1703–1789), Countess of
Albemarle* c.1745
oil on canvas 127.3 x 102.6
71/1948/1

Hudson, Thomas 1701–1779
*William Anne van Keppel (1702–1754), 2nd
Earl of Albemarle* c.1745
oil on canvas 127.4 x 101.2
71/1948/2

Hudson, Thomas 1701–1779
Anne, Countess of Dumfries (d.1811) 1763
oil on canvas 240 x 147.5
46/1968

Hudson, Thomas (circle of) 1701–1779
Portrait of a Lady (called 'Mrs
Adams') c.1740
oil on canvas 77.4 x 64.9
30/1970

Hughes, Arthur (attributed to) 1805–1838
Derwentwater, Cumberland 1836
oil on canvas 79.5 x 111
138/1975

Hughes, Robert Morson 1873–1953
The Old Cornish Tin Mine c.1938
oil on canvas 71.4 x 92
284/1982

**Hughes-Stanton, Herbert Edwin
Pelham** 1870–1937
Cader Idris 1918
oil on canvas 41.2 x 54.9
81/1918

Hulbert, Thelma 1913–1995
Dressing Table and Flowers 1939
oil on canvas 78 x 64
60/1998/1

Hulbert, Thelma 1913–1995
Green Shutters, France 1956
oil on canvas 118 x 91
60/1998/3

Hulbert, Thelma 1913–1995
Dead Leaves and Flowers 1957
oil on canvas 100 x 73
60/1998/4

Hulbert, Thelma 1913–1995
Sea and Rock, Italy c.1959
oil on canvas 81 x 127
60/1998/8

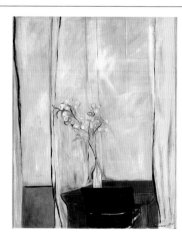

Hulbert, Thelma 1913–1995
Flight over Sea 1965
oil on canvas 93 x 123
60/1998/6

Hulbert, Thelma 1913–1995
Montage: Black and White c.1970
oil, fabric & fish bones on canvas 57 x 61
60/1998/10

Hulbert, Thelma 1913–1995
Honesty and Window 1972
oil on canvas 156 x 127
60/1998/7

Hulbert, Thelma 1913–1995
Room and Blossom 1975
oil on canvas 119 x 107
60/1998/9

Hulbert, Thelma 1913–1995
Blue Window, Fruit and Leaves 1976
oil on canvas 100 x 61
60/1998/11

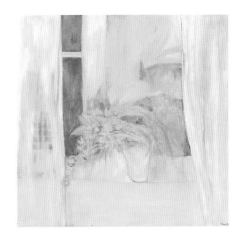

Hulbert, Thelma 1913–1995
Faded Flowers 1983
oil on canvas 116 x 131
60/1998/14

Humphry, Ozias (attributed to) 1742–1810
Mrs Archibald Hutcheson (c.1690–1781)
oil on canvas 76.8 x 64.1
82/1932

Hunter, Colin 1841–1904
Beer, Devon
oil on canvas 20.5 x 35.7
49/1949/150

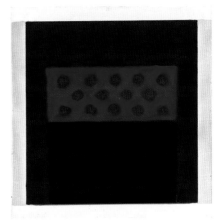

Illsley, Bryan b.1937
*Study in Green and Red with Black and
Brown* c.1965
oil on canvas mounted onto board 60.9 x 61
251/1972

Ipsen, Ernest Ludwig 1869–1951
John Lane (1854–1925) 1921
oil on canvas 111.8 x 81.8
111/1963

Jenkins, Charles (attributed to) c.1675–
1739
Nathaniel Newnham (1672–1760) c.1725
oil on canvas 121.9 x 110.6
618/1987

Jenkins, Thomas (attributed to) 1722–1798
*Sir William Morice of Werrington (d.1750),
MP*
oil on canvas 70.7 x 51.3
209/1981

Johns, Ambrose Bowden 1776–1858
Landscape in Devon (?)
oil on panel 39.3 x 54.3
106/1978x

Kemp-Welch, Lucy 1869–1958
*In Sight, Lord Dundonald's Dash on
'Ladysmith'* 1901
oil on canvas 151.6 x 305.8
1590/1909

Kite, Joseph Milner 1862–1946
Self Portrait 1922
oil on canvas 66 x 55
370/1971

Kneale, Bryan b.1930
Self Portrait 1955
acrylic on canvas 126.7 x 101.7
1064/1974

Kneller, Godfrey (follower of) 1646–1723
Portrait of a Gentleman (called 'Nicholas
Duck')
oil on canvas 74 x 62.5
165/1998

Knight, John Prescott 1803–1881
John Gendall of Exeter (1789–1865) c.1840
oil on canvas 76.2 x 63.8
33/1928

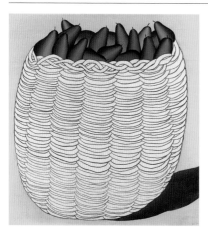

Knox, Jack b.1936
Big Basket, Pears and Shadow 1973
oil and charcoal on canvas 152.2 x 152.4
234/1975

Ladell, Edward 1821–1886
Still Life
oil on canvas 46.1 x 35.9
46/1941

Lamb, Henry 1883–1960
Military Exercise, Devonshire
oil on board 45 x 75.3
479/1977

Langhorne, Mary 1909–1984
Azaleas c.1945
oil on canvas 59.3 x 50.4
203/1981

Larivière, Charles Philippe Auguste de 1798–1876
The Prisoner (The Refugee)
oil on canvas 19.1 x 13.7
75/1917/73

Leakey, James 1775–1865
John White Abbott (1763–1851) c.1820
oil on panel 16.4 x 13.9
77/1937/2

Leakey, James 1775–1865
The Palmer Family c.1822
oil on panel 54.3 x 43.9
12/1955

Leakey, James 1775–1865
*Francis William Locke Ross (1793–1860),
Benefactor of the Royal Albert Memorial
Museum* c.1840–1850
oil on canvas 36.3 x 29.2
1895/3/10

Leakey, James 1775–1865
Devonshire Landscape
oil and pencil on panel 35.4 x 45.4
25/1999/3

Leakey, James 1775–1865
*Landscape with Figures and Cattle (Sea in
Distance)*
oil on canvas 53.5 x 77
47/1933/3

Leakey, James 1775–1865
Nadderwater, near Exeter, Devon
oil on canvas 62 x 92
47/1933/2

Leakey, James 1775–1865
Outside the Church, Dawlish, Devon
oil on panel 34.7 x 41.7
25/1999/2

Leakey, James 1775–1865
The Mill at Berry Pomeroy, Devon
oil & pencil on canvas 44.5 x 69.5
25/1999/4

Lee, Frederick Richard 1798–1879
A Devon Lane 1844
oil on panel 58.6 x 40.6
2/1941/1

Lee, Frederick Richard 1798–1879
Richmond Castle, Yorkshire 1862
oil on canvas 77 x 112.7
82/1941

Lee, Frederick Richard 1798–1879
View near Crediton, Devon 1867
oil on canvas 77.7 x 128.5
78/1918

Lee, Frederick Richard 1798–1879
Boys Bathing in a River
oil on panel 59.5 x 91.5
30/1941

Lee, Frederick Richard 1798–1879
The River Teign, South Devon
oil on card bonded to panel 25.3 x 35.5
80/1918

Lee, Frederick Richard 1798–1879
View near Crediton, Devon
oil on paper bonded to panel 25.3 x 35.2
79/1918

Lessore, John b.1939
Leon Kossoff (b.1926), with 'Cephalus and Aurora' c.1982
oil on board 60.9 x 71.2
203/1986

Linnell, John 1792–1882
Rustic Landscape with Sheep 1828
oil on canvas 26 x 35.6
40/1957/4

Facing page: Batoni, Pompeo, 1708–1787, *John Rolle Walter (1712–1779), MP for Exeter (1754–1776)*, 1753, Royal Albert Memorial Museum (p. 114)

John Rolle
Walter Esq

Loder, James 1784–1860
*Equestrian Portrait of William Stephens
(c.1784–1840)* 1836
oil on canvas 57.7 x 76
112/1933/1

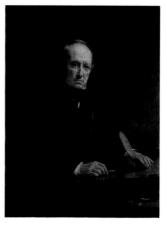

Long, Edwin 1829–1891
Samuel Cousins (1801–1887), RA 1882
oil on canvas 121.8 x 86.3
46/1925/14

Luny, Thomas 1759–1837
Coastal Scene 1791
oil on canvas 39.1 x 51.8
194

Luny, Thomas 1759–1837
In the Channel 1816
oil on canvas 61.3 x 86.8
1896/2

Luny, Thomas 1759–1837
A Fisherman's Cottage 1817
oil on canvas 26 x 35.8
1896/2/5

Luny, Thomas 1759–1837
A Ship of the Line off Plymouth, Devon 1817
oil on canvas 51 x 68.7
1896/2/2

Luny, Thomas 1759–1837
In the Channel 1817
oil on canvas 60.9 x 86.2
1896/3

Luny, Thomas 1759–1837
Dutch Coastal Scene with Shipping 1824
oil on canvas 22.6 x 30.6
219/1905

Luny, Thomas 1759–1837
St Michael's Mount, Cornwall 1825
oil on canvas 89.2 x 132.2
49/1935/1

Luny, Thomas 1759–1837
Coast Scene with Shipping and Figures 1829
oil on panel 30 x 40.6
1896/2/6

Luny, Thomas 1759–1837
*Fishing Scene, Teignmouth Beach and the
Ness, Devon* 1831
oil on panel 30.3 x 40.9
217/1905

Luny, Thomas 1759–1837
*A View of the River Teign, Looking up River
from Teignmouth towards Dartmoor,
Devon* c.1831
oil on canvas 60.5 x 85.7
285/1982

Luny, Thomas 1759–1837
*Shipping in Rough Seas, 1834 (Cape of Good
Hope)* 1834
oil on panel 30.1 x 41.1
150/1978x

Luny, Thomas 1759–1837
*Seascape with Shipping and Rowing
Boat* c.1834
oil on canvas 44.2 x 36.1
75/1917/4

Luny, Thomas 1759–1837
A View on the Coast of France
oil on canvas 38.1 x 50.8
221/1905

Luny, Thomas 1759–1837
Seascape, Shipping off the Coast in Rough Seas
oil on canvas 23.5 x 30.8
1896/1

Luny, Thomas 1759–1837
Shipping off the Eddystone
oil on canvas 86.9 x 130.1
220/1905

Luscombe, Henry Andrews 1820–1899
Coast Scene with Shipping 1871
oil on canvas 50.8 x 76.5
109/1978x

Manson, James Bolivar 1879–1945
Dartmouth, Devon c.1921
oil on panel 34.5 x 44.9
145/1969

Marks, Henry Stacey 1829–1898
A Bit of Blue 1877
oil on canvas 70.3 x 51
206/1911

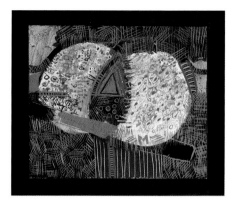

McNeish, Alexander 1932–2000
Landscape on a Bar c.1964
acrylic on panel 30.4 x 35.7
178/1968

Meninsky, Bernard 1891–1950
*Seascape (Project for a Ballet on Classical
Theme)*
oil on canvas 63.5 x 76.1
307/1976/2

Mieris, Willem van 1662–1747
The Poultry Seller 1710
oil on panel 37.8 x 29.6
66/1919/1

Miles, William active 1835–1860
The First Royal Devon Yeomanry 1840
oil on canvas 50.4 x 66.1
59/1938

Minton, John 1917–1957
Boy in a Landscape (Eric Verrico) 1948
oil on canvas 76.7 x 63.7
144/1969

Mogford, Thomas 1800–1868
Portrait of a Sister of Samuel Cousins c.1852
oil on canvas 127.4 x 101.7
32/1883

Mogford, Thomas 1800–1868
John Dinham (1785–1864) c.1855
oil on canvas 92 x 71.7
1892

Monamy, Peter 1681–1749
Shipping in a Calm
oil on canvas 42.7 x 59.8
86/1926

Monnington, Walter Thomas 1902–1976
Final Design of the Ceiling of the Chapel at the University of Exeter 1956
oil on board 44.3 x 111.7
308/1976/6

Nasmyth, Patrick (attributed to) 1787–1831
Landscape Study in Hampshire, 1821 1821
oil on canvas 17.8 x 24.2
228/1970

Newbery, Francis Henry 1855–1946
Portrait of a Devonian (Mrs Cleeve) c.1907
oil on canvas 114.4 x 95.1
35/1917

Northcote, James 1746–1831
Edmund Burke (1729–1797) c.1770–1780
oil on canvas 76.3 x 63.8
19/1948

Northcote, James 1746–1831
The Entry of Richard and Bolingbroke into London (from William Shakespeare's 'Richard II', Act V, Scene 2) 1793
oil on canvas 303.5 x 394
81/1975

Northcote, James 1746–1831
Moses Hawker 1808
oil on canvas bonded to panel 68.4 x 55.9
46/1925/9

Northcote, James 1746–1831
The Honourable Miss Caroline Fox (1767–1845) 1810
oil on canvas 76.5 x 63.6
274/1982

Northcote, James 1746–1831
Admiral Sir Michael Seymour (1768–1834), 1st Bt c.1815–1820
oil on canvas 76 x 63.8
46/1925/6

Northcote, James 1746–1831
Self Portrait as a Falconer 1823
oil on canvas 127.1 x 102
83/1947

Northcote, James 1746–1831
Portrait of the Artist at the Age of 81 1827
oil on canvas 76.8 x 64.4
24/1938

Opie, Edward 1810–1894
Mr J. C. Hay, Formerly Manager of Exeter Theatre, in His Celebrated Character of 'Jack Rag'
oil on canvas 65.9 x 42.7
46/1925/8

Opie, Edward (attributed to) 1810–1894
James Pearce of Falmouth c.1860
oil on canvas 161 x 130
214/1999

Opie, John (attributed to) 1761–1807
Lady Jane Buller c.1780
oil on canvas 102.7 x 68.3
47/1955

Opie, John (attributed to) 1761–1807
Major Daniel Hamilton (1722–1810) c.1786
oil on canvas 126.5 x 101.4
9/1894/2

Opie, John (attributed to) 1761–1807
Mrs Meymott c.1787
oil on canvas 76.2 x 62.8
55/1961

Organ, Robert b.1933
Natural History 1987
oil on canvas 151 x 303
1101/1988

Patch, Thomas 1725–1782
A Caricature Group in Florence c.1763
oil on canvas 83.6 x 118.7
61/1935

Patch, Thomas 1725–1782
*Portrait of a Gentleman on the Grand
Tour* 1769
oil on canvas laid on board 40 x 29
129/1993

Patch, Thomas 1725–1782
Italian Port Scene, Sunset 1770
oil on canvas 97.4 x 145.7
37/1938/2

Patch, Thomas 1725–1782
A View of Florence, Italy
oil on canvas 86.7 x 143
34/1944/1

Patch, Thomas 1725–1782
Italian Port Scene, Sunrise
oil on canvas 97.5 x 145.8
37/1938/1

Patch, Thomas (attributed to) 1725–1782
*Continental Coastal Scene (possibly an Italian
Castle, near Naples?)*
oil on canvas 69 x 81.9
75/1917/2

Payne, William c.1760–after 1830
View on the Wye c.1809–1810
oil on canvas 108.8 x 165.9
42/1950

Payne, William c.1760–after 1830
River in Devon
oil on canvas 32.3 x 47.2
106/1937/3

Pearse, Dennis Colbron 1883–1971
Early Tasmanian Canoes 1926
oil on board 29.6 x 41.6
25/1939

Pearson Hayward, L. F. active c.1890–1910
Her Majesty's Last Recruit 1901
oil on canvas 76.6 x 50.6
235/1905

Peters, Matthew William (attributed to) 1742–1814
Nelly
oil on canvas 91.3 x 70.9
K248

Piper, H. Wyatt
Portrait of a Lady c.1825
oil on panel 20.3 x 15.3
150/2004

Pissarro, Lucien 1863–1944
Apple Blossom, Riversbridge Farm, Blackpool, Devon 1921
oil on canvas 53.3 x 64.8
97/2005

Plimer, Andrew 1763–1837
Jane Kingdon (d.1816), Paternal Grandmother of Mr Kent Kingdon
oil on panel 29.5 x 25.5
K225

Ponsford, John 1790–1870
Mrs Bowditch (1756–1827), of Taunton 1821
oil on canvas 79 x 61
71/1927

Poynter, Edward John 1836–1919
Diadumene 1883
oil on canvas 51 x 50.9
77/1969

Prout, Samuel 1783–1852
Harbour Scene
oil on panel 16.4 x 21.8
60/1953/1

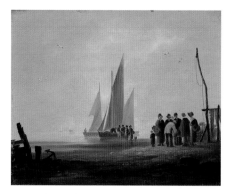

Prout, Samuel 1783–1852
Harbour Scene
oil on panel 16.4 x 21.8
60/1953/2

Pybus (attributed to)
Portrait of a Lady (possibly Mrs Richard Bird, d.1841) c.1840
oil on canvas 61.4 x 45.8
28/1919

Ramsay, Allan (attributed to) 1713–1784
*Portrait of an African (probably Ignatius
Sancho, 1729–1780)* c.1757–1760
oil on canvas 61.8 x 51.5
14/1943

Ramsay, James 1786–1854
James Northcote (1746–1831), Aged 78 1824
oil on canvas 75 x 62
213/1999

Reinagle, George Philip c.1802–1835
*A First Rate Man-of-War Driving on a Reef of
Rocks, and Foundering in a Gale* c.1826
oil on canvas 102 x 127.2
38/1928

Reynolds, Joshua 1723–1792
Captain Charles Proby (1725–1799) 1753
oil on canvas 76.2 x 63.5
51/1955

Reynolds, Joshua 1723–1792
*John Burridge Cholwich (c.1752–1835),
Unsuccessfully Contested the Exeter By-
Election (1776)* c.1776
oil on canvas 76.2 x 63.5
36/1961

Reynolds, Joshua 1723–1792
*Thomas Dawson (1726–1813), 1st Viscount
Cremorne*
oil on canvas 76.5 x 63.9
3/1948

Reynolds, Joshua (after) 1723–1792
*Portrait of a Girl (possibly Theophila Palmer,
1757–1848)* c.1767
oil on panel 31.9 x 26.2
13/1938

Rice, Brian b.1936
Devon 1996
mixed media on canvas 71 x 101.5
613/1997

Richards, Alan b.1932
After the Rain, Widecombe, Devon 1994
oil on canvas 48.5 x 58.7
84/2001

Richards, George active 19th C
Peter the Great of Russia (1672–1725)
oil on canvas 76.4 x 63.3
46/1925/12

Riviere, Briton 1840–1920
Pride of Place 1891
oil on canvas 44.4 x 29.1
62/1924/65

Riviere, Hugh Goldwin 1869–1956
Sir Harry Veitch (1840–1924) 1909
oil on canvas 105.9 x 76.6
62/1924/66

Rogers, Philip Hutchins c.1786–1853
Devon Landscape 1811
oil on canvas 43.9 x 62
125/1937/1

Rogers, Philip Hutchins c.1786–1853
Lake Scene 1812
oil on canvas 41.1 x 53.1
19/1950

Rosier, Amédée 1831–1898
Sunset Scene, Canal San Marco, Venice
oil on canvas 74.3 x 124.5
23/1915

Rouse
Interior of a Church
oil on paper bonded to board 20.2 x 27.2
3585

Say, Frederick Richard 1805–1868
*Sir William Webb Follet (1796–1845), MP for
Exeter (1835–1845)* c.1835
oil on canvas 126.8 x 101.3
11/1921

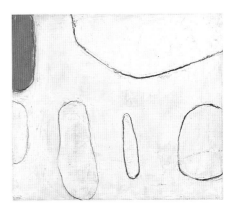

Scott, William George 1913–1989
Orange and White 1962
oil on canvas 30.4 x 36.7
75/1969/3

Facing page: British (English) School, *John Strange (1590–1646), Former Mayor of Bideford (1643–1646)*, c.1600, Bideford
Town Council (p. 38)

Shapland, John 1865–1929
The Quay, Exeter
oil on board 15.5 x 20.6
140/2004

Shaw, Walter James 1851–1933
Oceans, Mists and Spray
oil on canvas 91.7 x 152.7
93/1919

Shayer, William 1788–1879
Landscape with Cattle, Horses and Figures
oil on canvas 50.8 x 61
50/1943/7

Shuter, William active 1771–1799
Nathaniel Williams (1752–1797), of Exeter 1796
oil on panel 24.8 x 29.2
46/1925/3

Sickert, Walter Richard 1860–1942
Reclining Nude (Le lit de cuivre) c.1906
oil on canvas 40.9 x 50.9
121/1968

Smith, Hely Augustus Morton 1862–1941
Evelyn Phelps Morse (b.1861) c.1895
oil on canvas 74.5 x 62
286/1997

Smythe, Edward Robert 1810–1899
The Blacksmith's Shop
oil on canvas 75.2 x 97.8
23/1946/1

Spreat, William 1816–1897?
Ogwell Mill, Devon 1847
oil on canvas 77.9 x 92.7
113/1933

Spreat, William 1816–1897?
Bradley Vale, Newton Abbot, Devon
oil on canvas 78.6 x 93
71/1948/3

Spreat, William 1816–1897?
Holy Street Mill on the Teign, Devon
oil on canvas 50 x 76.5
32/1933

Stark, Arthur James 1831–1902
Dartmoor Drift, Devon
oil on canvas 104.4 x 183.5
5/1945

Swanenburgh, Isaac Claesz. (attributed to) 1537–1614
Nicklaes Warmondt (1540–1609), Burgomaster of Leiden 1607
oil on panel 109.8 x 76.8
118/1872

Tilson, Joe b.1928
Liknon, Egg and Pomegranate 1987
oil on canvas on wood relief 60 x 65.5
1106/1988

Towne, Francis 1739/1740–1816
Exeter from Exwick, Devon 1773
oil on canvas 116.4 x 163.1
10/1961

Towne, Francis 1739/1740–1816
At Tivoli, Mountain Landscape in the Alban Hills, Italy 1800
oil on panel 40 x 66
106/1937/1

Towne, Francis 1739/1740–1816
Roadside Scene in Rome (The Ancient Wall between Porta Salaria and Porta Pinciana, Rome) 1800
oil on panel 46.7 x 66
106/1937/2

Towne, Francis 1739/1740–1816
Landscape with a Castle
oil on panel 29.1 x 42.7
23/1948/1

Traies, Francis D. 1826–1857
Landscape with Figures and Animals, Collecting Heather 1852
oil on canvas 45.7 x 61.3
27/1934/1

Traies, William 1789–1872
*The Lime Kilns near Topsham on the Exe,
Devon, Lympstone and Exmouth in the
Distance* 1835
oil on canvas 71.1 x 91.1
83/1932/2

Traies, William 1789–1872
Landscape Composition 1838
oil on canvas 91.5 x 72.4
43/1936/2

Traies, William 1789–1872
Bridford Mill, Devon
oil on canvas 76.7 x 63.6
83/1932/3

Traies, William 1789–1872
Exeter from Exwick, Devon
oil on canvas 81.2 x 113.1
30/1933

Tucker, Charles W. J. 1920–1992
The Blitz c.1942
oil on board 40.5 x 60.3
159/1998/5

Tucker, Charles W. J. 1920–1992
The Farthing Breakfast
oil on board 46.8 x 65.4
159/1998/1

Tucker, Charles W. J. 1920–1992
The Soup Kitchen
oil on canvas 35 x 55.4
159/1998/2

Tucker, John Wallace 1808–1869
View at Berry Pomeroy, Devon 1830
oil on panel 25 x 32.9
28/1934/1

Tucker, John Wallace 1808–1869
*Cherry Bridge and the River Lynn, North
Devon* 1831
oil on panel 20 x 33.1
122/1978x

Tucker, John Wallace 1808–1869
Mill Stream at Pynes, Devon 1862
oil on canvas 33.4 x 46.2
63/1935

Tucker, John Wallace 1808–1869
Near Chulmleigh, Devon (Chulmleigh from the River Dart, Devon) 1862
oil on canvas 36.1 x 46.3
123/1978x

Tucker, John Wallace 1808–1869
Duncannon, on the River Dart, below Totnes, Devon 1866
oil on panel 25.2 x 35.4
57/1951/2

Tucker, John Wallace 1808–1869
On the River Dart between Totnes and Dartmouth, Devon 1869
oil on panel 25.4 x 35.7
57/1951/1

Tucker, John Wallace 1808–1869
Coastal Scene with Shipping and Figures
oil on panel 20.7 x 29.5
35/1935/1

Tucker, John Wallace 1808–1869
Landscape with a River Estuary
oil on panel 21.8 x 30.5
57/1951/3

Tucker, John Wallace 1808–1869
View on the Exe near Topsham, Devon
oil on canvas 45.5 x 63.5
467/1997

Virtue, John b.1947
Landscape No.440 1997–1998
acrylic, shellac & black ink on canvas 25.5 x 30.7
71/1999

Wainwright, John active 1855–1890
Primrose and Robin 1864
oil on canvas 45.6 x 35.4
K232

Wainwright, John active 1855–1890
Hawthorn and Chaffinch 1865
oil on canvas 25.4 x 33.1
K229

Wainwright, John active 1855–1890
*Still Life with Fruit and Flowers in a
Landscape* 1865
oil on canvas 46 x 36
K233

Webster, Thomas George 1800–1886
William Miles 1882
oil on panel 50.1 x 40
311/1907

Wells, Henry Tanworth (after) 1828–1903
(Walter) Percy Sladen (1849–1900)
oil on canvas 112.1 x 86.4
263/1903/A

Wells, Henry Tanworth (after) 1828–1903
Mrs Constance Sladen (d.1906)
oil on canvas 91.2 x 71.1
263/1903/B

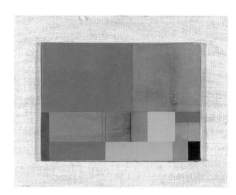

Wells, John 1907–2000
63/11 1962
acrylic on canvas 45.2 x 55.4
75/1969/4

White, John 1851–1933
*A Village Wedding, Shere Church,
Surrey* 1881
oil on canvas 170.9 x 117.2
22/1909

Widgery, Frederick John 1861–1942
Sky Study, Wind WSW 1911
oil on plywood panel 20 x 30.5
67/1931/481

Widgery, Frederick John 1861–1942
Sky Study
oil on board 15.6 x 25.7
67/1931/317

Widgery, Frederick John 1861–1942
William Widgery (1822–1893)
oil on canvas 91.4 x 71.3
1887/4/4

Widgery, William 1822–1893
Edward Adams (1823–1892), of Crediton 1856
oil on canvas 90 x 71.3
26/1978

Widgery, William 1822–1893
Fingle Bridge, Devon 1863
oil on canvas 70 x 90.9
45/1934

Widgery, William 1822–1893
Burdocks, Brambles and Furze 1868
oil on canvas 91.4 x 71.9
K245

Widgery, William 1822–1893
View in Gidley Park, Devon 1868
oil on canvas 91.3 x 71.6
K221

Widgery, William 1822–1893
Cross at Chagford, Devon 1869
oil on canvas 62.8 x 123.1
K230

Widgery, William 1822–1893
Scene near Holy Street Mill, Chagford, Devon 1869
oil on canvas 150 x 102.3
K213

Widgery, William 1822–1893
Swiss Lake Scene 1869
oil on canvas 70 x 113.2
221/1981

Widgery, William 1822–1893
Beechwood Scene 1870
oil on canvas 46.1 x 55.8
K217

Widgery, William 1822–1893
Bowerman's Nose, Dartmoor, Devon 1870
oil on canvas 91.4 x 71.9
K244

Widgery, William 1822–1893
A View off Teignmouth Bridge, Devon 1873
oil on board 21.2 x 47
K246

Widgery, William 1822–1893
Cranmere Pool, Dartmoor, Devon 1873
oil on board 21.2 x 45.5
K247

Widgery, William 1822–1893
On the Lyd, Devon 1873
oil on canvas 152.8 x 102.1
119/1935

Widgery, William 1822–1893
On the Lyd, Devon 1875
oil on canvas 45.8 x 30.7
141/1978x

Widgery, William 1822–1893
On the Lyd, Devon 1878
oil on canvas 45.8 x 30.6
K224

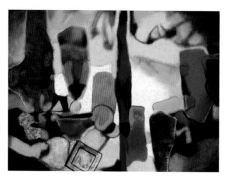

Widgery, William 1822–1893
Sharpitor Rocks, Dartmoor, Devon
oil on canvas 91.6 x 71.4
K220

Williams, Aubrey 1926–1990
Bonampak (Number 17) 1967
acrylic on canvas 137 x 182.5
208/1970

Williams, Howard 1909–1980
Exe Bridge from Gervase Avenue, Exeter, Devon 1963
oil on board 31.5 x 39.5
363/1979

Facing page: Knox, Jack, b.1936, *Big Basket, Pears and Shadow*, 1973, Royal Albert Memorial Museum (p. 142)

Williams, John Edgar c.1821–1891
*Charles John Follett (1838–1921), Mayor of
Exeter* 1875
oil on canvas 226.7 x 132.7
124/1978x

Williams, T. H. active 1801–1830
*Thomas Medland Kingdon (1783–
1832)* c.1820
oil on canvas 75 x 64
K215

Williams, William 1808–1895
View on the Fal, Cornwall 1842
oil on canvas 80 x 115.7
31/1933

Williams, William 1808–1895
Water Mill 1845
oil on panel 27.5 x 23.5
105/1939

Williams, William 1808–1895
*Morning after the Storm, Kenwick Cove, the
Lizard*
oil on canvas 77.2 x 127.4
3/1894/3

Williams, William 1808–1895
The Exe, near Topsham, Devon
oil on canvas 86.8 x 127.6
125/1978x

Williamson, William Henry 1820–1883
Near Clovelly, Devon 1875
oil on canvas 25.2 x 45.7
256/1972/1

Williamson, William Henry 1820–1883
Sunset on the Devonshire Coast 1875
oil on canvas 25.2 x 46.2
256/1972/2

Wilson, Richard 1712/1713–1782
Llyn Peris and Dolbadarn Castle c.1762–1765
oil on canvas 75.8 x 129.2
379/1971

Wootton, John c.1682–1764
Landscape with Angelica and Medaro
oil on canvas 104 x 101.5
617/1987

Wright, Joseph of Derby 1734–1797
Lake Albano and Castel Gandolfo, Italy 1792
oil on canvas 36.9 x 43.4
40/1957/3

Wyllie, Charles William 1853–1923
The Port of London
oil on canvas 80.5 x 127.2
514/1906

Royal Devon and Exeter Hospital

The Devon & Exeter Hospital was founded in 1741 and gained the title 'Royal' in 1899. The connection between art and health at the Hospital can be traced to the institution's very beginnings. The art of the portrait painter was the PR of the day. Benefactors and founding medical men had their portraits painted to signal to the City that the new hospital, one of the first modern hospitals outside of London, was open for business.

Every picture tells a story – so the saying goes. The portraits of the founders speak of a time of great development and change.

Alured Clarke, Dean of Exeter, is painted by James Wills. Clarke made the initial moves to establish the Hospital as he had done in Winchester during his time as Dean there. Clarke had received ecclesiastical training in London and must have been aware of the establishment of St Bartholomew's Hospital. As well as being one of the very earliest medical institutions of its kind, Bart's was also the scene of the first arts and health 'spat'. The founders of the Hospital, many of whom travelled the 'Grand Tour', realised the benefit of arts in the healing environment and commissioned leading continental artists to bring classical scenes to the Hospital. William Hogarth, who was born close by and was England's leading artist at the time, naturally took umbrage and insisted upon creating a huge work without fee in exchange for a seat on the board; presumably to ensure the Hospital commissioned more home-grown talent in the future.

The leading lights that Clarke recruited to establish the Hospital in Exeter were amongst the best business and scientific minds of the age in the region. John Tuckfield is shown in his portrait, painted by Thomas Hudson, with the original deed of the land he donated held aloft. Painted by William Hoare of Bath, Ralph Allen, the Bill Gates of his day, made his wealth by unifying and developing the postal service – the blueprint of mass communication to come. Reinvesting his money in quarrying, most of Bath was built of his stone. His comfort assured on earth, he set about buying his stairway to heaven by donating vast sums to establish hospitals in Exeter and Bath and to other social causes. John Patch Senior had learnt the art of surgery in Britain and on the continent. His portrait, by William Gandy, shows him resplendent in wig and frock coat lecturing on anatomy – with a drawing of a hand along with a flayed and dissected arm for emphasis. Beautifully painted of course, the work underlines the fact that the use of human remains for research was still somewhat taboo. Patch's son, also John, painted by John Opie, joined the family business and another family member Thomas, became an artist – and a rather good one at that!

In 1991 Exeter HealthCare Arts was established to deliver arts and cultural services within the Royal Devon & Exeter Hospital. The work includes the commissioning of public seating and landscaped areas – oases in which patients can withdraw from the clinical environment. The Hospital has a large collection of permanent works on display and a programme of changing exhibitions covering solo artist and group shows. The programme engages with regional artists and the staff communities. Hands-on, participatory schemes are a feature of working with young patients in the Hospital School. A recent project saw professional animators work alongside patients to create a five minute movie to introduce the children's ward to new patients via the Trust's website.

The contemporary collection includes a range of works donated, commissioned or on permanent loan. Lucy Willis' painting *Cliff Cottage* is on loan to the collection from the artist herself and another of her paintings, *The Walled Garden*, was commissioned for the Oncology department. Works are intended to take patients' minds off the immediate problems they may be facing. Relatives and other visitors use the artwork as a talking point, away from the medical conditions their loved ones may be contending with. When patients are recovering and regaining strength, often they will measure their recovery rate by the number of pictures or garden views they pass on a stroll away from the ward.

At a time when demands on staff are ever increasing, it is the improvements the arts make to the working environment that can provide respite from a busy and stressful day. In all of this, it is important to note that it is the arts community reaching out to the Hospital that helps it to become a hospitable place.

Stephen Pettet Smith, Head of Exeter HealthCare Arts

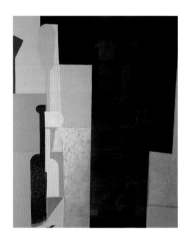

Baxter, Rod active 2003
Coffee Break
oil on canvas 99 x 79
PCF44

Bennett, William Mineard 1778–1858
Bartholemew Parr, Esq. (1713–1800), Surgeon (1741–1797) 1830
oil on canvas 75 x 62
PCF24

Bishop, Piran b.1961
Professor Ruth Hawker (b.1939), OBE, First Chairman of the Royal Devon and Exeter NHS Foundation Trust 2006
oil on canvas 71.2 x 51
PCF17

Bocos
Still Life with Flowers
oil on canvas 75.5 x 60.5
PCF5

Brice, Henry c.1831–1903
John Harris (1782–1855), Surgeon
oil on canvas 92 x 71
PCF22

British (English) School 19th C
Doctor Patrick Miller (1782–1871), Physician
(1809–1860)
oil on canvas 91 x 70
PCF26

British (English) School 19th C
Mr Samuel Barnes (1784–1858), Surgeon
(1813–1846)
oil on canvas 75 x 63
PCF32

British (English) School 19th C
William H. Elliot (1805–1874), Physician
(1860–1874)
oil on canvas 112 x 86
PCF34

Doyle, Anne Farrall b.1940
Woodland Path
oil on canvas 39 x 49
PCF15

Eastwood, Nicholas Anthony b.1942
Summer Stream
acrylic on board 120.3 x 142
PCF1

Gandy, William c.1655–1729
John Patch Senior (1691–1746), Surgeon
(1741–1746)
oil on canvas 121 x 82
PCF33

Hinds, Thorie Catherine b.1958
Thinking It Might 2004
oil on canvas 120.6 x 120.6
PCF14

Hinds, Thorie Catherine b.1958
A Little Bit Later
oil on canvas 103.6 x 103.6
PCF7

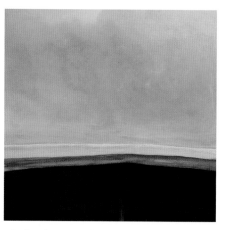

Hinds, Thorie Catherine b.1958
Settling Sky
oil on canvas 103.6 x 103.6
PCF8

Hoare, William 1706–1792
*Ralph Allen (1693–1764), President of the
Royal Devon and Exeter Hospital (1758), and
Benefactor*
oil on canvas 127 x 101
PCF21

Hudson, Thomas 1701–1779
*Doctor Michael Lee Dicker (1693–1752),
Physician (1741–1752)*
oil on canvas 125 x 99
PCF35

Hudson, Thomas 1701–1779
John Andrews, MD
oil on canvas 123.8 x 98.7
PCF46

Hudson, Thomas 1701–1779
*John Tuckfield (1717–1767), President of the
Royal Devon and Exeter Hospital (1748), and
Benefactor*
oil on canvas 126 x 100
PCF27

Jennison, Robert b.1933
Field Boundary (diptych)
oil on canvas 49.5 x 75.5
PCF41

Keenan, John active 1780–1819
*John Sheldon (1752–1808), Surgeon (1797–
1808)*
oil on canvas 125 x 100
PCF18

Keenan, John active 1780–1819
*John Sheldon (1752–1808), Surgeon (1797–
1808)*
oil on canvas 127 x 101
PCF31

Knight, John Prescott 1803–1881
Dr Thomas Shapter (1809–1902), Physician
oil on canvas 86 x 65
PCF25

Leakey, James 1775–1865
John Haddy James (1788–1869), Surgeon
(1816–1855)
oil on canvas 92 x 71
PCF28

Lester, James active 1985–2003
Sunrise
oil on canvas 59.7 x 49.5
PCF40

Mellings, Jenny b.1958
Decorated Wave
oil on canvas 125 x 165.2
PCF13

Miller, John 1931–2002
Penwith Sandspur, Cornwall 1994
oil on canvas 151 x 136
PCF4 (P)

Opie, John 1761–1807
Dr Thomas Glass (1709–1786), Physician
(1741–1775)
oil on canvas 125 x 99
PCF36

Opie, John 1761–1807
John Patch Junior (1723–1786), Surgeon
(1741–1786)
oil on canvas 74 x 61
PCF29

Reinagle, Ramsay Richard 1775–1862
Dr John Blackall (1771–1860)
oil on canvas 73 x 61
PCF30

Richards, Alan b.1932
Flowers for Seurat 1990
oil on canvas 102 x 76
PCF39

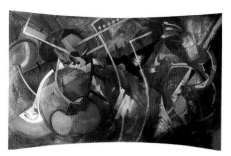

Richards, Alan b.1932
The Flowering of Art-Deco 1991
oil on canvas 90 x 69
PCF38

Richards, Alan b.1932
*Winter Afternoon, the Lake at Killerton House,
Devon* 1992
oil on canvas 59.5 x 75
PCF37

Romain, Ricky b.1948
Breath of Fire
oil on canvas 89 x 153
PCF2

Shiel, Mary Ode
Autumn Trees
oil on canvas 90.5 x 120.5
PCF43

Shiel, Mary Ode
Autumn Trees II
oil on canvas 101.5 x 152
PCF45

Smith, Ivy b.1945
Central Sterile Supply 1993
oil on canvas 202 x 90.2
PCF10

Smith, Ivy b.1945
The Catering Department 1993
oil on canvas 202 x 90.2
PCF11

Smith, Ivy b.1945
The Day Case Unit 1993
oil on canvas 202 x 90.2
PCF9

Smith, Ivy b.1945
The Physiotherapy Department 1993
oil on canvas 202 x 90.2
PCF12

Facing page: Chugg, Brian, 1926–2003, *Saunton Cliff, Devon*, 1958, Museum of Barnstaple and North Devon (p. 25)

Trist Newman, Beryl 1906–1991
Miss R. M. Furze, Matron, Royal Devon and Exeter Hospital (1958–1970) 1969
oil on canvas 74.5 x 60
PCF6

unknown artist
Dr Anthony Daly, MD, FRCP
oil on canvas 91.2 x 72
PCF19

Watts, George Frederick 1817–1904
Sir John Walrond (1818–1889), President of the Royal Devon and Exeter Hospital (1874), and Benefactor
oil on canvas 91 x 70.5
PCF23

Willis, Lucy b.1954
Cliff Cottage 1989
oil on canvas 150 x 256
PCF3 (P)

Willis, Lucy b.1954
The Walled Garden 1996
oil on canvas 101 x 167
PCF16

Wills, James active 1740–1777
Dean Alured Clarke (1696–1742), Dean of Exeter, Principal Founder and First President of Royal Devon and Exeter Hospital (1741)
oil on canvas 126 x 103
PCF20

The Devonshire and Dorset Regimental Charitable Trust

The history of British Army infantry regiments goes back to the seventeenth century and since then there have been numerous reorganisations, amalgamations and renamings.

The Devonshire and Dorset Regiment had its roots in the West Country when in 1685 The Duke of Beaufort's Musketeers were formed, later becoming The Devonshire Regiment, then the Devon and Dorsets in 1958. The explicit county titles were dispensed with upon the latest amalgamation in 2007 when The Rifles was formed. During the intervening three centuries the Regiment, and in particular the Officers' Messes of its constituent battalions, purchased a considerable amount of property, mostly in the form of silver, pictures and furniture. Many items, notably silver, were also presented by individual officers when they retired from the Regiment. As the

Regiment reduced over the years to a single battalion, many unwanted items, especially pieces of silver, were sold off and the funds invested. If the complete Regimental collection still existed it would be enormous, but it now comprises just enough to service a single battalion in a fixed location. It is owned by the Trustees of the Devonshire and Dorset Regiment and is effectively on permanent loan to the new Regiment, The Rifles.

Few oil paintings from before World War Two remain in the possession of the Trustees. It may be that there never were very many, but no records are known to exist. Certainly many battalions of the Regiment would have been stationed abroad where there may have been few artists of merit. Interestingly this was certainly not the case with silver, because the Regiment purchased many items of Burmese and Indian silver during what might be termed the Colonial Period. The majority of the Regiment's art collection dates from the second half of the twentieth century when there was a concerted effort to have notable battles and individuals reproduced on canvas. By this time the Regiment was based in the United Kingdom or West Germany for long periods, making the commissioning of paintings quite easy.

There was a tradition for some years of Commanding Officers presenting paintings to the Officers' Mess upon relinquishing command, while portraits of Colonels of the Regiment were also commissioned. All these are listed.

Lt. Col. G. S. Nicholls, Rifles Secretary

Burgh, Lydia de 1923–2007
The Mournes from Blackstaff Bridge
oil on canvas 45 x 59.4
PCF9

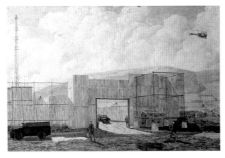

Hamilton, Lucius
Camp Monagh
oil on canvas 50 x 75
PCF8

Konkell, E.
Haystacks 1947
oil on board 48.2 x 34.7
PCF10

Lely, Peter (copy after) 1618–1680
*Henry Somerset (1629–1700), 1st Duke of
Beaufort*
oil on canvas 232.2 x 143.2
PCF1

Napolitano, J.
*Lieutenant Colonel L. H. M. Westropp
(1896–1991) of the Devonshire Regiment* 1945
oil on hardboard 65 x 51.4
PCF6

Pannett, Juliet Kathleen 1911–2005
*1st Battalion of the Dorset Regiment in the
Assault on Normandy, D Day, 6 June 1994*
oil on canvas 50.4 x 75.4
PCF7

Rowlands, David John b.1952
*'The Bloody Eleventh', Battle of Salamanca 22
July 1812* 1985
oil on canvas 82.5 x 138
PCF4

unknown artist
*Henry Somerset (1629–1700), 1st Duke of
Beaufort*
oil on canvas 60.4 x 52.6
PCF2

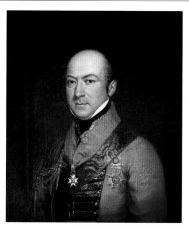

unknown artist
*Lieutenant General Sir Henry Tucker
Montresor (1767?–1837?), KCB, GCH*
oil on canvas 27.2 x 23.4
PCF5

unknown artist
Young Devon Soldier
oil on paper 60.2 x 51
PCF12

Wollen, William Barnes (copy after) 1857–
1936
*The Last Stand of the 2nd Devons at Bois-des-
Buttes, 27 May 1918*
oil on canvas 82.3 x 135.5
PCF3

Facing page: Lawrence, Thomas, 1769–1830, *John Rolle (1750–1842), Lord Rolle*, Great Torrington Almshouse, Town
Lands and Poors Charities (p. 225)

The Met Office

In November 2000, The Met Office announced its intention to relocate from Bracknell, Berkshire, to new, purpose-built accommodation in Exeter. We, in the project team, had the task of making this intention into a reality.

One of the key objectives of relocation was to create a working environment in which innovation, networking and communication could thrive. The architects have responded to this objective with a stunning design and we are now enjoying the benefits of its open working environment and plenty of communal spaces. However, from early on in the project it was clear that to fulfil this objective something more than just great architecture would be needed. We visited a range of new building projects, in both public and private sectors, and saw how art had been used in a variety of exciting ways to bring these new workplaces to life.

Since the mid-1980s, the Government, through the Department of Culture Media and Sport and the Arts Council of England, has promoted the concept of allocating a percentage of the capital building cost towards the commissioning of artists. Commissioned works of art, craft and design are incorporated into new building schemes to create a positive identity for the building, its users and the surrounding context.

Having observed the benefit of art in other new buildings, and in line with Government best practice, we initiated 'Art at The Met Office' with the aid of Maggie Bolt (Director of Public Art South West) in the Spring of 2002. Working with Tom Littlewood (Director of Gingko Projects) we developed a commissions plan, began the process of selecting artists and then set about building the trust needed on both sides to enable successful delivery of our commissions.

The programme generated huge interest among artists. The commissioning competition resulted in just fewer than 400 applications, from which we eventually selected the artists now featured in the installed commissions.

A key feature of the programme has been the placement of artists within The Met Office. The artworks are the result of a collaborative process which has enabled a wide range of staff to meet and work with the artists, informing and shaping their creative thinking, culminating in the commissions we now see installed in the building. It has been a revelation for us to see how artists, coming into The Met Office from a new and very different perspective, have responded to our work in their creativity.

It has been a pleasure and a privilege to work with the arts community in developing 'Art at The Met Office', and to see how art has indeed brought our new building to life.

These recently commissioned works include several paintings such as those by Michael Fairclough, Kurt Jackson and Rebecca MacPherson. They join the many fine paintings already existing in the art collection of The Met Office. These include paintings given by meteorological offices in Eastern Europe to celebrate the occasion of the 150th anniversary of The Met Office as well as portraits of ships and weather stations.

Rob Varley, Art at The Met Office Project Manager

Beck, Stuart 1903–2000
'Admiral Beaufort' 1979
oil on canvas 50 x 75
PCF7

Beck, Stuart 1903–2000
Atlantic Weather Ships Transferring Mail
oil on canvas 47.5 x 73.3
PCF6

Fairclough, Michael b.1940
Isle of Man Suite I – Langness 2004
mixed media & oil on canvas 112 x 122
PCF1

Fairclough, Michael b.1940
Isle of Man Suite II – Bradda Head 2004
mixed media & oil on canvas 112 x 132
PCF2

Fairclough, Michael b.1940
*Isle of Man Suite III – Niarbyl (Sun
Dogs)* 2004
mixed media & oil on canvas 112 x 142
PCF3

Fairclough, Michael b.1940
Isle of Man Suite IV – Blue Point 2004
mixed media & oil on canvas 112 x 132
PCF4

Fairclough, Michael b.1940
Isle of Man Suite V – Point of Ayre 2004
mixed media & oil on canvas 112 x 121.5
PCF5

Jackson, Kurt b.1961
Squall
oil on canvas 122 x 122
PCF9

Jay, Peter
Summer Landscape
tempera on board 14 x 14
PCF13

Jay, Peter
Winter Landscape
tempera on board 14 x 14
PCF14

MacPherson, Rebecca b.1967
Soft as Water Hard as Rock
oil on canvas 101.5 x 91
PCF8

Patzer, Ryszard b.1941
Krajobraz po Sztormie (After the Storm)
acrylic & oil on canvas 51.5 x 60.5
PCF10

unknown artist early 20th C
Sir Napier Shaw (1854–1945)
oil on canvas 74.5 x 61.8
PCF11

unknown artist
Birch Woods 2004
acrylic on canvas 50 x 70
PCF12

The Palace, Exeter

There has been a bishop in residence since the tenth century when the first Bishop of Exeter, Bishop Leofric, Chaplain to King Edward the Confessor, moved from Crediton to Exeter. However, it was not until the thirteenth century that the Palace was built by Bishop Brewer, the tenth bishop.

Since then the Palace has gone through many changes in its history with some bishops choosing to rebuild and remodel the building to suit their purpose. During World War One the Palace was taken over by the Ministry of Defence as a hospital for wounded soldiers, whilst in World War Two it was used as the Area Headquarters for the Ministry of Pensions, although the state rooms continued to be used by the bishops.

In 1948 ownership of the Palace was given to the Church Commissioners who chose to rebuild and remodel so that the sixty seventh bishop, Robert Mortimer, could take up residence in 1953. There has been a bishop in residence ever since. The present bishop, Michael Langrish, and his wife have lived here since 2000.

Within the Palace there are some 29 oil portraits of previous bishops; the earliest bishop represented is Seth Ward, the forty third bishop, who was in office from 1662. However, the collection is not complete: one painting in the collection is a copy of Gainsborough's *George Lavington (1684–1762), Bishop of Exeter (1746–1762)* by an artist from the British (English) School. The original now hangs in Auckland Art Gallery in New Zealand and was bought from Christies in London in the 1960s. The most recent portrait is *Hewlett Thomson (b.1929), Bishop of Exeter (1985–1999)*, the sixty ninth bishop, painted in 1998 by David Hankinson.

D. A. Carter, House Steward to the Bishop of Exeter

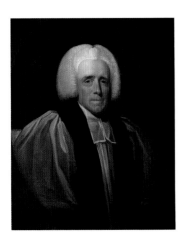

Abbott, Lemuel Francis 1760–1803
John Ross (1719–1792), Bishop of Exeter (1778–1792)
oil on canvas 74.5 x 62.5
PCF23

British (English) School 17th C
Anthony Sparrow (1612–1686), Bishop of Exeter (1667–1676)
oil on canvas 72 x 48
PCF27

British (English) School 17th C
Joseph Hall (1574–1656), Bishop of Exeter (1627–1641)
oil on canvas 63 x 54
PCF9

British (English) School 18th C
Edward Cotton, Grandson of William Cotton, Bishop of Exeter (1598–1621)
oil on canvas 72 x 60
PCF29

British (English) School 18th C
Seth Ward (1617–1688/9), Bishop of Exeter (1662–1667)
oil on canvas 74 x 62
PCF25

British (English) School 18th C
Thomas Lamplugh (1615–1691), Bishop of Exeter (1676–1688)
oil on canvas 72 x 61
PCF14

British (English) School 18th C
William Buller (1735–1796), Bishop of Exeter (1792–1797)
oil on canvas 126 x 100
PCF8

British (English) School mid-18th C
George Lavington (1684–1762), Bishop of Exeter (1746–1762)
oil on canvas 76 x 63
PCF2

British (English) School early 19th C
William Carey (1769–1846), Bishop of Exeter (1820–1830)
oil on canvas 73 x 60
PCF1

British (English) School 20th C
John Fisher (1748–1825), Bishop of Exeter (1803–1807)
oil on canvas 75 x 62
PCF30

Cope, Arthur Stockdale 1857–1940
Edward Henry Bickersteth (1825–1906), Bishop of Exeter (1895–1900) 1899
oil on canvas 109 x 85
PCF3

Dahl, Michael I (circle of) 1656/1659–1743
The Right Reverend Dr Ofspring Blackall (1655–1716), Late Lord Bishop of Exeter (1654–1716), Bishop of Exeter (1707–1716)
oil on canvas 124 x 100
PCF4

Dahl, Michael I (circle of) 1656/1659–1743
The Right Reverend Dr Ofspring Blackall
(1655–1716), Late Lord Bishop of Exeter
(1654–1716), Bishop of Exeter (1707–1716)
oil on canvas 125 x 100
PCF7

Dahl, Michael I (circle of) 1656/1659–1743
The Right Reverend Dr Ofspring Blackall
(1655–1716), Late Lord Bishop of Exeter
(1654–1716), Bishop of Exeter (1707–1716)
oil on canvas 74 x 61
PCF18

Dahl, Michael I (circle of) 1656/1659–1743
The Right Reverend Dr Ofspring Blackall
(1655–1716), Late Lord Bishop of Exeter
(1654–1716), Bishop of Exeter (1707–1716)
oil on canvas 74 x 63
PCF26

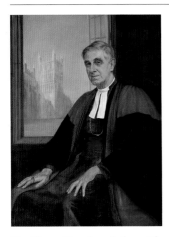

Davidson-Houston, Aubrey Claude 1906–
1995
Robert Cecil Mortimer (1902–1976), Bishop of
Exeter (1949–1973)
oil on canvas 110 x 84
PCF15

Frampton, Meredith 1894–1984
Lord William Cecil (1863–1936), Bishop of
Exeter (1916–1936) 1934
oil on canvas 170 x 124
PCF17

Hankinson, David
Hewlett Thomson (b.1929), Bishop of Exeter
(1985–1999) 1994
oil on canvas 136 x 90
PCF19

Kneller, Godfrey (follower of) 1646–1723
Jonathan Trelawny (1650–1721), Bishop of
Exeter (1688–1707) 18th C
oil on canvas 74 x 62
PCF24

Langworthy, Paddy
Eric A. C. Mercer (1917–2003), Bishop of
Exeter (1973–1985)
oil on canvas 76 x 63
PCF12

Loggan, David (after) 1634–1692
Peter Mews 'Black Spot', Bishop of Bath and
Wells (1672–1684)
oil on canvas 74 x 62
PCF21

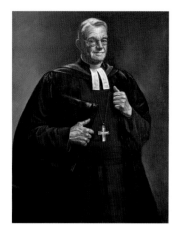

Mansbridge, John 1901–1981
Charles Edward Curzon (1878–1954), Bishop of Exeter (1936–1948)
oil on canvas 111 x 85
PCF10

Pond, Arthur 1701–1758
Stephen Weston (1665–1742), Bishop of Exeter (1724–1758)
oil on canvas 124 x 100
PCF13

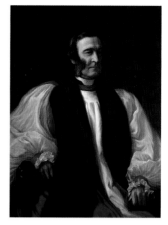

Prynne, Edward A. Fellowes 1854–1921
Frederick Temple (1821–1902), Bishop of Exeter (1869–1885) 1886
oil on canvas 111 x 85
PCF22

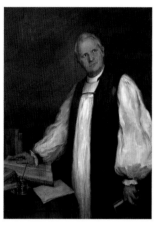

Robertson, A. (Miss)
Archibald Robertson (1853–1931), Bishop of Exeter (1903–1916) 1906
oil on canvas 152 x 114
PCF5

Romney, George (circle of) 1734–1802
The Honorable Frederick Keppel (d.1777), Bishop of Exeter (1762–1777)
oil on canvas 75 x 63
PCF28

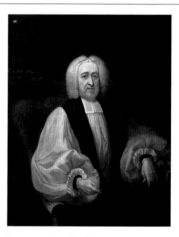

Seeman, Enoch the younger c.1694–1745
(attributed to) & **Seeman, Isaac** d.1751
(attributed to) *Lancelot Blackburne (1658–1743), Bishop of Exeter (...)* 1716
oil on canvas 124 x 100
PCF6

Trist Newman, Beryl 1906–1991
The Enthronement of Bishop Robert Mortimer, Bishop of Exeter (1948–1973) 1949
oil on canvas 90 x 70
PCF11

unknown artist
Henry Reginald Courtenay (1741–1803), DD, Bishop of Exeter (1797–1803)
oil on canvas 37.5 x 31.2
PCF16

Woolnoth, Thomas A. (attributed to) 1785–1857
Henry Phillpotts (1778–1869), Bishop of Exeter (1831–1869)
oil on canvas 117 x 90
PCF20

University of Exeter, Fine Art Collection

The University Collection has over 1,000 important and diverse artworks, including pictures and sculptures, which are distributed throughout the campuses. The art collection contains works bought, on loan, donated or bequeathed by friends of the University, often Honorary Graduates, alumni or lecturers who wish to give something back to the University. The policy of rotating certain artworks within the three campuses will, it is hoped, provide interest and stimulation, while helping to raise awareness of the art collection.

The development of the University's art collection began in 1959 when the then Vice-Chancellor, Dr James Cook, wrote: 'We are trying to build up a collection of works of art in the University. We have already made a modest start.' Art works were donated including a complete set of plates of J. M. W. Turner's *Liber Studiorum*. By the 1970s, as the acquisition programme gained momentum, the art collection acquired a painting by Patrick Heron entitled *Violet with Venetian Scarlet and Emerald*. Two paintings by Harold Harvey were bequeathed to the University and a previous Chancellor, Sir Rex Richards, donated four paintings by David Blackburn.

The University's art collection exists for the purpose of developing and cultivating in the individual student an appreciation of painting and sculpture. With the enthusiastic encouragement and support of the Vice-Chancellor, Professor Steve Smith, hopefully not only the students but all the staff associated with the University benefit visually. The establishment of this significant art collection demonstrates the University's commitment to the enjoyment, patronage and advancement of the visual arts in the West Country.

Gina Cox, Curator of Visual Arts

Al-Kilai, Mohammid
Street Scene
oil on canvas (?) 36 x 102.5
FAC01581

Al-Qasimi, Sheikha Hoor
Arab Boy
oil on board 44 x 51
FAC01582.6

Al-Qasimi, Sheikha Hoor
Arab Gentleman
oil on board 91.5 x 25.5
FAC01582.4

Al-Qasimi, Sheikha Hoor
Arab Girl
oil on board 44 x 51
FAC01582.5

Al-Qasimi, Sheikha Hoor
Arab Musician
oil on board 91.5 x 25.5
FAC01582.3

Al-Qasimi, Sheikha Hoor
Arab Woman
oil on canvas 147.5 x 25.5
FAC01582.1

Al-Qasimi, Sheikha Hoor
Arab Woman
oil on canvas 147.3 x 25.5
FAC01582.2

Apperley, Nigel
Dartmoor, Devon 1992
mixed media & oil on board 163.7
PCF61

Baird, J. Noel
*W. H. Reed, Alderman of Exeter Who
Bequeathed Reed Hall to the University in 1922*
oil on canvas 127 x 101.5
FAC00284

Ballantyne, John 1815–1897
*Miss Bertha Salter, Singer from North Devon
(1890s–1920s)* 1890
oil on canvas 106 x 68
FAC00306

Bampfylde, Coplestone Warre 1720–1791
Holy Trinity Church, Exmouth, Devon
oil on canvas 71.5 x 79.1
FAC00395

Barker, Elsie M.
*Mr John Lloyd, First University
Librarian* c.1960
oil on board 62.7 x 49.8
FAC00758 (P)

Facing page: Harvey, Harold C., 1874–1941, *Boys Loading Mangolds onto a Cart*, c.1920, University of Exeter, Fine Art
Collection (p. 196)

Bartlett, Alan G. active 1956–1968
Sandstone Cliffs, Devon Coast, Ladram 1956
oil on board 44.5 x 63.5
FAC00660

Bartlett, Alan G. active 1956–1968
River Dart, near Hexworthy, Devon 1960
oil on board 38 x 48
PCF22

Bartlett, Alan G. active 1956–1968
Höllental, Bavaria, Germany 1968
oil on board 59.8 x 59.5
FAC00680

Bartlett, Alan G. active 1956–1968
Channel Island Scene
oil on board 34 x 58
FAC00289

Bennett, Vincent 1910–1993
Suzannah and the Elders 1950s
oil on board 60.5 x 60
FAC00591

Bird
Waterfront
oil on board 42 x 78
FAC00398

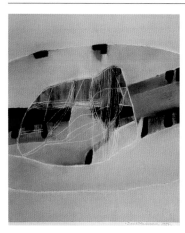

Blackburn, David b.1939
Boulder in Light 1997
acrylic on paper 42.5 x 36
FAC00927

Blackburn, David b.1939
Pale Beach, South Coast 1997
acrylic on paper 43.5 x 36
FAC00929

Blackburn, David b.1939
Sunlight, Early Morning 1997
acrylic on paper 42.5 x 36
FAC00928

Blackburn, David b.1939
Sea Window
acrylic on paper 37 x 43
FAC00930

Boundy, Joy active 1972–1999
Seven Ovals in Pink 1972
oil on canvas 106.5 x 87.5
PCF316

Boundy, Joy active 1972–1999
Crustacean Delight 1995
oil on board 53 x 124.5
FAC00790

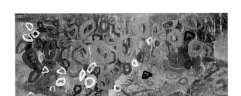

Boundy, Joy active 1972–1999
Presences at Bryce Canyon, USA 1999
oil on canvas 51 x 122 (E)
FAC00794

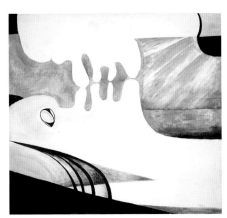

Boundy, Joy active 1972–1999
Sky Kiss 1999
oil on canvas 111.5 x 122
FAC00792

Boundy, Joy active 1972–1999
The Heavy Weight of Ignorance 1999
oil on canvas 121.5 x 117
FAC00795

Boundy, Joy active 1972–1999
Canto V
oil on board 99 x 168
FAC00894

Boundy, Joy active 1972–1999
Christ and the Four Apostles
oil on canvas 50.3 x 75.5
PCF38

Boundy, Joy active 1972–1999
Inferno
oil on board 100 x 110.5
FAC00893

Boundy, Joy active 1972–1999
Looking over to Baker Street from Gloucester Place, London, W1
oil on canvas 48 x 65.5
FAC00888

Boundy, Joy active 1972–1999
Poverty in Sicily
oil on board 76 x 122
FAC00891

Boundy, Joy active 1972–1999
Poverty in Sicily II
oil on board 59.7 x 90
FAC00892

Bourdillon, Frank Wright 1851–1924
Aboard the 'Revenge'
oil on canvas 135 x 210
FAC00259

Bower, Stephen b.1949
Circus Garden 1996
oil on board 81.5 x 56
FAC00777

Bower, Stephen b.1949
View of the Otter at Cadhay Bridge, Devon 2000
oil on canvas 61 x 76
FAC00980

Brougier, Adolf M. 1870–1962
Mountain Landscape
oil on board 35 x 45 (E)
PCF20

Canning, Neil b.1960
Axis 2000
oil on canvas 153 x 213
FAC00956

Canning, Neil b.1960
Breakaway 2003
oil on canvas 122 x 122
FAC00988 (P)

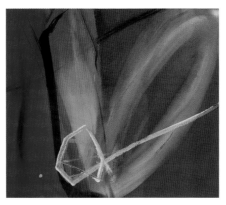

Canning, Neil b.1960
Catalyst 2003
oil on canvas 122 x 153
FAC00987 (P)

Canning, Neil b.1960
Challenge 2004
acrylic on paper 33 x 38
FAC01016 (P)

Canning, Neil b.1960
Reach 2004
acrylic on paper 55 x 75
FAC01017 (P)

Canning, Neil b.1960
Rising Spirit, 'Sperys dasserhy' 2005
oil on canvas 60 x 80
FAC03041

Cattermull, Caroline & **Cressell, Sarah**
Bass Player 2000
acrylic on board 61 x 61
PCF409

Cattermull, Caroline & **Cressell, Sarah**
Drummer 2000
acrylic on board 61 x 61
PCF408

Cattermull, Caroline & **Cressell, Sarah**
Saxophone Player 2000
acrylic on board 61 x 61
PCF406

Cattermull, Caroline & **Cressell, Sarah**
Trumpeter 2000
acrylic on board 61 x 61
PCF407

Cay, S.
Still Life with Two Blue Vases
oil on board 43.5 x 58.5
FAC00101

Clint, George 1770–1854
Caroline Orges
oil on canvas 106.5 x 81
FAC00130

Cook, Christopher b.1959
Death in the Valley c.1982
acrylic on canvas 178 x 203
FAC00729

Cook, Christopher b.1959
Burning Tyres 1986
oil on canvas 198 x 197.5
FAC00224

Cook, Christopher b.1959
Adolescent Landscape
acrylic on canvas 194.7 x 197
FAC00728 (P)

Cotton, Alan b.1938
*Harry Kay, Vice-Chancellor of the University
of Exeter (1973–1984)* 1970s
oil on canvas 100 x 75
FAC00358

Cotton, Alan b.1938
Hartland Point I, Devon 1977
oil on canvas 152 x 101.5
FAC00209

Cotton, Alan b.1938
Hartland Point II, Devon 1978
oil on canvas 101.5 x 152
FAC00210

Cotton, Alan b.1938
The Otter Valley, Devon 1979
oil on canvas 59.7 x 75
PCF17

Cotton, Alan b.1938
Hartland Point III, Devon 1981
oil on canvas 152 x 101.5
FAC00211

Cotton, Alan b.1938
Hartland Point IV, Devon 1981
oil on canvas 152 x 101.5
FAC00212

Cotton, Alan b.1938
Hartland Point V, Devon 1987
oil on canvas 76 x 60.5
FAC00240

Cotton, Alan b.1938
County Donegal, Ireland, Slieve League in Evening Light 2007
oil on canvas 101.5 x 126.5
FAC03044

Cotton, Alan b.1938
Harry Kay
oil on canvas 49.7 x 39.3
PCF16

Cotton, Alan b.1938
Hartland IV, Devon
oil on canvas 76 x 58 (E)
PCF28

Cotton, Alan b.1938
Summer Bank, Otter River, Devon
oil on canvas 83 x 106
PCF25

Creedy, John
William Francis Jackson Knight (1895–1964), Classical Scholar c.1950
oil on canvas 67.5 x 44.5
FAC00204

Crossland, James Henry 1852–1939
First Snow on Broughton Moor, Cumberland (Birks Bridge, Duddon Valley) 1890
oil on canvas 101.2 x 151
FAC00475

Crossland, James Henry 1852–1939
Dungeon Ghyll, Cumberland
oil on canvas 152 x 112.1 (E)
FAC00950

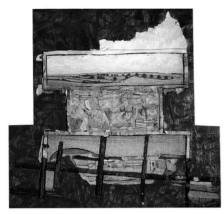

Cunliffe, Leslie b.1950
Covenant Landscape 1991
mixed media & oil on board 156.8 x 177.2
FAC00654

Cunliffe, Leslie b.1950
Scapegoat 1994
oil on board 23 x 17
FAC00653

David
Arthur Knott Woodbridge, MA c.1946
oil on canvas 55.2 x 39.5
PCF13

David
*T. Arnold Brown, MA, BSc, FRSE, FRAS,
Professor of Mathematics at the University of
Exeter (1923–1958)* c.1946
oil on canvas 54.5 x 39.1
FAC00171

Davis, Henry William Banks 1833–1914
Cattle in a Highland Loch
oil on canvas 25 x 49.5
FAC00311

Donaldson, David Abercrombie 1916–1996
Sir Hector Hetherington (1888–1965)
oil on canvas 75 x 62.5
FAC00421 (P)

Dutch School
*Portrait of a Young Lady with a Lace Collar
and a Fan* c.1650
oil on panel 113.8 x 89.5
FAC00202

Dutch School
Portrait of a Woman
oil on panel 68.2 x 52.8
PCF3

W. R. E.
A Country Road with a Distant Windmill
oil on canvas 95.2 x 121.7
FAC00823

Facing page: British (English) School, *Captain Cooke (1765–1841), Chief of the Exeter Javelin Men*, Royal Albert
Memorial Museum (p. 121)

Eastman, Frank S. 1878–1964
Sir Henry Lopes (1859–1938) 1932
oil on canvas 126 x 100.2
FAC00469

Eastman, Frank S. 1878–1964
Sir Henry Lopes (1859–1938) 1932
oil on canvas 72.2 x 60.1
FAC00470

Eastman, Frank S. 1878–1964
William Tatem (1868–1942), Lord Glanely, DL, JP, LLD, President of the University College of South Wales and (...) 1932
oil on canvas 124.5 x 100.5
FAC00156

Eastwood, Nicholas Anthony b.1942
Abstract in Blue, Red and Yellow 1980
oil on board 90 x 104
PCF312

Eastwood, Nicholas Anthony b.1942
Southern Landscape Series: Slow Thaw II 1980
oil on board 51.5 x 70
FAC00624

Evangeliemos, I. M. active 20th C
Icon of Christ Crucified
oil on panel 50.2 x 36
FAC03061

Eves, Reginald Grenville 1876–1941
John Murray, Principal of the UCSW (c.1930–c.1950) c.1935
oil on canvas 111 x 85
FAC00428

Fernee, Kenneth William A. 1926–1983
Dartmoor Stone Row, Devon
oil on board 49.5 x 60
FAC00410

Fisher, Alec active 20th C
Miss Murray
oil on canvas 68.7 x 56
FAC00439

Fishwick, Clifford 1923–1997
Sea Orb I 1966
oil on board 122 x 61
FAC00196

Fishwick, Clifford 1923–1997
Landscape 1992
oil on board 19.2 x 30
PCF309

Fletcher
Underground Crucifixion
oil on board 123 x 160 (E)
PCF44

Forbes, Stanhope Alexander (attributed to) 1857–1947
Feeding the Pigs 1921
oil on canvas 140 x 99
FAC00157

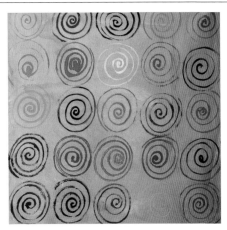

Frost, Terry 1915–2003
Arizona Spirals 1995
acrylic on paper 121 x 121
FAC00971

Frost, Terry 1915–2003
Timberain (triptych, left panel)
oil on canvas 207 x 120
FAC00974.2

Frost, Terry 1915–2003
Timberain (triptych, centre panel)
oil on canvas 207 x 120
FAC00974.1

Frost, Terry 1915–2003
Timberain (triptych, right panel)
oil on canvas 207 x 120
FAC00974.3

Garinei, E.
Italian Street
oil on board 19 x 12.8
FAC00290

Gaussen, Winifred
G. R. Champernowne 1930s
oil on canvas 91.8 x 86
FAC00283

Gaussen, Winifred
Still Life with a Violin
oil on board 90 x 120.5
PCF49

Gaussen, Winifred
The Scales
oil on board 118 x 90
FAC03059

Gilbert, Arthur 1819–1895
Pastoral Scene, River Scene 1855
oil on canvas 92.5 x 150
FAC00797

Gosslean, J. H.
Ravine with a Bridge c.1900
oil on canvas 150.7 x 120
FAC00129

Green, Anthony 1939–2003
Vessels Last Dance 1997
mixed media & oil on canvas 122.3 x 152.5
FAC00618

Harvey, Harold C. 1874–1941
Boys Loading Mangolds onto a Cart c.1920
oil on canvas 29.5 x 24
FAC00417 🐝

Harvey, Harold C. 1874–1941
Three Boys 1944
oil on canvas 39 x 28.5
FAC00207 🐝

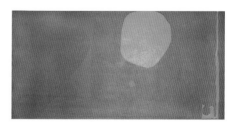

Heron, Patrick 1920–1999
Violet with Venetian Scarlet and Emerald 1971
oil on canvas 250 x 460
FAC00730

Hilliard, John Michael b.1945
Shades of Light, Gathering Storm
oil on canvas 182 x 221
FAC00993

Howell, June
Cups and a Milk Bottle
oil on canvas 119 x 121
FAC03060

Jackson, Kurt b.1961
Crushing and Screening Plant 1998
acrylic 23 x 23
FAC00941

Jackson, Kurt b.1961
Sun and Rain, Strong Winds, Drilling Carnsew Mine 1999
acrylic on paper 58 x 77.5
FAC00942

Jackson, Kurt b.1961
Catch the Light
mixed media & oil on canvas 152.4 x 152.4
FAC03048

Jeany, M. J.
Intérieure: Palette et pot de fleurs 1961
oil on board 46 x 39
FAC01019

Jennison, Robert b.1933
Hillside with Approaching Storm 1989
oil on board 41.7 x 56.5
FAC00245

Jewell, Catherine active 1978–2003
Symphony in Nature 1980
oil on board 41 x 57.5
FAC00357

Jewell, Catherine active 1978–2003
Mid the Flowers
oil on board 29 x 21
FAC00979

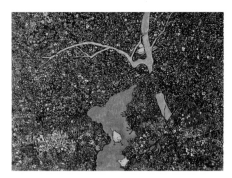

Jewell, Catherine active 1978–2003
Yellow Bird
oil on board 24 x 49
FAC00978

Johns, Ewart b.1923
Red Dance 1961
emulsion on board 61 x 244
FAC00941

Johns, Ewart b.1923
Sir James Cook 1964
oil on hardboard 101 x 74
FAC00328

Johns, Ewart b.1923
Blue and Black Abstract
oil on hardboard 120 x 79
FAC00825

Johns, Ewart b.1923
Devon Landscape
oil on board 212.5 x 398
FAC00222

Johns, Ewart b.1923
Three Figures
oil on board 73.5 x 43.5
FAC00637

Johnson, Colin Trevor b.1942
Coastline Collage 2006
oil & wood on board 27 x 73
FAC01590

Kinsella, Katherine
Still Life, Vase of Flowers 1909
oil on canvas 69.5 x 85
FAC00757

Logsdail, William 1859–1944
Venetian Scene, Canal
oil on panel 34 x 24
FAC00314

Long, Edwin 1829–1891
Sir Stafford Northcote (1818–1887), 1st Earl of Iddesleigh 1882
oil on canvas 118 x 80
FAC00394

Loon, Theodor van 1581/1582–1667
Portrait of a Young Girl in a White Dress and Crimson Overwrap 1652
oil on panel 72 x 58.8
FAC00286

Loon, Theodor van 1581/1582–1667
Portrait of a Young Girl in a Crimson Dress Wearing a Pearl Necklace
oil on panel 76.5 x 61.5
FAC00285

Maeckelberghe, Margo b.1932
Sea Green Winter 1979
oil on board 30 x 60
FAC03015

Maeckelberghe, Margo b.1932
Roller Coaster High 1991
oil on board 41.5 x 58
FAC03014

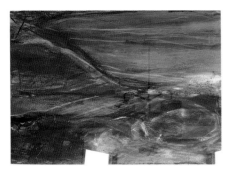

Maeckelberghe, Margo b.1932
Tin Mine Coast 1997
oil on board 73.5 x 58.5
FAC00957

Maeckelberghe, Margo b.1932
Valley to the Sea 2002–2003
oil on canvas 60 x 45
FAC03057

Maeckelberghe, Margo b.1932
Ancient Land I
oil on canvas 46 x 60.5
FAC03046

May, Christopher
The Author and MacHeath 1994
oil on canvas 182.5 x 123.5
PCF54

Miró, Joan (after) 1893–1983
Untitled
oil on canvas 183.5 x 152.5
FAC00799

Miskin, Lionel 1924–2006
Jack Clemo 1956
oil on board 66 x 44
FAC00747

Miskin, Lionel 1924–2006
Lionel Miskin's Mother (?) 1984
oil on board 33 x 28
FAC00560

Murillo, Bartolomé Esteban (after) 1618–1682
The Immaculate Conception 18th C
oil on canvas 149 x 99
FAC00218

Nash, Catte
Female Nude Study 1979
oil on board 76 x 62.5 (E)
FAC00879

Nisbet
Adam and Eve Expelled from the Garden
oil on canvas 102 x 80 (E)
PCF46

Nisbet
Christ and Three Men
oil on canvas 102 x 80 (E)
PCF45

Pankhurst, Andy b.1968
Robert Scott Alexander (1936–2005), Lord Alexander of Weedon, QC 2007–2010
oil on canvas 171 x 105
FAC03083

Pascoe, Ernest 1922–1996
The Roman Wall 1959
oil on canvas 70.5 x 91
FAC00355

Pragnall, G.
Duryard House, University of Exeter, Devon
oil on board 59 x 84.5
FAC03007

Ramsay, Allan b.1959
*Sir Rex Richards (b.1922), DSc, FBA, FRS,
Chancellor of the University (1982–
1998)* 1993
oil on canvas 85 x 69.7
FAC00411

Raphael (copy after) 1483–1520
Madonna della seggiola 19th C
oil on canvas 71
FAC00438

Roberts, L.
River Scene
oil on board 30 x 40 (E)
PCF19

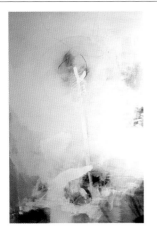

Rodrigues, Judy b.1960
Eyestone 2005
oil on canvas 183 x 122
FAC03047

Rubens, Peter Paul (attributed to) 1577–
1640
The Four Corners of the World
oil on canvas 245 x 368
FAC00453

Russell, Jack
Three People Scything Corn 1913
oil on board 31 x 38.5
FAC00602

Sattar, Al-Shaykh
Landscape 1969
oil on paper 30.5 x 49
FAC00976

Scholz, Heinz-Joachim
Buntheim Summer, 1954
oil on board 48.4 x 33.5
PCF29

Simmonds, Stanley b.1917
Winter Scene I 1983
oil on board 60.2 x 90.2
FAC00229 (P)

Smith, Anthony William David b.1962
Blue Seascape 2002
acrylic on paper 33 x 23
FAC00997

Smith, Anthony William David b.1962
Beach Scene 2004
acrylic on paper 31 x 15
FAC00998

Smith, Anthony William David b.1962
Black and White Seascape 2004
acrylic & paper on canvas 122 x 152
FAC00996

Spear, Ruskin 1911–1990
*Mary Cavendish (1895–1988), Duchess of
Devonshire in Chancellor's Robes* 1966
oil on canvas 101 x 75.5
FAC00331

Stephenson, Pippa
Sometimes I … 2006
acrylic on canvas 49.5 x 38.7
FAC01589

Stubley, Trevor 1932–2010
*David Harrison, DBE, SCD, Feng, Vice-
Chancellor of the University of Exeter
(1984–1994)* 1993
oil on canvas 90 x 75
FAC00412

Symonds, Ken b.1927
*Sir Geoffrey Holland (b.1938), Vice-Chancellor
of the University of Exeter* 2002
oil on canvas 98 x 77.5
FAC00346

Taffs, Charles Harold b.1876
Lady with a Fan in a Chair 1905
oil on panel 27.5 x 23.5
FAC00399

Facing page: Condy, Nicholas, 1793–1857, *Cleaning the Fish*, Royal Albert Memorial Museum (p. 126)

Timson, Bruce
Portrait of a Woman with a Book 1992
oil on canvas 129.5 x 90
PCF56

Tripp, Stella b.1954
Twister 1999
acrylic & mixed media on board 38 x 46
FAC01018

Trist, Brody
Eden Phillpotts, Esq. (1862–1960) 1937
oil on canvas 75 x 62
FAC00858

Tucker, John Wallace 1808–1869
Bramford Speke Bridge, River Exe, Devon 1860s
oil on panel 9.5 x 10.5
FAC00502.3

Tucker, John Wallace 1808–1869
Bramford Speke, River Exe, Devon 1860s
oil on panel 9.5 x 10.5
FAC00502.1

Tucker, John Wallace 1808–1869
Dittisham, River Dart, Devon 1860s
oil on panel 9.5 x 10.5
FAC00502.6

Tucker, John Wallace 1808–1869
Kingswear Mills, River Dart, Devon 1860s
oil on panel 9.5 x 10.5
FAC00502.5

Tucker, John Wallace 1808–1869
Kingswear, River Dart, Devon 1860s
oil on panel 9.5 x 10.5
FAC00502.7

Tucker, John Wallace 1808–1869
Near South Molton, Devon 1860s
oil on panel 9.5 x 10.5
FAC00502.8

Tucker, John Wallace 1808–1869
Red Rock, Bramford Speke, River Exe,
Devon 1860s
oil on panel 9.5 x 10.5
FAC00502.2

Tucker, John Wallace 1808–1869
Rewe, Devon 1860s
oil on panel 9.5 x 10.5
FAC00502.4

Tucker, John Wallace 1808–1869
Littleham, Devon 1867
oil on board 34.4 x 29.4
FAC00503

unknown artist
Portrait of a Gentleman, Aged 72 1655
oil on panel 71.5 x 55.5
FAC00201

unknown artist early 19th C
Miss Helen Hope, Who Donated Money in the
1920s for a Hall of Residence, Hope Hall
oil on canvas 75 x 57
FAC00436

unknown artist mid-19th C
Prince of Orange Landing at Torbay, Devon
oil on canvas 56 x 76
FAC00468

unknown artist
Laver Building, University of Exeter,
Devon 1966
oil on board 48 x 64
FAC00852

unknown artist 20th C
Colonel Mardon, Donor towards the Building
of Mardon Hall, a New Hall of Residence at
the University in 1933
oil on canvas 60 x 49.5
FAC00488

unknown artist
A Steppe Landscape
acrylic on canvas 49 x 68.7
FAC03105

unknown artist
Abstract Head
oil on board 74.5 x 60
FAC00865

unknown artist
Abstract in Blue and Black
oil on canvas 91.5 x 61.2
FAC00825

unknown artist
Abstract in Blue and White
oil on board 64.3 x 95
FAC_00830

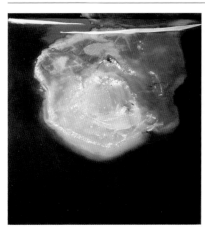

unknown artist
Abstract in Brown and Black
oil on canvas 182 x 171
PCF329

unknown artist
Abstraction in Pink
acrylic on canvas 100 x 100
PCF206

unknown artist
Abstraction in Pink
acrylic on canvas 100 x 100
PCF207

unknown artist
Abstraction in Pink
acrylic on canvas 100 x 100
PCF208

unknown artist
Australian Landscape
oil on canvas 60 x 74.3
FAC00267

unknown artist
Bird
oil on canvas 148.8 x 199.8
PCF330

unknown artist
Castle with a Lake
oil on panel 45 x 60
PCF48

unknown artist
City Corner
oil on canvas 59.5 x 49.1
PCF404

unknown artist
Classical Scene with a Waterfall
oil on panel 22.8 x 19.4
FAC00897

unknown artist
Donkey Following Two People
oil on board 59.5 x 102
FAC00833

unknown artist
Flower Painting
oil on canvas 49.3 x 59.2
FAC00418

unknown artist
Forest Tunnel
oil on canvas 151 x 122
PCF53

unknown artist
Gladys Hoopern Hogsbrawn
oil on canvas 36 x 30
FAC00658

unknown artist
Horse's Head
oil on canvas 54.4 x 53.3
FAC00605

unknown artist
Pastoral Abstract
acrylic & mixed media on paper 25 x 64.5
FAC00859

unknown artist
Portrait of a Gentleman
oil on canvas 109.5 x 82
PCF2

unknown artist
Portrait of a Gentleman with a Sword
oil on panel 102.4 x 90
PCF6

unknown artist
Portrait of a Lady with a Fan
oil on panel 105.2 x 91
PCF7

unknown artist
Portrait of a Mayor
oil on canvas 203.7 x 106.8
FAC00798

unknown artist
Portrait of a Woman
oil on canvas 106 x 82.5
PCF1

unknown artist
Religious Themes: Cross
oil & newsprint on panel 105.5 x 81
FAC_00828

unknown artist
Sir John Llewellyn, Vice Chancellor (1966–1972)
oil on board 101.5 x 73.5
PCF58

unknown artist
St Luke's, South Cloisters, University of Exeter
acrylic on canvas 60.6 x 183
PCF203

unknown artist
Still Life with Three Oranges
oil on canvas 75 x 63 (E)
FAC03092

unknown artist
Vegetables and a Cooking Pot
oil on canvas 76 x 91.5
FAC00863

Walker, Gregory b.1957
King's Wear 1979
acrylic on canvas 182 x 152
FAC00638

Webb, James 1825–1895
*The Old Castle Overlooking the Bay of Naples,
Italy* 1875
oil on canvas 55 x 85
FAC00322

West, F.
Gingjer, Cornwall 1920s
oil on canvas 66 x 48
FAC00476

Whittington-Ince, Richard 1934–1983
Woman, the Railway Cutting 1971
oil on board 61 x 61
FAC00579

Whittington-Ince, Richard 1934–1983
Railway Cutting
oil on board 86.5 x 102 (E)
FAC00824

Whittington-Ince, Richard 1934–1983
Scorrier, near Redruth, Cornwall
oil on board 86.5 x 102.5
PCF40

Whittington-Ince, Richard 1934–1983
Urban Scene from a Bridge
oil on board 105 x 118
FAC00791

Widgery, Frederick John 1861–1942
*Coastal View (Mouth of the Yealm,
Devon)* c.1940
oil on canvas 48 x 72.5
FAC00131

Widgery, William 1822–1893
River Scene
oil on canvas 74.5 x 151
FAC00298

Williamson, Mary
Mabel Early 1933
oil on canvas 34.8 x 30
FAC00241

Wood, Ron
Silver Moon 1981
tempera on paper 23.1 x 17.5
FAC00562

Wouwerman, Philips (after) 1619–1668
Village Scene
oil on canvas 52 x 67.5
FAC00420

Wreford-Clarke, W.
Still Life
oil on board 33 x 22.5
FAC00808

Facing page: unknown artist, *Portrait of a Gentleman, Aged 72*, 1655, University of Exeter, Fine Art Collection (p. 205)

Wonford House Hospital

In 1795, a bequest was made, by one Mr Pitfield, of £200 to enable the building of a 'lunatic ward' at the Devon and Exeter Hospital. In fact, rather than a ward at the existing hospital, the money, along with an additional £200 donated by Bishop Buller, was spent on adapting the fifteenth-century Bowhill House to become the separate St Thomas Hospital for Lunatics.

Surprisingly advanced for its time, the Hospital had three walled courts, three gardens and five indoor galleries. Recent research into exercise and mental health would seem to confirm what a sensible arrangement this was. Also surprisingly modern is the Hospital's 1801 constitution, which states that its function was to be the *cure* of its inmates; this at a time when insanity was generally held to be incurable. The Hospital's inheritors, Devon Partnership NHS Trust, maintain a similar commitment to recovery principles in working with mental health needs.

By 1842, the Metropolitan Commissioners in Lunacy found that the Hospital had outgrown its premises and recommended an increase in size, particularly of its grounds. Twenty acres of land were purchased on the other side of the city, at Wonford, and work commenced in October 1866. The architect, one Mr Cross, seems to have had visions of something like a French château, and the building's billiard and games room, ballroom and chapel make it clear that the hospital was primarily intended for gentlemen. Paupers could, however, be admitted by order of a Justice, clergymen or officer of their parish. The Hospital, then called Exe Vale Hospital, and accommodating 120 patients, was opened by the Earl of Devon in 1869.

There has always been a role for the arts and art-making in mental health services. Today, this ranges from their use as psychotherapies and in occupational therapy to the work undertaken by the Enhancing the Healing Environment programme, which helps to link mental health services to their communities. Incidentally, Exeter was also home to the Withymead Centre, which, from 1943 until the 1960s, was one of the earliest and most radical experiments in working with the arts and psychotherapy. The Centre was eventually absorbed into the NHS before its closure.

Some of the images reproduced here, such as the portrait of benevolent Victorian benefactor of Wonford House Hospital, James Manning, and the rather elegant picnic scene, *Tea on the Lawn in front of Wonford House Hospital*, both by unknown artists, reflect the Hospital's rich history. It has to be said that this Hospital was mainly intended for the middle classes; neighbouring facilities for the poor were not so appealing.

Other paintings in the collection are from very recent projects. Specifically, the works *Flowers*, *Trees I* and *Trees II*, which were executed in 2009/2010 and are collaborations between the artist Karen Huckvale of Insider Art and the staff and users of the Haldon Unit Eating Disorders Service at Wonford House. The opportunity for staff and patients to work alongside professional artists, to produce high-quality but inclusive art works, is very much a part of how the Trust hopes to develop recovery-based, inclusive and creative mental health services. Generating art works to improve healthcare environments, by working alongside the people who provide and use those services, echoes the creativity, resilience, ownership and pride that are the opposite of stigmatising mental health issues.

At the time of writing (October 2010), Devon Partnership NHS Trust continues to provide art and occupational therapy services at Wonford House. The Trust is currently working with community arts group Magic Carpet on artist residencies at the nearby Cedars inpatient unit, and has regularly changing art works in the corridors of what is now the Trust's administrative headquarters.

Malcolm Learmonth, Arts and Environments Development Lead, Devon Partnership NHS Trust

Cassidy, D.
Spiral 2008
acrylic on board 39.9 x 60.1
PCF20

Huckvale, Karen & **Haldon Unit Eating Disorders Service Staff & Users**
Flowers 2009/2010
mixed media & tempera on paper 68.6 x 68.6
PCF17

Huckvale, Karen & **Haldon Unit Eating Disorders Service Staff & Users**
Trees I 2009/2010
mixed media & tempera on board 48.9 x 68.9
PCF18

Huckvale, Karen & **Haldon Unit Eating Disorders Service Staff & Users**
Trees II 2009/2010
mixed media & tempera on board 48.9 x 68.9
PCF19

Knowles, Gwen
Lilies
acrylic on board 75.4 x 49.5
PCF23

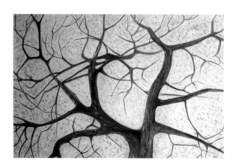

Knowles, Gwen
Tree in Winter
acrylic on board 49.3 x 74.7
PCF22

unknown artist
Quiet Light 2005
oil on board 50.6 x 40.5
PCF21

unknown artist
Abstract Landscape
acrylic on board 22.8 x 29.8
PCF10

unknown artist
Cactus
tempera on paper 16.3 x 14.8
PCF14

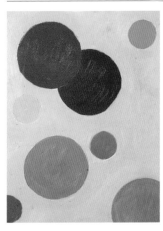

unknown artist
Circles
acrylic on board 30.2 x 22.7
PCF11

unknown artist
Fish
tempera on paper 14.7 x 20.8
PCF15

unknown artist
Head
oil on paper 24.7 x 20
PCF13

unknown artist
James Manning, Founder of Wonford House Hospital (1801)
oil on canvas 73.3 x 60.2
PCF16

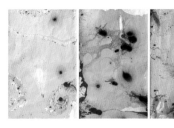

unknown artist
Marblised Triptych
oil on paper 39 x 64.4
PCF12

unknown artist
Spiral 1
oil on canvas 30.2 x 30.2
PCF1

unknown artist
Spiral 2
oil on canvas 30.2 x 30.2
PCF2

unknown artist
Spiral 3
oil on canvas 30.2 x 30.2
PCF3

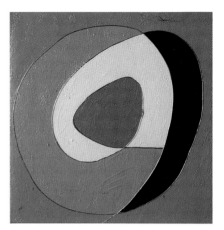

unknown artist
Spiral 4
oil on canvas 30.2 x 30.2
PCF4

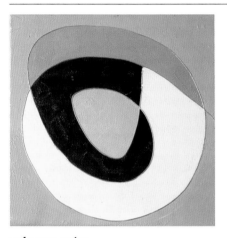

unknown artist
Spiral 5
oil on canvas 30.2 x 30.2
PCF5

unknown artist
Spiral 6
oil on canvas 30.2 x 30.2
PCF6

unknown artist
Tea on the Lawn in front of Wonford House Hospital, Devon
oil on board 35.9 x 56.3
PCF24

unknown artist
Three Gold Leaves
oil on canvas 30.2 x 30.2
PCF7

Exmouth Library

Cooke, William Edward active 1872–1898
Withycombe Mill, Devon 1898
oil on canvas 60.2 x 50
PCF6

Goodrich, J. B. active 1861–1884
Withycombe Brook, Devon 1884
oil on board 16.4 x 23.4
EXM00136

Goodrich, J. B. active 1861–1884
Exmouth, Devon, View of House on the Maer c.1884
oil on board 20.4 x 35.2
EXM00138

Goodrich, J. B. active 1861–1884
View of Estuary and Beacon from a Field, Devon
oil on canvas 44 x 59.4
PCF3

Green, Dorrie
Holy Trinity Church and Bicton Place, Exmouth, Devon 1983
oil on board 49 x 59
PCF4

Hullmandel, Charles Joseph (attributed to) 1789–1850
Combeinteignhead, View on the River Teign, Combe Cellars, Devon c.1820
oil on board 21 x 29.9
EXM01001

Hullmandel, Charles Joseph (attributed to) 1789–1850
Starcross, View of Starcorss on the River Exe, Devon c.1820
oil on board 21.4 x 30
EXM01000

Hynard, H.
Thomas Abel (1848–1943), MBE, JP
oil on canvas 62.3 x 49.6
PCF2

Lloyd, Julia
'Louisa Cottage', Exmouth, Devon 1942
oil on canvas 40.5 x 50
EXM01151

Sharp, Miles Balmford 1897–1973
Portrait of an Exmouth Lifeboatman c.1960
oil on board 50.6 x 40.6
EXM10242

Sharp, Miles Balmford 1897–1973
Portrait of an Exmouth Lifeboatman c.1960
oil on board 50.4 x 40.3
EXM10243

Sharp, Miles Balmford 1897–1973
View of the Strand Gardens, Exmouth, Devon
oil on board 60.6 x 76
PCF1

Strong, Charles Edward active 1851–1884
Ships in the Exe Estuary, Devon 1884
oil on canvas 59.4 x 89.9
PCF5

unknown artist
View from the Maer, Devon, out to Sea 1885
oil on board 16.5 x 34.1
EXM10265

Exmouth Museum

Exmouth Museum is a fully accredited museum of social history and was first opened in 1985. It is housed in early nineteenth-century council stables and an adjoining cottage, which was occupied by the Council Foreman and his family. It is now divided into three galleries, two on the ground floor and one on the first floor. The Museum is a lot larger than it appears from the road.

The Museum includes a small picture gallery, a 1930s dining room and a Victorian kitchen, with displays about the Second World War, lacemaking, local schools, old toys, the beach during the Victorian era, the local railway, local brick making, archaeology, famous ladies who lived in Exmouth, together with a local stationary steam engine and other changing displays.

Francis Danby A.R.A., the famous landscape artist, resided in Exmouth in his later years. He died in 1861 and is buried in a local parish churchyard.

We cater for school visits and provide education boxes for local schools. We also provide reminiscence boxes for rest homes if required. The Museum is run entirely by volunteers. For opening times and more information please see our website *www.devonmuseums.net/exmouth.*

Tom Haynes, Honorary Curator and Jean Haynes, Conservator

Cole, William d.late 1990s
Clock Tower, Exmouth, Devon
oil on board 83 x 64
PCF3

Cole, William d.late 1990s
Holy Trinity Church, Exmouth, Devon
oil on paper 50 x 147
5346

Cole, William d..late 1990s
Lane to Littleham, Exmouth, Devon
oil on paper 45.5 x 86
PCF1

Cole, William d..late 1990s
Prattshayes, Maer Lane, Littleham, Exmouth, Devon
oil on board 34 x 44.5
5345

Driver, Charles Percy 1911–1988
Chapel Street, Exmouth, Devon 1986
acrylic on panel 195 x 244
PCF4

Mair, Thomas active 1901–1924
Orcombe Point, Exmouth, Devon 1901
oil on canvas 24 x 45
0730

Maylor, D.
Lifeboat 'Carolyne Finch' on Call
oil on board 22 x 34
1778

Mordinoff, R. A.
Robert R. A. Tucker Pain 1923
oil on canvas 60 x 40
0044

Morgan, Trevor b.1929
Chapel Street, Exmouth, Devon 2008
acrylic on wooden door 196 x 92
PCF5

Morgan, Trevor b.1929
Mr Turnip
acrylic on board 96 x 26.5
PCF2

Morley, H. F.
Memories of a Happy Holiday: Exmouth Docks, Devon 1955
tempera on card 14.5 x 25
4883

Mortimore, A.
Dead Calm sunset in the Bight at Exmouth, Devon (copy after James Francis Danby) 1973
oil on plywood 34 x 49
4031

David Blackburn, 1997.

Pethybridge, D. C.
Annie Rowsell 1969
oil on board 34.5 x 45
1556

Stokes, Sybil
The Lane at Littleham Cross, Exmouth, Devon 1940
oil on canvas 39 x 49
3878

Tods
The Docks, Exmouth, Devon 1992
oil on board 39 x 50
3832

unknown artist
Colonel Thorneycroft
oil on canvas 76 x 63.3
0032

unknown artist
D'Arcy W. A. Hughes, First Headmaster of Exmouth Grammar School (1929–c.1957)
oil on canvas 78 x 64.6
0031

Whateley, John
Fireside Domestic Scene
acrylic on board 23 x 30.7
5308

Whateley, John
Six Gypsy Children
acrylic on board 23 x 30.3
5308.1

Facing page: Blackburn, David, b.1939, *Pale Beach, South Coast*, 1997, University of Exeter, Fine Art Collection (p. 186)

Exmouth Town Council

Cotton, Alan b.1938
Exmouth, Devon, from the Estuary 1981
oil on canvas 90.4 x 120.8
PCF1

Penn, William Charles 1877–1968
Portrait of a Gentleman 1940
oil on canvas 88 x 68.2
PCF4

Reeves, Tom b.1925
*Chapel Street, Exmouth, Devon (now
Magnolia Centre)* 1960
acrylic on board 50 x 75
PCF3

Strong, C. P.
*Exmouth Estuary with Custom House and
Shipyard from Manchester Quay, Devon* 1859
oil on canvas 90.4 x 151.5
PCF2

Great Torrington Almshouse, Town Lands and Poors Charities

The fine collection of paintings, displayed at present in the Assembly Rooms of Great Torrington Town Hall, are of both historic and artistic importance. Most of the paintings are from the eighteenth and nineteenth centuries and are portraits of dignitaries and aristocracy pertinent to local and national history. It is rare that a collection of this importance and size has not been dispersed over time and remains in situ in the town to which it has historical significance.

The collection, which has become known as the Rolle/Clinton Collection, was housed in Great Torrington Town Hall for safe keeping almost a century ago. Recently, Lord Clinton has made the collection over to the town in the custodianship of the the Great Torrington Almshouse, Town Lands and Poors Charities.

All the paintings are in need of restoration, ranging from simple cleaning to more major treatment. For their further care, provision is being made for their display in a refurbished Town Hall.

Whilst initial studies into the background of the subjects of the portraits have been made, it is hoped that further research will illuminate their history in greater detail. With the demise of the Rolle family line, there is indeed a large amount of research needed. The place of the Rolle family in the history of Great Torrington leads significantly onto international history, offering tantalising associations with early Australian government (Sir James Frederick Palmer) and the colonisation of Florida (Denys Rolle). There is also important work to be done on the wives and daughters featured in the portraits, about which little is known.

The gems of the collection are the two large and lustrous portraits of man and wife: *John Rolle (1750–1842), Lord Rolle* and *Lady Louisa Barbara Rolle (1796–1885)*. Both portraits are by Thomas Lawrence, but the latter was unfinished at his death and is thought to have been completed by Christina Robertson. Other fine works are portraits of Anne Rolle, Christiana Maria Rolle and Denys Rolle by Thomas Hudson, whose many pupils included Joshua Reynolds and Joseph Wright.

The collection once included a portrait of John Rolle Walter by the Italian painter Pompeo Batoni. Recently sold, this portrait happily remains in Devon and is now in the Royal Albert Memorial Museum in Exeter.

Other notable paintings are by Richard Cosway and from the studios of Sir Peter Lely and Johann Kerseboom, and the school of Godfrey Kneller.

The text of this foreword was adapted from the printed booklet 'The Portrait Collection of Great Torrington' by Mrs Cilla Bangay

British (English) School
Captain Thomas Colby (1782–1864)
oil on canvas 70.5 x 57.2
PCF16

British (English) School
Sir James Frederick Palmer (1804–1871)
oil on canvas 74.7 x 64.5
PCF14

Brooks, Henry Jamyn 1839–1925
*Alderman Nathaniel Chapple, Mayor of
Torrington (1871, 1879 and 1889)*
oil on canvas 90.4 x 69.4
PCF11

Brooks, Henry Jamyn 1839–1925
Alderman William Vaughan (1804–1871)
oil on canvas 90 x 70
PCF6

Collier, John 1850–1934
*The Honourable Mark George Kerr Rolle
(1835–1907)*
oil on canvas 125 x 100
PCF17

Cosway, Richard 1742–1821
John Rolle, Lord Rolle (1750–1842)
oil on canvas 233 x 157 (E)
PCF13

Doe (Miss)
The Bellman
oil on canvas 89.6 x 44.4
PCF15

Doe (Miss)
The Bellman
oil on canvas 63.5 x 76
PCF18

Hudson, Thomas 1701–1779
Anne Rolle (1722–1781)
oil on canvas 158 x 128
PCF12

Hudson, Thomas 1701–1779
Christiana Maria Rolle (1710–1780)
oil on canvas 127 x 102
PCF8

Hudson, Thomas 1701–1779
Denys Rolle (1720–1797)
oil on canvas 158 x 128 (E)
PCF4

Kerseboom, Johann d..1708
William Rolle
oil on canvas 127 x 102
PCF10

Kneller, Godfrey (attributed to) 1646–1723
Lady Ranleigh
oil on canvas 235 x 142
PCF1

Kneller, Godfrey (school of) 1646–1723
James II of England (1633–1701), King of England, Scotland and Ireland (1685–1688)
oil on canvas 235 x 142
PCF7

Kneller, Godfrey (school of) 1646–1723
Mary of Modena, Queen Mary II (1659–1718), Queen Consort of King James II of England
oil on canvas 235 x 142
PCF5

Lawrence, Thomas 1769–1830
John Rolle (1750–1842), Lord Rolle
oil on canvas 269 x 175.2
PCF9

Lawrence, Thomas 1769–1830 & **Robertson, Christina** active 1823–1850 **(attributed to)**
Lady Louisa Barbara Rolle (1796–1885)
oil on canvas 269 x 175.2
PCF3

Lely, Peter (studio of) 1618–1680
Catherine Noel (1657–1733), Duchess of Rutland
oil on canvas 127 x 99
PCF2

Great Torrington Heritage Museum and Archive

Barber, Judy d..2003
German Bomber over Torrington, Devon
acrylic on board 89.5 x 80
PCF6

Gay, Alfred 'Humpy' 1870–1916
Rothern Bridge, Devon
oil on canvas 25 x 30
PCF2

Gay, Alfred 'Humpy' 1870–1916
Viaduct for the Marland Railway, Devon
oil on canvas 25 x 30
PCF3

Klingenberg, I.
Breaking Waves
acrylic on board 29.8 x 39.8
PCF5

unknown artist
Torrington 'May Fair', Devon
acrylic on board 59.7 x 75.2
PCF4

Whitfield, W. (attributed to)
Castle Hill, Torrington, Devon
oil on canvas 59.2 x 89.8
PCF1

Holsworthy Museum

Bassett, William active 1850–1890
Elizabeth Fry, Aged 90 1859
oil on canvas 35.2 x 30.8
626

unknown artist
Derriton Viaduct, Holsworthy, Devon
oil on board 25.2 x 45.3
823

unknown artist
Dunsland House, Holsworthy, Devon
oil on canvas 12.8 x 17.8
1010

Allhallows Museum

Barton, Bernard Pawley 1912–1992
Joe Lake (1926–1998), Town Crier 1990
acrylic on board 50 x 40
2002.28

Hayes-Valentine, Mary
George Blagdon Westcott (1753–1798) 2000
acrylic on board 50 x 40
2001.015

Leyman, Alfred 1856–1933
Tracey Bridge, Honiton, Devon 1888
oil on canvas 19 x 37
2008.252

unknown artist
Bishop Edward Copleston (1776–1864)
oil on canvas 125 x 100
2001.027

unknown artist
John Gaius Copleston (1749–1831)
oil on canvas 90 x 70
2001.026

Honiton Hospital

Taylor, Jane R. b.1924
Stream
oil on board 24 x 29.2
PCF2

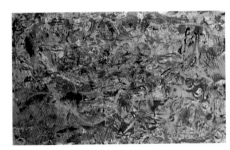

Thorne, Sheila J. b.1938
Festival 1
acrylic on canvas 62 x 102
PCF3

Thorne, Sheila J. b.1938
Festival 2
acrylic on canvas
PCF5

Thorne, Sheila J. b.1938
Wetlands
acrylic on canvas 65 x 95.5
PCF4

Williams, Avril b.1935
Portugese Fishermen
oil on board 29.5 x 39
PCF1

Facing page: Drummond, Malcolm, 1880–1945, *John Rolle (1750–1842), The Park Bench*, c.1910, Royal Albert Memorial Museum (p. 130)

Honiton Library

Batten, Jean
River Otter, Devon
oil on canvas 43.2 x 55
PCF1

Honiton Town Council

Gisol
Mézidon-Canon, France
oil on canvas 44.5 x 59.5
PCF3

Salter, William 1804–1875
The Entombment of Christ 1838
oil on canvas 262 x 185
PCF1

unknown artist
Juanita Maxwell Phillips (1880–1966)
oil on canvas 133.2 x 108
PCF2

Ilfracombe Museum

Bolton, Don
HMS 'Ilfracombe' 1987
oil on canvas 49.5 x 65
PCF4

Darton, J.
Lantern Hill, Ilfracombe, Devon
oil on panel 47 x 65.7
PCF3

Hoare, C. T.
Ilfracombe (The Cove) 1909
oil on canvas 46.5 x 75
ILFCM_2132

Rudd, B.
The 'Waverley' Coming under the Clifton Suspension Bridge 1909
oil on canvas 45 x 67.1
PCF1

unknown artist
Ilfracombe, Devon, Viewed from Above
oil on canvas 72.5 x 105
PCF2

unknown artist
Ilfracombe Harbour, Devon
oil on copper 20 x 30
ILFCM_1293

Ilfracombe Town Council

Jenkins, George Henry 1843–1914
Lantern Hill, Ilfracombe, Devon
oil on canvas 33.9 x 59.2
PCF4

Jenkins, George Henry 1843–1914
Lantern Hill, Ilfracombe, Devon
oil on canvas 54.6 x 90.4
PCF6

Jenkins, George Henry 1843–1914
The Quay, Ilfracombe, Devon
oil on canvas 33.9 x 59.2
PCF3

Naish, John George 1824–1905
Ilfracombe, Devon 1870
oil on canvas 77.7 x 138.5
PCF5

Sims, Thomas
Dr John Jones, Chairman of Ilfracombe Council (1859–1865)
oil on canvas 113 x 74.5
PCF1

unknown artist
Major F. H. Thomas, Chairman of Ilfracombe Council (1936–1938)
oil on canvas 76.1 x 63
PCF2

Cookworthy Museum

Crowdey (Miss)
Steve Hurrell (d. after 1915)
oil on canvas 40 x 30
KIXCM.4176

Gay, W. R.
Burgh Island and Bantham Bar 1900
oil on canvas 44.5 x 60
KIXCM.3250

Gay, W. R.
Thurlestone Rock, Devon 1900
oil on canvas 44.5 x 60
KIXCM.3249

Lidstone, W.
Hallsands, Devon 1869
oil on board 30 x 45
KIXCM.0910

Newman, Tom
Ella Trout Launching Out from Hallsands: The Men Said, 'Too rough to go out"
oil on hardboard 50 x 75
KIXCM.1311.1

Newman, Tom
Ella Trout Said, 'I picked him out of the sea like bass!'
oil on hardboard 50 x 75
KIXCM.1311.2

Newman, Tom
Ella Trout and the Boy Willie Trout, Age 10, in the 'Long Seas' Start Bay with the Rescued Man
oil on hardboard 50 x 75
KIXCM.1311.3

Newman, Tom
Ella Trout Transferring the Negro Fireman to ML49 off Start Point
oil on hardboard 50 x 75
KIXCM.1311.4

Pearce, Roger
The Fair on Kingsbridge Quay, Devon 1979–
1980
oil on hardboard 43.5 x 59.7
KIXCM.1310

unknown artist
*Bantham Bay, a View of Burgh Island and the
River Avon from the Village of Bantham,
Devon*
oil on canvas 22.5 x 36.7
KIXCM.0911

unknown artist
Kingsbridge Rea at High Tide, Devon
oil on canvas 23.5 x 43.5
KIXCM.1545

unknown artist
Thomas Crispin (1607–1690)
oil on canvas 214.5 x 124
PCF1

Kingsbridge Town Council

Bisgood, D.
Return from Alamein No.2 1974
acrylic on canvas 120.5 x 90
PCF3

Saunders, George active 1906–1918
*J. S. Hurrell, JP, CC, Chairman of Kingsbridge
Urban District Council* 1906
oil on canvas 110 x 84
PCF5

Saunders, George active 1906–1918
J. S. Hurrell, JP, CC, Chairman of Kingsbridge Urban District Council 1918
oil on canvas 59.5 x 44
PCF4

Williams-Lyouns, Herbert Francis 1863–1933
Devon Cliffs 1914
oil on canvas 201 x 304
PCF1

Williams-Lyouns, Herbert Francis 1863–1933
Watercress Seller
oil on canvas 101 x 75.2
PCF2

The Fairground Heritage Trust

Without doubt, the collection of fairground art at Dingles Fairground Heritage Centre in Devon is the most important in the country. It is a world-class collection of British fairground art from the 1880s to the 1980s.

Fairground art has long been neglected by historians, ethnologists and industrial archaeologists alike. Being neither the product of rural crafts nor the art school, it has, with rare exceptions, been ignored. Since the late 1970s, fairground artefacts such as carved horses and painted panels have gained museum status as they became highly collectable. Fairground art consists generally of large panels or banners that draw immediate attention to the form of entertainment they are promoting: live shows, games or rides. It was produced by relatively unsophisticated showmen and the artists and craftsmen they employed; it is essentially popular in form and spirit.

Fairground art was only intended to be in use for a short period of time. The peripatetic lifestyle of the showmen meant constant building up and pulling down of shows, games and riding machines. Exposure to the elements meant constant repairing and repainting. Established ride builders such as Savages, and Orton Sons & Spooner were originally concerned with the more prosaic activities of coachbuilding and agricultural engineering. As their fairground manufacturing increased, their workforce of craftsmen came to include scenic artists and signwriters.

The idea of a National Fairground Museum was first explored in the early 1980s and The Fairground Heritage Trust formed in 1986. At that time many fairground artefacts were being shipped, via the antiques trade, to the United States and others were lost due to poor storage conditions. The Trust was formed to preserve and exhibit the way of life of the travelling showman. Dingles Fairground Heritage Centre is the realisation of that vision. The Trust has had many false starts and the move to Devon was only planned during the past few years. The Centre is home to the National Fairground Collection.

The fairground was often at the forefront of popular entertainment. The moving picture show, for example, was first shown at a British fairground in 1897. It enjoyed a boom until the outbreak of the Great War, by which time most towns had a permanent cinema. The fairground showmen of the early twentieth century were masters at presenting illusion, sham-opulence and offering a glimpse of fantasy. The magic of coloured fairy lights, in a stark, harsh world, existed at the fairground before the use of electricity or running water in the home. In the early twentieth century, country folk from humble candle-lit cottages could board a richly upholstered Venetian gondola on a Switchback ride, assisted by uniformed attendants, and whirl around a steeply undulating track, around gilded carvings, bevelled mirrors and enjoy the latest music on a grand military band organ, all for tuppence a ride. The pennies added up to great fortunes in some cases and the showmen's dynasties that still exist today were founded.

By far the oldest ride in the Trust's collection is the legendary Rodeo Switchback. Believed to have been built by Savages of King's Lynn for James Pettigrove, possibly as a Velocipede in as early as 1880, this is the last remaining Spinning Top Switchback in existence, and probably also the oldest surviving fairground ride in the country. Its early history is shrouded in mystery. This, along with the rides once owned by the Edwards family of Swindon, forms the nucleus of the Trust's collection. It is unique in that a whole travelling fair has been preserved.

The name of Edwards was famous throughout Wiltshire and its neighbouring counties. The travelling fairground firm founded by Bob Edwards in the 1900s was not the largest, nor the one that travelled over the widest of areas, yet it was held in universal esteem by showmen, and occupied a very special place in the hearts of all who love the fair. The firm created five riding machines of such high quality that they form the core of our collection. The Dodgem, Super Chariot Racer Ark and Supersonic Skid are now in working order. These three rides contain very many fine examples of classic post-war fairground art. The art of the showman harnessed the power of hundreds of pulsing electric lamps to highlight the subtle use of metallic silver and gold. A fourth ride, a Brooklands Speedway of the 1930s, has yet to be re-assessed. The firm's original ride, a galloping horse roundabout, is on site and there are some wonderful carved horses and many painted panels on display.

At the end of the 1920s, the public were invited to crash cars into each other in relative safety, as the showman invested in the latest American novelty, the Dodgems. It was, in fact, a novelty that has never worn off. The vast area around the Dodgem car track gave the fairground artist great scope for huge pieces of public art. Initially, in the early 1930s, motor racing scenes were popular, but these, in turn, were replaced by the striking post-war images of speed lines and winged motifs in rich colours, making much use of gold and silver leaf. The favoured colours were creams, maroons and greens, and tone was even more important than colour.

The famous firm of Hall & Fowle was formed in the immediate post-war years and soon became the most sought after fairground decorators in the country. Fred Fowle, and Edwin and Billy Hall painted some fine examples that form part of The Fairground Heritage Trust's Collection.

Popular culture was soon incorporated into the artwork of the fair. Disney's Mickey Mouse was universally copied and Arnold Ridley's play, *The Ghost Train*, inspired the iconic dark ride on the fairground. Ghoulish montages, based on the creations of 1930s Hollywood soon appeared on the Ghost Train. The example at Dingles Fairground Heritage Centre is clearly signed by Hall & Fowle.

To find out more, *Fairground Art*, published in 1981 by The Fairground Heritage Trust trustees, Richard Ward and Geoff Weedon, remains the definitive work on the subject. It is available from Dingles Fairground Heritage Centre.

Guy Belshaw, Trustee and Honorary Press Officer

Barnes and Son Belper (Barrett)
Proctor's Hoopla: Landscape Scene, Dovedale, Derbyshire (rounding board)
oil on board 76 x 155
PCF40 (P)

Barnes and Son Belper (Barrett)
Proctor's Hoopla: Landscape Scene, Doveholes, Dovedale, Derbyshire (rounding board)
oil on board 76 x 155
PCF44 (P)

Barnes and Son Belper (Barrett)
Proctor's Hoopla: Landscape Scene, Monsal Dale, Buxton, Derbyshire (rounding board)
oil on board 76 x 155
PCF45 (P)

Barnes and Son Belper (Barrett)
Proctor's Hoopla: Landscape Scene, Pickering Tors, Derbyshire (rounding board)
oil on board 76 x 155
PCF43 (P)

Barnes and Son Belper (Barrett)
Proctor's Hoopla: Landscape Scene, Pickering Tors, Dovedale, Derbyshire (rounding board)
oil on board 76 x 155
PCF41 (P)

Barnes and Son Belper (Barrett)
Proctor's Hoopla:Lion's Head Rock, Dovedale, Derbyshire (rounding board)
oil on board 76 x 155
PCF42 (P)

Barnes and Son Belper (Barrett) (attributed to)
Landscape Scene (hoopla shutter)
oil on board 68 x 67
PCF92 (P)

Barnes and Son Belper (Barrett) (attributed to)
Landscape Scene (hoopla shutter)
oil on board 68 x 67
PCF93 (P)

Barnes and Son Belper (Barrett) (attributed to)
Street Scene (hoopla shutter)
oil on board 68 x 67
PCF94 (P)

Barnes and Son Belper (Barrett) (attributed to)
Townscape (hoopla shutter)
oil on board 68 x 67
PCF95 (P)

Carter, Richard
Ghost Train, Monsters (paybox, front panel) late 1970s
oil on metal 183 x 89.3
1994.5.7 (P)

Carter, Richard
Ghost Train, Monsters (paybox, side panel) late 1970s
oil on metal 169.11 x 150.5
1994.5.8 (P)

Carter, Richard
Ghost Train, Monsters (paybox, side panel) late 1970s
oil on metal 169.1 x 150.5
1994.5.9 (P)

Carter, Richard
Ghost Train, Monsters (paybox, back panel) late 1970s
  183 x 89.3
1994.5.10 (P)

Deacon, E.
Country Garden Scene (hoopla, rounding board)
oil on board 60 x 150
PCF114 (P)

Facing page: Morgan, Trevor, b.1929, *Chapel Street, Exmouth, Devon*, 2008, Exmouth Museum (p. 219)

Deacon, E.
Harbour Scene (hoopla, rounding board)
oil on board 60 x 150
PCF111 (P)

Deacon, E.
Landscape and Herons (hoopla, rounding board)
oil on board 60 x 150
PCF115 (P)

Deacon, E.
Landscape and Sailboats (hoopla, rounding board)
oil on board 60 x 150
PCF108 (P)

Deacon, E.
Landscape and Swans (hoopla, rounding board)
oil on board 60 x 150
PCF112 (P)

Deacon, E.
Landscape and Windmills (hoopla, rounding board)
oil on board 60 x 150
PCF110 (P)

Deacon, E.
Landscape in Autumn (hoopla, rounding board)
oil on board 60 x 150
PCF113 (P)

Deacon, E.
Landscape in Spring (hoopla, rounding board)
oil on board 60 x 150
PCF109 (P)

Farmer, Sid
Scott's 'Wonder Walters': Cellist and Mandolin (shutter, two panels) c.1955
oil on board 180 x 80; 180 x 80 (E)
D012.3 (P)

Farmer, Sid
Scott's 'Wonder Walters': Concertina Player and Mandolin (shutter, two panels) c.1955
oil on board 180 x 80; 180 x 80 (E)
D012.5 (P)

Farmer, Sid
Scott's 'Wonder Walters': Conductor and Mandolin (shutter, two panels) c.1955
oil on board 180 x 80; 180 x 80 (E)
D012.8 (P)

Farmer, Sid
Scott's 'Wonder Walters': Drummer and Mandolin (shutter, two panels) c.1955
oil on board 180 x 80; 180 x 80 (E)
D012.1 (P)

Farmer, Sid
Scott's 'Wonder Walters': Flute Player and Mandolin (shutter, two panels) c.1955
oil on board 180 x 80; 180 x 80 (E)
D012.7 (P)

Farmer, Sid
Scott's 'Wonder Walters': Saxophone Player and Mandolin (shutter, two panels) c.1955
oil on board 180 x 80; 180 x 80 (E)
D012.2 (P)

Farmer, Sid
Scott's 'Wonder Walters': Triangle Player and Mandolin (shutter, two panels) c.1955
oil on board 180 x 80; 180 x 80 (E)
D012.4 (P)

Farmer, Sid
Scott's 'Wonder Walters': Trumpeter and Mandolin (shutter, two panels) c.1955
oil on board 180 x 80; 180 x 80 (E)
D012.6 (P)

Farmer, Sid
Scott's 'Wonder Walters': Kentucky Waltz (shutter)
oil on metal 138 x 185
D110.3 (P)

Farmer, Sid
Scott's 'Wonder Walters': Young Man Dancing (false pillar)
oil on metal 200 x 38
D110.1 (P)

Fowle, Frederick George 1914–1983
Yogi Bear (centre panel from a juvenile ride) early 1960s
oil on board 113 x 65
PCF90 (P)

Fowle, Frederick George 1914–1983
Pixie (centre panel from a juvenile ride) early
1970s
oil on board 113 x 65
PCF89 (P)

Fowle, Frederick George 1914–1983
David Wallis's 'Super Walzer' (front) 1978
enamel on board 206 x 796
PCF20 (P)

Fowle, Frederick George 1914–1983
Lion 1982
oil on metal 90 x 155
D028 (P)

Fowle, Frederick George 1914–1983
Mercury Speed
oil on board 81 x 120
PCF23 (P)

Fowle, Frederick George 1914–1983
Spaceship
oil on board 83 x 125
D232 (P)

Gaze, Charles (Swindon)
*R. Edwards' 'Galloping Horses': Jungle
Animals, Bear and a Boa* (centre
shutter) 1928
oil on panel 118.3 x 59.5
PCF220

Gaze, Charles (Swindon)
*R. Edwards' 'Galloping Horses': Jungle
Animals, Cheetah* (centre shutter) 1928
oil on panel 118.3 x 59.5
PCF219

Gaze, Charles (Swindon)
*R. Edwards' 'Galloping Horses': Jungle
Animals, Giraffe* (centre shutter) 1928
oil on panel 118.3 x 59.5
PCF224

Gaze, Charles (Swindon)
*R. Edwards' 'Galloping Horses': Jungle
Animals, Lion* (centre shutter) 1928
oil on panel 118.3 x 59.5
PCF223

Gaze, Charles (Swindon)
R. Edwards' 'Galloping Horses': Jungle Animals, Lion (centre shutter) 1928
oil on panel 118.3 x 59.5
PCF225

Gaze, Charles (Swindon)
R. Edwards' 'Galloping Horses': Jungle Animals, Polar Bear (centre shutter) 1928
oil on panel 118.3 x 59.5
PCF222

Gaze, Charles (Swindon)
R. Edwards' 'Galloping Horses': Jungle Animals, Red Deer (centre shutter) 1928
oil on panel 118.3 x 59.5
PCF221

George Orton, Sons and Spooner Ltd
John Powell's 'Motorcyle Speedway': Motorcyclists (rounding board) 1936
oil on board 143 x 311
D238 (P)

George Orton, Sons and Spooner Ltd
John Powell's 'Monte Carlo Speedway': Winged Wheel (rounding board) 1936–1937
oil on board 107 x 229
PCF33

George Orton, Sons and Spooner Ltd
R. Edwards' 'Super Chariot Racer': Floral Scene (top centre) c.1936
oil on board 185 x 90; 185 x 90
119.27

George Orton, Sons and Spooner Ltd
R. Edwards' 'Super Chariot Racer': Floral Scene (top centre) c.1936
oil on board 185 x 90; 185 x 90
119.28

George Orton, Sons and Spooner Ltd
R. Edwards' 'Super Chariot Racer': Floral Scene (top centre) c.1936
oil on board 185 x 90; 185 x 90
119.3

George Orton, Sons and Spooner Ltd
R. Edwards' 'Super Chariot Racer': Floral Scene (top centre) c.1936
oil on board 185 x 90; 185 x 90
119.31

George Orton, Sons and Spooner Ltd
R. Edwards' 'Super Chariot Racer': Floral Scene
(top centre) c.1936
oil on board 185 x 90; 185 x 90
119.32

George Orton, Sons and Spooner Ltd
R. Edwards' 'Super Chariot Racer': Floral Scene
(top centre) c.1936
oil on board 185 x 90; 185 x 90
119.33

George Orton, Sons and Spooner Ltd
R. Edwards' 'Super Chariot Racer': Floral Scene
(top centre) c.1936
oil on board 185 x 90; 185 x 90
119.34

George Orton, Sons and Spooner Ltd
*R. Edwards' 'Super Chariot Racer': Floweral
Scene* (top centre) c.1936
oil on board 185 x 90; 185 x 90
119.29

George Orton, Sons and Spooner Ltd
*R. Edwards' Orton & Spooner 'Monte Carlo
Speedway': Winged Wheel* (rounding
board) 1938
oil on board 107 x 229
PCF155

**George Orton, Sons and Spooner Ltd,
Howell, A.** 1877–1959 & **Howell, A. S.**
1906–1966
R. Edwards' 'Super Chariot Racer' (...) 1946
oil on metal 210 x 3300
119.7

**George Orton, Sons and Spooner Ltd,
Howell, A.** 1877–1959 & **Howell, A. S.**
1906–1966
R. Edwards' 'Super Chariot Racer' (...) 1946
oil on metal
119.8

**George Orton, Sons and Spooner Ltd,
Howell, A.** 1877–1959 & **Howell, A. S.**
1906–1966
R. Edwards' 'Super Chariot Racer' (...) 1946
oil on metal
119.9

**George Orton, Sons and Spooner Ltd,
Howell, A.** 1877–1959 & **Howell, A. S.**
1906–1966
R. Edwards' 'Super Chariot Racer' (...) 1946
oil on metal
119.1

**George Orton, Sons and Spooner Ltd,
Howell, A.** 1877–1959 & **Howell, A. S.**
1906–1966
R. Edwards' 'Super Chariot Racer' (...) 1946
oil on metal
119.11

**George Orton, Sons and Spooner Ltd,
Howell, A.** 1877–1959 & **Howell, A. S.**
1906–1966
R. Edwards' 'Super Chariot Racer' (...) 1946
oil on metal
119.12

**George Orton, Sons and Spooner Ltd,
Howell, A.** 1877–1959 & **Howell, A. S.**
1906–1966
R. Edwards' 'Super Chariot Racer' (...) 1946
oil on metal
119.13

**George Orton, Sons and Spooner Ltd,
Howell, A.** 1877–1959 & **Howell, A. S.**
1906–1966
R. Edwards' 'Super Chariot Racer' (...) 1946
oil on metal
119.14

**George Orton, Sons and Spooner Ltd,
Howell, A.** 1877–1959 & **Howell, A. S.**
1906–1966
R. Edwards' 'Super Chariot Racer' (...) 1946
oil on metal
119.15

**George Orton, Sons and Spooner Ltd,
Howell, A.** 1877–1959 & **Howell, A. S.**
1906–1966
R. Edwards' 'Super Chariot Racer' (...) 1946
oil on metal
119.16

**George Orton, Sons and Spooner Ltd,
Howell, A.** 1877–1959 & **Howell, A. S.**
1906–1966
R. Edwards' 'Super Chariot Racer' (...) 1946
oil on metal
119.17

**George Orton, Sons and Spooner Ltd,
Howell, A.** 1877–1959 & **Howell, A. S.**
1906–1966
R. Edwards and Sons' 'Super Chariot (...)
oil on board 400 x 950 (E)
119

Hall, Edwin
John Holland's 'Super Dodgems' (rounding
board) 1952
oil on board 96 x 346
PCF21 (P)

Hall and Fowle
Brett's 'Ghost Train' (backdrop) 1948–1949
oil on metal 266 x 1792
1994.5.1a (P)

Hall and Fowle
Brett's 'Ghost Train' (backdrop) 1948–1949
oil on metal
1994.5.1b (P)

Hall and Fowle
Brett's 'Ghost Train' (backdrop) 1948–1949
oil on metal
1994.5.1c (P)

Hall and Fowle
Brett's 'Ghost Train' (backdrop) 1948–1949
oil on metal
1994.5.1d (P)

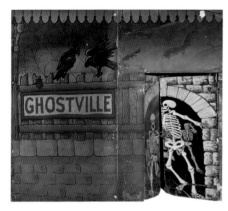

Hall and Fowle
Brett's 'Ghost Train' (backdrop) 1948–1949
oil on metal
1994.5.1e (P)

Hall and Fowle
Brett's 'Ghost Train' (backdrop)   1948–1949
oil on metal
1994.5.1f (P)

Hall and Fowle
Brett's 'Ghost Train' (showfront) (from a
design by Edwin Hall) 1948–1949
oil on metal 276 x 1463
1994.5a (P)

Hall and Fowle
Brett's 'Ghost Train' (showfront) (from a
design by Edwin Hall) 1948–1949
oil on metal
1994.5b (P)

Hall and Fowle
Brett's 'Ghost Train' (showfront) (from a
design by Edwin Hall) 1948–1949
oil on metal
1994.5c (P)

Facing page: Brockedon, William, 1787–1854, *Ossian Relating the Fate of Oscar to Malvina* (from 'The Poems of Ossian'
by James Macpherson), Totnes Guildhall (p. 302)

Hall and Fowle
Brett's 'Ghost Train' (showfront) (from a design by Edwin Hall) 1948–1949
oil on metal
1994.5d (P)

Hall and Fowle
Culine's Dodgems: Winged Wheel (rounding board) 1950s
oil on board 128 x 243
PCF14 (P)

Hall and Fowle
Victor Hart's Hoopla: Mercury (rounding board) early 1960s
oil on metal 61 x 248
PCF39

Hall and Fowle
Victor Hart's Hoopla: Mercury (shutter) early 1960s
oil on board 76 x 160
PCF38 (P)

Hall and Fowle
Andrew Simon's 'Juvenile': Monogramme 'AS' (rounding board)
oil on metal 74 x 172
PCF98 (P)

Hall and Fowle
Mrs Holland's 'Dogdems': Lion (rounding board)
oil on board 91 x 330
PCF22 (P)

Howell, A. S. 1906–1966
R. Edwards' 'Super Chariot Racer': Jungle Scene (shutter) c.1962
oil on board 117 x 175
119.1

Howell, A. S. 1906–1966
R. Edwards' 'Super Chariot Racer': Jungle Scene (shutter) c.1962
oil on board 120 x 220
119.2

Howell, A. S. 1906–1966
R. Edwards' 'Super Chariot Racer': Jungle Scene (shutter) c.1962
oil on board 93 x 220
119.3

Howell, A. S. 1906–1966
*R. Edwards' 'Super Chariot Racer': Jungle
Scene* (shutter) c.1962
oil on board 93 x 220
119.4

Howell, A. S. 1906–1966
*R. Edwards' 'Super Chariot Racer': Jungle
Scene* (shutter) c.1962
oil on board 120 x 220
119.5

Howell, A. S. 1906–1966
*R. Edwards' 'Super Chariot Racer': Jungle
Scene* (shutter) c.1962
oil on board 120 x 220
119.6

Howell, A. S. 1906–1966
*R. Edwards' 'Super Chariot Racer': Jungle
Scene* (shutter) c.1962
oil on board 117 x 175
119.21

Howell, A. S. 1906–1966
*R. Edwards' 'Super Chariot Racer': Jungle
Scene* (shutter) c.1962
oil on board 120 x 220
119.22

Howell, A. S. 1906–1966
*R. Edwards' 'Super Chariot Racer': Jungle
Scene* (shutter) c.1962
oil on board 93 x 220
119.23

Howell, A. S. 1906–1966
*R. Edwards' 'Super Chariot Racer': Jungle
Scene* (shutter) c.1962
oil on board 93 x 220
119.24

Howell, A. S. 1906–1966
*R. Edwards' 'Super Chariot Racer': Jungle
Scene* (shutter) c.1962
oil on board 120 x 220
119.25

Howell, A. S. 1906–1966
*R. Edwards' 'Super Chariot Racer': Jungle
Scene* (shutter) c.1962
oil on board 120 x 220
119.26

Lakin & Co., R. J. (Edwin Hall)
Ashley Brothers' 'Jungle Thriller' (rounding board) 1932
oil on board 165 x 1015
PCF2 (P)

Lakin & Co., R. J. (Edwin Hall)
Ashley Brothers' 'Jungle Thriller': Jungle Scene (rounding board) 1932
oil on board 188 x 301
PCF226 (P)

Lakin & Co., R. J. (Edwin Hall)
Bull Fighting Scene (front proscenium) 1932
oil on board 335 x 1040
D202 (P)

Lakin & Co., R. J. (Edwin Hall)
Jungle Scene with a Baboon (rounding board) 1932
oil on board 167 x 253
PCF148 (P)

Lakin & Co., R. J. (Edwin Hall)
Jungle Scene with a Bear (rounding board)
oil on board 167 x 253
PCF151 (P)

Lakin & Co., R. J. (Edwin Hall)
Jungle Scene with a Leopard (rounding board) 1932
oil on board 167 x 253
PCF147 (P)

Lakin & Co., R. J. (Edwin Hall)
Jungle Scene with a Lynx (rounding board) 1932
oil on board 167 x 253
PCF146 (P)

Lakin & Co., R. J. (Edwin Hall)
Jungle Scene with a McCaw (rounding board) 1932
oil on board 167 x 253
PCF153 (P)

Lakin & Co., R. J. (Edwin Hall)
Jungle Scene with a Monkey (rounding board) 1932
oil on board 167 x 253
PCF149

Lakin & Co., R. J. (Edwin Hall)
Jungle Scene with a Monkey (rounding board) 1932
oil on board 167 x 253
PCF150 (P)

Lakin & Co., R. J. (Edwin Hall)
Jungle Scene with a Wild Cat and Its Kill (rounding board) 1932
oil on board 167 x 253
PCF152 (P)

Lakin & Co., R. J. (Edwin Hall)
Parrots (top centre panel from Wroot's 'Ben Hur') 1936
oil on board 127 x 86.5
PCF11 (P)

Lakin & Co., R. J. (Edwin Hall)
Sam Crow's 'Dodgem Track': Racecars (front proscenium) 1938
oil on board 178 x 978
D023 (P)

Lakin & Co., R. J. (Edwin Hall)
Sam Crow's 'Dodgem Track': Racing Car No.2 1938
oil on board 116 x 336
D023.2 (P)

Lakin & Co., R. J. (Edwin Hall)
Sam Crow's 'Dodgem Track': Racing Car No.3 1938
oil on board 114 x 244
D023.1 (P)

Lakin & Co., R. J. (Edwin Hall)
Sam Crow's 'Dodgem Track': Racing Car No.8 1938
oil on board 116 x 336
D023.3 (P)

Lakin & Co., R. J. (Edwin Hall)
Front Proscenium with Ben Hur (G. Heath & Sons) 1945
oil on board 234 x 1015
PCF13 (P)

Lakin & Co., R. J. (Edwin Hall)
T. Whitelegg's 'No.2 Dodgems': Pegasus (rounding board)
oil on metal 91 x 323
PCF16 (P)

Lakin & Co., R. J.
Brett's 'Skid': Mercury (figure from a handrail) 1949
oil on metal 75 x 160 (E)
D115 (P)

Lakin & Co., R. J.
Hummingbird (top centre panel from Wroot's Ben Hur)
oil on board 128 x 90
PCF88 (P)

Lakin & Co., R. J.
Silcock's 'Skid': Trumpeting Girl (top centre)
oil on board 122 x 119
PCF86 (P)

Postlethwaite, Victoria
William Wilson's 'Rodeo Switchback': Cowboy Scene (shutter)
oil on wood panels 210 x 188
1993.1.2a

Postlethwaite, Victoria
William Wilson's 'Rodeo Switchback': Cowboy Scene (shutter)
oil on wood panels 188 x 210
1993.1.2b

Postlethwaite, Victoria
William Wilson's 'Rodeo Switchback': Cowboy Scene (shutter)
oil on wood panels 210 x 188
1993.1.2c

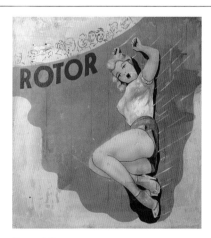

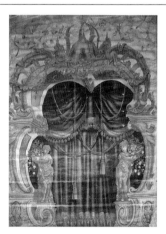

Pratt, Albert
The Gee Gees, Girl Riding on a Merry-Go-Round (shutter from Saunt's Hoopla)
oil on board 135 x 79
PCF63 (P)

Pratt, Albert
The Rotor, Girl on a Spinning Fairground Ride (shutter from Saunt's Hoopla)
oil on board 79 x 135
PCF64 (P)

Sconce, Walter & Sons 1855–1925
Bioscope Show Banner with a Theatre Stage Scene
oil on canvas 536 x 360
1994.23 (P)

Sconce, Walter & Sons 1855–1925
Bioscope Show Banner with a Theatre Stage Scene
oil on canvas 536 x 360
1994.24 (P)

Sconce, Walter & Sons 1855–1925
Landscape with a Lake (banner)
oil on canvas 91 x 348
PCF117 (P)

Smith, A. V. (Camberwell) active late 19th C
Wild Boy (banner)
oil on canvas 256 x 229
L26 (P)

Smith, Alfred (Junior) active late 19th C
Salome (banner)
oil on canvas 210 x 207 (E)
L1 (P)

Tei, Peter
Mercury
oil on board 65 x 130 (E)
PCF001a (P)

unknown artist late 19th C
French Beauty Show (banner)
oil on canvas 210 x 207
PCF15 (P)

unknown artist
Billy Wood and Son 'Boxing Booth': Boxer Lee Savold
oil on board 288 x 89.3
1994.11.1 (P)

unknown artist
Billy Wood and Son 'Boxing Booth': Boxers Joe Louis and Joe Walcott
oil on board 217.4 x 305
1994.11.2 (P)

unknown artist
Billy Wood and Son 'Boxing Booth' (believed to be of Billy Wood) (showfront) (polyptych, panel 1 of 5) 1930s
oil on board 263 x 1525 (E)
1994.11a (P)

unknown artist
*Billy Wood and Son 'Boxing Booth': Fight
between Phil Scott and Larry Gains, 1931*
(showfront) (polyptych, panel 2 of 5)
oil on board
1994.11b (P)

unknown artist
*Billy Wood and Son 'Boxing Booth': Fight
between Dave Shade and Len Harvey, 1930*
(showfront) (polyptych, panel 3 of 5)
oil on board
1994.11c (P)

unknown artist
*Billy Wood and Son 'Boxing Booth': Fight
between Billy Wood and Arnold 'Kid' Shepherd*
(showfront) (polyptych, panel 4 of 5)
oil on board
1994.11d (P)

unknown artist
*Billy Wood and Son 'Boxing Booth': Unnamed
Boxer* (showfront) (polyptych, panel 5 of 5)
oil on board
1994.11e (P)

unknown artist
*Donald Ive's 'Ark': Lion Leaping through a
Burning Hoop* (dragon chariot rear
panel) 1930s
oil on board 66 x 132
PCF37 (P)

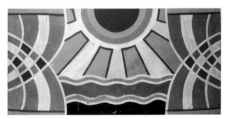

unknown artist
*John Liny's Hoopla (Chicken Joe): Art Deco
Sun* (shutter) late 1920s–early 1930s
oil on board 60 x 110
PCF65 (P)

unknown artist
Barney and Fred (coconut shy, two panels)
oil on metal 91.3 x 30; 91.3 x 30
PCF215 (P)

unknown artist
Flo and Tom Cat (coconut shy, two panels)
oil on metal 91.3 x 30; 91.3 x 30
PCF214 (P)

unknown artist
Huckleberry Hound and Yogi Bear (coconut
shy, two panels)
oil on metal 91.3 x 30; 91.3 x 30
PCF216 (P)

unknown artist
Officer Dibble and Tom Cat (coconut shy, two
panels)
oil on metal 91.3 x 30; 91.3 x 30
PCF213 (P)

unknown artist
Humphries' 'Shooting Gallery': Lion (shutter)
oil on board 51 x 153
PCF157 (P)

unknown artist
Humphries' 'Shooting Gallery': Tiger (shutter)
oil on board 51 x 153
PCF156 (P)

unknown artist
Landscape Scene (hoopla upright)
oil on board 15 x 4.5
PCF66 (P)

unknown artist
Landscape Scene (hoopla upright)
oil on board 15 x 4.5
PCF67 (P)

unknown artist
Landscape Scene (hoopla upright)
oil on board 15 x 4.5
PCF69 (P)

unknown artist
Landscape Scene (hoopla upright)
oil on board 15 x 4.5
PCF70 (P)

unknown artist
Landscape Scene (hoopla upright)
oil on board 15 x 4.5
PCF71 (P)

unknown artist
Landscape Scene (hoopla upright)
oil on board 15 x 4.5
PCF72 (P)

unknown artist
Landscape Scene (hoopla upright)
oil on board 15 x 4.5
PCF73 (P)

unknown artist
Landscape Scene (rounding board)
oil on board 15 x 4.5
PCF68 (P)

unknown artist
Noyce's 'Shooting Gallery': Gorilla
lights & oil on board 230 x 105
PCF158 (P)

unknown artist
Noyce's 'Shooting Gallery': Walrus
oil & lights on board 230 x 105
PCF159 (P)

unknown artist
Psychedelic Face
oil on board 61 x 163
PCF12 (P)

unknown artist
R. Edwards' 'Galloping Horses': Birds (organ
panel)
oil on board 74 x 32
1986.2a

unknown artist
R. Edwards' 'Galloping Horses': Birds (organ
panel)
oil on board 74 x 32
1986.2b

unknown artist
*R. Edwards' 'Galloping Horses': Chariot Race
with Cherubs* (organ panel)
oil on board 45 x 104
1986.2c

unknown artist
*R. Edwards' 'Galloping Horses': Mythological
Scene* (organ panel)
oil on board 50 x 170
1986.2d

Facing page: Wood, Tim G., c.1929–1998, *Dartmouth Castle, Devon*, Britannia Royal Naval College (p. 76)

unknown artist
Spinner Figure, Butterfly
oil on board 46 x 60
L4 (P)

Whiting, Henry 1839–1931
Hatwell's 'Gallopers': Woman Seated in a Tree
(centre panel in the shape of a crown) c.1980
oil on panel 80 x 50
1986.34.1

Whiting, Henry 1839–1931
Hatwell's 'Gallopers': Cowboy Chased by Indians (bottom centre panel)
oil on panel 78 x 61
L39 (P)

Whiting, Henry 1839–1931
Hatwell's 'Gallopers': Fox Hunt (bottom centre panel)
oil on panel 78 x 61
L38 (P)

Whiting, Henry 1839–1931
Hatwell's 'Gallopers': Hippopotamus Hunt (bottom centre panel)
oil on panel 78 x 61
1986.34.13

Whiting, Henry 1839–1931
Hatwell's 'Gallopers': Horse and a Cyclist (bottom centre panel)
oil on panel 78 x 61
1986.34.15

Whiting, Henry 1839–1931
Hatwell's 'Gallopers': Man Wrestling an Alligator (bottom centre panel)
oil on panel 78 x 61
1986.34.11

Whiting, Henry 1839–1931
Hatwell's 'Gallopers': Tiger Hunt (bottom centre panel)
oil on panel 78 x 61
1986.34.16

Whiting, Henry 1839–1931
Hatwell's 'Gallopers': Wild Dogs Attacking Antelope (bottom centre panel)
oil on panel 76 x 61
1986.34.12

Whiting, Henry 1839–1931
Hatwell's 'Gallopers': Wolves Hunting Deer
(bottom centre panel)
oil on panel 78 x 61
1986.34.14

Whiting, Henry (attributed to) 1839–1931
Hatwell's 'Gallopers': Seated Woman with a Cherub (centre panel in the shape of a crown) c.1890
oil on panel 80 x 50
1986.34.9

Whiting, Henry (attributed to) 1839–1931
Hatwell's 'Gallopers': Woman and an Eagle (centre panel in the shape of a crown) c.1890
oil on panel 80 x 50
1986.34.3

Whiting, Henry (attributed to) 1839–1931
Hatwell's 'Gallopers': Woman and Two Cherubs (centre panel in the shape of a crown) c.1890
oil on panel 80 x 50
1986.34.4

Whiting, Henry (attributed to) 1839–1931
Hatwell's 'Gallopers': Woman Holding a Cupid's Arrow (centre panel in the shape of a crown) c.1890
oil on panel 80 x 50
1986.34.8

Whiting, Henry (attributed to) 1839–1931
Hatwell's 'Gallopers': Woman Holding a Fan (centre panel in the shape of a crown) c.1890
oil on panel 80 x 50
1986.34.7

Whiting, Henry (attributed to) 1839–1931
Hatwell's 'Gallopers': Woman Holding a Scythe and a Sheaf of Wheat (centre panel in the shape of a crown) c.1890
oil on panel 80 x 50
1986.34.10

Whiting, Henry (attributed to) 1839–1931
Hatwell's 'Gallopers': Woman in a Green Dress (centre panel in the shape of a crown) c.1890
oil on panel 80 x 50
1986.34.5

Whiting, Henry (attributed to) 1839–1931
Hatwell's 'Gallopers': Woman Playing the Violin (centre panel in the shape of a crown) c.1890
oil on panel 80 x 50
1986.34.6

Whiting, Henry (attributed to) 1839–1931
Hatwell's 'Gallopers': Woman with Cherubs and a Cornucopia (centre panel in the shape of a crown) c.1890
oil on panel 80 x 50
1986.34.2

Wilson, George (Wrexham) 1874– 1944
Tiger and Panther (banner)
oil on canvas 196 x 217 (E)
L16 (P)

Wilson, George (Wrexham) 1874– 1944
Tiger and Snake (banner)
oil on canvas 196 x 217 (E)
L15 (P)

Wright, Paul b.1954
John Walter Shaw's 'Easyrider': Elvis (centre shutter, recto) late 1970s
oil on metal 168 x 51
PCF36 (P)

Wright, Paul b.1954
John Walter Shaw's 'Easyrider': George Michael (centre shutter, verso) late 1970s
oil on metal 168 x 51
PCF96 (P)

Wright, Paul b.1954
John Walter Shaw's 'Easyrider': Madonna (centre shutter, recto) late 1970s
oil on metal 168 x 51
PCF97 (P)

Wright, Paul b.1954
John Walter Shaw's 'Easyrider': Tina Turner (centre shutter, verso) late 1970s
oil on metal 168 x 51
PCF36 (P)

Wright, Paul b.1954
Brett's 'Ghost Train': Skeleton (false pillar) early 1980s
oil on metal 268.7 x 30.7
1994.5.5 (P)

Wright, Paul b.1954
Brett's 'Ghost Train': Skeleton (false pillar) early 1980s
oil on metal 268.7 x 30.7
1994.5.6 (P)

Wright, Paul b.1954
Brett's Ghost Train': Skeleton in Shackles (false
pillar) early 1980s
oil on metal 268.7 x 30.7
1994.5.2 (P)

Wright, Paul b.1954
Brett's Ghost Train': Skeleton in Shackles (false
pillar) early 1980s
oil on metal 268.7 x 30.7
1994.5.4 (P)

Wright, Paul b.1954
Brett's Ghost Train': Vampire (false
pillar) early 1980s
oil on metal 268.7 x 30.7
1994.5.3 (P)

Wright, Paul b.1954
Showman's Guild Showfront (detail) 1989
house paint on board 366 x 2571
1994.26

Wright, Paul b.1954
Caryatid (false pillar) 1990s
oil on board 170 x 40
PCF91 (P)

Wright, Paul b.1954
Thor Holding Lightning Rods
oil on cardboard 85 x 122
PCF19

Wright, Paul b.1954
Thor Power Lightning
oil on cardboard 85 x 122
PCF18

Lynton and Lynmouth Town Council

Calvert, Samuel 1828–1913
Rhenish Tower, Lynmouth, Devon
oil on canvas 39.5 x 54.7
PCF2

Ethelston, Ellen
The Bridge and Part of the Village of Lynmouth, North Devon 1845
oil on canvas 44.5 x 63.6
PCF1

Eves, Reginald Grenville 1876–1941
John Ward Holman, Esq., OBE
oil on canvas 60 x 50
PCF5

Gilson, Marjorie
Queen Elizabeth II (b.1926), Jubilee Year, 1977 1977
acrylic on board 60 x 44.5
PCF8

Lee, Arthur active mid-19th C
Rhenish Tower, Lynmouth, Devon
oil on canvas 39.7 x 60
PCF3

Schofield, John William 1865–1944
Lieutenant Colonel W. W. Lean, Fifth Bengal Cavalry 1903
oil on canvas 206 x 98
PCF7

unknown artist
Stag 1888
oil on canvas 126.5 x 102
PCF6

unknown artist
Castle Rock, Lynton, Devon
oil on canvas 83 x 128.7
PCF12

unknown artist
Lady Fanny Hewitt
oil on canvas 73 x 60 (E)
PCF9 (P)

unknown artist
Lynmouth Harbour, Devon
oil on canvas 59.8 x 90.3
PCF4

unknown artist
Lynmouth Harbour, Devon
oil on canvas 86.5 x 106 (E)
PCF13

unknown artist
Sir Thomas Hewitt
oil on canvas 84 x 68 (E)
PCF10 (P)

unknown artist
Vellacott Pool on the East Lyn
oil on canvas 89.5 x 117 (E)
PCF11

Moretonhamp-
stead Hospital

Wiley, R. D.
Summer Flowers
oil on board 50 x 39.5
PCF1

Moretonhamp-
stead Library

Dover, J.
George Parker Bidder (1806–1878) 1864
oil on canvas 148.6 x 113
PCF2

unknown artist
Sir Thomas B. Bowring (1847–1915)
oil on canvas 101.5 x 79
PCF1

Ball Clay Heritage
Society

Cox, Frederick C. B. b.1939
*Inclined Shaft, Ball Clay Mining, Peters
Marland, North Devon* 1981
oil on canvas 49 x 75
PCF3

Cox, Frederick C. B. b.1939
Ball Clay Mining, Kingsteignton, Devon 1995
oil on canvas 49 x 75
PCF1

Cox, Frederick C. B. b.1939
Ball Clay Mining, Kingsteignton, Devon 1995
oil on canvas 49 x 75
PCF2

Facing page: Beechey, William, 1753–1839, *Frederick Hodgson, Esq. (d.1854)*, Barnstaple Town Council (p. 14)

Ilford Park Polish Home

Cymbrykiewicz, Maria 1910–2005
The Blessed Sacrament 1997
oil on board 76 x 50
PCF3

Cymbrykiewicz, Maria 1910–2005
*The Immaculate Conception of the Blessed
Virgin Mary* 1997
oil on board 75 x 62
PCF4

Dobrawolska
Icon of the Blessed Virgin
oil on canvas 44 x 34
PCF2

Sobkowiak-Mozdzer, Emilia
The Deposition of Christ 1993
oil on canvas 49 x 99
PCF5

unknown artist
Christ Blessing
oil on board 75 x 62
PCF1

unknown artist
Christ Preaching
oil on canvas 79 x 80
PCF6

unknown artist
Polish Man in Traditional Highland Dress
oil on black fabric 67 x 41
PCF7

unknown artist
Polish Woman in Traditional Highland Dress
oil on black fabric 67 x 41
PCF8

Newton Abbot Town & GWR Museum

The Newton Abbot Town & GWR Museum has a small painting collection which reflects the growth and importance of the town and its light industries from the late 1800s.

In 1928 Sydney Hacker, Chairman of the Newton Abbot Urban District Council, donated a large oil painting by his brother Arthur Hacker (1858–1919) a prominent British artist, entitled *The Hours*. The subjects of the painting were 'The Hours' the daughters of Zeus and Themis. They were named Eunomia (Order), Dice (Justice) and Eirene (Peace).

Sydney Hacker's intention was that a public gallery should be established in the town. The painting was hung together with others given to the town in the Lecture Room of the Library (Reference: *Devon and Newton Times*, 9th March 1929). The proposed gallery was never built and the paintings were eventually donated to the Museum in 1988. The Museum has continued to accept paintings that fall into the Museum collections policy: paintings that reflect the history of the town and the Great Western Railway.

Felicity Cole, Curator

Armfield, George 1810–1893
A Spaniel and a Terrier
oil on canvas 30 x 35
1988.139

Armfield, George 1810–1893
Terriers Ratting
oil on canvas 30 x 35
1988.131

Cox, Frederick C. B. b.1939
Departure to Plymouth, Devon 1985
acrylic on canvas 69.5 x 120
PCF8

Gaunt, Ray
Supermarine Spitfire P8655 'Newtonia'
acrylic on board 49.8 x 39.5
PCF2

Hacker, Arthur 1858–1919
The Hours 1906
oil on canvas 123.5 x 213.5
1997.134

Hall, Gordon
Dartmoor Granite Railway at Haytor, Devon 2000
acrylic on board 45.1 x 60
PCF1

Houghton, Ruth
Familiar Ways, Newton Abbot, Devon 1970s
oil on board 49 x 64.2
2004.96

Price, C.
Great Western 1, The Early Years (1840–1902) 1985
oil on board 61 x 81.2
PCF6

Price, C.
Great Western 2, Churchward (1902–1921) 1985
oil on board 61 x 81.2
PCF5

Price, C.
Great Western 3, Zenith (1921–1949) 1985
oil on board 61 x 81.2
PCF4

Price, C.
Great Western 4, Modern Times (1950–1985) 1985
oil on board 61 x 81.2
PCF3

Rhys, Oliver b.c.1858
A Cavalry Camp
oil on copper 18.5 x 15
1988.134

Stacey, Walter Sydney 1846–1929
St Peter's Church, Tiverton, Devon
oil on canvas 58.5 x 48.5
1988.14

Tyler, L. M.
St Mary's Parish Church, Wolborough, Devon
oil on canvas 31.4 x 44
1988.142

Newton Abbot Town Council

Lawrence, David
Synchro Pain and Caterpillar Loop
acrylic on board 39 x 59.5
PCF2

Members of the Newton Abbot Women's Institute
Parish Map
pearlescent acrylic on paper 91
PCF5

Smith, Keith A.
The Clock Tower, Newton Abbot, Devon
oil on board 37.4 x 27.8
PCF1

Stacey, Walter Sydney 1846–1929
Rough Courting 1884
oil on canvas 111 x 87.5
PCF3

Whitehead, Frederick William Newton 1853–1938
Cattle in a Country Lane at Kenilworth, Warwickshire
oil on canvas 30.5 x 46
PCF4

Teignbridge
District Council

Carter, Ken active 1986–1987
Estuary View 1986
oil on board 11.5 x 15.5
PCF15

Carter, Ken active 1986–1987
Exe Scene I 1986
oil on board 11.6 x 17.8
PCF11

Carter, Ken active 1986–1987
Exe Scene III 1986
oil on board 13.1 x 20
PCF13

Carter, Ken active 1986–1987
Haldon Moor, Teignmouth, Devon 1986
oil on board 15.7 x 21.5
PCF14

Carter, Ken active 1986–1987
Exe Scene II Sunset 1987
oil on board 21.5 x 20
PCF12

Cotton, Alan b.1938
*Golden Harvest Landscape, near Gordes,
Provence, France* 1989
oil on canvas 59.5 x 74.7
PCF10

Green, John
*Charles I (1600–1649) (after Gerrit van
Honthorst)* 1997
oil on canvas 66 x 50
PCF2

Holden, M. G.
Forde House, Newton Abbot, Devon 2001
acrylic on board 34 x 44.4
PCF3

Holden, M. G.
Charles I (1600–1649)
acrylic on board 38.5 x 28
PCF4

Jansch, Heather b.1948
Out of a Winter Sea 1990
oil, driftwood & wire on board 128.8 x 153
PCF6

Lloyd, Reginald James b.1926
Dawlish Warren I, Devon 1989
oil on board 61.5 x 69.5
PCF7

Lloyd, Reginald James b.1926
Dawlish Warren II, Devon 1989
oil on board 61.5 x 69.5
PCF8

Lloyd, Reginald James b.1926
Haytor Quarry, Dartmoor, Devon 1989
oil on canvas 61.5 x 69.5
PCF9

Salisbury, Frank O. 1874–1962
*Lady Gertrude E. Smith (Lady Ben), Member
of Newton Abbot Rural District Council
(1965–1975)*
oil on canvas 74.5 x 62.5
PCF5

unknown artist
Portrait of a Gentleman
oil on canvas 139 x 119.5
PCF1

Museum of Dartmoor Life, Okehampton

Holding, Emmanuel (attributed to)
Okehampton with a View of the Parish Church of All Saints' 1880s
oil on canvas 70 x 105 (E)
PCF2

Widgery, Frederick John 1861–1942
In the Gorge, Lydford, Devon
oil on canvas 69 x 103
PCF1 (P)

Okehampton Town Council

Ash, Thomas Morris 1851–1935
From Box Hill, Surrey
oil on canvas 38 x 60.5
PCF6

Barrett, John 1822–1893
Wooded Vale
oil on canvas 30.5 x 44
PCF16

Crayer, Gaspar de (attributed to) 1584–1669
Memento mori
oil on panel 97.4 x 56.2
PCF10

Heem, Cornelis de 1631–1695
Still Life with Grapes, Peaches and a Bohemian Glass Goblet
oil on canvas 62.2 x 75
PCF7

Herring, John Frederick I (style of) 1795–1865
Farmyard
oil on canvas 55 x 82.5
PCF4

Kurzweil, T.
Good Morning
oil on canvas 111.5 x 81
PCF8

Leader, Benjamin Williams 1831–1923
Riverside Cottages at Dusk 1887
oil on canvas 51 x 76
PCF3

Linnell, James Thomas 1826–1905
Thro' the Fields , a Landscape at Harvest Time 1869
oil on canvas 53 x 75
PCF5

Russ II, Franz 1844–1906
Young Girl Holding a Spray of Jasmine 1886
oil on panel 49.3 x 38.7
PCF14

Sinoir, M.
Bridge Scene
oil on canvas 32.2 x 44.5
PCF15

Widgery, Frederick John 1861–1942
Okehampton Castle, Devon
oil on canvas 74.4 x 105.2
PCF2

Widgery, William 1822–1893
A Boy by a Rocky Wooded Stream
oil on canvas 59.7 x 89.6
PCF1

Widgery, William 1822–1893
A Bridge over a Dartmoor Stream
oil on canvas 44.8 x 29.8
PCF9

Woodville, Richard Caton 1856–1927
A Cavalry Charge 1892
oil on panel 40 x 31.2
PCF13

Woodville, Richard Caton 1856–1927
Napolean and His Marshals Watching a Battle 1892
oil on panel 34.7 x 26.3
PCF11

Woodville, Richard Caton 1856–1927
Saladin's Cavalry Charging the Crusaders 1892
oil on panel 44 x 36.5
PCF12

Ottery St Mary Hospital

Entwhistle, Tom
Boats on a Beach 1996
oil on canvas 29.5 x 40
PCF2

Wilkins, Julie
West Hill from East Hill Garden
oil on board 39 x 49
PCF1

Dartmoor Prison Museum

These few paintings that we have here in our Museum are small in number compared to the total that must have been created over the 200 years of this Prison's existence and, certainly, during the period since 1850. We have little idea of how many remain or where they may be.

Brian Dingle, Curator

Facing page: Larivière, Charles Philippe Auguste de, 1798–1876, *The Prisoner (The Refugee)*, Royal Albert Memorial Museum (p. 143)

L. B.
Windmill 1972
oil on board 59 x 75.5
PCF9

Coles, E. P. active 1969–1970
French Prisoners of War Being Transported
across the Moors on the 24 May, 1809 1969
oil on board 90 x 180.5
PCF6

Coles, E. P. active 1969–1970
The Prison Hulks, Devonport, Devon 1970
oil on board 90 x 180
PCF7

Coles, E. P. active 1969–1970
Market Square, Dartmoor Prisoner of War
Depot
oil on board 86 x 175
PCF2

Duckett, Lewis 1892–1977
Mounted Prison Patrol Officer on Dartmoor
oil on board 56 x 83.4
PCF8

unknown artist
Dartmoor Prison
oil on board 81 x 102
PCF1

Wanmantle, James
My Lord and My God 1954
oil on slate flooring slab 132.2 x 99.7
PCF3

Wanmantle, James
The Last Supper 1954
oil on slate flooring slab 127 x 196.5
PCF4

Wanmantle, James
Thou Art the Christ, the Son of the Living
God 1954
oil on slate flooring slab 132.1 x 100.2
PCF5

Seaton Hospital

Fletcher, Mollie
Gladioli
oil on board 68 x 35.6
PCF3

Knightly, L. M. (Mrs)
Farningham Mill, Kent
oil on board 48.7 x 97.3
PCF5

Knightly, L. M. (Mrs)
St Michael's Mount, Cornwall
oil on board 59.5 x 90
PCF4

Neale, George Hall 1863–1940
Portrait of a Doctor's Wife
oil on canvas 116.5 x 86.5
PCF1

Page, Will
Devon Coast
oil on board 49 x 74.5
PCF8

Robertson, Kit b.1915
In the Hedgerow
oil on board 43.2 x 32.5
PCF6

unknown artist
Stream
oil on board 44 x 55
PCF7

Wilde, Ron
Rain Approaching Axmouth 1988
oil on board 69.5 x 89
PCF2

Sidmouth Museum

Sidmouth Museum, Devon is a small independent Museum staffed by volunteers. As such it is part of the Sid Vale Association, the first civic society in Britain, which was founded in 1846. The Museum is fully accredited by the Museums, Libraries and Archives Council.

Housed in Hope Cottage, alongside the Parish Church, the Museum plays a major role in the interpretation of the local history of Sidmouth and the Sid Valley. Recently, the Museum has come to provide a centre for the understanding of the Jurassic Coast World Heritage Site.

The collections are particularly rich in artefacts relating to the growth of the town from a small fishing village to Regency splendour and Victorian establishment. There are, therefore, extensive collections of early newspapers, late nineteenth-century photographs, lace, local ephemera and more.

The art collection consists of several works by artists of the Victorian age. These mostly depict views of the surrounding countryside and the stunning cliff scenery. Worthy of mention is *Sidmouth Beach and Cliffs, Devon* by Hopkins Horsley Hobday Horsley (1807–1890). A major project is in currently underway studying the watercolours of the Victorian antiquary Peter Orlando Hutchinson.

At present, we have a policy of adding paintings by local, modern artists so our holdings have been considerably strengthened. A secondary acquisition policy involves adding paintings showing views and features of the Jurassic Coast. As a small museum with a limited budget, the art collection grows slowly mostly through donations but some purchases are made, usually through auction.

Dr Robert Symes, OBE, Honorary Curator

Adams, Margaret
That Was the Coastal Path!
acrylic on board 60 x 45
2007–148

Allinson, Adrian Paul 1890–1959
Geranium Plant (Painted from the Ground Floor of No.9 Fortfield Terrace)
oil on canvas 60 x 51
2007–149

Antony
Looking over High Peak, Sidmouth, Devon
oil on canvas 39.1 x 29
PCF14

Dorrington, Edna b.1934
Monmouth Beach, Lyme Regis
acrylic on paper 29 x 38
2007–279

Dunning, John Thomson 1851–1931
*Clifton Place Cottages, Sidmouth,
Devon* before 1902
oil on canvas 30.8 x 51
2007–91

Horsley, Hopkins Horsley Hobday 1807–
1890
Sidmouth Beach and Cliffs, Devon 1880
oil on canvas 45 x 55 (E)
PCF4

Horsley, Hopkins Horsley Hobday 1807–
1890
The Belmont, Sidmouth Seafront, Devon
oil on panel 39 x 61.7
PCF1

Horsley, Hopkins Horsley Hobday 1807–
1890
Sidmouth from Salcombe Hill, Devon
oil on canvas 39 x 61.7
PCF2

Leask, William 1892–1977
Fisherman's Beacon, Sidmouth, Devon 1945–
1949
oil on board 67.2 x 52.5
1994–173

Moysey, Kathleen
Jim Smith c.1965
oil on canvas 51.1 x 35.7
2007–81

Sweetapple, E. F.
The 'Duchess of Devonshire' 1993
oil on board 34.5 x 24
PCF5

Tucker, John Wallace 1808–1869
*Sidmouth Harbour, Devon (Clifton
Beach)* 1840
oil on panel 14.5 x 19.7
2005–260

unknown artist
Bob Wooley, a Sidmouth Fisherman
oil on canvas 35 x 29
1977–506

unknown artist
Mouth of the Sid, Devon
oil on canvas 84 x 127.8 (E)
PCF3

unknown artist
Toll Gate, Sidmouth, Devon
oil on canvas 24.6 x 39.7
2007–97

White, Gerald Ewart b.1932
Standing Stones on Mutter's Moor, Sidmouth, Devon 2003
oil on hardboard 55.3 x 75
2009–168

Woodley, Maureen
Hope Cottage, Sidmouth, Devon (Sidmouth Museum)
acrylic on board 44.5 x 60.5
2007–108

Sidmouth Victoria Hospital

Firth, Irene
Sidmouth Cliffs Looking East, Devon
oil on board 34 x 44.7
PCF2

Macfadyan, Evan
Still Life with Flowers 1980
acrylic on board 64.2 x 49.1
PCF1

Tavistock Subscription Library

unknown artist
John Commins (1776–1859)
oil on canvas 70 x 54.5
PCF1

unknown artist
John Russell (1766–1839), 6th Duke of Bedford
oil on canvas 75.2 x 62
PCF2

unknown artist
*The Original Tavistock Subscription Library,
Devon (also known as 'The Propylaeum')*
oil on canvas 42 x 52
PCF3

Tavistock Town Hall

Over the years there have been many who, attending a function in the Town Hall, felt themselves to be under inspection from at least one of the pairs of eyes that gaze down from the walls. Nineteen heads keep a constant vigil, and they exercise restraint under the most provocative of circumstances (though some claim to have seen movement at the end of a long civic ball). They all, of course, commemorate men and women with local connections.

Only two portraits, *Sir Francis Drake (1540–1596)* and *John Pym (1584–1643)*, both by Lady Arthur Russell, depict sitters who could be said to have played a major part in English history, although at least two others made a significant impact at national level in their own times. Seven of the portraits are members of the Russell family. No fewer than 13, including four of the Russells, represented Tavistock in Parliament. Their lives cover a period from the fifteenth to the twentieth century. Only two are women, and they married

Russells. One of these, painted by an unknown artist, is the lady to whom we owe the bulk of the collection. Lady Laura Russell painted 10 of the 19 portraits. But for her skill and generosity we would not have what the Town Hall provides; a portrait gallery that tells us so much about 500 years of our history.

G. Woodcock, Historian

Croft, M. D.
Town Criers 2001
oil on canvas 50 x 75
PCF18

Hawkins, Jane
Lady Laura Russell (c.1850–1910)
oil on canvas 74 x 55
PCF11

Lane, F.
Hugh Fownes-Luttrell (1857–1918), MP for Tavistock (1892–1900 & 1906–1910)
oil on canvas 83 x 60 (E)
PCF5

Lane, F.
John Hornbrook Gill (1787–1874)
oil on canvas 128 x 103
PCF10

Prynne, Edward A. Fellowes 1854–1921
John Ward Spear (1848–1921), MP for Tavistock (1900–1906 & 1910–1918)
oil on canvas 235 x 125 (E)
PCF3

Read, Arthur James 1932–2006
Tavistock Town Hall, Devon
acrylic on canvas 90 x 121
PCF17

Facing page: Poynter, Edward John, 1836–1919, *Diadumene*, 1883, Royal Albert Memorial Museum (p. 152)

Russell, Laura c.1850–1910
*John Pym (1584–1643), MP for Tavistock
(1624–1643) (after Cornelis Janssens van
Ceulen)* 1866
oil on canvas 103 x 84
PCF12

Russell, Laura c.1850–1910
Sir Francis Drake (1540–1596) 1867
oil on canvas 103.5 x 78.4
PCF15

Russell, Laura c.1850–1910
Colonel John Russell (1618–1687)
oil on canvas 90 x 70
PCF8

Russell, Laura c.1850–1910
*Elizabeth Keppell (1739–1768), Marchioness of
Tavistock (copy of Thomas Gainborough)*
oil on canvas 80 x 60 (E)
PCF16

Russell, Laura c.1850–1910
*Francis Russell (1788–1861), 7th Duke of
Bedford*
oil on canvas 130 x 100
PCF9

Russell, Laura c.1850–1910
*George Byng (1830–1898), Viscount Enfield,
MP for Tavistock (1852–1857)*
oil on canvas 79 x 70
PCF13

Russell, Laura c.1850–1910
John Russell (1710–1771), 4th Duke of Bedford
oil on canvas 112 x 77 (E)
PCF4

Russell, Laura c.1850–1910
John Russell (1766–1839), 6th Duke of Bedford
oil on canvas 76 x 61
PCF14

Russell, Laura c.1850–1910
*Sir John Trelaway (1816–1885), MP for
Tavistock (1843–1852 & 1857–1865)*
oil on canvas 92 x 72 (E)
PCF1

Russell, Laura c.1850–1910
William Lord Russell (1639–1683)
91 x 70
PCF21

unknown artist
*John Rundle (1791–1864), MP for Tavistock
(1835–1843)* 1856
oil on canvas 135 x 105 (E)
PCF2

unknown artist
Alfred Rooker (1814–1875)
oil on canvas 87 x 70
PCF7

unknown artist
Portrait of a Gentleman
oil on canvas 73 x 60
PCF19

unknown artist
Portrait of a Gentleman
oil on canvas 74 x 61
PCF20

unknown artist
Sir Richard Edgcumbe (1440–1489)
oil on canvas 90 x 60 (E)
PCF6

Teignmouth &
Shaldon Museum:
Teign Heritage

Armstrong, Thomas 1832–1911
The Ness, Teignmouth, Devon 1904
oil on canvas 36 x 49
TEGNM.2072

Chatfield, Donald Graham 1933–2007
*Fokke Wulfe German Aircraft Approaching
Teignmouth* 1976
oil on canvas 30 x 45
TEGNM.1369

Francis, B.
The Newquay Inn
oil on board 32 x 47
TEGNM.879

Lawrence, Thomas 1769–1830
The Right Honourable Edward Pellew
(1757–1833), 1st Viscount Exmouth, Vice-
Admiral of England 1818
oil on canvas 125 x 110
TEGNM.2152 (P)

Luny, Thomas 1759–1837
Teignmouth Beach and Ness Point,
Devon 1829
oil on panel 28.5 x 39
TEGNM.1178

Luny, Thomas (circle of) 1759–1837
Teignmouth Regatta, Devon
oil on canvas 29 x 48.5
TEGNM.1740

Teignmouth Town Council

Egginton, Wycliffe 1875–1951
Autumn Splendour
oil on canvas 135.8 x 181.4
PCF5

Haywood, Michael Graham b.1950
Admiral Sir Edward Pellew (1757–1833), 1st
Viscount Exmouth (after Samuel Drummond)
oil on canvas 75 x 59.5
PCF10

Huggins, William John 1781–1845
*HMS 'Indefatigable' Accompanied by HM
'Amazon' Attacking the French Ship 'Les droits
des hommes'*
oil on canvas 58.6 x 89.3
PCF2

Loos, John Frederick active 1861–1902
The Barque 'Eldra' 1902
oil on canvas 62 x 75.7
PCF8

Luny, Thomas 1759–1837
Off Dartmouth, Devon 1821
oil on panel 28.4 x 39
PCF4

Luny, Thomas 1759–1837
Shipwreck at Teignmouth, Devon 1825
oil on canvas 60 x 85.5
PCF9

Luny, Thomas 1759–1837
*Figures on a Beach Unloading Barrels from a
Small Boat* 1828
oil on panel 24.4 x 34.5
PCF6

Luny, Thomas 1759–1837
Fishing Boats in Teignmouth Harbour, Devon
oil on canvas 58.7 x 84.3
PCF1

Luny, Thomas (attributed to) 1759–1837
Self Portrait
oil on canvas 59 x 48.4
PCF7

Moyle, J. Alfred active late 19th C
Tol-Pedn-Penwith, Porthgwarra, Cornwall
oil on canvas 152 x 121.2
PCF11

Walter, Joseph (style of) 1783–1856
The 'Eliza' of Teignmouth in an Open Sea
oil on canvas 39.4 x 54.3
PCF3

Anglo-Polish Organisation

The Anglo-Polish Organisation was created in 2007 to support the Polish community, promote Polish culture and preserve its heritage in Devon. We run regular drop-in surgeries for practical support, develop education materials for schools, organise social events and activities and have started up a small subscription library.

The members of the management committee, as well as being keen to support new Polish arrivals to the UK, have always been interested in the rich and influential Polish heritage of Devon, which put down its roots here during the Second World War. It was during this period that many Polish men and women came to Britain to fight alongside Allied forces in the war against Germany. Unable, or unwilling, to return to Poland under communist rule after the war, thousands of displaced Poles established themselves in resettlement camps around Britain. One of those camps was Stover Camp outside Newton Abbot in Devon.

Stover Camp was the last Polish Resettlement Camp in Britain to close in 1992. Its aging community were relocated to Ilford Park Polish Home, a purpose built accommodation adjacent to the camp, and whose paintings, some by its former residents, also appear in this catalogue. The seventeen-acre Stover Camp site was left to fall into dereliction until it was finally demolished in January 2010. Prior to the removal of the 30 plus buildings, however, members of the Anglo-Polish Organisation, having received permission from Gilpin Demolition, went on to the site to salvage the papers and artefacts left behind by its former residents.

The artefacts, books and documents they salvaged form an important repository of information that goes some way to preserve the rich heritage of the Polish people of Devon that would otherwise have been lost. The eight, charming, hand-made folk paintings in this collection were among the items salvaged from the floor of one of the buildings at Stover Camp. Meticulously and lovingly made they preserve a piece of Polish folk art tradition that lives on in Devon through the Polish community that has arrived recently. These are joined by a more recent painting, *Krakow Market, Poland*, by an unknown artist, a gift to the organisation that brightens our Tiverton offices.

Przemek Jonczyk and Caroline Nicholson, Joint Directors

K., D. active 2005
Krakow Market, Poland 2005
oil on canvas 22 x 27.3
APL_010

unknown artist
Folk Painting with Birds
ink and tempera on paper 14 x 8.5
APL_003

unknown artist
Folk Painting with Cockerels
tempera on paper 9 x 14
APL_006

unknown artist
Folk Painting with Deer
tempera on paper 14 x 9
APL_007

unknown artist
Folk Painting with Flowers
ink and tempera on paper 9.5 x 13.7
APL_001

unknown artist
Folk Painting with Flowers
tempera on paper 14 x 9
APL_004

unknown artist
Folk Painting with Flowers
ink and tempera on paper 12 x 8.5
APL_008

unknown artist
Folk Painting with Flowers
ink & tempera on paper 14 x 9
APL009

unknown artist
Folk Painting with Sunflowers
tempera on paper 8.5 x 14
APL_005

Tiverton Museum of Mid Devon Life

Armstrong, Gordon
The Angel Hotel, the Square, Witheridge, Devon (painted in Starkey, Knight and Ford colours) 1968
oil on board 34.4 x 44.5
2006.57

Day, George
Thomas Gamlen, Esq. (1759–1835), of Hayne (copy of an original painting by Ayerst) 1909
oil on canvas 55 x 46
1987.739.1

Greenhalgh, Stephanie
Mr James Mclachlan, Former Honorary President of Tiverton Museum (d.1998)
oil on paper 74.3 x 49.7
1999.39.1a-b

Hudson (Mrs)
G. C. Greenway 1822
oil on canvas 74.5 x 60.5
1988.863.12

Palce, John
Portrait of a Man (said to be the last of the woolen weavers of Tiverton) 1661
oil on panel 18.9 x 13.5
1977.347

Pembrey, R. G.
View of Collipriest Walk and a Bridge over a River, Tiverton, Devon 1957
oil on canvas 44 x 32
1985.278

unknown artist
'Glory', Devon Longwool Ram 1854
oil on canvas 53.3 x 64
1977.1132

unknown artist
'Matchless' 1859
oil on canvas 49 x 59.3
1977.1131

unknown artist
15lb Pike Caught in Tiverton Canal in 1905
oil on canvas 35 x 118.4
1988.849.6

unknown artist
22lb Pike Caught in Tiverton Canal in 1906
oil on canvas 55.8 x 125
1988.849.3

Wannell, F.
Tiverton Railway Station, Devon
acrylic on board 35 x 50
1988.1183

Weatherley, Dudley Graham 1912–2004
*The Grand Western Canal at Snake
Wood* c.1982
oil on board 39.8 x 49.8
1999.137a-c

Weatherley, Dudley Graham 1912–2004
*Panoramic View of Tiverton, Devon, Seen from
the High Ground at Ashley, Showing the River
Exe and Local Landmarks* 1985
oil on canvas 81.3 x 119.5
2001.12 (P)

Wickham, Peter 1934–2009
Tiverton Townscape, Devon 1993–1995
acrylic, gouache & collage on board 27 x 37.5
1998.132.2.a-b

Woolnar, John
*Derick Heathcoat-Amory (1899–1981), 1st
Viscount Amory* 1979
oil on canvas 45.6 x 35.4
1988.1090.6

Woolnar, John
*John Heathcoat-Amory (1829–1914), 1st
Bt* 1979
oil on canvas 45.5 x 35
1988.1090.4

Tiverton Town Hall

Tiverton Town Hall was designed by Henry Lloyd, who also designed Exeter St David's railway station. It was built by Samuel Garth, who was Mayor of Tiverton from 1861 to 1862, and was opened in May 1864. Some of the paintings in the Town Hall, however, are far older than the building. Many of these would have also been displayed in the Guildhall, which was demolished to allow the present building to be erected.

Of the pictures on display, one is *Henry John Temple (1784–1865), 3rd Viscount Palmerston, KG, GCB, PC, Prime Minister (1835–1865)* by William Thomas Roden. Palmerston was one of the two MPs for the area. He was the first Liberal Prime Minister and indeed was Prime Minister when the building was opened. For many years there was a hotel in Fore Street in Tiverton which carried his name.

In the Mayoralty Room is *Sir John Heathcoat, Esq., JP, MP for Tiverton (1832–1959)*, painted by an unknown artist. At the age of 32 he bought a redundant mill in the town and set up the Heathcoat Lace Factory. This was to be one of the most significant events in the town's history. As John Heathcoat prospered so did Tiverton. Many of the houses in the area were built by Heathcoat for his workers and he even built a school so that when the young people came to work in the factory they were able to read and write. There are a number of pictures of the Heathcoat-Amory family on the walls of the Town Hall.

Sir Joshua Reynolds' painting *George III (1738–1820)* takes pride of place, looking over those who attend meetings and functions in the Mayoralty Room. Also displayed in this room are pictures of two ships with strong links to the town: *HMS 'Hermes' after Conversion to Commando Carrier and Anti-Submarine Helicopter Ship* is by John Webster; *HMS 'Enterprise'*, is executed in watercolour and so is not reproduced here. HMS *Hermes* was a sister ship to HMS *Ark Royal* and was given the Freedom of Tiverton. When the ship was decommissioned, its bell was presented to the Council and now sits in the Mayoralty Room. In more recent times, HMS *Enterprise*, built in Appledore and based in Plymouth, was also given the Freedom of Tiverton.

John Vanderwolfe, Town Clerk

Facing page: Reynolds, Joshua, 1723–1792, *George III (1738–1820)*, Tiverton Town Hall (p. 294)

Eastman, Mary b.1921
*Sir Derick Heathcoat-Amory (1899–1981), 4th
Bt, Viscount Amory* 1965
oil on canvas 90 x 70
PCF13

Eastman, Mary b.1921
*Sir John Heathcoat-Amory (1894–1972), 3rd
Bt* 1965
oil on canvas 90 x 70
PCF14

Kneller, Godfrey (after) 1646–1723
George I (1720–1727)
oil on canvas 214 x 153
PCF9

Mercier, Charles 1834–1909
*Right Honourable W. N. Massey, MP for
Tiverton (1872–1880)*
oil on canvas 189 x 143 (E)
PCF1

Ramsay, Allan 1713–1784
*George III (1738–1820) (when Prince
Regent)* c.1780
oil on canvas 74 x 60 (E)
PCF4

Reynolds, Joshua 1723–1792
George III (1738–1820)
oil on canvas 77 x 64
PCF8

Roden, William Thomas 1817–1892
*Henry John Temple (1784–1865), 3rd Viscount
Palmerston, KG, GCB, PC, Prime Minister
(1835–1865)*
oil on canvas 214 x 153
PCF10

unknown artist
Portrait of a Gentleman c.1770
oil on board 75 x 62 (E)
PCF5

unknown artist
Portrait of a Gentleman c.1800
oil on canvas 170 x 130 (E)
PCF3

unknown artist
Francis Hole, Esq., JP, Mayor of Tiverton
oil on canvas 140 x 110
PCF17

unknown artist
George II (1727–1760)
oil on canvas 75 x 62
PCF16

unknown artist
George W. Cockram, JP, Mayor of Tiverton (1875–1877)
oil on canvas 101 x 85
PCF11

unknown artist
Sir John Heathcoat, Esq., JP, MP for Tiverton (1832–1959)
oil on canvas 143 x 120
PCF6

unknown artist
Sir John Heathcoat-Amory (1829–1914), Bt, MP for Tiverton (1868–1885)
oil on canvas 200 x 130 (E)
PCF2

unknown artist
Thomas Ford, JP, Mayor of Tiverton (1881–1883)
oil on canvas 101 x 95
PCF7

unknown artist
William Hornsey Gamlen, Esq., of Hayne Aged 29, Mayor of Tiverton (1843–1844)
oil on canvas 60 x 50
PCF15

Webster, John b.1932
HMS 'Hermes' after Conversion to a Commando Carrier and an Anti-Submarine Helicopter Ship 1973
oil on canvas 39 x 59
PCF12

Topsham Museum

Miss Dorothy Holman (1888–1983) created a very personal museum for Topsham in 1967 in the sail loft at the rear of her home. The Museum gathered together a collection of objects relating to her great-grandfather, who owned important sailing shipyards in the port of Topsham, as well as many items belonging to Topsham's maritime history. In her will, she left the whole property to continue as a more extensive museum for Topsham and expressed her hope that the house itself would be used to demonstrate the home of a Topsham seafaring family.

The Museum is fully accredited by the Museums, Libraries and Archives Council and managed by the Topsham Museum Society, whose purpose is to enable the public to explore the history of Topsham and the Exe Estuary and to experience a typical Topsham merchant's house of 1680–1750. Since 1986, the Society has acquired more works, including some with the assistance of the Art Fund.

As well as paintings of Topsham and the Exe Estuary in various media, the collections include a representative selection of works by artists who lived and worked in the communities bounding the estuary. Portraits of members of significant Topsham families, and vessels that were built in Topsham shipyards, or owned by Topsham families, also form part of the collection.

Rachel Nichols, Volunteer Collections Manager

Boyle, Geraldine Lilian (attributed to) 1899–1992
Portrait of a Man in a Green Jacket over a Pullover 1973
oil on board 49.5 x 39.5
1512

Brice, Henry c.1831–1903
Jane Bramah Popham (1841–1874) 1874
oil on canvas 110 x 85
2977

Croos, Pieter van der (school of) 1609–1701
River Landscape with Travellers near a Wood 17th C
oil on canvas 46 x 64
4023

Cullin, E. M.
George Henry Voysey (1902–1975), a Topsham Fisherman
oil on board 35 x 25
2698

Elliott, Robinson 1814–1894
Francis Robert Newton Haswell (1834–1912) and Eleanor Mary Haswell (1837–1917), later Holman 1844
oil on canvas 59.4 x 49.4
3010

Harding, Sophie 1902–1995
Dorothy Holman (1888–1983), Founder of Topsham Museum 1980s
oil on canvas 49 x 39
2565

Harding, Sophie 1902–1995
Morice Parsons (1913–1998) c.1991
oil on board 48 x 38
2948.1

Hiscocks, John
Tom Putt Apples
acrylic on board 12.6 x 16.3
7410

Holman, Dorothy A. 1888–1983
Mrs Sophia Hawkes Holman, née Andrew (1863–1928), Lady in an Armchair
oil on canvas 50 x 39
3121

Holman, Dorothy A. 1888–1983
Welsh Pony 'Bessie'
oil on canvas 39.3 x 49.5
3029

Hughes, Nathaniel John Baird 1865–1936
Mrs Sophia Hawkes Holman, née Andrew (1863–1928), Lady in a Red Dress
oil on canvas 110 x 83
3030

King, Christopher active 1987
Three Tom Putt Apples
oil on board 16 x 21
2105

Reynolds, Joshua (copy after) 1723–1792
Nativity Scene
oil on canvas 92 x 62
869

Simmonds-Roads, Juliette 1900–1995
Roofs of Topsham, Devon
oil on board 33 x 43
133

unknown artist
Barque 'Hugh Fortescue', Built in Topsham in 1865 by John Holman & Sons for the China Trade 1866
oil on board 45 x 58
108

unknown artist
Steamship 'Sam Handford' 1897 (?)
oil on canvas 60 x 90
2146.1

unknown artist mid 19th C
John Westcott (c.1794–1878), Shapter St Gardens, Grower of Excelsior Strawberry
oil on board 71 x 51
186

unknown artist
Screw-Powered Schooner 'City of Exeter', Built in 1870 for John Holman and Sons
oil on canvas 60 x 95.5
109

unknown artist
Thomas Andrew (1831–1902), Maternal Grandfather of Dorothy Holman
oil on canvas 34 x 27
3171

Voysey, Eric b.1930
Fast and Free
oil on board 59 x 75
227

Totnes
Elizabethan
House Museum

Barker, Benjamin II 1776–1838
Town Mills, Totnes, Devon 1827
oil on canvas 26.6 x 34.7
PCF5

Clark, A.
'Phantom' 1855
oil on canvas 49.3 x 59
TOTEH1963.111

Hendry, William Leslie 1891–1981
Totnes, Devon, Goes Elizabethan c.1971
acrylic on board 49 x 59
PCF6

Hilliard, Nicholas 1537–1619
Christopher Wise (c.1566–1628), Mayor of Totnes (1605 & 1621)
oil on canvas 112.5 x 87
TOTEH1963.128

King, Edward R. 1863–after 1924
River Dart 1922
oil on board 34.5 x 51.8
TOTEH1983.024

Maclagan, Philip Douglas 1901–1972
View from Shell Field, Totnes, Devon 1972
oil on board 34.4 x 44.2
PCF1

Morgan, T.
Rosina, Mrs W. Cole
acrylic on canvas 45.7 x 30.5
TOTEH2004.013

Morgan, T. C.
Totnes House, Devon
oil on board 37 x 51.5
TOTEH2004.016

Pitman, William
Ruined Gate
oil on board 39.2 x 53.5
PCF4

Pitman, William
The Walk, Totnes, Devon
oil on board 34.5 x 50
PCF3

Snowden, Hilda Mary 1910–1997
Beachy Head, East Sussex
acrylic on paper 24.8 x 35
PCF12

Sulway, Joy
Two Owls
acrylic on board 25.3 x 35.7
PCF2

unknown artist
The Town Mill 1982
oil on board 37.5 x 48.5
TOTEH2004.015

unknown artist
John Trist of Hannaford
oil on canvas 60 x 55
TOTEH1988.297 (P)

unknown artist
Reverend John Trist (1718–1781), MA, Vicar of Veryan
oil on canvas 82.5 x 59.3
TOTEH1988.297 (P)

unknown artist
Totnes Town Mill, Devon
oil on board 38.5 x 50
TOTEH2004.014

Facing page: Lely, Peter, 1618–1680, *Princess Henrietta (1644–1670), Daughter of Charles I*, Exeter Guildhall (p. 105)

Totnes Guildhall

Brockedon, William 1787–1854
*Ossian Relating the Fate of Oscar to Malvina
(from 'The Poems of Ossian' by James
Macpherson)*
oil on canvas 233.5 x 195.4
3007.377

Brockedon, William 1787–1854
Self Portrait
oil on panel 74.5 x 62.5
3007.379

Ford, E. C.
*Charles Stanley Jacka (1893–1970), Mayor of
Totnes (1950–1951)*
oil on canvas 101.6 x 62.4
3007.066

Honeywill, Paul Douglas 1949–2002
*Councillor Rendle Crang (1933–2005), Town
Mayor (1986–1988) and Mrs Eileen Crang
(b.1935), Mayoress (1997–1999)* 2001
acrylic on board 86 x 60
3007.067

Norman, A.
Councillor Bill Bennett (1927–2004), MBE
oil on board 59.8 x 44.8
3007.068

Simpson, Doris
The Butterwalk, Totnes, Devon
acrylic on board 39.2 x 49.4
PCF11

unknown artist
Captain William Short (1762–1825)
oil on canvas 73.8 x 61.4
3007.386

unknown artist
*Christopher Maynard (1577–1635), Mayor of
the Borough of Totnes (1632) or Christopher
Maynard (d.1669), Mayor of the Borough (...)*
oil on canvas 111.5 x 90
3007.378

unknown artist
Frederick Bowden (1819–1903), Mayor of
Totnes (1883)
oil on canvas 60 x 50
3007.331

unknown artist
Portrait of a Man
oil on canvas 74.8 x 62.5
3007.391

unknown artist
Portrait of a Woman
oil on canvas 74.8 x 62.5
3007.392

Totnes Hospital

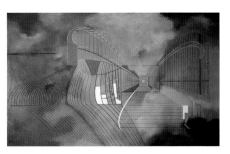

Carter, Peter J.
Architectural Abstract 1973
oil on board 76 x 122
PCF2

Carter, Peter J.
Steamer Quay, Totnes, Devon
oil on board 57.5 x 100
PCF1

Kirk, R.
Totnes, Devon 1982
acylic on paper 134 x 160
PCF3

Paintings Without Reproductions

This section lists all the paintings that have not been included in the main pages of the catalogue. They were excluded as it was not possible to photograph them for this project. Additional information relating to acquisition credit lines or loan details is also included. For this reason the information below is not repeated in the Further Information section.

Britannia Royal Naval College

Clegg, Ernest active 1951, *SMS 'Moltke' (polyptych, panel 3 of 6)*, 44 x 68.5, oil on board, A706_3, presented by the artist, 1951, lost

Dawlish Museum Society

Elliott, Les *Dawlish Seafront, Devon*, 2004, 99 x 168, oil on plywood, PCF13, gift from the artist, not available at the time of photography

Dawlish Town Council

Barker (attributed to) *Heron Hunt*, PCF5, unknown acquisition method, not available at the time of photography

Luny, Thomas (attributed to) 1759–1837, *Beach Scene*, PCF4, unknown acquisition method, not available at the time of photography

Luny, Thomas (attributed to) 1759–1837, *River Scene*, PCF3, unknown acquisition method, not available at the time of photography

unknown artist *Portrait*, PCF6, unknown acquisition method, not available at the time of photography

unknown artist *View of Old Dawlish, Devon*, PCF2, unknown acquisition method, not available at the time of photography

unknown artist *View towards Exmouth, Devon*, oil, PCF1, unknown acquisition method, not available at the time of photography

Royal Albert Memorial Museum

Bampfylde, Coplestone Warre 1720–1791, *The Hamoaze and Dock, Plymouth, Devon*, 38 x 60.3, oil on panel, 51/1953, purchased with the assistance of the Kent Kingdon Bequest, 1953, not available at the time of photography

Barker, John Joseph 1824–1904, *Cavalier Troops Mustering Outside the Guildhall, Exeter, Devon*, 1886, 243.7 x 152, oil on canvas, 93/1978x, not available at the time of photography

Barker, John Joseph 1824–1904, *Landscape with a Battle between Cavaliers and Roundheads*, 1886, 151.9 x 243.5, oil on canvas, 92/1978x, not available at the time of photography

Beeson, Jane 1930–2006, *Winter I*, 1963, 173.4 x 172.9, oil on canvas, 111/2002, purchased from the artist, 2001, not available at the time of photography

Bomberg, David 1890–1957, *Bideford, Devon*, 1946, 64.8 x 71.1, oil on canvas, PCF1, accepted by HM Government in lieu of inheritance tax and allocated to the Royal Albert Memorial Museum, 2010, not available at the time of photography

British (English) School *Richard Somers Gard (1797–1868)*, c.1860, 124.7 x 99.4, oil on canvas, 208/1911, bequeathed by Miss Outhwaite, 1911, not available at the time of photography

British (English) School 19th C, *Shipping in Harbour at Plymouth, Devon*, 38.5 x 53.9, oil on canvas, 143/1978x, not available at the time of photography

Dutch School 17th C, *General Ottavio Piccolomini (1599–1656) (formerly called 'Sir Thomas Denys')*, 210.5 x 126.9, oil on canvas, 466/1997, transferred from the Guildhall, Exeter, 1971, not available at the time of photography

Freebairn, Robert 1764–1808, *Ruins of an Ancient Temple on Lake Avernus, near Naples, Italy*, 1806, 92.4 x 123, oil on canvas, K219, bequeathed by Kent and Jane Kingdon, 1892, not available at the time of photography

Gandy, William c.1655–1729, *Portrait of a Gentleman (called 'Reverend Henry Walrond')*, 42.9 x 34.6, oil on canvas, 28/1970, purchased from Whitton & Laing,

Exeter, 1970, not available at the time of photography

Gendall, John 1790–1865, *Landscape with a River and Trees*, 62.2 x 82.8, oil on canvas, 447/1980, gift from Devon County Council Social Services Department, 1980, not available at the time of photography

Gibbons, William active 1870–1890, *Seascape*, 1880, 113.6 x 183.8, oil on canvas, 27/1934/2, purchased, 1934, not available at the time of photography

Goodall, Frederick 1822–1904, *Pastoral Scene near Cairo, Egypt, Evening*, 1895, 38.1 x 92, oil on canvas, 100/1970, purchased from Chamberlain Bros & Michelmore, 1970, not available at the time of photography

Gorman, Michael b.1938, *Flowers for the Composer (Igor Stravinsky)*, 1971, 90.5 x 153.3, Aquatec on canvas, 108/1973, purchased from the artist, 1971, not available at the time of photography

Hillier, Tristram Paul 1905–1983, *Beach with an Old Breakwater*, 1977, 51.4 x 76.3, oil on canvas, 338/1979, purchased from John Linfield with the assistance of the Victoria and Albert Museum Purchase Grant Fund, 1979, not available at the time of photography

Hudson, Thomas 1701–1779, *Richard Osbaldeston (1691–1764)*, 1764, 128.6 x 118.6, oil on canvas, 46/1925/25, bequeathed by John Lane, 1925, not available at the time of photography

Hulbert, Thelma 1913–1995, *Leaves and Bottles*, 1980, 141 x 140, oil on canvas, 60/1998/13, gift from the Thelma Hulbert Memorial Fund, 1998, not available at the time of photography

Leakey, James 1775–1865, *John White Abbott (1763–1851)*, 1825, 32.2 x 23.5, oil on panel, 28/1952, purchased, 1952, , not available at the time of photography

Leakey, James 1775–1865, *Landscape with Cattle and Figures*,

58.7 x 93.4, oil on canvas, 47/1933/1, gift from Mr W. H. Moore, 1933, not available at the time of photography

Leakey, James 1775–1865, *Waiting for the Ferry*, 63.5 x 78.6, oil on canvas, 25/1999/1, gift from Mrs M. K. B. Blight, 1999, not available at the time of photography

Leakey, James (attributed to) 1775–1865, *Portrait of a Child*, 10.1 x 9, oil & pencil on panel, 43/1999/7, gift from Mrs M. K. B. Blight, 1999, not available at the time of photography

Lee, Frederick Richard 1798–1879, *Above Yeoford, Devon*, 59.5 x 65.2, oil on canvas, 137/1991, bequeathed by Geoffrey W. Clarke, 1991, not available at the time of photography

Luny, Thomas 1759–1837, *Tantallon Castle and the Bass Rock*, 1835, 22.6 x 30.7, oil on panel, 1896/2/3, bequeathed by Edwin Lawrence White, 1896, not available at the time of photography

Mackenzie, Kenneth active 1884–1899, *Meadow and Moorland*, 214.1 x 137.4, oil on canvas, 110/1978x, purchased with the assistance of the Kent Kingdon Bequest, not available at the time of photography

Merriott, Jack 1901–1968, *Storm over Dartmoor, Devon*, 71 x 91.2, oil on board, 219/1970, gift from the Jack Merriott Memorial Committee, 1970, not available at the time of photography

Northcote, James 1746–1831, *The Northcote Family*, c.1780, 101.7 x 127.3, oil on canvas, 46/1925/31, bequeathed by John Lane, 1925, not available at the time of photography

O'Connor, James Arthur 1791–1841, *Moonlight, the Castle of Blarney, Ireland*, 14 x 18.2, oil on panel, 50/1943/8, bequeathed by Lady Lockyer, 1943, not available at the time of photography

Olsson, Albert Julius 1864–1942, *Near Newquay, Cornwall*, 76.6 x

102, oil on canvas, 110/1920, purchased with the assistance of the Kent Kingdon Bequest, 1920, not available at the time of photography

Opie, John 1761–1807, *Isabella Wyatt-Edgell*, c.1783, 74.7 x 62.2, oil on canvas, 143/1993/3FA, bequeathed by Pamela Mary Thompson, 1993, not available at the time of photography

Opie, John 1761–1807, *The Reverend Micaiah Towgood (1700–1792)*, c.1783, 101 x 128, oil on canvas, 146/2006/1, bequeathed by Mrs Joyce Witherington Hanson, 2006, not available at the time of photography

Opie, John 1761–1807, *Lady Hoare (1736–1800)*, c.1785, 74.7 x 62.2, oil on canvas, 143/1993/2FA, bequeathed by Pamela Mary Thompson, 1993, not available at the time of photography

Opie, John 1761–1807, *Sir Richard Hoare (1735–1787), Bt*, c.1785, 74.5 x 62, oil on canvas, 143/1993/1FA, bequeathed by Pamela Mary Thompson, 1993, not available at the time of photography

Patch, Thomas 1725–1782, *A View of Fiesole, near Florence, Italy*, 86.7 x 143.3, oil on canvas, 34/1944/2, purchased from Sir Alec and Lady Martin with the assistance of the National Art Collections Fund, 1944, not available at the time of photography

Sharland, William *Reuben Phillips (c.1746–1833)*, 239.7 x 149.6, oil on canvas, 469/1997, transferred from the Guildhall, Exeter, 1970s, not available at the time of photography

Traies, William 1789–1872, *Landscape Composition*, 106.3 x 96.2, oil on canvas, 43/1936/1, gift from Robert Worthington, 1936, not available at the time of photography

Tremlett, James c.1810–1879, *George Shears (d.1839)*, c.1820–1830, 10.9 x 9.2, oil on card, 193/1915, gift from Samuel Commin, 1915, not available at the time of photography

Tremlett, James c.1810–1879, *Mr Commin (1774–1835), of North Street*, c.1825–1835, 8.2 x 6.7, oil on card, 192/1915, gift from Samuel Commin, 1915, not available at the time of photography

Tucker, John Wallace 1808–1869, *The Parson and Clerk, Teignmouth, Devon*, 15 x 20.3, oil on panel, 65/1935, gift from Robert Worthington, 1935, not available at the time of photography

Widgery, Frederick John 1861–1942, *Coastal Scene*, 183 x 107, oil on canvas, 259/2008, gift from the artist, 1931, not available at the time of photography

Widgery, Frederick John 1861–1942, *Untitled, Moorland Scene*, 110.5 x 161.5, oil on canvas, 257/2008, gift from the artist (?), 1931, not available at the time of photography

Widgery, William 1822–1893, *Confines of Dartmoor, Devon*, 1873, 120.5 x 153, K212, oil on canvas, bequeathed by Kent and Jane Kingdon, 1892, not available at the time of photography

Widgery, William 1822–1893, *A Scene on the Lyd, Devon*, 122.8 x 183.1, oil on canvas, 37/1916, gift from Reverend Langford, 1916, not available at the time of photography

Widgery, William 1822–1893, *Ancient Cross on Whitchurch Down near Tavistock, Devon*, 77.2 x 150, oil on canvas, K218, bequeathed by Kent and Jane Kingdon, 1892, not available at the time of photography

Widgery, William 1822–1893, *Fingle Bridge, Dartmoor, Devon*, 122 x 182.7, oil on canvas, 46/1922/1, bequeathed by H. D. Thomas, 1922, not available at the time of photography

Widgery, William 1822–1893, *On the Tavy, Devon*, 131.7 x 182.6, oil on canvas, 46/1922/2, bequeathed by H. D. Thomas, 1922, not available at the time of photography

Widgery, William 1822–1893, *Woodland Scene with Cattle*, 102.4 x 153, oil on canvas, 139/1978x, not available at the time of photography

Williams, William 1808–1895, *Royal William Victualling Yard, Plymouth, Devon*, 1894, 20 x 38.2, oil on canvas bonded to board, 118/1933, gift from Miss M. E. Harding, 1933, not available at the time of photography

Williams, William 1808–1895, *Whiddon Park on the Teign, Devon*, 60.5 x 60.9, oil on canvas, 91/1868, gift from the artist, 1868, not available at the time of photography

University of Exeter, Fine Art Collection

Al-Kilai, Mohammid *Streetfood Vendor*, oil on board, FAC01580, unknown acquisition method, not available at the time of photography

Bennett, Vincent 1910–1993, *Shop Front*, 1975, 38 x 49, oil on canvas, FAC00508, purchased by the Fine Art and Exhibition Advisory Group, not available at the time of photography

Bestard, D. *Old Street, Looe, Cornwall*, 1974–1975, 35 x 27, oil on canvas, FAC00427, presented by Stephen, Gertrude and Karin Fisher, 1975, not available at the time of photography

Boundy, Joy active 1972–1999, *Westward Ho!*, 1999, 109 x 89.5, oil on canvas, FAC00786, purchased by the Fine Art and Exhibition Advisory Group, not available at the time of photography

Boundy, Joy active 1972–1999, *Canto V*, 173 x 101, oil on board, FAC00890, purchased by the Fine Art and Exhibition Advisory Group, not available at the time of photography

Boundy, Joy active 1972–1999, *Post USA 1*, 129.5 x 104, oil on canvas, FAC00936, unknown acquisition method, not available at the time of photography

Boundy, Joy active 1972–1999, *Post USA 2*, 129.5 x 104, oil on canvas, FAC00937, unknown acquisition method, not available at the time of photography

Boundy, Joy active 1972–1999, *Ultima cena (Last Supper)*, 76 x 124.5, oil on hardboard, FAC00886, purchased by the Fine Art and Exhibition Advisory Group, not available at the time of photography

Bower, Stephen b.1949, *Rue Lepic, Montmartre, Paris*, 1994, 61 x 49.5, oil on canvas, FAC00189, purchased by the Fine Art and Exhibition Advisory Group, not available at the time of photography

Bower, Stephen b.1949, *Bizarre Garden*, 2003, 58.5 x 58.5, oil on copper, FAC01007, purchased by the Fine Art and Exhibition Advisory Group, not available at the time of photography

Bower, Stephen b.1949, *Swing Garden*, 2003, 51 x 51, oil on copper, FAC01008, purchased by the Fine Art and Exhibition Advisory Group, not available at the time of photography

Brougier, H. *Landscape*, 43 x 35.5, oil on canvas, FAC00756, unknown acquisition method, not available at the time of photography

Brozier, W. *Pastoral Scene, French Mountain*, 34 x 46, oil on hardboard, FAC00810, unknown acquisition method, not available at the time of photography

Carter, Brenda *Bowl of Cherries*, 1995, oil on canvas, FAC00953, purchased by the Fine Art and Exhibition Advisory Group, not available at the time of photography

Clement, Bob *Spring Road to Great Sherberton, Devon*, 1997, 67 x 80, acrylic, FAC00955, purchased by the Fine Art and Exhibition Advisory Group, not available at the time of photography

Craig, Frank 1874–1918, *He Saw Barbie Spreading Her Linen*, 1908, 56 x 69, mixed media, FAC00676, unknown acquisition method, not available at the time of photography

Daveney, Jean *Three Sails*, 50 x 68, oil on canvas, FAC03012, gift from Professor Tom Daveney, not available at the time of photography

Dix, Brian *Red Gate*, 1970s, 99.5 x 144, acrylic, FAC00737, purchased by the Fine Art and Exhibition Advisory Group, not available at the time of photography

Dutch School 17th C, *Portrait of a Gentleman, Head and Shoulders and Holding Staff*, 113 x 90, oil on panel, FAC00201, bequeathed by D. Brendon of Sherbourne, not available at the time of photography

Eastwood, Nicholas Anthony b.1942, *Sketch for a Large Work*, 2003, 30.5 x 30.5, oil on hardboard, FAC00984, not available at the time of photography

Hudson, Thomas (school of) 1701–1779, *Lawrence Sterne (1713–1768)*, 18th C, 25.5 x 30.5, oil on canvas laid on panel, FAC00499, unknown acquisition method, not available at the time of photography

Jennison, Robert b.1933, *Trunks, Broken Sunlight*, 2000, 61 x 61, oil on canvas, FAC00778, purchased by the Fine Art and Exhibition Advisory Group, not available at

the time of photography

Jewell, Catherine active 1978–2003, *Opium Fantasy*, 1978, 64 x 51, oil, FAC00181, purchased by the Fine Art and Exhibition Advisory Group, not available at the time of photography

Jewell, Catherine active 1978–2003, *Tapestry of Flowers*, 2003, 30.5 x 20, oil on canvas, FAC00983, purchased by the Fine Art and Exhibition Advisory Group, not available at the time of photography

Johns, Ewart b.1923, *Woman in a Sun Shower*, 1950s, 91.5 x 61, oil on canvas, FAC00745, presented by H. Halberstan, not available at the time of photography

Loon, Theodor van 1581/1582–1667, *Portrait of a Gentleman*, 1650, 71.5 x 55.5, oil on panel, FAC00353, presented by Mrs D. Brendon of Sherbourne, not available at the time of photography

Loon, Theodor van 1581/1582–1667, *Portrait of a Lady with a Fan*, 114 x 90, oil on panel, FAC00307, bequeathed by D. Brendon of Sherbourne, not available at the time of photography

Loon, Theodor van 1581/1582–1667, *Portrait of a Young Girl*, 72 x 55, oil on panel, FAC00285, bequeathed by D. Brendon of Sherbourne, not available at the time of photography

Lublinski, David active 1968–1997, *Your Feet Are Killing Me*, 1968, 55 x 80, acrylic on hardboard, FAC00670, presented by the artist, 1997, not available at the time of photography

Malone, Ray b.1939, *Untitled*, 1998, 32 x 40.5, acrylic & graphite on paper, FAC00921, purchased by the Fine Art and Exhibition Advisory Group, not available at the time of photography

Malthouse, Eric James 1914–1997, *Above Orange*, 1960, 68.5 x 89, oil on canvas, FAC00934, unknown acquisition method, not available at the time of photography

Malthouse, Eric James 1914–1997, *Untitled*, 1960, 119 x 58, oil on canvas, FAC00266, purchased by the Fine Art and Exhibition Advisory Group, not available at the time of photography

Mellings, Jenny b.1958, *Dying Swan (Stone Bird?)*, 178 x 193, oil on canvas, FAC00731, unknown acquisition method, not available at the time of photography

Milne, Joseph 1857/1860–1911, *Sheep Grazing in a Water Meadow*, 1911, 40 x 60, oil on canvas, FAC00305, presented by Principal Murray, 1949, not available at the time of photography

Munnings, Alfred James 1878–1959, *Building Hayricks*, 24 x 34, oil on wood, FAC00510, unknown acquisition method, not available at the time of photography

Richards, Alan *Summer Landscape, Christow, Devon*, 1990, 61 x 66, oil on canvas, FAC00170, purchased by the Fine Art and Exhibition Advisory Group, not available at the time of photography

Scholz, Heinz-Joachim (follower of) *Street Scene, Bentheum*, 1954, 48 x 34.5, oil on hardboard, FAC00491, unknown acquisition method, not available at the time of photography

Stirland, Derek *Moor*, 30 x 47, acrylic on hardboard, FAC03006, unknown acquisition method, not available at the time of photography

Thorpe, Deborah *Remembrance of Nothing*, 1993, 184 x 154, oil on canvas, FAC00287, purchased by the Fine Art and Exhibition Advisory Group, not available at the time of photography

Thursby, Peter 1930–2011, *White Intrusion*, 1966, 53.5 x 40.5, mixed media, FAC00711, on loan from the Guild of Students, not available at the time of photography

unknown artist 17th C, *Portrait of a Lady with a Fan*, 53.5 x 68.5, oil on wood, FAC00835, unknown acquisition method, not available at the time of photography

unknown artist 17th C, *Portrait of a Young Girl, Half-Length with a Crimson Dress and a Pearl Necklace*, 56 x 72, oil on panel, FAC00951, unknown acquisition method, not available at the time of photography

unknown artist 17th C–18th C, *Portrait*, 81 x 106.5, oil on canvas, FAC00834, unknown acquisition method, not available at the time of photography

unknown artist 18th C, *Landscape with a Mountain, a River and a Waterfall*, 23 x 19, oil on canvas, FAC00291, unknown acquisition method, not available at the time of photography

unknown artist *Lakeside Scene*, 1914, 51 x 33, oil on canvas, FAC00869, unknown acquisition method, not available at the time of photography

unknown artist *Cairo, Egypt*, 1973, 76 x 61, oil on canvas, FAC01579, unknown acquisition method, not available at the time of photography

unknown artist *Portrait of Claire*, 1990s, 92 x 61.5, oil, FAC00253, unknown acquisition method, not available at the time of photography

unknown artist *Donkey*, 71 x 24, acrylic on canvas, FAC00751, unknown acquisition method, not available at the time of photography

unknown artist *Pastoral Scene*, 41 x 26, oil on canvas, FAC01576, gift from Ms Hamida Sagar, not available at the time of photography

unknown artist *Portrait Angel (?)*, 81 x 46, acrylic on hardboard, FAC00867, unknown acquisition method, not available at the time of photography

unknown artist *Stripes 1*, 178 x 456.5, oil on canvas, PCF59, unknown acquisition method, not available at the time of photography

unknown artist *Stripes 2*, 178 x 456.5, oil on canvas, PCF60, unknown acquisition method, not available at the time of photography

unknown artist *Study of People*, 185.5 x 153.5, oil on canvas, FAC00889, unknown acquisition method, not available at the time of photography

Walker, Gregory b.1957, *When Did You Last See Your Father?*, 1979, 170.5 x 138.5, oil on canvas, FAC00750, purchased by the Fine Art and Exhibition Advisory Group, not available at the time of photography

Weeks, David *For You Blue (To Dave)*, 1973, 70 x 180, acrylic, FAC00144, acquired by the Fine Arts Advisory Group from the Guild, not available at the time of photography

Weeks, David *Savoy Truffle (To Jim)*, 1973, 70 x 180, acrylic, FAC00145, acquired by the Fine Arts Advisory Group from the Guild, not available at the time of photography

Whittington-Ince, Richard 1934–1983, *Abstract Woman (The Railway Cutting)*, 1971, 68 x 88.5, oil on hardboard, FAC00579, unknown acquisition method, not

available at the time of photography

Widgery, William 1822–1893, *River Scene, Dartmoor in the Background*, 100.3 x 151.5, oil on canvas, FAC00298, unknown acquisition method, not available at the time of photography

William, W. active late 19th C, *Landscape with Two Figures and Sheep*, 43 x 58.5, oil on canvas, FAC00310, unknown acquisition method, not available at the time of photography

Wood, Ron *Trio One*, 1981, 20 x 18, acrylic on paper, FAC00563, unknown acquisition method, not available at the time of photography

The Fairground Heritage Trust

George Orton, Sons and Spooner Ltd *R. Edwards' 'Super Chariot Racer': Jungle Scene (rounding board)*, 93 x 220, oil on board, 119.36, unknown acquisition method, not available at the time of photography

George Orton, Sons and Spooner Ltd *R. Edwards' 'Super Chariot Racer': Jungle Scene (rounding board)*, 120 x 220, oil on board, 119.37, unknown acquisition method, not available at the time of photography

George Orton, Sons and Spooner Ltd *R. Edwards' 'Super Chariot Racer': Jungle Scene (rounding board)*, 120 x 220, oil on board, 119.38, unknown acquisition method, not available at the time of photography

unknown artist *Scott's 'Wonder Walter's': Guitarist and Mandolin (shutter, two panels)*, 180 x 80; 180 x 80 (E), oil on board, D012.11, unknown acquisition method, not available at the time of photography

unknown artist *Scott's 'Wonder Walter's': Pianist and Mandolin (shutter, two panels)*, 180 x 80; 180 x 80 (E), oil on board, D012.10, unknown acquisition method, not available at the time of photography

unknown artist *Scott's 'Wonder Walter's': Singer and Mandolin (shutter, two panels)*, 180 x 80; 180 x 80 (E), oil on board, D012.12, unknown acquisition method, not available at the time of photography

unknown artist *Scott's 'Wonder Walter's': Violinist and Mandolin (shutter, two panels)*, 180 x 80; 180 x 80 (E), oil on board, D012.9,

unknown acquisition method, not available at the time of photography

unknown artist *William Wilson's 'Rodeo Switchback': Cowboy Scene (rounding board)*, 210 x 188, oil on wood panels, 1993.1.1, unknown acquisition method, not available at the time of photography

Further Information

The paintings listed in this section have additional information relating to one or more of the five categories outlined below. This extra information is only provided where it is applicable and where it exists. Paintings listed in this section follow the same order as in the illustrated pages of the catalogue.

I The full name of the artist if this was too long to display in the illustrated pages of the catalogue. Such cases are marked in the catalogue with a (...).

II The full title of the painting if this was too long to display in the illustrated pages of the catalogue. Such cases are marked in the catalogue with a (...).

III Acquisition information or acquisition credit lines as well as information about loans, copied from the records of the owner collection.

IV Artist copyright credit lines where the copyright owner has been traced. Exhaustive efforts have been made to locate the copyright owners of all the images included within this catalogue and to meet their requirements. Any omissions or mistakes brought to our attention will be duly attended to and corrected in future publications.

V The credit line of the lender of the transparency if the transparency has been borrowed. Bridgeman images are available subject to any relevant copyright approvals from the Bridgeman Art Library at www.bridgemanart.com

Appledore Library

Clark, E. L *Seascape*, unknown acquisition method
Mead, Geraldine active 2000, *Portrait of a Vicar of Appledore*, unknown acquisition method
unknown artist *Garden Gate*, unknown acquisition method

North Devon Maritime Museum

Braund, P. *A Topsail Schooner*, gift from R. G. Jockes
Chinese School *The Ship 'Glamorganshire'*, gift from Mrs D. Connor
Cockell, Herb *The Five Masted Barque 'France'*, unknown acquisition method
Cockell, Herb *The Four Masted Barque 'Rewa'*, unknown acquisition method
Day, Archibald McCullum c.1852–1923, *The Four Masted Ship 'Falls of Dee', 1896*, gift from R. M. Day
Harris, L. (?) *The 'Pace di Fiume' Ashore at Westward Ho!*, gift from Mrs R. Doran, 2008
Heard, Joseph 1799–1859, *The Brig 'Star' of Bideford, Devon*, bequeathed by the Croscombe Family
Heard, Joseph (attributed to) 1799–1859, *The Barque 'Hugenot' in a Gale*, bequeathed by the Croscombe family
Jamieson, A. *The Four Masted Barque 'Colonial Empire'*,

unknown acquisition method
T. M. *The Topsail Schooner 'Kate'*, unknown acquisition method
Myers, Mark Richard b.1945, *A Medieval Ship, Boat and Coaster in the Taw*, gift from the artist, 1977, © the artist
Myers, Mark Richard b.1945, *The 'Prudence' Prize at Barnstaple Quay, 1590*, gift from the artist, 1977, © the artist
Myers, Mark Richard b.1945, *The Relief of the 'Investigator' 1853*, bequeathed by Captain C. C. Lowry, 2001, © the artist
Myers, Mark Richard b.1945, *The 'Volunteer' Service to the 'Daniel', 1829*, bequeathed by Captain C. C. Lowry, 2001, © the artist
Quance, G. M. *The Ketch 'Minnie Flossie'*, gift from Mr T. Andrews
Ross, George active 1904–1912, *The Four Masted Barque 'Loch Torridon'*, gift from Mrs D. Connor
Ross, George active 1904–1912, *The Schooner 'Madeleine' Ashore*, gift from Mrs D. Connor
Ross, George active 1904–1912, *A Yacht Race off the Isle of Wight*, gift from Mrs D. Connor
Ross, George active 1904–1912, *The Ketch 'Johnny Toole'*, gift from Mrs D. Connor
Semple, Joseph 1830–1877, *The Barque 'Edmund Preston'*, bequeathed by the Croscombe family
Smith, Ivor *A Tribute to Bravery*, unknown acquisition method

unknown artist *A Sailing Boat in a Fresh Breeze*, unknown acquisition method
unknown artist *A View of Bideford, Devon, from the East*, unknown acquisition method
unknown artist *Braunton Burrows Lighthouse, Devon*, unknown acquisition method
unknown artist *Portrait of a Gentleman (probably Mr Alexander Beara)*, gift from Miss D. Beara
unknown artist *Portrait of a Mariner (associated with Philip R. Dart, mariner of Bideford)*, unknown acquisition method
unknown artist *The Ketch 'Margaret'*, gift from Mrs C. J. Burt, 2004
unknown artist *The Smack 'BE1'*, unknown acquisition method

Ashburton & Buckfastleigh Community Hospital

Crowley, A. M. (Miss) *Bridge at Nantes, France*, unknown acquisition method

Axminster Guildhall

Gill, William active 1826–1871, *View of Axminster, Devon**, presented by Mrs William Gill

Axminster Heritage

Hudson, Esdaile active 2004–2005, *An Artist's Impression of Thomas*

Whitty (1716–1792), gift from the artist, 2005
Lynch, Kate Mary b.1949, *Carpet Weaving, Axminster Carpets, Axminster, Devon*, gift from the artist, 2010, © the artist
Lynch, Kate Mary b.1949, *The Twister Attending His Bobbins of Plying Yarn, Buckfast Spinning Mill, Buckfastleigh, Devon*, gift from the artist, 2010, © the artist

Axminster Hospital

Clark, B. *Nyman's Gardens, West Sussex*, unknown acquisition method
Cole, Susan *Flowers*, unknown acquisition method
B. H. *Roses*, unknown acquisition method
B. H. *Poppies*, unknown acquisition method
Humphries, Amelia *The Spinney*, unknown acquisition method
Martens *Still Life with a Magnifying Glass*, unknown acquisition method
Morris, M. E. (Mrs) *Toller Fratrum Farmhouse, Dorset*, unknown acquisition method
Morris, Peter *View to the Obelisk*, unknown acquisition method
Pickard, Daphne Eileen b.1921, *Axminster Market, Devon*, unknown acquisition method, © the artist
Ridgeway, C. J. *Riverside Cottages*, unknown acquisition method

Stalman, Joy active 1996–1998, *Francesca's Camellias*, unknown acquisition method
Stalman, Joy active 1996–1998, *Dorset Hills*, unknown acquisition method
unknown artist *Dr Jacinth Morton*, unknown acquisition method
unknown artist *Harvest*, unknown acquisition method
unknown artist *Woodland*, unknown acquisition method
White, Margaret *Garden Corner*, unknown acquisition method

Axminster Museum

Gill, William active 1826–1871, *East Devon Farm*, presented to Axminster Museum by Mrs William Gill, 1994
Gill, William active 1826–1871, *Still Life with Flowers*, presented to the museum by Mrs L. M. Robertson, 1994

Barnstaple Town Council

Adcock, Mollie *Portrait of a Bearded Cleric*, unknown acquisition method
Beechey, William 1753–1839, *Frederick Hodgson, Esq.*, presented to the Town Council by his nephew, the Reverend Christopher Haggard, 1885
British (English) School *Richard Bremridge, Mayor of Barnstaple (1829 & 1859)*, unknown acquisition method

British (English) School 19th C, *Gilbert Inner Wallas, MA*, unknown acquisition method

British (English) School 19th C, *Lionel T. Bencraft, Mayor of Barnstaple (1883)*, unknown acquisition method

British (English) School 19th C, *Portrait of a Young Soldier Officer Wearing a Uniform*, unknown acquisition method

British (English) School 19th C, *Stephen Bencraft*, unknown acquisition method

Gould, Alexander Carruthers 1870–1948, *Francis Carruthers Gould (1844–1925), at His Desk*, unknown acquisition method

Graves, Henry Richard 1818–1882, *The Honourable Mark George Kerr Rolle (1835–1907), High Steward (1861–1908)*, unknown acquisition method

Hudson, Thomas (attributed to) 1701–1779, *Benjamin Incledon, Recorder (1758–1796)*, unknown acquisition method

Hudson, Thomas (attributed to) 1701–1779, *Reverend Robert Luck, Master of the Grammar School (1698–1740)*, unknown acquisition method

Hudson, Thomas (studio of) 1701–1779, *Alexander Webber, Mayor of Barnstaple (1737)*, unknown acquisition method

Hudson, Thomas (studio of) 1701–1779, *Charles Marshall, Mayor of Barnstaple (1748)*, unknown acquisition method

Hudson, Thomas (studio of) 1701–1779, *Charles Velly, Mayor of Barnstaple (1734 & 1749)*, unknown acquisition method

Hudson, Thomas (studio of) 1701–1779, *Charles Wright, Mayor of Barnstaple (1744)*, unknown acquisition method

Hudson, Thomas (studio of) 1701–1779, *George Score, Mayor of Barnstaple (1730)*, unknown acquisition method

Hudson, Thomas (studio of) 1701–1779, *George Wickey, Mayor of Barnstaple (1739)*, unknown acquisition method

Hudson, Thomas (studio of) 1701–1779, *Gregory Anthony, Town Clerk of Barnstaple (1733–1747)*, unknown acquisition method

Hudson, Thomas (studio of) 1701–1779, *Henry Beavis, Mayor of Barnstaple (1738 & 1751)*, unknown acquisition method

Hudson, Thomas (studio of) 1701–1779, *Henry Drake (1745–1806), Town Clerk of Barnstaple*, unknown acquisition method

Hudson, Thomas (studio of) 1701–1779, *Henry Wickey, Councillor*, unknown acquisition method

Hudson, Thomas (studio of) 1701–1779, *John Baker, Mayor of Barnstaple (1715 & 1729)*, unknown acquisition method

Hudson, Thomas (studio of) 1701–1779, *John Fraine, Mayor of Barnstaple (1740 & 1752)*, unknown acquisition method

Hudson, Thomas (studio of) 1701–1779, *John Gaydon (1685–1732), Mayor of Barnstaple (1726)*, unknown acquisition method

Hudson, Thomas (studio of) 1701–1779, *John Swayne, Councillor*, unknown acquisition method

Hudson, Thomas (studio of) 1701–1779, *Mark Slee, Mayor of Barnstaple (1747)*, unknown acquisition method

Hudson, Thomas (studio of) 1701–1779, *Marshall Swayne, Mayor of Barnstaple (1746)*, unknown acquisition method

Hudson, Thomas (studio of) 1701–1779, *Matthew Rock, Mayor of Barnstaple (1741 & 1753)*, unknown acquisition method

Hudson, Thomas (studio of) 1701–1779, *Nicholas Glass, Mayor of Barnstaple (1787 & 1804)*, unknown acquisition method

Hudson, Thomas (studio of) 1701–1779, *Paul Tucker, Mayor of Barnstaple (1736)*, unknown acquisition method

Hudson, Thomas (studio of) 1701–1779, *Reverend Thomas Steed, Vicar of Barnstaple*, unknown acquisition method

Hudson, Thomas (studio of) 1701–1779, *Richard Chapple, Mayor of Barnstaple (1742, 1762 & 1781)*, unknown acquisition method

Hudson, Thomas (studio of) 1701–1779, *Richard Knight, Mayor of Barnstaple (1735, 1750 & 1761)*, unknown acquisition method

Hudson, Thomas (studio of) 1701–1779, *Richard Mervyn, Deputy Recorder and Mayor of Barnstaple*, unknown acquisition method

Hudson, Thomas (studio of) 1701–1779, *Richard Newell, Mayor of Barnstaple (1728)*, unknown acquisition method

Hudson, Thomas (studio of) 1701–1779, *Robert Incledon, Deputy Recorder and Mayor of Barnstaple (1712)*, unknown acquisition method

Hudson, Thomas (studio of) 1701–1779, *Robert King, Mayor of Barnstaple (1745)*, unknown acquisition method

Hudson, Thomas (studio of) 1701–1779, *Samuel Berry, Mayor of Barnstaple (1731)*, unknown acquisition method

Hudson, Thomas (studio of) 1701–1779, *Thomas Harris, Mayor of Barnstaple (1733)*, unknown acquisition method

Hudson, Thomas (studio of) 1701–1779, *William Lantrow, Councillor*, unknown acquisition method

Hudson, Thomas (style of) 1701–1779, *Reverend Samuel*

Thompson, Vicar of Barnstaple, unknown acquisition method

Janssens van Ceulen, Cornelis (style of) 1593–1661, *John Penrose (1778–1859)*, unknown acquisition method

Janssens van Ceulen, Cornelis (style of) 1593–1661, *John Penrose (1778–1859)*, unknown acquisition method

Kennedy, Joseph c.1838–1893, *Old Guildhall, Barnstaple, Devon*, unknown acquisition method

Kennedy, Joseph c.1838–1893, *Old Northgate and the Bluecoat School, Barnstaple, Devon*, unknown acquisition method

Kennedy, Joseph c.1838–1893, *The Strand, Barnstaple, Devon*, unknown acquisition method

Reid, F. Michael P. *St Cuthbert Mayne, Born Shirwell, Barnstaple, Martyred 1577*, unknown acquisition method

Richardson, Jonathan the elder (style of) 1664/1665–1745, *John Gay (1685–1732), Poet and Author*, unknown acquisition method

Rutherford, R. G. *Long Bridge, Barnstaple, Devon*, presented in memory of John Bryon Cruse, MBE, TD, JP, FCA, Mayor of Banstaple (1952–1953), Chamberlain of the Long Bridge Trust (1945–1984)

Thomas, Brian Dick Lauder 1912–1989, *A View in the Roman Campagna*, unknown acquisition method

Thomas, Brian Dick Lauder 1912–1989, *Ascension of Christ, Cartoon for the New Shrine of the Order of the British Empire in St Paul's Cathedral*, unknown acquisition method

Thomas, Brian Dick Lauder 1912–1989, *Clouded Yellow Butterfly*, unknown acquisition method

Thomas, Brian Dick Lauder 1912–1989, *Dr F. L. Thomas, Mayor of Barnstaple (1922)*, presented by the artist, 1985

Thomas, Brian Dick Lauder 1912–1989, *Meadow Brown Butterfly*, unknown acquisition method

Thomas, Brian Dick Lauder 1912–1989, *Mrs F. L. Thomas (Margaret), Mayoress*, presented by the artist, 1985

Thomas, Brian Dick Lauder 1912–1989, *Red Admiral Butterfly*, unknown acquisition method

Thomas, Brian Dick Lauder 1912–1989, *The Entombment, Cartoon for the New Shrine of the Order of the British Empire in St Paul's Cathedral*, unknown acquisition method

unknown artist *Spring Plowing*, unknown acquisition method

unknown artist *A Three-Masted Vessel in a Swell*, unknown acquisition method

unknown artist *Bruce Oliver, Mayor of Barnstaple (1931)*, unknown acquisition method

unknown artist *Reverend Henry Nicholls, Mayor of Barnstaple (1826)*, unknown acquisition method

Vanderbank, John (after) 1694–1739, *John Gay (1685–1732), Poet and Dramatist*, presented by the Western Morning News Company, Sir Richard Harmsworth and Mr G. A. Harmsworth, 1928

Williams, John Edgar c.1821–1891, *Mrs Payne (1811–1890)*, unknown acquisition method

Williams, John Edgar c.1821–1891, *Wiliam Frederick Rock (1802–1890)*, unknown acquisition method

Museum of Barnstaple and North Devon

Beattie, A. active 1840–1856, *The Valley of the Taw, Devon*, on loan from the North Devon Athenaeum

Briggs, Henry Perronet 1791/1793–1844, *Frederick R. Lee, (1798–1879), RA*, on loan from the North Devon Athenaeum

G. C. active 20th C, *Country Scene with a River and a Bridge*, on loan from the North Devon Athenaeum

Chugg, Brian 1926–2003, *Coast Guard Lookout, Used as Target 1943, Baggy Point, Devon (Area F, US Army ATC) (painted on the spot)*, gift from the estate of the artist, 2004, © the artist's estate

Chugg, Brian 1926–2003, *Reinforced Concrete, Strong Point 1943, Baggy Point, Devon*, gift from the estate of the artist, 2004, © the artist's estate

Chugg, Brian 1926–2003, *Hovering Rock No.1*, gift from the estate of the artist, 2006, © the artist's estate

Chugg, Brian 1926–2003, *Continental Shelf*, gift from the estate of the artist, 2006, © the artist's estate

Chugg, Brian 1926–2003, *Saunton Rock and Atomic Cloud (Nuclear Dissolution)*, gift from the estate of the artist, © the artist's estate

Chugg, Brian 1926–2003, *Raised Beach*, gift from the estate of the artist, 2006, © the artist's estate

Chugg, Brian 1926–2003, *Rampart*, gift from the estate of the artist, 2006, © the artist's estate

Chugg, Brian 1926–2003, *Saunton Cliff, Devon*, gift from the estate of the artist, 2006, © the artist's estate

Chugg, Brian 1926–2003, *Atlantic Coast*, gift from the estate of the artist, 2006, © the artist's estate

Chugg, Brian 1926–2003, *Giant's Cave No.2*, gift from the estate of the artist, 2006, © the artist's estate

Chugg, Brian 1926–2003, *The Gulf Dream*, gift from the estate of the artist, 2006, © the artist's estate

Chugg, Brian 1926–2003, *Atlantic No.4*, gift from the estate of the artist, 2006, © the artist's estate

Chugg, Brian 1926–2003, *Form Experiment No.4*, gift from the

estate of the artist, 2006, © the artist's estate

Chugg, Brian 1926–2003, *Rock Form No.1*, gift from the estate of the artist, 2006, © the artist's estate

Chugg, Brian 1926–2003, *Developing Rock No.3*, gift from the estate of the artist, 2006, © the artist's estate

Chugg, Brian 1926–2003, *Evolving Rock No.4*, gift from the estate of the artist, 2006, © the artist's estate

Chugg, Brian 1926–2003, *Devonian Outcrop No.6*, gift from the estate of the artist, 2006, © the artist's estate

Chugg, Brian 1926–2003, *Composite of Beach Defences I*, gift from the estate of the artist, 2004; accessioned, 2005, © the artist's estate

Chugg, Brian 1926–2003, *Composite of Beach Defences II*, gift from the estate of the artist, 2004; accessioned, 2005, © the artist's estate

Chugg, Brian 1926–2003, *Rocks at Saunton, Devon*, gift from the estate of the artist, 2006, © the artist's estate

Falcon, Thomas Adolphus 1872–1944, *Appledore Shore with Boats, Devon*, purchased with the assistance of the Art Fund; originally from Sharlands House, Braunton

Foster, J. J. *Henry Rock (1774–1846), Father of William Frederick Rock*, on loan from the North Devon Athenaeum

Gould, Francis Carruthers 1844–1925, *John Penrose (d.1624) (copy after an earlier painting in the Penrose Almshouses)*, on loan from the North Devon Athenaeum

Hopwood *Isaac Clark, Esq.*, on loan from the North Devon Athenaeum

Jack, Richard 1866–1952, *Lady Barclay Black of Yelland Manor*, unknown acquisition method, © the artist's estate

Kennedy, Joseph c.1838–1893, *Barnstaple and the River Taw, Devon*, on loan from the North Devon Athenaeum

Kennedy, Joseph c.1838–1893, *North Gate and Rolle Quay, Barnstaple*, on loan from the North Devon Athenaeum

Kennedy, Joseph c.1838–1893, *The 'Star Inn'*, on loan from Anne Bainbridge

Kennedy, Joseph c.1838–1893, *River Taw from Rock Park, Devon*, unknown acquisition method

Kennedy, Joseph c.1838–1893, *The Construction of the Railway Bridge at Pottington, Devon*, unknown acquisition method

Kennedy, Joseph c.1838–1893, *Mill*, unknown acquisition method

Kennedy, Joseph c.1838–1893, *Raleigh Mill from the River Yeo*, on loan from the North Devon Athenaeum

Kennedy, Joseph c.1838–1893, *The Old Guildhall, Barnstaple, Devon*,

on loan from Anne Bainbridge
Kennedy, Joseph c.1838–1893, *Town Mill with Ship*, on loan from the North Devon Athenaeum
Kennedy, Joseph (attributed to) c.1838–1893, *Barnstaple North Gate, Devon (detail)*, presented by Miss L. Baker; on loan from the North Devon Athenaeum
Lee, Frederick Richard 1798–1879, *View from the River, Barnstaple, Devon*, unknown acquisition method
Lee, Frederick Richard 1798–1879, *River Taw and the Railway, Bishop's Tawton, near Barnstaple, Devon*, on loan from Whitton and Laing, Exeter
Lee, Frederick Richard 1798–1879, *West Lyn, Lynton, Devon*, on loan from the North Devon Athenaeum
Lely, Peter 1618–1680, *Portrait of a Lady with a Bouquet*, on loan from the North Devon Athenaeum
Nasmyth, Patrick (attributed to) 1787–1831, *Lime Kilns*, donation
Perrett, J. *The Old Mill, Lynmouth, Devon*, on loan from Mr P. Mewton
Shaddick, G. *The Castle, Barnstaple, Devon*, unknown acquisition method
Shaw, George 1843–1915, *Doone Valley, Devon*, on loan from the North Devon Athenaeum
Stiles, Peter b.1959, *Phillip Gosse Finding a Chrysaora Cyclonota in a Pool Below the Tunnels at Ilfracombe, Devon, 14 September 1852*, purchased, 2009, © the artist
unknown artist *Barnstaple from Sticklepath, Devon*, on loan from the North Devon Athenaeum
unknown artist *West Hill Farm, Braunton, Devon*, unknown acquisition method
unknown artist *Barnstaple Leat, Devon*, gift from the Misses Shaplands, 1995
unknown artist *Hugh Fortescue (1783–1861), 2nd Earl Fortescue*, on loan from the North Devon Athenaeum
unknown artist *Hugh Fortescue (1818–1905), 3rd Earl Fortescue*, on loan from the North Devon Athenaeum
unknown artist *John Abbott of Culley, Frithelstock (1639–1727), Sculptor*, on loan from the Royal Albert Memorial Museum, Exeter
unknown artist *John Roberts Chanter (1816–1895), Originator and First Honorary Secretary of the Barnstaple Literary and Scientific Institute (1845–1861)*, unknown acquisition method
unknown artist *Mr Rendle*, unknown acquisition method
unknown artist *Mrs Prudence Hartree Rock (1770–1846)*, on loan from the North Devon Athenaeum
unknown artist *Mrs Prudence Payne (1810–1890), Sister of William Frederick Rock*, on loan from the North Devon Athenaeum
unknown artist *Mrs Rendle*, unknown acquisition method

unknown artist *Penrose Almshouses, Litchdon Street, Barnstaple, Devon*, unknown acquisition method
unknown artist *'Poltimore Arms', Boutport Street, Barnstaple*, on loan from the North Devon Athenaeum
unknown artist *Portrait of a Man with Beard in Profile*, unknown acquisition method
unknown artist *Reverend Jonathan Hanmer (1606–1687), MA, St John's College Cambridge, One of Two Thousand Clergy Ejected from the Church of England in 1662*, presented to the Cross Street Congregational Church, Barnstaple, by Gay Neville Carleton-Stiff, 1956
unknown artist *Reverend Jonathan Hanmer (1606–1687), MA, St John's College, Cambridge*, presented to the Cross Street Congregational Church, Barnstaple, by Gay Neville Carleton-Stiff, 1956
unknown artist *River with a House and Church*, on loan from the North Devon Athenaeum
unknown artist *The 'Exeter Inn'*, unknown acquisition method
unknown artist *The Rhenish Tower, Lynmouth, Devon*, purchased, 1988
unknown artist *Three Tuns*, unknown acquisition method
unknown artist *Three Tuns*, unknown acquisition method
unknown artist *View of Barnstaple from Fort Hill, Devon*, on loan from the North Devon Athenaeum
unknown artist *William Avery (1812–1893), Mayor (1846, 1851, 1875 & 1878–1880)*, on loan from the North Devon Athenaeum
unknown artist *William Frederick Rock (1802–1890), Aged 35*, on loan from the North Devon Athenaeum
Vanderbank, John 1694–1739, *John Gay (1685–1732)*, on loan from the North Devon Athenaeum
Warren, M. F. J. *The Old Smithy, North Molton, Devon (reputed to be associated with the fictional character Tom Faggus, in the book, 'Lorna Doone', by R. D. Blackmore)*, unknown acquisition method
Williams, John Edgar c.1821–1891, *William Frederick Rock (1802–1890)*, presented by the artist to the Barnstaple Literary and Scientific Institution, 1863; on loan from the North Devon Athenaeum

North Devon Athenaeum

Kennedy, Joseph c.1838–1893, *The Fish Shambles, St Nicholas' Chapel and 'The Old Star' Inn, Barnstaple, Devon*, unknown acquisition method
Lee, Frederick Richard 1798–1879, *Bideford, Devon*, unknown acquisition method
Lee, Frederick Richard 1798–1879, *Devon Cottages*, unknown

acquisition method
Slade, R. W. *The Square, Braunton, North Devon*, unknown acquisition method
unknown artist *William Frederick Rock (1802–1890)*, unknown acquisition method

North Devon Council

Golds, Christopher Charles b.1936, *Brig Rounding a Cape*, presented by the artist, 1980

Penrose Almshouses

Hasler, F. *Penrose Almshouses, Barnstaple, Devon*, unknown acquisition method
Janssens van Ceulen, Cornelis 1593–1661, *John Penrose, Aged 26*, unknown acquisition method
unknown artist *Mr Gilbert Paige*, presented by John Gould King

Bideford Library

Bowyer, Alan J. active 1956–1969, *Miss M. E. Abbott, Founder and Headmistress of West Bank School, Bideford (1896–1938)*, presented to the West Bank School, 1956
Mead, Geraldine active 2000, *Sand Dunes*, donated by the artist
Mead, Geraldine active 2000, *The Quay at Bideford, Devon*, donated by the artist
Mead, Geraldine active 2000, *Under Construction, Kenwith Viaduct, Devon*, unknown acquisition method
Pearce, Jon *The Frozen Torridge, Devon*, donated by the artist's family
Williams, John Edgar c.1821–1891, *Edward Capern (1819–1895), Bideford Postman Poet*, transferred from Bideford Museum Collection to Devon County Council, 1974

Bideford Town Council

British (English) School *John Strange (1590–1646), Former Mayor of Bideford (1643–1646)*, unknown acquisition method
British (English) School 19th C, *John Willcock (b.1736), Mayor of Bideford (1783 & 1800)*, unknown acquisition method
British (English) School 19th C, *Charles Carter (1771–1862)*, unknown acquisition method
British (English) School 19th C, *Josias Wren, Mayor of Bideford (1842)*, unknown acquisition method
Dosser, Marguerite b.1942, *La Maison du Haut, Landivisau, France*, unknown acquisition method, © the artist
Dyer, Edmund active c.1820–1875, *Sir Richard Grenville (1542–1591)*, purchased by public subscription

and presented to the town of Bideford by Mayor H. W. Greenwood, 1938
Hoare, William (school of) 1706–1792, *Portrait of a Gentleman*, unknown acquisition method
King, Charles b.1912, *William Ewart Ellis (1884–1958), Mayor of Bideford (1934–1935)*, unknown acquisition method
Opie, John (school of) 1761–1807, *John Chanter, Mayor of Bideford (1815–1816)*, unknown acquisition method
Romney, George (follower of) 1734–1802, *George Stucley Buck (1754–1791)*, unknown acquisition method
Sandercock, M. *Bideford Quay, Devon*, unknown acquisition method
Sutton, Fran *Fred Pitfield Bailey (1915–1987), Mayor of Bideford (1979)*, unknown acquisition method

Burton Art Gallery and Museum

Beresford-Williams, Mary b.1931, *Summer on the Dart*, donated by the artist, © the artist
Braund, Allin 1915–2004, *Copse Path, April 1940*, donated, © the artist's estate
Braund, Allin 1915–2004, *Pebble and Seaweed*, donated by the artist, 2001, © the artist's estate
Braund, Allin 1915–2004, *Kelp*, gift from the Friends of the Burton Art Gallery and Museum, 1985, © the artist's estate
Braund, Allin 1915–2004, *Seascape with a White Bird*, donated, 2001, © the artist's estate
Carpenter, Margaret Sarah 1793–1872, *Study of a Girl in a Red Cloak*, bequeathed from the Hubert Coop Collection, 1951
Charles, James 1851–1906, *The Home Field*, bequeathed from the Hubert Coop Collection, 1951
Chugg, Brian 1926–2003, *Marine Organism*, gift from Mary Chugg Cooper, 2006, © the artist's estate
Clausen, George 1852–1944, *A Little Brook in Essex*, bequeathed from the Hubert Coop Collection, 1951, © Clausen estate
Coop, Hubert 1872–1953, *Chalk at Dover, Kent*, bequeathed from the Hubert Coop Collection, 1951
Coop, Hubert 1872–1953, *Hanging Cloud, Silver and Anglesey, and Beyond*, bequeathed from the Hubert Coop Collection, 1951
Cooper, Thomas Sidney 1803–1902, *Three Cows*, donated by Commander Didham, 1980
Correggio (after) c.1489–1534, *Meditation (based on the painting 'The Penitent Magdalene')*, gift from Thomas Burton, 1951
Dutch School 18th C, *Still Life with Fruit (in the style of the 17th century)*, bequeathed from the

Hubert Coop Collection, 1951
Ellis, Edwin 1842–1895, *Running for Shelter*, bequeathed from the Hubert Coop Collection, 1951
Ellis, Edwin 1842–1895, *Study of a Lobster*, bequeathed from the Hubert Coop Collection, 1951
Ellis, Edwin 1842–1895, *The Old Breakwater Walderswick, Suffolk*, bequeathed from the Hubert Coop Collection, 1951
Fisher, Mark 1841–1923, *Algerian Landscape*, bequeathed from the Hubert Coop Collection, 1951
Fisher, Mark 1841–1923, *Essex Marshes*, bequeathed from the Hubert Coop Collection, 1951
Fisher, Mark 1841–1923, *Essex Meadows*, bequeathed from the Hubert Coop Collection, 1951
Fisher, Mark 1841–1923, *Great Elms*, bequeathed from the Hubert Coop Collection, 1951
Fisher, Mark 1841–1923, *Spring in Orchard*, bequeathed from the Hubert Coop Collection, 1951
Fisher, Mark 1841–1923, *Still Life with Flowers*, bequeathed from the Hubert Coop Collection, 1951
Fisher, Mark 1841–1923, *Vasouy near Honfleur, France*, bequeathed from the Hubert Coop Collection, 1951
Friedenson, Arthur A. 1872–1955, *Belstone near Okehampton, Devon*, bequeathed from the Hubert Coop Collection, 1951, © the artist's estate
Friedenson, Arthur A. 1872–1955, *Evening over the Isles of Purbesck, Dorset*, bequeathed from the Hubert Coop Collection, 1951, © the artist's estate
Friedenson, Arthur A. 1872–1955, *Landscape, Corfe Castle, Dorset*, bequeathed from the Hubert Coop Collection, 1951, © the artist's estate
Friedenson, Arthur A. 1872–1955, *On the River at Wareham, Dorset*, bequeathed from the Hubert Coop Collection, 1951, © the artist's estate
Furse, Patrick John Dolignon 1918–2005, *Lady in a Hat*, donated by Mrs A. Furse, 2010, © the artist's estate
Girling, William H. 1913–1991, *Still Life 1*, gift from Mrs P. Girling, 1991
Hall, Oliver 1869–1957, *Entrance to Egdean Wood, West Sussex*, bequeathed from the Hubert Coop Collection, 1951, © the artist's estate
Hayward, Alfred Frederick William 1856–1939, *Bucks Mills, Devon*, donated by Ackland Edwards Trust, 1996
Heard, Hugh Percy 1866–1940, *Sea and Landscape*, bequeathed from the Hubert Coop Collection, 1951
Heard, Hugh Percy 1866–1940, *Stormy Sea*, gift
Hunt, Edgar 1876–1953, *Tangier, Morocco*, donated by Christopher Whitehouse

Hunt, Edward Aubrey 1855–1922, *A Tidal River*, bequeathed from the Hubert Coop Collection, 1951
Hunt, Edward Aubrey 1855–1922, *An Old Dutch Town*, bequeathed from the Hubert Coop Collection, 1951
Hunt, Edward Aubrey 1855–1922, *Broadly That's It*, bequeathed from the Hubert Coop Collection, 1951
Hunt, Edward Aubrey 1855–1922, *Cattle in a Field*, donated by Christopher Whitehouse Oakland
Hunt, Edward Aubrey 1855–1922, *Cows and a Village*, bequeathed from the Hubert Coop Collection, 1951
Hunt, Edward Aubrey 1855–1922, *Desert Camels near Tangiers, Morocco*, bequeathed from the Hubert Coop Collection, 1951
Hunt, Edward Aubrey 1855–1922, *Mrs Howard Stormont and Her Pikinese 'Prince Pri'*, bequeathed from the Hubert Coop Collection, 1951
Hunt, Edward Aubrey 1855–1922, *Off the Moroccan Coast*, bequeathed from the Hubert Coop Collection, 1951
Hunt, Edward Aubrey 1855–1922, *On the Marne above Nogent, France*, bequeathed from the Hubert Coop Collection, 1951
Hunt, Edward Aubrey 1855–1922, *River Scene*, bequeathed from the Hubert Coop Collection, 1951
Hunt, Edward Aubrey 1855–1922, *Sallee Rover*, bequeathed from the Hubert Coop Collection, 1951
Hunt, Edward Aubrey 1855–1922, *Silver Sky and Shining Sands*, bequeathed from the Hubert Coop Collection, 1951
Hunt, Edward Aubrey 1855–1922, *Study of Cattle by a Clump of Willows*, bequeathed from the Hubert Coop Collection, 1951
Hunt, Edward Aubrey 1855–1922, *Study of Cattle in the Shade of a Large Willow Tree*, bequeathed from the Hubert Coop Collection, 1951
Hunt, Edward Aubrey 1855–1922, *The Drinking Place*, bequeathed from the Hubert Coop Collection, 1951
Hunt, Edward Aubrey 1855–1922, *The White Pony*, bequeathed from the Hubert Coop Collection, 1951
Hunter, Colin 1841–1904, *Kelp Gatherers*, bequeathed from the Hubert Coop Collection, 1951
Hunter, Colin 1841–1904, *Summer Fishing, Skye*, bequeathed from the Hubert Coop Collection, 1951
James, Clifford Boucher d.1913, *The Wail of the Banshee, Waving Her Hands and Chanting a Sweet Song of Life*, bequeathed from the Hubert Coop Collection, 1951
Jones, Patrick b.1948, *Pilaster*, donated, 2006, © the artist
Knight, John William Buxton 1842/1843–1908, *Building the Rick*, bequeathed from the Hubert Coop Collection, 1951

Knight, John William Buxton 1842/1843–1908, *Loading the Haywain*, bequeathed from the Hubert Coop Collection, 1951
Lavery, John 1856–1941, *E. Aubrey Hunt (1855–1922)*, bequeathed from the Hubert Coop Collection, 1951, © by courtesy of Felix Rosenstiel's Widow and Son Ltd, London on behalf of the estate of Sir John Lavery
Littlejohns, John b.1874, *Bruges, Belgium*, bequeathed from the Hubert Coop Collection, 1951
Lloyd, Reginald James b.1926, *Estuary*, gift from the Friends of the Burton Art Gallery and Museum, 1992, © the artist
Mead, Geraldine active 2000, *Still Life in Silver and Grey*, gift from the artist, 2000
Milne, William Watt 1865–1949, *A Corner of the Farmyard*, bequeathed from the Hubert Coop Collection, 1951
Milne, William Watt 1865–1949, *Corner of the Farmyard*, bequeathed from the Hubert Coop Collection, 1951
Mumford, Howard *Elizabeth Athrens, Died Aged 98*, gift from the family of the sitter
Opie, John 1761–1807, *Doctor Burton*, bequeathed from the Hubert Coop Collection, 1951
Ousey, Buckley 1850–1889, *The Tail End of a Blow, Bull Bay, Anglesey*, bequeathed from the Hubert Coop Collection, 1951
Owen, William 1769–1825, *The Rest by the Wayside*, bequeathed by Ernest E. Cook through the National Art Collections Fund, 1955
Peacock, Ralph 1868–1946, *Master Wilson*, donated by Marjorie Richards
Peacock, Ralph 1868–1946, *Miss Wilson*, donated by Marjorie Richards, the sitter
Pipkin, James Edward b.1945, *The Sunset Line*, donated by the artist in memory of his father, © the artist
Prance, Bertram 1889–1958, *Winter Scene*, unknown acquisition method
Reid, Peter *A Letter to Peter Reid*, gift from the Friends of the Burton Art Gallery and Museum, 1980
Reid, Peter *Appledore Shipyard, Devon*, gift from the Friends of the Burton Art Gallery and Museum, 1976
Reynolds, Joshua 1723–1792, *Mrs John Clevland of Tapley*, on permanent loan from H. J. I. Meredith, Esq.
Sadler, Walter Dendy 1854–1923, *The Attorney*, bequeathed from the Hubert Coop Collection, 1951
Sadler, Walter Dendy 1854–1923, *There's Joy in Remembrance (Portrait of a Lady at Her Desk)*, bequeathed from the Hubert Coop Collection, 1951
Shayer, William 1788–1879, *The Stable*, donated by Mr and Mrs

Thomas Burton, 1951
Shayer, William 1788–1879, *Travellers by a Gypsy Encampment*, donated by Mr and Mrs Thomas Burton, 1960
Sims, Charles 1873–1928, *April*, bequeathed from the Hubert Coop Collection, 1951
Trefusis, Hilda 1891–1980, *Self Portrait*, donated to the Friends of Burton Art Gallery and Museum by Jack Trefusis; donated
unknown artist *A View of Bideford from Upcott Hill, Devon*, donated by Bideford Museum, 1991
unknown artist *Bertha Burton*, donated by Mrs Cooper
unknown artist *Edward Capern (1819–1894), Postman Poet*, presented by Alderman J. W. Narraway, 1906
unknown artist *Thomas Burton*, donated by Mrs Cooper
Wilson, Richard 1712/1713–1782, *Lake Nemi Showing Castel Gandolfo and the Barberini Palace, Italy*, bequeathed from the Hubert Coop Collection, 1951

Bovey Tracey Heritage Trust

Elphick, David b.1942, *Bovey Signal Box, Devon*, gift from the artist, 2004, © the artist
Malpass, I. *Kelly Cottage, Bovey Tracey, Devon*, unknown acquisition method
Yendall, Arthur active c.1935–1965, *The Bovey Pottery, Devon*, gift from Edith Yendall, 1996
Yendall, Arthur active c.1935–1965, *Bovey Station, Devon*, gift from Edith Yendall, 1996
Yendall, Arthur active c.1935–1965, *'Church Steps', Bovey Tracey, Devon*, unknown acquistion method
Yendall, Arthur active c.1935–1965, *Waiting for the Train at Bovey Station, Devon*, gift from Edith Yendall, 1996

Braunton & District Museum

Adams, Arthur b.1930, *Knowle, Devon*, unknown acquisition method
Cabot *Under Sail (possibly 'Bessie Clarke')*, gift from Alan Tucker, 1994
Dye, Lewis G. d. late 1960s, *Braunton, Devon: An English Village*, gift from Miss Dye, 1993
Dye, Lewis G. d. late 1960s, *Buckland Farm Cottages*, gift from Miss Dye, 1993
Dye, Lewis G. d. late 1960s, *North Devon Coast Scene*, gift from Miss Dye, 1993
Dye, Lewis G. d. late 1960s, *Rocks of Saunton, Devon*, gift from Miss Dye, 1993
Dye, Lewis G. d. late 1960s, *Winter, North Street, Braunton, Devon*, gift from Miss Dye, 1993

Falcon, Thomas Adolphus 1872–1944, *Braunton, Devon, View from East Hill*, gift from Brian and Mary Chugg, 1997
Falcon, Thomas Adolphus 1872–1944, *North Devon Coast View*, gift from Brian and Mary Chugg, 1997
Falcon, Thomas Adolphus 1872–1944, *View across Braunton with Estuary and Great Field in the Distance*, gift from Brian and Mary Chugg, 1997
unknown artist *Mariners' Close, South Street, Braunton, Devon*, gift from the warden of Mariners' Close Sheltered Accommodation, 2000
Wilson, L. *View of Braunton, Devon, with Two Bridges*, donated by Francis Gerald Wigley

Buckfastleigh Town Hall

Mann, Warwick Henry 1838–1910, *John Hamlyn (1816–1878)*, unknown acquisition method
unknown artist 19th C, *William Hamlyn (b.1852)*, unknown acquisition method
Vigard, W. active 1886–1889, *Joseph Hamlyn (1809–1888)*, unknown acquisition method

Budleigh Salterton Town Council

Dennys, Joyce 1893–1991, *Above Steamer Steps*, gift from the artist
Dennys, Joyce 1893–1991, *Beach Party, the Old Capstan*, gift from the artist
Dennys, Joyce 1893–1991, *Eating Ice Creams on Budleigh Seafront, Devon*, gift from the artist
Dennys, Joyce 1893–1991, *Fore Street Hill, Budleigh Salterton, Devon*, gift from the artist
Dennys, Joyce 1893–1991, *The Coffee Morning, 'Markers' Restaurant*, gift from the artist
Dennys, Joyce 1893–1991, *The Longboat Café*, gift from the artist

Fairlynch Museum

Carpenter, George Ellis 1891–1971, *Rainy Day*, gift, 2007, © the artist's estate
Cotton, Alan b.1938, *Otter Valley, Devon, Evening Light*, bequeathed by Mrs Clayden, 2001, © the artist
Dennys, Joyce 1893–1991, *Family on the Beach at Budleigh Salterton, Devon*, gift from P. Hull, 1999
Dennys, Joyce 1893–1991, *Flower Painting*, bequeathed by F. Van Meter, 1994
Dennys, Joyce 1893–1991, *On the Parade*, on loan from Budleigh Salterton Town Council
Dennys, Joyce 1893–1991, *Still Life with Flowers*, on loan from the Methodist Church, Budleigh

Salterton
Goodhall, Peter b.1957, *A Revenue Cutter Apprehends the Smuggler Jack Rattenbury off Budleigh Salterton*, © the artist
Goodhall, Peter b.1957, *The Dutch Privateer 'Zeuse' Brought as a Prize into Exmouth by the 'Defiance' after a Two Hour Action in the Bay, June 1782*, unknown acquisition method, © the artist

Crediton Area History and Museum Society

unknown artist *Marjorie Jago, Music Teacher at Queen Elizabeth School, Crediton, Devon and Choir Mistress at the Parish Church*, gift from Queen Elizabeth School
unknown artist *Pauls and Whites, Crediton Mill, Devon*, gift from Pauls and Whites Ltd

Britannia Royal Naval College

Abbott, Lemuel Francis 1760–1803, *Captain Thomas Masterman Hardy (1769–1839)*, presented by the 1st Viscount Rothermere in memory of his eldest son, Captain the Honorable H. A. V. St G. Harmsworth, MC, Irish Guards (who died of his wounds, February 1918, aged 23), 1925
Armitage, Edward 1817–1896, *The Death of Nelson*, presented by Mrs G. de Wilton, a direct descendant of the artist
Bambridge, Arthur Leopold 1861–1923, *Alfred Ernest Albert (1844–1900), Duke of Saxe-Coburg and Gotha, Duke of Edinburgh*, presented by the Duchess of Saxe-Coburg and Gotha, 1903
Birley, Oswald Hornby Joseph 1880–1952, *George VI (1895–1952)*, commissioned by the Wardroom at the Royal Naval College Greenwich, © the artist's estate
Birley, Oswald Hornby Joseph 1880–1952, *Admiral of the Fleet Sir Max Horton (1883–1951), GCB*, commissioned by the Wardroom at the Royal Naval College Greenwich, 1998, © the artist's estate
Birley, Oswald Hornby Joseph 1880–1952, *Admiral Sir Algernon Willis (1889–1976)*, commissioned by the Wardroom at the Royal Naval College Greenwich, 1998, © the artist's estate
Birley, Oswald Hornby Joseph 1880–1952, *Admiral Sir Henry Harwood (1888–1950), KCB*, commissioned by the Wardroom at the Royal Naval College Greenwich, 1998, © the artist's estate
Birley, Oswald Hornby Joseph 1880–1952, *Admiral Sir Percy Noble (1880–1955)*, commissioned by the Wardroom at the Royal

Naval College Greenwich, 1998, © the artist's estate

Birley, Oswald Hornby Joseph 1880–1952, *Admiral of the Fleet Earl Viscount Mountbatten of Burma (1900–1979), KC*, commissioned by the Wardroom at the Royal Naval College Greenwich, 1998, © the artist's estate

Birley, Oswald Hornby Joseph 1880–1952, *Admiral of the Fleet Lord Tovey (1885–1971), GCB*, commissioned by the Wardroom at the Royal Naval College Greenwich, 1998, © the artist's estate

Birley, Oswald Hornby Joseph 1880–1952, *Admiral of the Fleet Sir Charles Forbes (1880–1960), GCB*, commissioned by the Wardroom at the Royal Naval College Greenwich, 1998, © the artist's estate

Birley, Oswald Hornby Joseph 1880–1952, *Admiral of the Fleet Sir James Somerville (1882–1949), GCB*, commissioned by the Wardroom at the Royal Naval College Greenwich, 1998, © the artist's estate

Birley, Oswald Hornby Joseph 1880–1952, *Admiral of the Fleet The Earl of Mountbatten*, presented by Major General Sir Harold Wernher, GCVO and officers who served on Admiral Mountbatten's staff when he was Chief of Combined Operations, 1941–1943, in memory of the part played by the College in Combined Operations, 1942–1945, © the artist's estate

Birley, Oswald Hornby Joseph 1880–1952, *Admiral of the Fleet Viscount Cunningham (1883–1963)*, commissioned by the Wardroom at the Royal Naval College Greenwich, 1998, © the artist's estate

Birley, Oswald Hornby Joseph 1880–1952, *Admiral Sir Bertram Ramsay (1883–1945), KCB*, commissioned by the Wardroom at the Royal Naval College Greenwich, 1998, © the artist's estate

Birley, Oswald Hornby Joseph 1880–1952, *Admiral Sir John Cunningham (1885–1962), GCB*, commissioned by the Wardroom at the Royal Naval College Greenwich, 1998, © the artist's estate

Birley, Oswald Hornby Joseph 1880–1952, *Lord Fraser (1888–1981)*, commissioned by the Wardroom at the Royal Naval College Greenwich, 1998, © the artist's estate

Birley, Oswald Hornby Joseph 1880–1952, *Sir Bernard Rawlings (1889–1962)*, commissioned by the Wardroom at the Royal Naval College Greenwich, 1998, © the artist's estate

Birley, Oswald Hornby Joseph 1880–1952, *Admiral of the Fleet Sir*

Neville Syfret (1889–1972), KCB, commissioned by the Wardroom at the Royal Naval College Greenwich, 1998, © the artist's estate

Birley, Oswald Hornby Joseph 1880–1952, *Sir Phillip Vian (1894–1968)*, commissioned by the Wardroom at the Royal Naval College Greenwich, 1998, © the artist's estate

Birley, Oswald Hornby Joseph 1880–1952, *Admiral of the Fleet Dudley-Pound (1877–1943)*, commissioned by the Wardroom at the Royal Naval College Greenwich, 1998, © the artist's estate

Birley, Oswald Hornby Joseph 1880–1952, *Admiral Sir Arthur J. Power (1889–1960)*, commissioned by the Wardroom at the Royal Naval College Greenwich, 1998, © the artist's estate

Boel, Maurice 1913–1998, *Abstraction*, unknown acquisition method

Bolwell, Norman William 1938–2009, *Battle Group South Atlantic*, presented by the artist, © the artist's estate

Brie, Anthony de 1854–1921, *Admiral George Legge (c.1647–1691), Lord Dartmouth (after Joseph Vivien)*, presented by the 6th Earl of Dartmouth, 1914

British (English) School *HMS 'Britannia' and HMS 'Trafalgar' at Portland*, presented by the Admiralty, 1928

Brooks, Frank 1854–1937, *His Royal Highness The Duke of Windsor (1894–1972)*, purchased by Britannia Royal Naval College, 1962

Bumford, Frederick W. active 1979–1986, *HMS 'Thunderer' Devastation Class, 1877*, unknown acquisition method

Bumford, Frederick W. active 1979–1986, *HMS 'Thunderer' Orion Class, 1912*, unknown acquisition method

Bumford, Frederick W. active 1979–1986, *HMS 'Thunderer' Culloden Class, 1781*, unknown acquisition method

Bumford, Frederick W. active 1979–1986, *HMS 'Thunderer' Lion Class, 1939*, unknown acquisition method

Burke, Terry b.1927, *Dartmouth, Devon*, unknown acquisition method

Carmichael, John Wilson 1799–1868, *The Battle of Copenhagen, 16 August–5 September 1807*, bequeathed by Baron Winster, 1998

Clarke, Sarah d.c.2001, *Britannia Royal Naval College*, presented by PMO-Surgeon Lieutenant Commander John Clarke, husband of the artist, 2001

Clegg, Ernest active 1951, *HMS 'Cardiff' (polyptych, panel 1 of 6)*, presented by the artist, 1951

Clegg, Ernest active 1951, *SMS 'Seydlitz' (polyptych, panel 2 of 6)*, presented by the artist, 1951

Clegg, Ernest active 1951, *SMS 'Derfflinger' (polyptych, panel 4 of 6)*, presented by the artist, 1951

Clegg, Ernest active 1951, *SMS 'Hindenburg' (polyptych, panel 5 of 6)*, presented by the artist, 1951

Clegg, Ernest active 1951, *SMS 'Von der Tann' (polyptych, panel 6 of 6)*, presented by the artist, 1951

Cobb, Charles David b.1921, *Operation Loyalty*, unknown acquisition method, © the artist

Collins, William Wiehe 1862–1951, *The Channel Squadron, 1898*, presented to RNC Osborne in 1904 by the artist; transferred to Britannia Royal Naval College, 1921

Condy, Nicholas Matthew 1816–1851, *HMS 'Pike'*, bequeathed by Mrs C. I. Heath, 1972

Cope, Arthur Stockdale 1857–1940, *Edward VII (1841–1910)*, presented by George V, 1911

Cope, Arthur Stockdale 1857–1940, *George V (1865–1936)*, presented by the Prince of Wales (later Edward VIII), 1913

Cundall, Charles Ernest 1890–1971, *Dunkirk*, commissioned for presentation to Lord Gort, who died before its completion; purchased by the Nuffield Trust for HMS 'St George', the Special Duties Officers School; transferred to the College when HMS 'St George' moved to Dartmouth, 1973, © the artist's estate/Bridgeman Art Library

De Lacy, Charles John 1856–1936, *HMS 'Vindictive' Storming Zeebrugge Mole*, unknown acquisition method

Dodd, Robert (attributed to) 1748–1815, *HMS 'Victory' at Spithead, 1791 (The British fleet under Lord Hood: The Russian Armament, 1791)*, presented by Miss C. M. York, 1948

Drew, Pamela 1910–1989, *Prince Philip Presents the Queen's Colour to the Britannia Royal Naval College, Dartmouth, Devon 1 July 1958*, unknown acquisition method, © the artist's estate

Eves, Reginald Grenville 1876–1941, *The Admiral of the Fleet John Rushworth Jellicoe (1859–1935), OM, 1st Earl Jellicoe*, gift from Mrs Margaret Wilson, 2002

Fearnley, Alan b.1942, *HMS 'Bacchante' Conducting PWD Firings against Shelduck X2538 off Gibraltar on 25 October 1978*, presented to the Fleet Target Group by Aerial Targets LTD and Northrop Corporation Ventura Division to mark the 20th anniversary of the first launch of a KD2R–5 Shelduck in Royal Navy Service in 1959, 1979, © the artist

Fildes, Denis 1889–1974, *Elizabeth II (b.1926)*, commissioned, 1959

Fildes, Denis 1889–1974, *The Duke of Edinburgh (b.1921)*, commissioned, 1961

Fisher, Roger Roland Sutton 1919–1992, *HMS 'Manchester' on Armilla Patrol*, presented by the artist, 1992, © the artist's estate

Fleck, J. *The First Battle Cruiser Squadron*, presented, 2009

Fleck, J. *First Battle Cruiser Squadron Returning from Jutland, June 1916*, presented, 2009

Gardner, Derek George Montague 1914–2007, *San Carlos, Falkland Islands, May 1982*, commissioned

George, Colin *Moorland Fire*, presented by the artist, 1993

Goodwin, Albert 1845–1932, *The Invincible Armada*, presented to RNC Osborne in 1915, by Ian D. Elliot, grandson of the painter; transferred to Britannia Royal Naval College, 1921

Goodwin, Albert 1845–1932, *The Phantom Ship*, presented by Mr I. Sansom, 1949

Green, George Pycock Everett c.1811–1893, *The Deposition of Christ (after Peter Paul Rubens)*, presented to the College Chapel by Dr and Mrs Gow in memory of their son, Lieutenant Roderick Gow, Royal Navy, who was killed in HMS 'Defence' at the Battle of Jutland, 1916

Gribble, Bernard Finnigan 1872–1962, *Nelson's First Prize*, presented by the Admiralty, 1923, © the artist's estate

Gribble, Bernard Finnigan 1872–1962, *The Doomed Raider*, presented by the artist, 1927, © the artist's estate

Guzzardi, Leonardo active 1798–1800, *Horatio Nelson (1758–1805), 1st Viscount Nelson*, presented by Sir Robert Harmsworth in memory of his nephew Lieutenant the Hon V. S. T. Harmsworth, Royal Naval Division, formerly Midshipman RN (who was killed at the Battle of Beaumont Hamel in 1916, aged 21), 1918

Hailstone, Bernard 1910–1987, *Charles, Prince of Wales (b.1948)*, presented by Mrs Julius Grant in memory of her late husband, Commander J. H. Carrow, Royal Navy (1890–1923), 1977, © the artist's estate

Hailstone, Bernard 1910–1987, *Prince Andrew (b.1960)*, presented by an anonymous donor, 1982, © the artist's estate

Hailstone, Bernard 1910–1987, *Princess Anne (b.1950)*, presented by the artist, 1977, © the artist's estate

Halliday, Edward Irvine 1902–1984, *Her Royal Highness Princess Elizabeth (b.1926) and the Duke of Edinburgh (b.1921)*, unknown acquisition method, © the artist's estate

Herkomer, Herman 1863–1935, *Admiral of the Fleet Sir Edward Seymour (1840–1929)*, presented by Captain Meyer, RN, c.1998

Higson, Max *Chipmunks over Dartmouth, Devon*, presented by the artist

Johnson, Desmond b.1922, *SMS 'Moltke' (after Ernest Clegg)*, commissioned as a replacement for panel 3 of the 6-panelled polyptych by Ernest Clegg, the original having been lost, © the artist

Johnson, Desmond b.1922, *Sailing in Dartmouth Harbour*, gift from Mrs Rosemary Deeprose in memory of her husband Derrick Deeprose, lecturer at the College, 1996, © the artist

Lady Abercromby *Admiral Lord Duncan (after Joshua Reynolds)*, presented by the Earl of Camperdown, c.1913

Langmaid, Rowland 1897–1956, *Battle Fleet*, unknown acquisition method

Leigh-Pemberton, John 1911–1997, *George VI (1895–1952) (copy after Oswald Hornby Joseph Birley)*, on loan from Her Majesty the Queen, since 1961, © the artist's estate

Long, Leonard Hugh b.1911, *Creswell Naval College, Jervis Bay, Australia*, presented by the Royal Australian Naval College, 1965

Luny, Thomas 1759–1837, *The Battle of Trafalgar, 21 October 1805*, presented by Major-General F. G. Cotter in memory of his son, Sub Lieutenant F. J. A. Cotter of HMS 'Good Hope', killed in action at the Battle of Coronel on 1 November 1914, 1920

Mason, Frank Henry 1876–1965, *HMS 'Superb'*, on loan from the Imperial War Museum

McDowell, William 1888–1950, *HMS 'Liverpool'*, unknown acquisition method

Mendoza, June b.1945, *Admiral of the Fleet Sir Michael Le Fanu (1913–1970)*, commissioned with the assistance of a bequest from Miss Alice Fawcett Walker, 1978, © the artist

Mendoza, June b.1945, *Admiral of the Fleet the Earl Mountbatten of Burma (1900–1979)*, commissioned by Britannia Royal Naval College, 1982, © the artist

Menzies, William A. active 1886–1928, *Lord Nelson (1758–1805), after Copenhagen (copy after John Hoppner)*, presented by the first and last Lord Leith of Fyvie (d.1925), probably before 1914

Minderhout, Hendrik van 1632–1696, *View of Bruges Harbour*, presented by Her Royal Highness the Princess Louise, Duchess of Argyll, 1925

Mitchell, A. L. *Admiral Sir William Parker (1781–1866), GCB*, unknown acquisition method

Mitchell, F. *The Red Fleet, 1781,* unknown acquisition method

Neate, Andrew *Britannia Royal Naval College,* gift from the Brooke family in memory of Commander H. J. A. Brooke, 2007

Nibbs, Richard Henry 1816–1893, *HMS 'Bombay',* presented to RNC Osborne by Commander H. Blackett, 1906; transferred, 1921

Noakes, Michael b.1933, *Admiral of the Fleet Terence Thornton Lewin, Baron Lewin (1920–1999), Chief of the Defence Staff,* commissioned, © the artist

Noble, John Rushton b.1927, *Destroyer Screen,* purchased from a private collection in Plymouth, 1969

Phillips, Rex b.1931, *Helicopter,* unknown acquisition method, © the artist

Phillips, Rex b.1931, *Jellicoe Crosses the 'T', Jutland 31 May 1916,* presented by the artist, 1992, © the artist

Pocock, Nicholas (after) 1740–1821, *The Capture of 'L'Étoile',* presented by Mr H. F. Frazer

Poole, Burnell 1884–1933, *Sixth Battle Squadron, Grand Fleet Rear Admiral Hugh Rodman, United States Navy Commanding,* presented to the British Admiralty by the officers and men of the Sixth Battle Squadron, 1917–1918

Powell, Charles Martin 1775–1824, *HMS 'Enchantress' in the River Dart,* purchased with the assistance of the National Art Collections Fund, 1951

Riley, James Lewis b.1925, *Mountbatten at Singapore,* presented by the artist, © the artist

Robins, Henry 1820–1892, *HMS 'Britannia' and 'Hindostan',* offered to Britannia Royal Naval College by Commander John Lee in exchange for a wooden bust of Admiral Lord Nelson, 1974

Rosse, Nicholas St John b.1945, *Admiral of the Fleet Lord Fieldhouse (1928–1992), Commander-in-Chief Fleet,* commissioned, 1998, © the artist

Rosse, Nicholas St John b.1945, *Admiral Sir Henry Leach (b.1923), First Sea Lord,* commissioned, 2000, © the artist

Saumarez, Marion 1885–1978, *Admiral James Saumarez (1757–1836), 1st Baron de Saumarez (copy after Thomas Phillips),* unknown acquisition method

Swan, Robert John 1888–1980, *Admiral of the Fleet Andrew Browne Cunningham (1873–1968), PC, GCB, OM, 1st Viscount Cunningham of Hyndhope,* presented in memory of Captain J. A. A. Morris, Royal Navy, Commander of the College (1922–1926), by his daughter, Mrs Ann Keen, and other members of the family

Swan, Robert John 1888–1980, *Admiral of the Fleet Andrew Browne Cunningham, 1st Viscount Cunningham of Hyndhope,* commissioned, 1964

Swan, Robert John 1888–1980, *Admiral of the Fleet Lord Fisher of Kilverstone (1841–1920) (copy after Hubert von Herkomer),* commissioned, 1965

Taylor, Robert b.1946, *HMS 'Kelly',* on loan from the Imperial War Museum, © the Military Gallery, Wendover, UK

unknown artist *Admiral Edward Russell (1653–1727) (copy after an earlier painting by unknown artist),* presented by the 11th Duke of Bedford, 1906

unknown artist *Admiral of the Fleet George Anson (1697–1762), 1st Baron Anson,* unknown acquisition method

unknown artist *Admiral Sir David Milne (1763–1845), GCB,* unknown acquisition method

unknown artist *Portsmouth Harbour,* bequeathed by an anonymous donor from Shepton Mallet

unknown artist *Seascape,* bequeathed by Baron Winster, 1998

unknown artist *Seascape,* bequeathed by Baron Winster, 1998

unknown artist *Seascape,* bequeathed by Baron Winster, 1998

unknown artist *The Last of the 'Revenge' (triptych, left wing),* unknown acquisition method

unknown artist *The Last of the 'Revenge' (triptych, centre panel),* unknown acquisition method

unknown artist *The Last of the 'Revenge' (triptych, right wing),* unknown acquisition method

Velde II, Willem van de (school of) 1633–1707, *Large Seascape,* presented by Mr H. F. Frazer

Vincent *HMS 'Sheffield',* unknown acquisition method

Watherston, Evelyn Mary 1880–1952, *William Howard (c.1510–1573), 1st Baron Howard of Effingham (copy after Daniel Mytens),* presented by the 15th Duke of Norfolk and members of the Howard family, 1913

Webster, John b.1932, *Entering Dartmouth Harbour,* gift from the artist, 1992, © the artist

Webster, John b.1932, *HMS 'Westminster' off Greenwich,* gift from the artist, c.2004, © the artist

Wilcox, Leslie Arthur 1904–1982, *Admiral of the Fleet Earl Jellicoe (1858–1935) (copy after Reginald Grenville Eves),* commissioned through the Royal Society of Portrait Painters, 1963, © trustees of the estate of L. A. Wilcox

Wilkinson, Norman 1878–1972, *HMS 'Lion', Battlecruiser,* presented to the cruiser Lion in 1968; on loan to Britannia Royal Naval College, since 1982, © the

Norman Wilkinson estate

Wilkinson, Norman 1878–1972, *The Normandy Landings, 1944,* purchased, 1965, © the Norman Wilkinson estate

Wood, Frank Watson 1862–1953, *HMS 'Renown' with HMS 'Terrible' in Company Leaving Portsmouth Harbour,* purchased from the artist by RNC Osborne, 1906; transferred, 1921

Wood, Tim G. c.1929–1998, *Dartmouth Castle, Devon,* purchased

Wyllie, William Lionel 1851–1931, *The Battle of Trafalgar, 21 October 1805,* purchased by the College, 1965

Wyllie, William Lionel 1851–1931, *The Destruction of the German Raider 'Leopard' by His Majesty's Ships 'Achilles' and 'Dundee', 16 March 1917,* on loan from the Imperial War Museum

Dartmouth and Kingswear Hospital

Beulke, Reinhardt 1926–2008, *Devil's Marbles, Australia,* unknown acquisition method, MR - see http://www.turosshead.org/ Artists/ReinhardtBeulke.htm

Donaldson, John b.1945, *Dartmouth Harbour Scene, Devon,* unknown acquisition method, © the artist

Tiffen, S. *Riders in a Wood,* gift in memory of Dr Betty Hobbs

Dartmouth Guildhall

Campbell, T. H. *Sir Thomas Wilton, Mayor of Dartmouth (1900–1901 & 1914–1919),* unknown acquisition method

Girard, Michel b.1939, *A French Fishing Port,* unknown acquisition method

Harris, George Frederick 1856–1926, *Sir Henry Paul Seale (1806–1897), Bt, Mayor of Dartmouth,* unknown acquisition method

unknown artist *Arthur Howe Holdsworth (1780–1860), Governor of Dartmouth Castle (1807–1857),* unknown acquisition method

unknown artist *Elizabeth Kennicott, Mayoress of Dartmouth (1683),* unknown acquisition method

unknown artist *Francis Charles Simpson, Mayor of Dartmouth (1882–1891),* unknown acquisition method

unknown artist *George Kennicott, Mayor of Dartmouth (1683),* unknown acquisition method

unknown artist *Hercules Hoyles, BA Oxon, Clerk of Dartmouth (1695),* unknown acquisition method

unknown artist *Reverend John Flavel (c.1630–1691), BA Oxon, Rector of Dartmouth (1656–1662),*

unknown acquisition method

unknown artist *Robert Cranford, Mayor of Dartmouth (1871–1872),* unknown acquisition method

unknown artist *Samuel Were Prideaux (1803–1874),* unknown acquisition method

unknown artist *William Smith, Mayor of Dartmouth (1891–1893),* unknown acquisition method

Way, William Hopkins 1812–1891, *Charles Chalker, First Postmaster of Dartmouth (1870),* unknown acquisition method

Wimbush, John L. c.1854–1914, *Charles Peek, Mayor of Dartmouth (1911–1914 & 1919–1921),* unknown acquisition method

Wray, G. *John Morgan Puddicombe, Mayor of Dartmouth (1873–1876),* unknown acquisition method

Dartmouth Museum

A. H. *'Annie', Yarmouth, Isle of Wight,* gift

Assar, W. *Dartmouth from King's Quay, Devon (after Clarkson Stansfield),* purchased by the Friends of Dartmouth Museum, 1955

Beavis, Hubert E. b.1925, *Motor Torpedo Boat MTB 777,* gift, 2009, © the artist

Butler, Gustav *The 'Dittisham Flyer', Lilienthal's Aerostat in Fields,* unknown acquisition method

Holwill, Fred Cyril 1887–1980, *Morning Departure, 'Mayflower II 'Leaving Dartmouth, 19 April 1957,* gift from the artist's son, Bruce Blackmore Holwill, 1960, © the artist's estate

Hunt, C. B. (Miss) *Higher Street Looking South, 'The Old Shambles', Dartmouth, Devon,* gift from J. H. Smith, probably 1949

Ing, Harold Vivian 1900–1973, *Lightship under Repair, HMS 'Venus' in the Background,* gift, probably 1956

Ing, Harold Vivian 1900–1973, *Tall Ships in Dartmouth Harbour, Devon, Prior to a Race,* purchased by the Friends of Dartmouth Museum, 1957

Luny, Thomas 1759–1837, *HMS 'Dartmouth',* purchased by the Friends of Dartmouth Museum, 1951

Luny, Thomas 1759–1837, *Mouth of the Dart with a Merchant Ship Entering,* purchased by the Friends of Dartmouth Museum, 1953

Mackay, K. (Miss) *New Ground Bridge and Plumleigh Conduit, Dartmouth, Devon,* gift from Dr Taylor, 1950

Mackay, K. (Miss) (copy of) *New Ground Bridge and Plumleigh Conduit, Dartmouth, Devon,* on loan from the Trustees of the Henley Collection

Myers, A. *Hurricane Fighting Dornier over Dartmouth Harbour, Devon in 1940,* gift

Payne, Charles *'Dawn Exercise', Blackpool Sands, near Dartmouth, Devon, April 1944,* unknown acquisition method

Tucker, Edward c.1825–1909, *Dartmouth Harbour from Castle Walk, Devon,* purchased by the Friends of Dartmouth Museum, 1963

unknown artist *Dartmouth Castle, Devon,* on loan from the Trustees of the Henley Collection

unknown artist *Ellen Langley, Aged 5,* bequeathed by Mrs E. G. Couldrey via Messrs Bearnes, 1998

unknown artist *HMT 'Himalaya', Hong Kong, China, 1922, January,* unknown acquisition method

unknown artist *Mountain Landscape,* gift from Lewis Stock, 1972

unknown artist *Portrait of a Gentleman,* on loan from the Trustees of the Henley Collection

unknown artist *Portrait of a Gentleman,* unknown acquisition method

unknown artist *Ship,* gift from Lewis Stock, 1972

Way, William Hopkins 1812–1891, *Bayard's Cove, Devon,* gift from the Friends of Dartmouth Museum, 1962

Wimbush, John L. c.1854–1914, *Portrait of a Girl,* on loan from the Trustees of the Henley Collection

Wimbush, John L. c.1854–1914, *The Jester,* on loan from the Trustees of the Henley Collection

Wood, Tim G. c.1929–1998, *Townstal Hill, Dartmouth,* gift from Mrs E. B. Holliwell

Dawlish Community Hospital

Stacey, Andrew b.1951, *Dawlish Warren Seascape, Devon (triptych, left wing),* presented by David Hoare of Luscombe Castle to the League of Friends, 1998, © the artist

Stacey, Andrew b.1951, *Dawlish Warren Seascape, Devon (triptych, centre panel),* presented by David Hoare of Luscombe Castle to the League of Friends, 1998, © the artist

Stacey, Andrew b.1951, *Dawlish Warren Seascape, Devon (triptych, right wing),* presented by David Hoare of Luscombe Castle to the League of Friends, 1998, © the artist

Stacey, Andrew b.1951, *Seascape 1,* purchased by the Dawlish Hospital League of Friends, 1998, © the artist

Stacey, Andrew b.1951, *Seascape 2,* purchased by the Dawlish Hospital League of Friends, 1998, © the artist

Stacey, Andrew b.1951, *Dawlish Seascape, Devon,* purchased by the Dawlish Hospital League of Friends, 1998, © the artist

Stacey, Andrew b.1951, *Dawlish Seascape, Devon,* purchased by the

Dawlish Hospital League of Friends, 1998, © the artist
Stacey, Andrew b.1951, *Dawlish Seascape, Devon*, purchased by the Dawlish Hospital League of Friends, 1998, © the artist
Stacey, Andrew b.1951, *Dawlish Seascape, Devon*, purchased by the Dawlish Hospital League of Friends, 1998, © the artist
Stacey, Andrew b.1951, *Dawlish Seascape, Devon*, purchased by the Dawlish Hospital League of Friends, 1998, © the artist
Stacey, Andrew b.1951, *Dawlish Seascape, Devon*, purchased by the Dawlish Hospital League of Friends, 1998, © the artist

Dawlish Museum Society

Chapman, L. *Eventide with Fishing Boats*, donated
Chapman, L. *Eventide with Fishing Boats*, donated
Elliott, Les *Cows on a Hill above Dawlish, Devon*, gift from the artist
Elliott, Les *Dawlish Black Swan*, gift from the artist
Elliott, Les *Jubilee Bridge at Dawlish, Devon*, gift from the artist
Elliott, Les *The Brook at Dawlish, Devon*, gift from the artist
Elliott, Les *The Mill at Dawlish, Devon*, gift from the artist
Godfrey, Elsa 1900–1991, *Southwood Farm, Dawlish, Devon*, presented to the museum by Judith Godfrey, daughter of the artist
Godfrey, Elsa 1900–1991, *The Coast at Dawlish, Devon*, presented to the museum by F. C. Parsons, 1984
Hutchings, E. A. *The Atmospheric Railway, Starcross, Devon*, donated
Hutchings, E. A. *The Cow's Hole*, donated
Hutchings, E. A. *The Lawn at Dawlish, Devon*, donated
Sanders, L. M. *Landscape with a Church*, donated
Sanders, L. M. *Landscape with a Farm*, donated
unknown artist *Cold: Dawlish Fountain Frozen in Winter, Devon*, donated
unknown artist *St Mark's Church, Dawlish, Devon*, donated
unknown artist *William Cousins, Esq. (1780–1871) of Langdon House, Dawlish*, gift from Dawlish Hospital, 2009

Bicton College

Burbidge, Gill b.1946, *Bicton House, Devon*, commissioned © the artist
Burbidge, Gill b.1946, *Aunty Mary's Hat*, commissioned © the artist
Burbidge, Gill b.1946, *Young People's Refectory Series*, commissioned © the artist
Burbidge, Gill b.1946, *Young People's Refectory Series*,

commissioned © the artist
Burbidge, Gill b.1946, *Young People's Refectory Series*, commissioned © the artist
Burbidge, Gill b.1946, *Young People's Refectory Series*, commissioned © the artist
Burbidge, Gill b.1946, *Young People's Refectory Series*, commissioned © the artist
Burbidge, Gill b.1946, *Young People's Refectory Series*, commissioned © the artist
Burbidge, Gill b.1946, *Young People's Refectory Series*, commissioned © the artist
Burbidge, Gill b.1946, *Young People's Refectory Series*, commissioned © the artist
Burbidge, Gill b.1946, *Young People's Refectory Series*, commissioned © the artist
Burbidge, Gill b.1946, *Young People's Refectory Series*, commissioned © the artist
Burbidge, Gill b.1946, *Young People's Refectory Series*, commissioned © the artist
Burbidge, Gill b.1946, *Young People's Refectory Series*, commissioned © the artist
Burbidge, Gill b.1946, *Devon Summer*, commissioned © the artist
Deakins, George 1911–1981, *Village Scene*, presented by students of Bicton College, 1967
Debeuf, A. *Woodland in Sunset*, unknown acquisition method
Dyson, Collette *Sunset*, gift from the artist
Miller, Shannon Frances b.1963, *Friesian Calves*, on loan from the artist © the artist
Miller, Shannon Frances b.1963, *Sheep*, on loan from the artist © the artist

Dean and Chapter, Exeter Cathedral

Davies, Janet M. b.1939, *The Very Reverend Marcus Knight (1903–1988), Dean of Exeter (1960–1972)*, unknown acquisition method
Halls, John James 1776–1853, *The Very Reverend John Garnett, D. D., Dean of Exeter (1810–1813)*, unknown acquisition method
Knapton, George 1698–1778, *Sir Philip Sidney (after Isaac Oliver)*, unknown acquisition method
Knight, Harold 1874–1961, *Spencer Cecil Carpenter (1877–1959), Dean of Exeter (1950–1960)*, unknown acquisition method, reproduced with permission of the estate of Dame Laura Knight, DBE, RA, 2012. All rights reserved
Raphael (after) 1483–1520, *Madonna and Child, Madonna del Granduca*, unknown acquisition method

unknown artist *Unknown Dean*, unknown acquisition method
unknown artist *George III (1738–1820)*, unknown acquisition method
unknown artist *The Very Reverend Alured Clarke, Dean of Exeter (1740–1741)*, unknown acquisition method
unknown artist *The Very Reverend Dr Whittington Landon, Dean of Exeter (1813–1838)*, unknown acquisition method
unknown artist *William of Orange*, unknown acquisition method

Devon & Somerset Fire & Rescue Service

Ford, Fred *The Burning of the Theatre Royal, Exeter, 3 September 1887*, unknown acquisition method
Lynham, J. 1864–1942, *Somerset Fire Brigade at Hestercombe*, commissioned by Chief Fire Officer Musselwhite, 1989
Olsson, Albert Julius 1864–1942, *Sea and Rocks, Moonlight*, purchased, 1926
Spear, Ruskin 1911–1990, *Mr William Herbert Barratt, Chief Fire Officer, Somerset Fire Brigade (1948–1959)*, commissioned by members of the Somerset Fire Brigade, 1960

Devon County Council

Buhler, Robert A. 1916–1989, *Sir George C. Hayter-Hames, Kt, Chairman of Devon County Council (1955–1965)*, unknown acquisition method, © the artist's estate/Bridgeman Art Library
Dring, William D. 1904–1990, *John Adam Day (1901–1966), Chairman of Devon County Council (1965–1966)*, unknown acquisition method, © the artist's estate/Bridgeman Art Library
Dring, William D. 1904–1990, *Eric Palmer, Chairman of Devon County Council (1971–1974)*, unknown acquisition method, © the artist's estate/Bridgeman Art Library
Dring, William D. 1904–1990, *Charles Arthur Ansell, Chairman of Devon County Council (1973–1977)*, unknown acquisition method, © the artist's estate/Bridgeman Art Library
Dring, William D. 1904–1990, *Gerald Whitmarsh, Chairman of Devon County Council (1966–1971)*, unknown acquisition method, © the artist's estate/Bridgeman Art Library
Gurney, Hugh b.1932, *Landscape at Odam Bridge, Devon*, gift from the artist, © the artist
Gurney, Hugh b.1932, *The River Mole near Meethe, Devon*, gift from the artist, © the artist
Neale, Maud Hall 1869–1960, *Sir John F. Shelley, Bt, Chairman of*

Devon County Council (1946–1955), unknown acquisition method
Tollet-Loeb, Jacqueline b.1931, *Calvados Townscape, France*, presented by Calvados Council, © the artist SINGLE CONSENT
Weatherley, Dudley Graham 1912–2004, *Warnicombe Bridge, the Grand Western Canal, Devon*, on loan from Mr C. R. Weatherley, © the artist's estate

Devon Record Office

Brice, Henry c.1831–1903, *Sir John Bowring (1792–1872)*, unknown acquisition method
Brockedon, William 1787–1854, *Miss Louisa Champernowne (b.1809)*, unknown acquisition method
Chatterton, Henrietta Georgiana Maria Lascelles Iremonger 1806–1867, *Ernest Lane and His Sister*, unknown acquisition method
Kieling, M. *J. Watkins, Aged 77 3/4, Author of the History of Devon*, unknown acquisition method
Logsdail, William 1859–1944, *Agnes Elizabeth, only Daughter of William Reginald and Mother of Charles Frederick Lindley Wood, Viscount Halifax*, gift to Exeter City Library from Charles Frederick Lindlay Wood, c.1940, © the artist's estate/Bridgeman Art Library
Swan, E. active 1937–1944, *Portrait of a Judge*, unknown acquisition method
unknown artist *Billy Wotton, the Last Exeter Water-Catcher*, unknown acquisition method
unknown artist *Captain Thomas Tanner, HEICS, Mayor of Exeter (1858)*, presented by Miss Tanner
unknown artist *Mr John Score (b.c.1680), Woolmerchant of Exe Island, Exeter*, unknown acquisition method
unknown artist *Mr Smith, Headmaster of St John's Hospital School*, unknown acquisition method
unknown artist *Portrait of a Bearded Gentleman*, unknown acquisition method
unknown artist *Portrait of a Gentleman*, unknown acquisition method
unknown artist *Portrait of a Gentleman*, unknown acquisition method
unknown artist *Portrait of a Gentleman*, unknown acquisition method
unknown artist *Portrait of a Gentleman Holding a Letter*, unknown acquisition method
unknown artist *Portrait of a Gentleman Wearing a Red Coat*, unknown acquisition method

unknown artist *Portrait of a Gentleman Wearing a Tartan Waistcoat*, unknown acquisition method
unknown artist *Portrait of a Girl and Her Dog*, unknown acquisition method
unknown artist *Portrait of a Lady in a Lace Bonnet*, unknown acquisition method
unknown artist *Portrait of a Lady Wearing a Pearl Necklace*, unknown acquisition method
unknown artist *Portrait of a Seated Lady*, unknown acquisition method
unknown artist *Portrait of a Young Girl with a Basket of Flowers*, unknown acquisition method
unknown artist *Portrait of a Young Man with a Cane*, unknown acquisition method
Williams, M. F. A. *Portrait of a Lady Wearing a Headband*, unknown acquisition method
Woollatt, Leighton Hall 1905–1974, *Parish Church of Clyst St George, Devon, North East View*, gift from Mrs Woollatt, wife of the artist, 1974
Woollatt, Leighton Hall 1905–1974, *Parish Church of Clyst St George, Devon, Looking East through the Tower*, gift from Mrs Woollatt, wife of the artist, 1974
Woollatt, Leighton Hall 1905–1974, *Behind Sidwell Street, Exeter, Devon*, gift from Mrs Woollatt, wife of the artist, 1974
Woollatt, Leighton Hall 1905–1974, *Church of St Lawrence, High Street, Exeter, Devon*, gift from Mrs Woollatt, wife of the artist, 1974
Woollatt, Leighton Hall 1905–1974, *Exeter Cathedral, Devon, from Catherine Street*, gift from Mrs Woollatt, wife of the artist, 1974
Woollatt, Leighton Hall 1905–1974, *Interior, Lower Market, Exeter, Devon*, gift from Mrs Woollatt, wife of the artist, 1974
Woollatt, Leighton Hall 1905–1974, *Looking from Castle Street across High Street, Exeter, Devon*, gift from Mrs Woollatt, wife of the artist, 1974
Woollatt, Leighton Hall 1905–1974, *Post Eleven Speaking*, gift from Mrs Woollatt, wife of the artist, 1974
Woollatt, Leighton Hall 1905–1974, *Remains of the General Post Office, High Street, Exeter, Devon*, gift from Mrs Woollatt, wife of the artist, 1974
Woollatt, Leighton Hall 1905–1974, *South Chancel, Exeter Cathedral, Devon*, gift from Mrs Woollatt, wife of the artist, 1974
Woollatt, Leighton Hall 1905–1974, *Sun Street, Exeter, Devon*, gift from Mrs Woollatt, wife of the artist, 1974

Exeter Guildhall

Bird, Isaac Faulkner 1803–1884, *View from the Castle Wall Looking towards Southernhay, Exeter, Devon*, presented by Mr W. Pinson
Gainsborough, Thomas (circle of) 1727–1788, *John Rolle Walter, Esq. (1712–1779), MP for Exeter (1754–1776)*, presented to the Mayor and Chamber by the Right Honourable John Rolle, Lord Rolle, 1835
Hudson, Thomas 1701–1779, *Sir Charles Pratt (1714–1794), Lord Chief Justice of the Common Pleas*, gift from John Walter, Esq. in memory of the Great Asserter of the English Laws and Liberties
Hudson, Thomas 1701–1779, *George II (1683–1760)*, presented by the artist
Hudson, Thomas 1701–1779, *John Tuckfield, Esq., MP for Exeter (1745–1776)*, unknown acquisition method
Hudson, Thomas (attributed to) 1701–1779, *Thomas Heath, Mayor and Sheriff of Exeter*, unknown acquisition method
Leakey, James 1775–1865, *Henry Blackall, Esq. (1770–1845), Thrice Mayor of Exeter*, unknown acquisition method
Lely, Peter 1618–1680, *General Monck (1608–1670), 1st Duke of Albermarle, KG*, unknown acquisition method
Lely, Peter 1618–1680, *Princess Henrietta (1644–1670), Daughter of Charles I*, unknown acquisition method
Mogford, Thomas 1800–1868, *H. W. Hooper, Mayor of Exeter (1843), Sheriff of Exeter (1849), Builder of the Exeter Market*, unknown acquisition method
Mogford, Thomas 1800–1868, *William Page Kingdom*, presented by the family of the sitter
Northcote, James (attributed to) 1746–1831, *The Duke of Wellington (1769–1852), Mounted on a Grey Charger*, unknown acquisition method
Pine, Robert Edge c.1720/1730–1788, *Benjamin Heath (d.1766), LLD, Town Clerk of Exeter for Fourteen Years*, unknown acquisition method
Salisbury, Frank O. 1874–1962, *Lady J. Kirk Owen, Mayoress (1914–1915)*, purchased by private subscription and presented to the Corporation of Exeter in recognition of the conspicuous service rendered by the sitter during the Great War in ministering to the comfort of our soldiers and sailors and prisoners of war, © estate of Frank O. Salisbury. All rights reserved, DACS 2012
Salisbury, Frank O. 1874–1962, *Sir James Owen*, purchased by private subscription and presented to the Corporation of Exeter in recognition of the great services

rendered by the sitter as Mayor during the Great War, © estate of Frank O. Salisbury. All rights reserved, DACS 2012

Exeter Royal Academy for Deaf Education

Burlton *R. E. Olding, OBE, Headmaster of the Royal West of England Residential School for the Deaf (1965–1985)*, gift from the governors of the Royal West of England Residential School for the Deaf
Burlton *H. P. Jones, Headmaster of the Royal West of England Residential School for the Deaf (1985–1996)*, gift from the governors of the Royal West of England Residential School for the Deaf
unknown artist *H. P. Bingham, Headmaster of the Royal West of England Residential School for the Deaf (1827–1834)*, presented by J. T. Brownse Mason
Whinney, Maurice 1911–1997?, *Sir Paul H. W. Studholme, Treasurer of the Royal West of England Residential School for the Deaf (1973–1990), President of the Royal West of England Residential School for the Deaf (1968 & 1969)*, gift from the governors of the Royal West of England Residential School for the Deaf

Larkbeare House

Copnall, Frank Thomas 1870–1949, *Sir Henry Hepburn, Kt, Chairman of Devon County Council (1916)*, unknown acquisition mnethod
Crealock, John 1871–1959, *Portrait of a Judge*, unknown acquisition method
Jenkins, George Henry 1843–1914, *Cart Travelling across Dartmoor, Devon*, unknown acquisition method
Jenkins, George Henry 1843–1914, *Dartmoor, Devon*, unknown acquisition method
Neale, George Hall 1863–1940, *Sir Henry Yarde Buller Lopes (1859–1938), Chairman of Devon County Council (1916–1937)*, unknown acquisition method
Neale, Maud Hall 1869–1960, *Sir John Daw, Kt, Chairman of Devon County Council (1938–1946)*, unknown acquisition method
Shaw, George 1843–1915, *Dartmoor, Devon*, unknown acquisition method
unknown artist *Albert Edmund Parker (1843–1905), 3rd Earl of Morley, Chairman of Devon County Council (1901–1904)*, unknown acquisition method
unknown artist *Charles Henry Rolle Hepburn-Stuart-Forbes-Trefusis (1834–1904), 20th Baron Clinton, Chairman of Devon*

County Council (1889–1901), unknown acquisition method
unknown artist *Hugh Fortescue (1854–1932), 4th Earl Fortesque, Chairman of Devon County Council (1904–1916)*, unknown acquisition method
Widgery, Frederick John 1861–1942, *Devon Seascape*, unknown acquisition method
Widgery, Frederick John 1861–1942, *Dartmoor, Devon*, unknown acquisition method

Royal Albert Memorial Museum

Abbott, John White 1763–1851, *The High Street, Exeter, Devon, in 1797*, gift from the Misses Abbott, 1883
Abbott, John White 1763–1851, *The Old Lime-Kilns near Topsham on the Exe, Devon*, bequeathed by Mrs G. A. Abbott, 1937
Abbott, John White 1763–1851, *Portrait of the Artist's Daughter, Elizabeth, Aged 18*, purchased at Sotheby's with the assistance of the Victoria and Albert Museum Purchase Grant Fund and the Friends of Exeter Museums and Art Gallery, 1993
Abbott, John White 1763–1851, *Landscape with Figures and Cattle at a Stream*, gift from Sir Leicester Harmsworth, 1933
Abbott, John White 1763–1851, *The Stepping Stones*, gift from Mrs Emma Prevost, 1929
Abbott, John White 1763–1851, *Jaques and the Wounded Stag*, gift from Mrs Emma Prevost, 1929
Abbott, John White 1763–1851, *Landscape with Abraham and Isaac*, gift from Mrs Emma Prevost, 1929
Adams, John Clayton 1840–1906, *The Golden Vale (Junction of the Wye and Irfran near Builth Wells, Powys)*, purchased with the assistance of the Kent Kingdon Bequest, before 1902
Baird, Nathaniel Hughes John 1865–1936, *A Devonshire Stream*, gift from Miss A. Baird, 1973
Baird, Nathaniel Hughes John 1865–1936, *Evening Sunlight*, gift from Miss A. Baird, 1973
Baird, Nathaniel Hughes John 1865–1936, *The Bison Hunters*, gift from A.T. Loram
Ball, Wilfred Williams (attributed to) 1853–1917, *Large Falcons of the Palearctic*
Barker, Thomas (attributed to) 1769–1847, *Scotsman in a Cottage Interior*, purchased from Whitton & Laing, Exeter, 1969
Barker, Thomas (attributed to) 1769–1847, *Scotswoman with Cabbages, in Cottage Interior*, purchased from Whitton & Laing, Exeter, 1969
Barret the elder, George 1728/1732–1784, *Llyn Nantlle*, purchased from Thomas Agnew & Sons with the assistance of the

Victoria and Albert Museum Purchase Grant Fund and the Veitch Bequest, 1971
Batoni, Pompeo 1708–1787, *John Rolle Walter (1712–1779), MP for Exeter (1754–1776)*, purchased from Great Torrington Almshouse, Town Lands and Poors Charities with the assistance of the Heritage Lottery Fund, the Art Fund, the Museums, Libraries and Archives Council/Victoria and Albert Museum Purchase Grant Fund, Devon County Council, the
Bayes, Walter (attributed to) 1869–1956, *Victoria Station, London, Troops Leaving for the Front*, purchased from Thomas Agnew & Sons with the assistance of the Victoria and Albert Museum Purchase Grant Fund, 1975, © the artist's estate
Beale, Mary (attributed to) 1633–1699, *Portrait of a Lady (called 'Mrs Walkey of Alphington')*, bequeathed by John Lane, 1925
Beeson, Jane 1930–2006, *Still Life with Pots*, gift from the artist, 2002
Bennett, Frank Moss 1874–1952, *Conscience*, © the artist's estate
Bennett, William Mineard 1778–1858, *Self Portrait*, purchased, 1938
Bennett, William Mineard 1778–1858, *Self Portrait*, gift from Mr S. Seguin, 1979
Berchem, Nicolaes (attributed to) 1620–1683, *Landscape with Cattle and Sheep at a Fountain*, bequeathed by Kent and Jane Kingdon, 1892
Bevan, Robert Polhill 1865–1925, *A Devonshire Valley, Number 1*, purchased from Thomas Agnew & Sons with the assistance of the Victoria and Albert Museum Purchase Grant Fund, the National Art Collections Fund and the Veitch Bequest, 1968
Bird, Isaac Faulkner 1803–1884, *Henry Matthews (1793–1842), Druggist of Exeter*, bequeathed by Miss Matthews, 1923
Bird, Isaac Faulkner 1803–1884, *View from the Castle Wall, Looking towards Southernhay, Exeter, Devon*, gift from Mr W. Pinson, 1913
Birkmyer, James Bruce 1834–1899, *When the Tide Is Low, Maer Rocks, Exmouth, Devon*, gift from the artist, 1891
Birkmyer, James Bruce (attributed to) 1834–1899, *Landscape with a Gate and Buildings*, gift from Mr Francis R. J. England, 2000
Brice, Henry c.1831–1903, *Sir John Bowring (1792–1872)*, bequeathed by Lady Bowring, 1902
British (English) School *Joan Tuckfield (1506–1573)*, transferred from the Guildhall, Exeter, 1971
British (English) School *William Hurst (d.1568)*, transferred from the Guildhall, Exeter, 1971
British (English) School *Lawrence Atwill (or Atwell) (c.1511–1588)*,

transferred from the Guildhall, Exeter, 1971
British (English) School *Mrs Browne*, gift from Mrs D. Mostyn, 1946
British (English) School *John Hoker (or Hooker) (c.1527–1601)*, transferred from the Guildhall, Exeter, 1971
British (English) School *Lady Browne*, gift from Mrs D. Mostyn, 1946
British (English) School *Nicholas Spicer (1581–1647)*, purchased (?) from the Spicer Family, 1978
British (English) School *John Perriam (1540–after 1616)*, transferred from the Guildhall, Exeter, 1971
British (English) School *Walter Borough (1554–1632)*, transferred from the Guildhall, Exeter, 1970s
British (English) School *Elizabeth Flaye (1587–1673)*, transferred from the Guildhall, Exeter, 1971
British (English) School *Thomas Jefford (d.1703)*, transferred from the Guildhall, Exeter, 1970s
British (English) School *17th C, Portrait of a Gentleman in a Landscape*, gift from Mrs D. Mostyn, 1946
British (English) School *17th C, Portrait of a Lady*
British (English) School *17th C, Portrait of a Lady and Her Dog*, bequeathed by Kent and Jane Kingdon, 1892
British (English) School *17th C, Portrait of a Lady in a Landscape*, purchased from Whitton & Laing, Exeter, 1970
British (English) School *John Gay (1685–1732)*, bequeathed by John Lane, 1925
British (English) School *A Gentleman of the Needham Family of Melton Mowbray*, bequeathed by Stanley Reynolds Chard, 1974
British (English) School *Samuel Taunton (b.1749), as a Child*, bequeathed by James Moly, 1910
British (English) School *Thomas Taunton (1744–1828), as a Child*, bequeathed by James Moly, 1910
British (English) School *Henry Langford Brown (b.1721), of Combsatchfield and Kingskerswell*, gift from Mr T. H. L. Brown, 1957
British (English) School *John Campion (1742–1822)*, bequeathed by Mrs I. L. M. Coombes, 1996
British (English) School *18th C, Alexander Pope (1688–1744)*, bequeathed by John Lane, 1925
British (English) School *18th C, Commander Robert Bastin (1786–1854), RN*, gift from Spink & Sons, 1917
British (English) School *18th C, Landscape near Pope's House on the Thames at Twickenham (?)*, purchased, 1948
British (English) School *18th C, Landscape, Woodland Glade*, gift from Percy Moore Turner, 1934
British (English) School *18th C, Portrait of a Gentleman*

British (English) School 18th C, *Portrait of a Lady*

British (English) School 18th C, *Portrait of a Lady*, bequeathed by James Moly, 1910

British (English) School 18th C, *Portrait of a Lady of the Brown Family*, gift from Mr T. H. L. Brown, 1957

British (English) School 18th C, *Portrait of a Naval Officer*

British (English) School 18th C, *Study of a Monk*, bequeathed by James Moly, 1910

British (English) School 18th C, *The Flight into Egypt*, gift from Dr J. MacGregor, 1936

British (English) School 18th C, *William Kennaway, Senior (1718–1793)*, purchased from Bently, Agents & Valuers, 1976

British (English) School *Judge John Heath (1736–1816)*, gift from Dr Norman Duggan, c.1954–1955

British (English) School *The Fight on the Bridge*, gift from Percy Moore Turner, 1947

British (English) School *Carter, the Mail Coach Driver*, gift from A. Selby, 1933

British (English) School *Tommy Osborne (d.1823), Itinerant Bookseller of Exeter*, gift from E. C. Perry, JP, 1921

British (English) School *Charles Lewis, Secretary of the West of England Fire and Life Insurance Company (1810–1850)*, gift from the Norwich Union Insurance Company, 2003

British (English) School *William Matthews (d.1839), Woollen Merchant of Exeter*, bequeathed by Miss Matthews, 1923

British (English) School *Clementina Hooper, née Burnside (b.1803)*, gift from Mrs Dorothy Mayers, 1971

British (English) School *Captain Cooke (1765–1841), Chief of the Exeter Javelin Men*, gift from Chief Constable A. E. Rowsell, 1951

British (English) School *J. B. and Mary Davey*

British (English) School *Mrs Hanford Waters*, bequeathed by Lady Helen Mary Thomas, 1946

British (English) School *Portrait of a Young Man (possibly Thomas Latimer, 1803–1888, JP)*, gift from the Devonshire Liberal Club, 1923

British (English) School *Richard Somers Gard (1797–1868)*, bequeathed by Miss Outhwaite, 1911

British (English) School *Mr Thomas Camble of the West of England Fire Brigade, Exeter*, gift from the Norwich Union Insurance Company

British (English) School *The Guildhall on Election Night, 1880*, purchased from Mr Bill West, 1976

British (English) School 19th C, *Benjamin Floud*, bequeathed by Mrs Christine Isobel Heath, 1972

British (English) School 19th C, *Churchyard*

British (English) School 19th C, *History*

British (English) School 19th C, *John Hoker (or Hooker) (c.1527–1601)*, purchased from the Honiton Galleries, 1980

British (English) School 19th C, *John Veitch (1752–1839)*, bequeathed by Miss E. P. Veitch,1934

British (English) School 19th C, *Lake Scene*

British (English) School 19th C, *Landscape*

British (English) School 19th C, *Lighthouse and Ships*, bequeathed by Mr J. Brooking- Rowe, 1917

British (English) School 19th C, *Old Heavitree Church, Exeter, Devon*, gift from W. R. Park, 1913

British (English) School 19th C, *Old Houses, Exeter, Devon (demolished for St Edmund's Church, c.1870)*, purchased, 1929

British (English) School 19th C, *Plymouth, Devon*, bequeathed by John Lane, 1925

British (English) School 19th C, *Plymouth Harbour, Devon, with Shipping*, bequeathed by John Lane, 1925

British (English) School 19th C, *Portrait of a Gentleman*

British (English) School 19th C, *Portrait of a Gentleman*

British (English) School 19th C, *Portrait of a Gentleman (possibly Solomon Floud)*, bequeathed by Mrs Christine Isobel Heath, 1972

British (English) School 19th C, *Portrait of a Lady*

British (English) School 19th C, *St Lawrence Church, High St, Exeter, Devon*, acquired from an unknown source, c.1982

British (English) School 19th C, *Still Life with Roses*

British (English) School 19th C, *Study of the Interior of a Church (possibly in Heavitree, Exeter, Devon)*

British (English) School 19th C, *The College of Vicars' Choral, Exeter, Devon*, purchased, 1929

British (English) School *Floor Boards*, purchased from the Spacex Gallery, Exeter, 1991

British School 19th C, *Unknown Warrior (possibly Robert the Bruce, 1274–1329)*

Brooking, Charles (attributed to) 1723–1759, *Ship on Fire*, gift from James Carrall Wilcocks, 1869

Brown, John Alfred Arnesby 1866–1955, *Autumn Morning*, purchased, 1950

Cagnacci, Guido 1601–1681, *The Young Martyr (possibly St Martina)*, gift from Lady Lockyer and Miss Annie Leigh Browne, 1931

Carter, Sydney 1874–1945, *Reverend Sabine Baring-Gould (1834–1924)*, on loan from Devon Record Office, Exeter

Carter, Sydney 1874–1945, *Richard Carter, Father of the Artist*, gift from Miss Jessie Rodford, 1997

Caunter, Henry (attributed to) active c.1846–c.1850, *Abraham Cann (1794–1864), the Last Champion in Devon-Style Wrestling*, purchased, 1959

Cawse, John (attributed to) 1779–1862, *James Northcote (1746–1831), painting Sir Walter Scott (1771–1832)*, purchased, 1949

Christen, Rodolphe 1859–1906, *A Man Preparing Microscope Slides*, purchased

Clack, Richard Augustus 1801–1880, *Thomas Gray (1788–1848), the Railway Pioneer*, bequeathed by the artist, 1881

Clack, Richard Augustus 1801–1880, *Self Portrait*, gift from Colonel Thomas Stanley Clack, 1937

Clack, Richard Augustus 1801–1880, *William Wills Hooper (1807–1872), Mayor of Exeter (1850–1851 & 1851–1852)*, gift from Squadron Leader A. F. A. Hooper, 1923

Clack, Richard Augustus 1801–1880, *The Reverend Frederick Bell, Chaplain of His Majesty's Forces in Exeter for Many Years*, bequeathed by Dr Charles Edward Wallace Bell, 1930

Clack, Richard Augustus 1801–1880, *Henry Langford Brown (1802–1857)*, gift from Mr T. H. L. Brown, 1957

Clack, Richard Augustus 1801–1880, *Self Portrait by Sir Joshua Reynolds in the robes of a DCL Oxford (copy of Joshua Reynolds)*, gift from the artist, 1869

Codrington, Isabel 1874–1943, *Morning*, gift from the artist, 1934

Collins, Cecil 1908–1989, *By the Waters of Babylon*, bequeathed by Mrs Elisabeth Collins, 2001, © Tate, London 2012

Condy, Nicholas 1793–1857, *Cleaning the Fish*, purchased at Christie's, 1951

Condy, Nicholas 1793–1857, *Nicholas Matthew Condy (1816–1851)*, gift from Miss Bertha Duncan, 1964

Condy, Nicholas 1793–1857, *Old Man Smoking*, bequeathed by Kent and Jane Kingdon, 1892

Condy, Nicholas Matthew 1816–1851, *Harbour Scene*, purchased from Mr W. Park Little, 1935

Condy, Nicholas Matthew 1816–1851, *HMS 'Warspite' 50 Guns Conveying Lord Ashburton on a Special Mission to the United States, Beating Down the Channel*, purchased with assistance from the Friends of Exeter Museums and Art Gallery, 1950

Condy, Nicholas Matthew 1816–1851, *The Spinnaker Sail (Cutter with a Spinnaker Set)*, purchased, 1935

Coombes, George *Thomas Osborne (d.1823), Itinerant Bookseller of Exeter*, gift from Miss E. Chester, 1929

Coombes, George *Thomas Osborne (d.1823), the Bookseller*, gift from Miss E. Chester, 1929

Corri, F. J. *West Front of Exeter Cathedral, Devon*, purchased, 1934

Cortona, Pietro da (follower of) 1596–1669, *The Discovery of Moses in the Bulrushes*

Cosway, Richard 1742–1821, *Master Carew (probably Sir Henry Carew, 1779–1830)*, purchased from Mr W. Park Little, 1941

Cosway, Richard (attributed to) 1742–1821, *Portrait of the Artist (Self Portrait with Mahl Stick and Brush)*, gift from Percy Moore Turner, 1935

Cotton, Alan b.1938, *Hartland Quay, North Devon*, gift from the artist, 1978, © the artist

Cox, W. H. (attributed to) *The First Paddle Steamer to Navigate the Exe up to Exeter*, purchased from Mr Norman S. Leslie, 1929

Cranch, John 1751–1821, *The Village Cooper*, purchased at Christie's, 1950

Cranch, John 1751–1821, *The Carrier's Cart*, purchased from Gooden & Fox, 1937

Cranch, John 1751–1821, *The Miser*, purchased from R. G. Rummery, 1968

Cranch, John 1751–1821, *The Village Baker*, purchased, 1949

Cranch, John 1751–1821, *The Village Butcher*, purchased, 1949

Critz, John de the elder (after) 1551/1552–1642, *Sir Thomas White (1495–1567)*, transferred from the Guildhall, Exeter, 1971

Crome, John Berney 1794–1842, *Tell's Chapel, Lake of Lucerne, Switzerland*, bequeathed by Mr G. N. Hooper, 1915

Crosse, Richard 1742–1810, *Self Portrait*, purchased from Lieutenant-Colonel Reeder Crosse-Upcott with the assistance of the Veitch Bequest, 1962

Dabos, Laurent (attributed to) 1761–1835, *Napoléon Bonaparte (1769–1821)*, gift from James Carrall Wilcocks, 1869

Danby, Francis 1793–1861, *Dead Calm, Sunset at the Bight of Exmouth*, purchased from Thomas Agnew & Sons with the assistance of the Victoria and Albert Museum Purchase Grant Fund, the National Art Collections Fund and the Veitch Bequest, 1976

Dawson, Henry 1811–1878, *Dartmouth from St Petrox Churchyard, Devon*, purchased from Philip Mould Historical Portraits with the assistance of the Museums, Libraries and Archives Council/Victoria and Albert Museum Purchase Grant Fund, the Reynolds Chard Bequest, the Kent Kingdon Bequest and the Friends of Exeter Museums and Art Gallery, 1950

De Passe, Willem 1598–c.1637 (after) & Van De Passe, Magdalena 1600–1638 (after) *John Rainolds (1549–1607), DD*, gift from Aaron Reynolds, 1920

Dicksee, Thomas Francis

1819–1895, *Study of a Lady's Head*, gift from Miss M. E. Harding, 1933

Dingle, Thomas 1818–after 1900, *Winter*, bequeathed by Kent and Jane Kingdon, 1892

Downman, John (attributed to) 1750–1824, *Dr Hugh Downman (1740–1809), Physician and Author, Exeter, Devonshire*, bequeathed by John Lane, 1925

Drummond, Malcolm 1880–1945, *The Park Bench*, purchased from Thomas Agnew & Sons with the assistance of the Victoria and Albert Museum Purchase Grant Fund, 1969, © the artist's estate

Drummond, Samuel 1765–1844, *Admiral Edward Pellew (1757–1833), 1st Viscount Exmouth*, bequeathed by Lord Exmouth, 1876

Dutch School *Flower Piece*, bequeathed by Miss St Leger Good, 1970

Eastlake, Charles Lock 1793–1865, *Contemplation*, gift from the Western Morning News Company, 1933

Eastlake, Charles Lock 1793–1865, *Cypresses at L'Ariccia, Italy*, purchased at Sotheby's with the assistance of the Veitch Bequest, 1955

Elford, William c.1749–1837, *Landscape, Sheepstor, near Burrator Reservoir, Devon*, gift from Robert Worthington, 1934

Etty, William 1787–1849, *Andromeda, Perseus Coming to Her Rescue*, purchased from Thomas Agnew & Sons with the assistance of the Victoria and Albert Museum Purchase Grant Fund, 1972

Fischer, Karl 1862–1940, *The Church of St Mary Steps, Exeter, Devon*, gift from Mrs Strother, 1928

Fisher, Mark 1841–1923, *River Landscape*, gift from Percy Moore Turner, 1940

Fisher, Mark 1841–1923, *The Bridge*, gift from Percy Moore Turner, 1940

Fishwick, Clifford 1923–1997, *Secret Cove*, purchased from the artist, 1968, © the artist's estate

Forbes, Stanhope Alexander 1857–1947, *The 22 January 1901 (Reading the News of the Queen's Death in a Cornish Cottage)*, purchased from the artist, 1902, © the artist's estate/Bridgeman Art Library

Foweraker, Albert Moulton 1873–1942, *Afterglow, the Alhambra and Sierra Nevada, Granada, Spain*, gift from friends of the artist, 1910

French School 18th C or Italian (Venetian) School *Perseus and Andromeda*, bequeathed by Miss Mabel Petty, 1971

Friedman, J. *The Castle*

Frith, William Powell 1819–1909, *The Fair Toxophilites (English Archers, Nineteenth Century)*, purchased from Edgar Sheppard with the assistance of the Victoria and Albert Museum Purchase Grant Fund and the Veitch Bequest, 1976

Frost, Terry 1915–2003, *Lemon and White, Spring '63*, purchased from Justin Knowles with the assistance of the Victoria and Albert Museum Purchase Grant Fund, 1969, © estate of Terry Frost. All rights reserved, DACS 2012

Gainsborough, Thomas 1727–1788, *William Jackson (1730–1803)*, bequeathed by Ernest E. Cook, 1950

Gandy, James 1619–1689, *Deborah Hopton (c.1627–1702), and Her Son*, gift from A. P. Good, 1945

Gandy, William c.1655–1729, *Matthew Pear (1694–1765), Sword-Bearer of Exeter, and His Brother Philip Pear (b.1696)*, gift from Alfred H. Pear, 1893

Gandy, William c.1655–1729, *Sir Henry Langford (d.1725), Bt*, gift from Mr T. H. L. Brown, 1957

Gandy, William c.1655–1729, *Philippa Brown, née Musgrave (c.1699–1735), Wife of Thomas Brown*, gift from Mr T. H. L. Brown, 1957

Gandy, William c.1655–1729, *Thomas Brown (1691–1728), Son of Susannah Brown of Combsatchfield*, gift from Mr T. H. L. Brown, 1957

Gandy, William c.1655–1729, *Thomas Brown (1691–1728), Son of Susannah Brown of Combsatchfield*, gift from Mr T. H. L. Brown, 1957

Gandy, William (attributed to) c.1655–1729, *Benjamin Oliver (1601–1672)*, transferred from the Guildhall, Exeter, 1971

Garstin, Norman 1847–1926, *Oudenarde, Belgium*, gift from the Contemporary Art Society, 1981

Garstin, Norman 1847–1926, *The Pardon of Saint Barbe, Brittany, France*, gift from the Contemporary Art Society, 1981

Gheeraerts, Marcus the younger (attributed to) 1561/1562–1635/1636, *Portrait of a Lady (probably Mary Hungate)*, gift from Mrs D. Mostyn, 1946

Gendall, John 1790–1865, *Lydford Bridge on the Avon, Brent, Devon*, bequeathed by Kent and Jane Kingdon, 1892

Gendall, John 1790–1865, *Bridge near South Brent, Devon (Didsworthy Bridge?)*, bequeathed by Reverend James Ford, 1894

Gendall, John 1790–1865, *Children Spinning Tops*, gift from Robert Worthington, 1938

Gendall, John 1790–1865, *Landscape, River Scene*

Gendall, John 1790–1865, *River and Bridge*, purchased, 1940

Gendall, John 1790–1865, *View on the Avon*, bequeathed by Kent and Jane Kingdon, 1892

Gendall, John 1790–1865, *View on the Dart*, gift from Robert Worthington, 1935

Giannicola di Paolo (after) c.1460–1544, *The Annunciation*,

gift from Mayor Russell Coombe, 1919

Gilman, Harold 1876–1919, *Girl Combing Her Hair*, purchased from Thomas Agnew & Sons with the assistance of the Victoria and Albert Museum Purchase Grant Fund and the Veitch Bequest, 1968

Ginner, Charles 1878–1952, *Clayhidon, Devon*, purchased from Anthony d'Offay with the assistance of the Victoria and Albert Museum Purchase Grant Fund and the Friends of Exeter Museums and Art Gallery, 1983

Gore, Spencer 1878–1914, *Panshanger Park, Hertfordshire*, purchased from the Redfern Gallery with the assistance of the Victoria and Albert Museum Purchase Grant Fund, the National Art Collections Fund and the Veitch Bequest, 1968

Gould, Alexander Carruthers 1870–1948, *Sir Francis Carruthers Gould (1844–1925)*, bequeathed by John Lane, 1925

Gowing, Lawrence 1918–1991, *Judith at Sixteen*, purchased from Thomas Agnew & Sons with the assistance of the Victoria and Albert Museum Purchase Grant Fund and the Veitch Bequest, 1968, © estate of Sir Lawrence Gowing

Grant, Duncan 1885–1978, *Reclining Nude*, purchased from the artist, 1969, © 1978 estate of Duncan Grant

Hainsselin, Henry 1815–1886, *Friesland Boer Skating*, gift from William Williams, 1894

Hallett, William H. 1810–1858, *View of Exmouth from the Beacon Walls, Devon*, gift from the Western Times Company, 1952

Halnon, Frederick James (attributed to) 1881–1958, *Portrait of a Boy in a Boating Cap*, gift from the artist

Hart, F. active 19th C, *Study of a Dodo*, gift from Mrs Ross, 1865

Hart, Solomon Alexander 1806–1881, *Self Portrait*, bequeathed by John Lane, 1925

Hawker, Thomas (attributed to) c.1640–c.1725, *Dr William Musgrave (1655–1721)*, gift from Mr T. H. L. Brown, 1957

Haydon, Benjamin Robert 1786–1846, *Self Portrait as the Spirit of the Vine*, purchased from Gooden & Fox, 1952

Haydon, Benjamin Robert 1786–1846, *The Mock Election*, purchased with the assistance of the Kent Kingdon Bequest, 1943

Haydon, Benjamin Robert 1786–1846, *Chairing the Member*, purchased with the assistance of the Veitch Bequest, 1943

Haydon, Benjamin Robert 1786–1846, *Henrietta Nelson Noble*, gift from Mrs E. T. Foweraker, 1921

Haydon, Benjamin Robert 1786–1846, *Curtius Leaping into the Gulf*, purchased with the

assistance of the Kent Kingdon Bequest, 1933

Hayman, Francis 1708–1776, *Portrait of a Lady (probably the wife of the artist)*, purchased from Philip Mould Historical Portraits with the assistance of the Museums, Libraries and Archives Council/Victoria and Albert Museum Purchase Grant Fund, the Art Fund and the Friends of Exeter Museums and Art Gallery, 2007

Hayman, Francis 1708–1776, *Self Portrait of the Artist in His Studio*, purchased from Ronald Lee with the assistance of the Veitch Bequest, 1963

Hayman, Francis 1708–1776, *Grosvenor Bedford and His Family*, purchased from Christie's with the assistance of the Kent Kingdon Bequest, 1939

Hayman, Francis 1708–1776, *Portrait of the Artist at His Easel*, gift from the National Art Collections Fund, 1953

Hayman, Francis 1708–1776, *The Muses Paying Homage to Frederick, Prince of Wales and Princess Augusta (The Artists Presenting a plan for an Academy to Frederick, Prince of Wales and Princess Augusta)*, purchased from Raymond Head, 1974

Hayman, Francis 1708–1776, *Don Quixote Knighted by the Innkeeper*, purchased from Ronald Lee with the assistance of the Veitch Bequest, 1963

Hayman, Francis 1708–1776, *Don Quixote Attacking the Barber to Capture the Basin*, purchased from Ronald Lee with the assistance of the Veitch Bequest, 1963

Hayman, Francis 1708–1776, *Don Quixote Brought Home by the Peasant after the Tilt with the Toledo Merchant*, purchased from Ronald Lee with the assistance of the Veitch Bequest, 1963

Hayman, Francis 1708–1776, *Don Quixote Disputing with the Mad Cardenio*, purchased from Ronald Lee with the assistance of the Veitch Bequest, 1963

Hayman, Francis 1708–1776, *Don Quixote's Battle with the Wine Skins*, purchased from Ronald Lee with the assistance of the Veitch Bequest, 1963

Hayman, Francis 1708–1776, *The Barber Reclaiming His Basin from Don Quixote*, purchased from Ronald Lee with the assistance of the Veitch Bequest, 1963

Hayman, Francis (attributed to) 1708–1776, *The Wagg Family of Windsor*, purchased from Gooden & Fox, 1951

Hayman, John *East View of the East Gate, Exeter, Devon*, transferred from the Guildhall, Exeter, 2004

Hayman, John *West View of East Gate, Exeter, Devon*, transferred from the Guildhall, Exeter, 2004

Hayter, Stanley William

1901–1988, *Rippled Water*, gift from the Contemporary Art Society, 1968, © ADAGP, Paris and DACS, London 2012

Heron, Patrick 1920–1999, *Two Vermilions, Green and Purple in Red*, purchased from Justin Knowles with the assistance of the Victoria and Albert Museum Purchase Grant Fund, 1969, © Susanna Heron. All rights reserved, DACS 2012

Holder, Edward Henry 1847–1922, *A Cottage Home in Surrey*, gift from Miss Blanche F. Wright, 1921

Holl, Frank 1845–1888, *The Song of the Shirt*, purchased from Thomas Agnew & Sons with the assistance of the Victoria and Albert Museum Purchase Grant Fund, 1975

Hoppner, John 1758–1810, *Henry Langford (1758–1800)*, gift from Mr T. H. L. Brown, 1957

Howard-Jones, Ray 1903–1996, *Bird in a Landscape*, purchased from Thomas Agnew & Sons, 1991, © Amgueddfa Cymru - National Museum Wales and Nicola Howard-Jones

Hudson, Thomas 1701–1779, *Frances Brown, née Tucker (d.1769)*, gift from Mr T. H. L. Brown, 1957

Hudson, Thomas 1701–1779, *Anne van Keppel (1703–1789), Countess of Albemarle*, gift from Sir Harold Harmsworth, 1948

Hudson, Thomas 1701–1779, *William Anne van Keppel (1702–1754), 2nd Earl of Albemarle*, gift from Sir Harold Harmsworth, 1948

Hudson, Thomas 1701–1779, *Anne, Countess of Dumfries (d.1811)*, purchased from Thomas Agnew & Sons, 1968

Hudson, Thomas (circle of) 1701–1779, *Portrait of a Lady (called 'Mrs Adams')*, purchased from Whitton & Laing, Exeter, 1970

Hughes, Arthur (attributed to) 1805–1838, *Derwentwater, Cumberland*, bequeathed by Mabel Cameron Alexander, 1975

Hughes, Robert Morson 1873–1953, *The Old Cornish Tin Mine*, purchased from Phillips, 1982, © the artist's estate

Hughes-Stanton, Herbert Edwin Pelham 1870–1937, *Cader Idris*, purchased with the assistance of the Kent Kingdon Bequest, 1918

Hulbert, Thelma 1913–1995, *Dressing Table and Flowers*, gift from the Thelma Hulbert Memorial Fund, 1998

Hulbert, Thelma 1913–1995, *Green Shutters, France*, gift from the Thelma Hulbert Memorial Fund, 1998

Hulbert, Thelma 1913–1995, *Dead Leaves and Flowers*, gift from the Thelma Hulbert Memorial Fund, 1998

Hulbert, Thelma 1913–1995, *Sea and Rock, Italy*, gift from the

Thelma Hulbert Memorial Fund, 1998

Hulbert, Thelma 1913–1995, *Flight over Sea*, gift from the Thelma Hulbert Memorial Fund, 1998

Hulbert, Thelma 1913–1995, *Montage: Black and White*, gift from the Thelma Hulbert Memorial Fund, 1998

Hulbert, Thelma 1913–1995, *Honesty and Window*, gift from the Thelma Hulbert Memorial Fund, 1998

Hulbert, Thelma 1913–1995, *Room and Blossom*, gift from the Thelma Hulbert Memorial Fund, 1998

Hulbert, Thelma 1913–1995, *Blue Window, Fruit and Leaves*, gift from the Thelma Hulbert Memorial Fund, 1998

Hulbert, Thelma 1913–1995, *Faded Flowers*, gift from the Thelma Hulbert Memorial Fund, 1998

Humphry, Ozias (attributed to) 1742–1810, *Mrs Archibald Hutcheson (c.1690–1781)*, gift from the Misses Bailey, 1932

Hunter, Colin 1841–1904, *Beer, Devon*, gift from Mr Roland and Mrs Gertrude McAlpine Woods, 1949

Illsley, Bryan b.1937, *Study in Green and Red with Black and Brown*, gift from the Contemporary Art Society, 1972, © the artist

Ipsen, Ernest Ludwig 1869–1951, *John Lane (1854–1925)*, gift from Sir Allen Lane, 1963

Jenkins, Charles (attributed to) c.1675–1739, *Nathaniel Newnham (1672–1760)*, purchased from Martin Taylor with the assistance of the Victoria and Albert Museum Purchase Grant Fund, 1987

Jenkins, Thomas (attributed to) 1722–1798, *Sir William Morice of Werrington (d.1750), MP*, purchased from the Gavin Graham Gallery with the assistance of the Victoria and Albert Museum Purchase Grant Fund, 1981

Johns, Ambrose Bowden 1776–1858, *Landscape in Devon (?)*, purchased

Kemp-Welch, Lucy 1869–1958, *In Sight, Lord Dundonald's Dash on 'Ladysmith'*, purchased from the artist, 1909, © David Messum

Kite, Joseph Milner 1862–1946, *Self Portrait*, gift from Mrs Behrens, 1971

Kneale, Bryan b.1930, *Self Portrait*, gift from Lady Amory, 1974, © the artist

Kneller, Godfrey (follower of) 1646–1723, *Portrait of a Gentleman (called 'Nicholas Duck')*, transferred from the Guildhall, Exeter, 1970

Knight, John Prescott 1803–1881, *John Gendall of Exeter (1789–1865)*, gift from Philip Willmot, 1928

Knox, Jack b.1936, *Big Basket, Pears and Shadow*, gift from the

1869–1956, *Sir Harry Veitch (1840–1924)*, bequeathed by the sitter, 1924, © the artist's estate

Rogers, Philip Hutchins c.1786–1853, *Devon Landscape*, gift from the Western Times Company, 1937

Rogers, Philip Hutchins c.1786–1853, *Lake Scene*, purchased, 1950

Rosier, Amédée 1831–1898, *Sunset Scene, Canal San Marco, Venice*, bequeathed by Mr G. N. Hooper, 1915

Rouse *Interior of a Church*

Say, Frederick Richard 1805–1868, *Sir William Webb Follet (1796–1845), MP for Exeter (1835–1845)*, gift from Robert William Webb Follett and J. Spenser Follett, 1921

Scott, William George 1913–1989, *Orange and White*, purchased from Justin Knowles with the assistance of the Victoria and Albert Museum Purchase Grant Fund, 1969, © estate of William Scott 2012

Shapland, John 1865–1929, *The Quay, Exeter*, gift from Joyce Percival, 1985 (?)

Shaw, Walter James 1851–1933, *Oceans, Mists and Spray*, gift from Captain H. G. Hawker, 1919

Shayer, William 1788–1879, *Landscape with Cattle, Horses and Figures*, bequeathed by Lady Lockyer, 1943

Shuter, William active 1771–1799, *Nathaniel Williams (1752–1797), of Exeter*, bequeathed by John Lane, 1925

Sickert, Walter Richard 1860–1942, *Reclining Nude (Le lit de cuivre)*, purchased from Thomas Agnew & Sons with the assistance of the Victoria and Albert Museum Purchase Grant Fund and the Veitch Bequest, 1968, © estate of Walter R. Sickert. All rights reserved, DACS 2012

Smith, Hely Augustus Morton 1862–1941, *Evelyn Phelps Morse (b.1861)*, gift from Mrs Frank Woolley, 1989

Smythe, Edward Robert 1810–1899, *The Blacksmith's Shop*, bequeathed by Lady Helen Mary Thomas, 1946

Spreat, William 1816–1897?, *Ogwell Mill, Devon*, gift from T. Poocke, 1933

Spreat, William 1816–1897?, *Bradley Vale, Newton Abbot, Devon*, gift from Sir Harold Harmsworth, 1948

Spreat, William 1816–1897?, *Holy Street Mill on the Teign, Devon*, gift from T. Poocke, 1933

Stark, Arthur James 1831–1902, *Dartmoor Drift, Devon*, gift from Mr J. A. Stark, 1945

Swanenburgh, Isaac Claesz. (attributed to) 1537–1614, *Nicklaes Warmondt (1540–1609), Burgomaster of Leiden*, gift from Mrs H. Bellfield Lefevre, 1872

Tilson, Joe b.1928, *Liknon, Egg and Pomegranate*, gift from the

Contemporary Art Society, 1988, © Joe Tilson 2012. All rights reserved, DACS

Towne, Francis 1739/1740–1816, *Exeter from Exwick, Devon*, purchased, 1961

Towne, Francis 1739/1740–1816, *At Tivoli, Mountain Landscape in the Alban Hills, Italy*, gift from Robert Worthington, 1937

Towne, Francis 1739/1740–1816, *Roadside Scene in Rome (The Ancient Wall between Porta Salaria and Porta Pinciana, Rome)*, gift from Robert Worthington, 1937

Towne, Francis 1739/1740–1816, *Landscape with a Castle*, gift from F. J. Nettlefold, 1948

Traies, Francis D. 1826–1857, *Landscape with Figures and Animals, Collecting Heather*, purchased, 1934

Traies, William 1789–1872, *The Lime Kilns near Topsham on the Exe, Devon, Lympstone and Exmouth in the Distance*, gift from Robert Worthington, 1932

Traies, William 1789–1872, *Landscape Composition*, gift from Robert Worthington, 1936

Traies, William 1789–1872, *Bridford Mill, Devon*, gift from Robert Worthington, 1932

Traies, William 1789–1872, *Exeter from Exwick, Devon*, purchased, 1933

Tucker, Charles W. J. 1920–1992, *The Blitz*, gift from Miss S. E. J. Tucker, 1998

Tucker, Charles W. J. 1920–1992, *The Farthing Breakfast*, gift from Miss S. E. J. Tucker, 1998

Tucker, Charles W. J. 1920–1992, *The Soup Kitchen*, gift from Miss S. E. J. Tucker, 1998

Tucker, John Wallace 1808–1869, *View at Berry Pomeroy, Devon*, gift from Robert Worthington, 1934

Tucker, John Wallace 1808–1869, *Cherry Bridge and the River Lynn, North Devon*

Tucker, John Wallace 1808–1869, *Mill Stream at Pynes, Devon*, gift from Mr W. Park Little, 1935

Tucker, John Wallace 1808–1869, *Near Chulmleigh, Devon (Chulmleigh from the River Dart, Devon)*, purchased (?), 1930s

Tucker, John Wallace 1808–1869, *Duncannon, on the River Dart, below Totnes, Devon*, purchased, 1951

Tucker, John Wallace 1808–1869, *On the River Dart between Totnes and Dartmouth, Devon*, purchased, 1951

Tucker, John Wallace 1808–1869, *Coastal Scene with Shipping and Figures*, purchased, 1935

Tucker, John Wallace 1808–1869, *Landscape with a River Estuary*, purchased, 1951

Tucker, John Wallace 1808–1869, *View on the Exe near Topsham, Devon*

Virtue, John b.1947, *Landscape No.440*, purchased from Spacex Gallery, Exeter with the assistance

of the Kent Kingdon Bequest, 1999, © John Virtue. All Rights Reserved, DACS 2012

Wainwright, John active 1855–1890, *Primrose and Robin*, bequeathed by Kent and Jane Kingdon, 1892

Wainwright, John active 1855–1890, *Hawthorn and Chaffinch*, bequeathed by Kent and Jane Kingdon, 1892

Wainwright, John active 1855–1890, *Still Life with Fruit and Flowers in a Landscape*, bequeathed by Kent and Jane Kingdon, 1892

Webster, Thomas George 1800–1886, *William Miles*, bequeathed by Mrs Miles, 1907

Wells, Henry Tanworth (after) 1828–1903, *(Walter) Percy Sladen (1849–1900)*, gift from Mrs Percy Sladen, 1903

Wells, Henry Tanworth (after) 1828–1903, *Mrs Constance Sladen (d.1906)*, gift from Mrs Percy Sladen, 1903

Wells, John 1907–2000, *63/11*, purchased from Justin Knowles with the assistance of the Victoria and Albert Museum Purchase Grant Fund, 1969, © the estate of John Wells

White, John 1851–1933, *A Village Wedding, Shere Church, Surrey*, gift from Alderman James G. Commin, 1909

Widgery, Frederick John 1861–1942, *Sky Study, Wind W S W*, gift from the artist, 1931

Widgery, Frederick John 1861–1942, *Sky Study*, gift from the artist, 1931

Widgery, Frederick John 1861–1942, *William Widgery (1822–1893)*, gift from Colonel A. Wyatt-Edgell, 1887

Widgery, William 1822–1893, *Edward Adams (1823–1892), of Crediton*, purchased from Sotheby Bearne with the assistance of the Friends of Exeter Museums and Art Gallery, 1978

Widgery, William 1822–1893, *Fingle Bridge, Devon*, purchased, 1934

Widgery, William 1822–1893, *Burdocks, Brambles and Furze*, bequeathed by Kent and Jane Kingdon, 1892

Widgery, William 1822–1893, *View in Gidley Park, Devon*, bequeathed by Kent and Jane Kingdon, 1892

Widgery, William 1822–1893, *Cross at Chagford, Devon*, bequeathed by Kent and Jane Kingdon, 1892

Widgery, William 1822–1893, *Scene near Holy Street Mill, Chagford, Devon*, bequeathed by Kent and Jane Kingdon, 1892

Widgery, William 1822–1893, *Swiss Lake Scene*, purchased from Phillips, 1981

Widgery, William 1822–1893, *Beechwood Scene*, bequeathed by Kent and Jane Kingdon, 1892

Widgery, William 1822–1893,

Bowerman's Nose, Dartmoor, Devon, bequeathed by Kent and Jane Kingdon, 1892

Widgery, William 1822–1893, *A View off Teignmouth Bridge, Devon*, bequeathed by Kent and Jane Kingdon, 1892

Widgery, William 1822–1893, *Cranmere Pool, Dartmoor, Devon*, bequeathed by Kent and Jane Kingdon, 1892

Widgery, William 1822–1893, *On the Lyd, Devon*, purchased, 1935

Widgery, William 1822–1893, *On the Lyd, Devon*

Widgery, William 1822–1893, *On the Lyd, Devon*, bequeathed by Kent and Jane Kingdon, 1892

Widgery, William 1822–1893, *Sharpitor Rocks, Dartmoor, Devon*, bequeathed by Kent and Jane Kingdon, 1892

Williams, Aubrey 1926–1990, *Bonampak (Number 17)*, purchased from the artist with the assistance of the Victoria and Albert Museum Purchase Grant Fund, 1970, © Aubrey Williams. All rights reserved, DACS 2012

Williams, Howard 1909–1980, *Exe Bridge from Gervase Avenue, Exeter, Devon*, purchased from the artist, 1979

Williams, John Edgar c.1821–1891, *Charles John Follett (1838–1921), Mayor of Exeter*, acquired by Exeter City Council via public subscription, 1876

Williams, T. H. active 1801–1830, *Thomas Medland Kingdon (1783–1832)*, bequeathed by Kent and Jane Kingdon, 1892

Williams, William 1808–1895, *View on the Fal, Cornwall*, purchased, 1933

Williams, William 1808–1895, *Water Mill*, purchased, 1939

Williams, William 1808–1895, *Morning after the Storm, Kenwick Cove, the Lizard*, gift from the artist, 1894

Williams, William 1808–1895, *The Exe, near Topsham, Devon*, gift from the artist (?), 1894

Williamson, William Henry 1820–1883, *Near Clovelly, Devon*, purchased from Mr Keith Lightbown, 1969

Williamson, William Henry 1820–1883, *Sunset on the Devonshire Coast*, purchased from Mr Keith Lightbown, 1969

Wilson, Richard 1712/1713–1782, *Llyn Peris and Dolbadarn Castle*, purchased from Thomas Agnew & Sons with the assistance of the Victoria and Albert Museum Purchase Grant Fund, the National Art Collections Fund and the Veitch Bequest, 1971

Wootton, John c.1682–1764, *Landscape with Angelica and Medaro*, purchased from Thomas Agnew & Sons with the assistance of the Victoria and Albert Museum Purchase Grant Fund, the National Art Collections Fund and the Veitch Bequest, 1987

Wright, Joseph of Derby 1734–1797, *Lake Albano and Castel Gandolfo, Italy*, bequeathed by Miss Annie Moseley, 1957

Wyllie, Charles William 1853–1923, *The Port of London*, purchased with the assistance of the Kent Kingdon Bequest, 1906

Royal Devon and Exeter Hospital

Baxter, Rod *Coffee Break*, gift from the artist, 2003

Bennett, William Mineard 1778–1858, *Bartholemew Parr, Esq. (1713–1800), Surgeon (1741–1797)*, commissioned by the Trustees of the Devon and Exeter Hospital, 1830 (?)

Bishop, Piran b.1961, *Professor Ruth Hawker (b.1939), OBE, First Chairman of the Royal Devon and Exeter NHS Foundation Trust*, commissioned and presented by Doctor Imraan Jhetam, Governor, Royal Devon and Exeter NHS Foundation Trust, 2006, © the artist

Bocos *Still Life with Flowers*, presented by the members of the Royal Devon and Exeter Hospitals Nurse's League, 1974

Brice, Henry c.1831–1903, *John Harris (1782–1855), Surgeon*, commissioned byJohn Delpratt Harris; presented to the Trustees of the Devon and Exeter Hospital, 1889

British (English) School 19th C, *Doctor Patrick Miller (1782–1871), Physician (1809–1860)*, commissioned by the Trustees of the Devon and Exeter Hospital

British (English) School 19th C, *Mr Samuel Barnes (1784–1858), Surgeon (1813–1846)*, commissioned by the Trustees of the Devon and Exeter Hospital

British (English) School 19th C, *William H. Elliot (1805–1874), Physician (1860–1874)*, commissioned by the Trustees of the Devon and Exeter Hospital

Doyle, Anne Farrall b.1940, *Woodland Path*, gift from the artist, who was a patient in 2008, to the Oncology Centre in recognition of the immense care and kindness by all the staff, 2008, © the artist

Eastwood, Nicholas Anthony b.1942, *Summer Stream*, gift from the artist, © the artist

Gandy, William c.1655–1729, *John Patch Senior (1691–1746), Surgeon (1741–1746)*, commissioned by the Trustees of the Devon and Exeter Hospital

Hinds, Thorie Catherine b.1958, *Thinking It Might*, gift from the artist, 2001, © the artist

Hinds, Thorie Catherine b.1958, *A Little Bit Later*, gift from the artist, 2001, © the artist

Hinds, Thorie Catherine b.1958,

Settling Sky, gift from the artist, 2001, © the artist

Hoare, William 1706–1792, *Ralph Allen (1693–1764), President of the Royal Devon and Exeter Hospital (1758), and Benefactor*, commissioned by the Trustees of the Devon and Exeter Hospital

Hudson, Thomas 1701–1779, *Doctor Michael Lee Dicker (1693–1752), Physician (1741–1752)*, commissioned by the Trustees of the Devon and Exeter Hospital

Hudson, Thomas 1701–1779, *John Andrews, MD*, commissioned by the Trustees of the Devon and Exeter Hospital

Hudson, Thomas 1701–1779, *John Tuckfield (1717–1767), President of the Royal Devon and Exeter Hospital (1748), and Benefactor*, commissioned by the Trustees of the Devon and Exeter Hospital

Jennison, Robert b.1933, *Field Boundary (diptych)*, gift from the artist, 2003, © the artist

Keenan, John active 1780–1819, *John Sheldon (1752–1808), Surgeon (1797–1808)*, commissioned by the Trustees of the Devon and Exeter Hospital

Keenan, John active 1780–1819, *John Sheldon (1752–1808), Surgeon (1797–1808)*, commissioned by the Trustees of the Devon and Exeter Hospital

Knight, John Prescott 1803–1881, *Dr Thomas Shapter (1809–1902), Physician*, commissioned by the Trustees of the Devon and Exeter Hospital

Leakey, James 1775–1865, *John Haddy James (1788–1869), Surgeon (1816–1855)*, commissioned by the Trustees of the Devon and Exeter Hospital

Lester, James active 1985, *Sunrise*, gift from the artist, 2003

Mellings, Jenny b.1958, *Decorated Wave*, gift from the artist, 1995, © the artist

Miller, John 1931–2002, *Penwith Sandspur, Cornwall*, on loan from the artist's estate, © the artist's estate

Opie, John 1761–1807, *Dr Thomas Glass (1709–1786), Physician (1741–1775)*, commissioned by the Trustees of the Devon and Exeter Hospital

Opie, John 1761–1807, *John Patch Junior (1723–1786), Surgeon (1741–1786)*, commissioned by the Trustees of the Devon and Exeter Hospital

Reinagle, Ramsay Richard 1775–1862, *Dr John Blackall (1771–1860)*, commissioned by the Trustees of the Devon and Exeter Hospital

Richards, Alan b.1932, *Flowers for Seurat*, gift from the artist, 2000, © the artist

Richards, Alan b.1932, *The Flowering of Art-Deco*, gift from the artist, 1998, © the artist

Richards, Alan b.1932, *Winter*

Afternoon, the Lake at Killerton House, Devon, gift from the artist, 1999, © the artist

Romain, Ricky b.1948, *Breath of Fire*, gift from the artist, 2000, © the artist, www.rickyromain.com

Shiel, Mary Ode *Autumn Trees*, gift from the artist's estate, 2001

Shiel, Mary Ode *Autumn Trees II*, gift from the artist's estate, 2001

Smith, Ivy b.1945, *Central Sterile Supply*, commissioned by Exeter Health Care Arts for the Royal Devon and Exeter Healthcare NHS Trust, 1994, © the artist

Smith, Ivy b.1945, *The Catering Department*, commissioned by Exeter Health Care Arts for the Royal Devon and Exeter Healthcare NHS Trust, 1994, © the artist

Smith, Ivy b.1945, *The Day Case Unit*, commissioned by Exeter Health Care Arts for the Royal Devon and Exeter Healthcare NHS Trust, 1994, © the artist

Smith, Ivy b.1945, *The Physiotherapy Department*, commissioned by Exeter Health Care Arts for the Royal Devon and Exeter Healthcare NHS Trust, 1994, © the artist

Trist Newman, Beryl 1906–1991, *Miss R. M. Furze, Matron, Royal Devon and Exeter Hospital (1958–1970)*, commissioned, 1969

unknown artist *Dr Anthony Daly, MD, FRCP*, commissioned by the Trustees of the Devon and Exeter Hospital, 2005

Watts, George Frederick 1817–1904, *Sir John Walrond (1818–1889), President of the Royal Devon and Exeter Hospital (1874), and Benefactor*, commissioned by the Trustees of the Devon and Exeter Hospital

Willis, Lucy b.1954, *Cliff Cottage*, on loan from the artist, © the artist

Willis, Lucy b.1954, *The Walled Garden*, commissioned by exeter Healthcare Arts to celebrate the opening of the new Radiotherapy department, 1995, © the artist

Wills, James active 1740–1777, *Dean Alured Clarke (1696–1742), Dean of Exeter, Principal Founder and First President of Royal Devon and Exeter Hospital (1741)*, commissioned by the Trustees of the Devon and Exeter Hospital

The Devonshire and Dorset Regimental Charitable Trust

Burgh, Lydia de 1923–2007, *The Mournes from Blackstaff Bridge*, presented by Lieutenant Colonel P. D. King-Fretts, 1984 © the copyright holder

Hamilton, Lucius *Camp Monagh*, purchased by the Officers' Mess of the 1st Battalion of the Devonshire and Dorset Regiment, 1974

Konkell, E. *Haystacks*, presented by Major U. B. Burke

Lely, Peter (copy after) 1618–1680,

Henry Somerset (1629–1700), 1st Duke of Beaufort, unknown acquisition method

Napolitano, J. *Lieutenant Colonel L. H. M. Westropp (1896–1991) of the Devonshire Regiment*, unknown acquisition method

Pannett, Juliet Kathleen 1911–2005, *1st Battalion of the Dorset Regiment in the Assault on Normandy, D Day, 6 June 1994*, unknown acquisition method, © the artist's estate

Rowlands, David John b.1952, *'The Bloody Eleventh', Battle of Salamanca 22 July 1812*, presented by The Devonshire Regiment Old Comrades Association, 1985, © the artist

unknown artist *Henry Somerset (1629–1700), 1st Duke of Beaufort*, unknown acquisition method

unknown artist *Lieutenant General Sir Henry Tucker Montresor (1767?–1837?), KCB, GCH*, unknown acquisition method

unknown artist *Young Devon Soldier*, unknown acquisition method

Wollen, William Barnes (copy after) 1857–1936, *The Last Stand of the 2nd Devons at Bois-des-Buttes, 27 May 1918*, unknown acquisition method

The Met Office

Beck, Stuart 1903–2000, *'Admiral Beaufort'*, unknown acquisition method

Beck, Stuart 1903–2000, *Atlantic Weather Ships Transferring Mail*, unknown acquisition method

Fairclough, Michael b.1940, *Isle of Man Suite I – Langness*, purchased through the Met Office Relocation Fund, 2004, © the artist

Fairclough, Michael b.1940, *Isle of Man Suite II – Bradda Head*, purchased through the Met Office Relocation Fund, 2004, © the artist

Fairclough, Michael b.1940, *Isle of Man Suite III – Niarbyl (Sun Dogs)*, gift from Peter Ewins, 2004, © the artist

Fairclough, Michael b.1940, *Isle of Man Suite IV – Blue Point*, purchased through the Met Office Relocation Fund, 2004, © the artist

Fairclough, Michael b.1940, *Isle of Man Suite V – Point of Ayre*, purchased through the Met Office Relocation Fund, 2004, © the artist

Jackson, Kurt b.1961, *Squall*, purchased through the Met Office Relocation Fund, 2004, © the artist

Jay, Peter *Summer Landscape*, unknown acquisition method

Jay, Peter *Winter Landscape*, unknown acquisition method

MacPherson, Rebecca b.1967, *Soft as Water Hard as Rock*, purchased through the Met Office Relocation Fund, © the artist

Patzer, Ryszard b.1941, *Krajobraz po Sztormie (After the Storm)*, gift on the occasion of the 150th

anniversary of the Met Office from the Institute of Meteorology and Water Management, Poland, 2004

unknown artist early 20th C, *Sir Napier Shaw (1854–1945)*, unknown acquisition method

unknown artist *Birch Woods*, gift from Russia on the occasion of the 150th anniversary of the Met Office

The Palace, Exeter

Abbott, Lemuel Francis 1760–1803, *John Ross (1719–1792), Bishop of Exeter (1778–1792)*, unknown acquisition method

British (English) School 17th C, *Anthony Sparrow (1612–1686), Bishop of Exeter (1667–1676)*, unknown acquisition method

British (English) School 17th C, *Joseph Hall (1574–1656), Bishop of Exeter (1627–1641)*, unknown acquisition method

British (English) School 18th C, *Edward Cotton, Grandson of William Cotton, Bishop of Exeter (1598–1621)*, unknown acquisition method

British (English) School 18th C, *Seth Ward (1617–1688/9), Bishop of Exeter (1662–1667)*, unknown acquisition method

British (English) School 18th C, *Thomas Lamplugh (1615–1691), Bishop of Exeter (1676–1688)*, unknown acquisition method

British (English) School 18th C, *William Buller (1735–1796), Bishop of Exeter (1792–1797)*, unknown acquisition method

British (English) School mid-18th C, *George Lavington (1684–1762), Bishop of Exeter (1746–1762)*, unknown acquisition method

British (English) School early 19th C, *William Carey (1769–1846), Bishop of Exeter (1820–1830)*, unknown acquisition method

British (English) School 20th C, *John Fisher (1748–1825), Bishop of Exeter (1803–1807)*, unknown acquisition method

Cope, Arthur Stockdale 1857–1940, *Edward Henry Bickersteth (1825–1906), Bishop of Exeter (1895–1900)*, acquired in commemoration of fifty years of faithful labour by the sitter, 1899

Dahl, Michael I (circle of) 1656/1659–1743, *The Right Reverend Dr Ofspring Blackall (1655–1716), Late Lord Bishop of Exeter (1654–1716), Bishop of Exeter (1707–1716)*, unknown acquisition method

Dahl, Michael I (circle of) 1656/1659–1743, *The Right Reverend Dr Ofspring Blackall (1655–1716), Late Lord Bishop of Exeter (1654–1716), Bishop of Exeter (1707–1716)*, unknown acquisition method

Dahl, Michael I (circle of) 1656/1659–1743, *The Right Reverend Dr Ofspring Blackall (1655–1716), Late Lord Bishop of

Exeter (1654–1716), Bishop of Exeter (1707–1716)*, unknown acquisition method

Dahl, Michael I (circle of) 1656/1659–1743, *The Right Reverend Dr Ofspring Blackall (1655–1716), Late Lord Bishop of Exeter (1654–1716), Bishop of Exeter (1707–1716)*, unknown acquisition method

Davidson-Houston, Aubrey Claude 1906–1995, *Robert Cecil Mortimer (1902–1976), Bishop of Exeter (1949–1973)*, unknown acquisition method, © the artist's estate

Frampton, Meredith 1894–1984, *Lord William Cecil (1863–1936), Bishop of Exeter (1916–1936)*, unknown acquisition method, © the artist's estate

Hankinson, David *Hewlett Thomson (b.1929), Bishop of Exeter (1985–1999)*, unknown acquisition method

Kneller, Godfrey (follower of) 1646–1723, *Jonathan Trelawny (1650–1721), Bishop of Exeter (1688–1707)*, unknown acquisition method

Langworthy, Paddy *Eric A. C. Mercer (1917–2003), Bishop of Exeter (1973–1985)*, unknown acquisition method

Loggan, David (after) 1634–1692, *Peter Mews 'Black Spot', Bishop of Bath and Wells (1672–1684)*, unknown acquisition method

Mansbridge, John 1901–1981, *Charles Edward Curzon (1878–1954), Bishop of Exeter (1936–1948)*, unknown acquisition method

Pond, Arthur 1701–1758, *Stephen Weston (1665–1742), Bishop of Exeter (1724–1758)*, unknown acquisition method

Prynne, Edward A. Fellowes 1854–1921, *Frederick Temple (1821–1902), Bishop of Exeter (1869–1885)*, presented by some Devonshire friends to Mrs Temple for her lifetime then to be placed in the Palace of Exeter in perpetuity

Robertson, A. (Miss) *Archibald Robertson (1853–1931), Bishop of Exeter (1903–1916)*, unknown acquisition method

Romney, George (circle of) 1734–1802, *The Honorable Frederick Keppel (d.1777), Bishop of Exeter (1762–1777)*, unknown acquisition method

Seeman, Enoch the younger c.1694–1745 (attributed to) & **Seeman, Isaac** d.1751 (attributed to) *Lancelot Blackburne (1658–1743), Bishop of Exeter (1717–1724)*, unknown acquisition method

Trist Newman, Beryl 1906–1991, *The Enthronement of Bishop Robert Mortimer, Bishop of Exeter (1948–1973)*, unknown acquisition method

unknown artist *Henry Reginald Courtenay (1741–1803), DD, Bishop of Exeter (1797–1803),* presented by Jan-Eric Osterlund, 2010

Woolnoth, Thomas A. (attributed to) 1785–1857, *Henry Phillpotts (1778–1869), Bishop of Exeter (1831–1869)*, unknown acquisition method

University of Exeter, Fine Art Collection

Al-Kilai, Mohammid *Street Scene*, unknown acquisition method

Al-Qasimi, Sheikha Hoor *Arab Boy*, gift from the Ruler of Sharjah, United Arab Emirates

Al-Qasimi, Sheikha Hoor *Arab Gentleman*, gift from the Ruler of Sharjah, United Arab Emirates

Al-Qasimi, Sheikha Hoor *Arab Girl*, gift from the Ruler of Sharjah, United Arab Emirates

Al-Qasimi, Sheikha Hoor *Arab Musician*, gift from the Ruler of Sharjah, United Arab Emirates

Al-Qasimi, Sheikha Hoor *Arab Woman*, gift from the Ruler of Sharjah, United Arab Emirates

Al-Qasimi, Sheikha Hoor *Arab Woman*, gift from the Ruler of Sharjah, United Arab Emirates

Apperley, Nigel *Dartmoor, Devon*, unknown acquisition method

Baird, J. Noel *W. H. Reed, Alderman of Exeter Who Bequeathed Reed Hall to the University in 1922*, presented to University College of the South West by the Vice-President, 1922

Ballantyne, John 1815–1897, *Miss Bertha Salter, Singer from North Devon (1890s–1920s)*, unknown acquisition method

Bampfylde, Coplestone Warre 1720–1791, *Holy Trinity Church, Exmouth, Devon*, gift

Barker, Elsie M. *Mr John Lloyd, First University Librarian*, on loan from the late Mrs Lloyd

Bartlett, Alan G. active 1956–1968, *Sandstone Cliffs, Devon Coast, Ladram*, unknown acquisition method

Bartlett, Alan G. active 1956–1968, *River Dart, near Hexworthy, Devon*, unknown acquisition method

Bartlett, Alan G. active 1956–1968, *Höllental, Bavaria, Germany*, unknown acquisition method

Bartlett, Alan G. active 1956–1968, *Channel Island Scene*, unknown acquisition method

Bennett, Vincent 1910–1993, *Suzannah and the Elders*, unknown acquisition method

Bird *Waterfront*, unknown acquisition method

Blackburn, David b.1939, *Boulder in Light*, presented by Sir Rex Richards, © the artist

Blackburn, David b.1939, *Pale Beach, South Coast*, presented by Sir Rex Richards, © the artist

Blackburn, David b.1939, *Sunlight, Early Morning*, presented by Sir Rex Richards, © the artist

Blackburn, David b.1939, *Sea Window*, presented by Sir Rex

Richards, © the artist

Boundy, Joy active 1972–1999, *Seven Ovals in Pink*, unknown acquisition method

Boundy, Joy active 1972–1999, *Crustacean Delight*, purchased by the Fine Art and Exhibition Advisory Group

Boundy, Joy active 1972–1999, *Presences at Bryce Canyon, USA*, purchased by the Fine Art and Exhibition Advisory Group

Boundy, Joy active 1972–1999, *Sky Kiss*, purchased by the Fine Art and Exhibition Advisory Group

Boundy, Joy active 1972–1999, *The Heavy Weight of Ignorance*, purchased

Boundy, Joy active 1972–1999, *Canto V*, purchased by the Fine Art and Exhibition Advisory Group

Boundy, Joy active 1972–1999, *Christ and the Four Apostles*, unknown acquisition method

Boundy, Joy active 1972–1999, *Inferno*, purchased by the Fine Art and Exhibition Advisory Group

Boundy, Joy active 1972–1999, *Looking over to Baker Street from Gloucester Place, London, W1*, purchased by the Fine Art and Exhibition Advisory Group

Boundy, Joy active 1972–1999, *Poverty in Sicily*, purchased by the Fine Art and Exhibition Advisory Group

Boundy, Joy active 1972–1999, *Poverty in Sicily II*, purchased by the Fine Art and Exhibition Advisory Group

Bourdillon, Frank Wright 1851–1924, *Aboard the 'Revenge'*, unknown acquisition method

Bower, Stephen b.1949, *Circus Garden*, purchased by the Fine Art and Exhibition Advisory Group, © the artist

Bower, Stephen b.1949, *View of the Otter at Cadhay Bridge, Devon*, unknown acquisition method, © the artist

Brougier, Adolf M. 1870–1962, *Mountain Landscape*, unknown acquisition method

Canning, Neil b.1960, *Axis*, purchased, c.2000, © the artist

Canning, Neil b.1960, *Breakaway*, on loan from the artist, © the artist

Canning, Neil b.1960, *Catalyst*, on loan from the artist, © the artist

Canning, Neil b.1960, *Challenge*, on loan from the artist, © the artist

Canning, Neil b.1960, *Reach*, on loan from the artist, © the artist

Canning, Neil b.1960, *Rising Spirit, 'Sperys dasserhy'*, gift from the artist to the University of Exeter, Tremough Campus, © the artist

Cattermull, Caroline & Cressell, Sarah *Bass Player*, commissioned

Cattermull, Caroline & Cressell, Sarah *Drummer*, commissioned

Cattermull, Caroline & Cressell, Sarah *Saxophone Player*, commissioned

Cattermull, Caroline & Cressell, Sarah *Trumpeter*, commissioned

Cay, S. *Still Life with Two Blue Vases*, unknown acquisition method

Clint, George 1770–1854, *Caroline Orges*, unknown acquisition method

Cook, Christopher b.1959, *Death in the Valley*, purchased by the Fine Art and Exhibition Advisory Group, © the artist

Cook, Christopher b.1959, *Burning Tyres*, purchased by the Fine Art and Exhibition Advisory Group, © the artist

Cook, Christopher b.1959, *Adolescent Landscape*, on loan from the artist, © the artist

Cotton, Alan b.1938, *Harry Kay, Vice-Chancellor of the University of Exeter (1973–1984)*, commissioned, © the artist

Cotton, Alan b.1938, *Hartland Point I, Devon*, purchased, © the artist

Cotton, Alan b.1938, *Hartland Point II, Devon*, purchased, © the artist

Cotton, Alan b.1938, *The Otter Valley, Devon*, bequeathed by Mary Cotton, © the artist

Cotton, Alan b.1938, *Hartland Point III, Devon*, purchased, © the artist

Cotton, Alan b.1938, *Hartland Point IV, Devon*, purchased, © the artist

Cotton, Alan b.1938, *Hartland Point V, Devon*, purchased, © the artist

Cotton, Alan b.1938, *County Donegal, Ireland, Slieve League in Evening Light*, unknown acquisition method, © the artist

Cotton, Alan b.1938, *Harry Kay*, bequeathed by Mary Cotton, © the artist

Cotton, Alan b.1938, *Hartland IV, Devon*, unknown acquisition method, © the artist

Cotton, Alan b.1938, *Summer Bank, Otter River, Devon*, unknown acquisition method, © the artist

Creedy, John *William Francis Jackson Knight (1895–1964), Classical Scholar*, donated by the Jackson Knight Estate

Crossland, James Henry 1852–1939, *First Snow on Broughton Moor, Cumberland (Birks Bridge, Duddon Valley)*, unknown acquisition method

Crossland, James Henry 1852–1939, *Dungeon Ghyll, Cumberland*, unknown acquisition method

Cunliffe, Leslie b.1950, *Covenant Landscape*, purchased by the Fine Art and Exhibition Advisory Group, © the artist

Cunliffe, Leslie b.1950, *Scapegoat*, purchased by the Fine Art and Exhibition Advisory Group, © the artist

David *Arthur Knott Woodbridge, MA*, unknown acquisition method

David *T. Arnold Brown, MA, BSc, FRSE, FRAS, Professor of Mathematics at the University of*

Exeter (1923–1958), unknown acquisition method

Davis, Henry William Banks 1833–1914, *Cattle in a Highland Loch*, bequeathed by Sir Henry Veitch

Donaldson, David Abercrombie 1916–1996, *Sir Hector Hetherington (1888–1965)*, on permanent loan from A. Hetherington, © the artist's estate

Dutch School *Portrait of a Young Lady with a Lace Collar and a Fan*, bequeathed by D. Brendon of Sherbourne

Dutch School *Portrait of a Woman*, bequeathed by D. Brendon of Sherbourne

W. R. E. *A Country Road with a Distant Windmill*, unknown acquisition method

Eastman, Frank S. 1878–1964, *Sir Henry Lopes (1859–1938)*, unknown acquisition method

Eastman, Frank S. 1878–1964, *Sir Henry Lopes (1859–1938)*, unknown acquisition method

Eastman, Frank S. 1878–1964, *William Tatem (1868–1942), Lord Glanely, DL, JP, LLD, President of the University College of South Wales and Monmouthshire (1919–1924)*, unknown acquisition method

Eastwood, Nicholas Anthony b.1942, *Abstract in Blue, Red and Yellow*, unknown acquisition method, © the artist

Eastwood, Nicholas Anthony b.1942, *Southern Landscape Series: Slow Thaw II*, purchased by the Fine Art and Exhibition Advisory Group, © the artist

Evangeliemos, I. M. active 20th C, *Icon of Christ Crucified*, donated

Eves, Reginald Grenville 1876–1941, *John Murray, Principal of the UCSW (c.1930–c.1950)*, unknown acquisition method

Fernee, Kenneth William A. 1926–1983, *Dartmoor Stone Row, Devon*, unknown acquisition method

Fisher, Alec active 20th C, *Miss Murray*, unknown acquisition method

Fishwick, Clifford 1923–1997, *Sea Orb I*, purchased by the Fine Art and Exhibition Advisory Group, © the artist's estate

Fishwick, Clifford 1923–1997, *Landscape*, unknown acquisition method, © the artist's estate

Fletcher *Underground Crucifixion*, unknown acquisition method

Forbes, Stanhope Alexander (attributed to) 1857–1947, *Feeding the Pigs*, presented by Roland Glave Saunders, © the artist's estate/Bridgeman Art Library

Frost, Terry 1915–2003, *Arizona Spirals*, purchased by the Fine Art and Exhibition Advisory Group, © estate of Terry Frost. All rights reserved, DACS 2012

Frost, Terry 1915–2003, *Timberain (triptych, left panel)*, gift from the artist, © estate of Terry Frost. All

rights reserved, DACS 2012

Frost, Terry 1915–2003, *Timberain (triptych, centre panel)*, gift from the artist, © estate of Terry Frost. All rights reserved, DACS 2012

Frost, Terry 1915–2003, *Timberain (triptych, right panel)*, gift from the artist, © estate of Terry Frost. All rights reserved, DACS 2012

Garinei, E. *Italian Street*, unknown acquisition method

Gaussen, Winifred *G. R. Champernowne*, presented by L. Elmhirst

Gaussen, Winifred *Still Life with a Violin*, unknown acquisition method

Gaussen, Winifred *The Scales*, unknown acquisition method

Gilbert, Arthur 1819–1895, *Pastoral Scene, River Scene*, unknown acquisition method

Gosslean, J. H. *Ravine with a Bridge*, unknown acquisition method

Green, Anthony 1939–2003, *Vessels Last Dance*, purchased by the Fine Art and Exhibition Advisory Group

Harvey, Harold C. 1874–1941, *Boys Loading Mangolds onto a Cart*, bequeathed by Roland Glave Saunders, © the artist's estate/Bridgeman Art Library

Harvey, Harold C. 1874–1941, *Three Boys*, bequeathed by Roland Glave Saunders, © the artist's estate/Bridgeman Art Library

Heron, Patrick 1920–1999, *Violet with Venetian Scarlet and Emerald*, purchased with funds from an anonymous donor, © Susanna Heron. All rights reserved, DACS 2012

Hilliard, John Michael b.1945, *Shades of Light, Gathering Storm*, purchased by the English Department following an exhibition in the Atelier Gallery, © the artist

Howell, June *Cups and a Milk Bottle*, unknown acquisition method

Jackson, Kurt b.1961, *Crushing and Screening Plant*, purchased out of the Registrar's Discretionary Fund, 2000, © the artist

Jackson, Kurt b.1961, *Sun and Rain, Strong Winds, Drilling Carnsew Mine*, purchased by the Fine Art and Exhibition Advisory Group and the Registrar's Discretionary Fund, © the artist

Jackson, Kurt b.1961, *Catch the Light*, gift from the artist, © the artist

Jeany, M. J. *Intérieure: Palette et pot de fleurs*, unknown acquisition method

Jennison, Robert b.1933, *Hillside with Approaching Storm*, purchased by the Fine Art and Exhibition Advisory Group, © the artist

Jewell, Catherine active 1978–2003, *Symphony in Nature*, purchased by the Fine Art and Exhibition Advisory Group

Jewell, Catherine active 1978–2003, *Mid the Flowers*, purchased by the Fine Art and Exhibition Advisory Group

Jewell, Catherine active 1978–2003, *Yellow Bird*, purchased by the Fine Art and Exhibition Advisory Group

Johns, Ewart b.1923, *Red Dance*, unknown acquisition method © the artist

Johns, Ewart b.1923, *Sir James Cook*, unknown acquisition method © the artist

Johns, Ewart b.1923, *Blue and Black Abstract*, unknown acquisition method © the artist

Johns, Ewart b.1923, *Devon Landscape*, unknown acquisition method © the artist

Johns, Ewart b.1923, *Three Figures*, unknown acquisition method © the artist

Johnson, Colin Trevor b.1942, *Coastline Collage*, purchased by the Fine Art and Exhibition Advisory Group, © the artist

Kinsella, Katherine *Still Life, Vase of Flowers*, unknown acquisition method

Logsdail, William 1859–1944, *Venetian Scene, Canal*, bequeathed by Sir Henry Veitch, © the artist's estate/Bridgeman Art Library

Long, Edwin 1829–1891, *Sir Stafford Northcote (1818–1887), 1st Earl of Iddesleigh*, presented to Lady Northcote by Devonshire Friends, 1883

Loon, Theodor van 1581/1582–1667, *Portrait of a Young Girl in a White Dress and Crimson Overwrap*, bequeathed by D. Brendon of Sherbourne

Loon, Theodor van 1581/1582–1667, *Portrait of a Young Girl in a Crimson Dress Wearing a Pearl Necklace*, bequeathed by D. Brendon of Sherbourne

Maeckelberghe, Margo b.1932, *Sea Green Winter*, purchased from the artist, 2008

Maeckelberghe, Margo b.1932, *Roller Coaster High*, purchased from the artist, 2008

Maeckelberghe, Margo b.1932, *Tin Mine Coast*, purchased by the Fine Art and Exhibition Advisory Group

Maeckelberghe, Margo b.1932, *Valley to the Sea*, purchased from the artist, 2004

Maeckelberghe, Margo b.1932, *Ancient Land I*, purchased from the artist

May, Christopher *The Author and MacHeath*, unknown acquisition method

Miró, Joan (after) 1893–1983, *Untitled*, unknown acquisition method

Miskin, Lionel 1924–2006, *Jack Clemo*, gift from the sitter, © the artist's estate

Miskin, Lionel 1924–2006, *Lionel Miskin's Mother (?)*, donated by Jack Clemo, © the artist's estate

Murillo, Bartolomé Esteban (after) 1618–1682, *The Immaculate Conception*, gift

Nash, Catte *Female Nude Study*, unknown acquisition method

Nisbet *Adam and Eve Expelled from the Garden*, unknown acquisition method

Nisbet *Christ and Three Men*, unknown acquisition method

Pankhurst, Andy b.1968, *Robert Scott Alexander (1936–2005), Lord Alexander of Weedon, QC*, commissioned, 2010

Pascoe, Ernest 1922–1996, *The Roman Wall*, unknown acquisition method, © the artist's estate

Pragnall, G. *Duryard House, University of Exeter, Devon*, unknown acquisition method

R. B. *Deer by a Lakeside*, unknown acquisition method

Ramsay, Allan b.1959, *Sir Rex Richards (b.1922), DSc, FBA, FRS, Chancellor of the University (1982–1998)*, unknown acquisition method

Raphael (copy after) 1483–1520, *Madonna della seggiola*, unknown acquisition method

Roberts, L. *River Scene*, unknown acquisition method

Rodrigues, Judy b.1960, *Eyestone*, purchased, © the artist

Rubens, Peter Paul (attributed to) 1577–1640, *The Four Corners of the World*, unknown acquisition method

Russell, Jack *Three People Scything Corn*, unknown acquisition method

Sattar, Al-Shaykh *Landscape*, unknown acquisition method

Scholz, Heinz-Joachim *Buntheim Summer, 1954*, unknown acquisition method

Simmonds, Stanley b.1917, *Winter Scene I*, on loan from Dr Coleman

Smith, Anthony William David b.1962, *Blue Seascape*, gift from the artist, © the artist

Smith, Anthony William David b.1962, *Beach Scene*, purchased by the Fine Art and Exhibition Advisory Group, © the artist

Smith, Anthony William David b.1962, *Black and White Seascape*, gift from the artist, © the artist

Spear, Ruskin 1911–1990, *Mary Cavendish (1895–1988), Duchess of Devonshire in Chancellor's Robes*, commissioned, © the artist's estate/Bridgeman Art Library

Stephenson, Pippa *Sometimes I …*, purchased by the Fine Art and Exhibition Advisory Group

Stubley, Trevor 1932–2010, *David Harrison, DBE, SCD, Feng, Vice-Chancellor of the University of Exeter (1984–1994)*, unknown acquisition method, © the artist's estate

Symonds, Ken b.1927, *Sir Geoffrey Holland (b.1938), Vice-Chancellor of the University of Exeter*, commissioned, © the artist

Taffs, Charles Harold b.1876, *Lady with a Fan in a Chair*, unknown acquisition method

Timson, Bruce *Portrait of a Woman with a Book*, unknown acquisition method

Tripp, Stella b.1954, *Twister*, purchased by the Fine Art and Exhibition Advisory Group, © the artist

Trist, Brody *Eden Phillpotts, Esq. (1862–1960)*, unknown acquisition method

Tucker, John Wallace 1808–1869, *Bramford Speke Bridge, River Exe, Devon*, presented by G. J. Abell, JP

Tucker, John Wallace 1808–1869, *Bramford Speke, River Exe, Devon*, presented by G. J. Abell, JP

Tucker, John Wallace 1808–1869, *Dittisham, River Dart, Devon*, presented by G. J. Abell, JP

Tucker, John Wallace 1808–1869, *Kingswear Mills, River Dart, Devon*, presented by G. J. Abell, JP

Tucker, John Wallace 1808–1869, *Kingswear, River Dart, Devon*, presented by G. J. Abell, JP

Tucker, John Wallace 1808–1869, *Near South Molton, Devon*, presented by G. J. Abell, JP

Tucker, John Wallace 1808–1869, *Red Rock, Bramford Speke, River Exe, Devon*, presented by G. J. Abell, JP

Tucker, John Wallace 1808–1869, *Rewe, Devon*, presented by G. J. Abell, JP

Tucker, John Wallace 1808–1869, *Littleham, Devon*, presented by G. J. Abell, JP

unknown artist *Portrait of a Gentleman, Aged 72*, bequeathed by D. Brendon of Sherbourne

unknown artist early 19th C, *Miss Helen Hope, Who Donated Money in the 1920s for a Hall of Residence, Hope Hall*, unknown acquisition method

unknown artist mid-19th C, *Prince of Orange Landing at Torbay, Devon*, unknown acquisition method

unknown artist *Laver Building, University of Exeter, Devon*, unknown acquisition method

unknown artist 20th C, *Colonel Mardon, Donor towards the Building of Mardon Hall, a New Hall of Residence at the University in 1933*, unknown acquisition method

unknown artist *A Steppe Landscape*, unknown acquisition method

unknown artist *Abstract Head*, unknown acquisition method

unknown artist *Abstract in Blue and Black*, unknown acquisition method

unknown artist *Abstract in Blue and White*, unknown acquisition method

unknown artist *Abstract in Brown and Black*, unknown acquisition method

unknown artist *Abstraction in Pink*, unknown acquisition method

unknown artist *Abstraction in Pink*, unknown acquisition method

unknown artist *Abstraction in Pink*, unknown acquisition method

unknown artist *Australian Landscape*, unknown acquisition method

unknown artist *Bird*, unknown acquisition method

unknown artist *Castle with a Lake*, unknown acquisition method

unknown artist *City Corner*, unknown acquisition method

unknown artist *Classical Scene with a Waterfall*, unknown acquisition method

unknown artist *Donkey Following Two People*, unknown acquisition method

unknown artist *Flower Painting*, unknown acquisition method

unknown artist *Forest Tunnel*, unknown acquisition method

unknown artist *Gladys Hooper Hogsbrawn*, unknown acquisition method

unknown artist *Horse's Head*, unknown acquisition method

unknown artist *Pastoral Abstract*, unknown acquisition method

unknown artist *Portrait of a Gentleman*, unknown acquisition method

unknown artist *Portrait of a Gentleman with a Sword*, unknown acquisition method

unknown artist *Portrait of a Lady with a Fan*, unknown acquisition method

unknown artist *Portrait of a Mayor*, unknown acquisition method

unknown artist *Portrait of a Woman*, unknown acquisition method

unknown artist *Religious Themes: Cross*, unknown acquisition method

unknown artist *Sir John Llewellyn, Vice Chancellor (1966–1972)*, commissioned

unknown artist *St Luke's, South Cloisters, University of Exeter*, unknown acquisition method

unknown artist *Still Life with Three Oranges*, unknown acquisition method

unknown artist *Vegetables and a Cooking Pot*, unknown acquisition method

Walker, Gregory b.1957, *King's Wear*, purchased by the Fine Art and Exhibition Advisory Group © the copyright holder

Webb, James 1825–1895, *The Old Castle Overlooking the Bay of Naples, Italy*, unknown acquisition method

West, F. *Gingjer, Cornwall*, unknown acquisition method

Whittington-Ince, Richard 1934–1983, *Woman, the Railway Cutting*, unknown acquisition method

Whittington-Ince, Richard

Whittington-Ince, Richard 1934–1983, *Railway Cutting*, unknown acquisition method

Whittington-Ince, Richard 1934–1983, *Scorrier, near Redruth, Cornwall*, unknown acquisition method

Whittington-Ince, Richard 1934–1983, *Urban Scene from a Bridge*, unknown acquisition method

Widgery, Frederick John 1861–1942, *Coastal View (Mouth of the Yealm, Devon)*, gift from Dr and Mrs De Newman

Widgery, William 1822–1893, *River Scene*, unknown acquisition method

Widgery, William 1822–1893, *River Scene, Dartmoor in the Background*, unknown acquisition method

Williamson, Mary *Mabel Early*, gift from the sitter

Wood, Ron *Silver Moon*, acquired, 1981

Wouwerman, Philips (after) 1619–1668, *Village Scene*, gift

Wreford-Clarke, W. *Still Life*, unknown acquisition method

Wonford House Hospital

Cassidy, D. *Spiral*, unknown acquisition method

Huckvale, Karen & Haldon Unit Eating Disorders Service Staff & Users *Flowers*, unknown acquisition method

Huckvale, Karen & Haldon Unit Eating Disorders Service Staff & Users *Trees I*, unknown acquisition method

Huckvale, Karen & Haldon Unit Eating Disorders Service Staff & Users *Trees II*, unknown acquisition method

Knowles, Gwen *Lilies*, unknown acquisition method

Knowles, Gwen *Tree in Winter*, unknown acquisition method

unknown artist *Quiet Light*, unknown acquisition method

unknown artist *Abstract Landscape*, unknown acquisition method

unknown artist *Cactus*, unknown acquisition method

unknown artist *Circles*, unknown acquisition method

unknown artist *Fish*, unknown acquisition method

unknown artist *Head*, unknown acquisition method

unknown artist *James Manning, Founder of Wonford House Hospital (1801)*, unknown acquisition method

unknown artist *Marblised Triptych*, unknown acquisition method

unknown artist *Spiral 1*, unknown acquisition method

unknown artist *Spiral 2*, unknown acquisition method

unknown artist *Spiral 3*, unknown acquisition method

unknown artist *Spiral 4*, unknown acquisition method
unknown artist *Spiral 5*, unknown acquisition method
unknown artist *Spiral 6*, unknown acquisition method
unknown artist *Tea on the Lawn in front of Wonford House Hospital, Devon*, unknown acquisition method
unknown artist *Three Gold Leaves*, unknown acquisition method

Exmouth Library

Cooke, William Edward active 1872–1898, *Withycombe Mill, Devon*, purchased with the assistance of the Thomas Abell Reference Library Foundation from the illustrations collection of his son, George Abell (?)
Goodrich, J. B. active 1861–1884, *Withycombe Brook, Devon*, purchased with the assistance of the Thomas Abell Reference Library Foundation from the illustrations collection of his son, George Abell (?)
Goodrich, J. B. active 1861–1884, *Exmouth, Devon, View of House on the Maer*, purchased with the assistance of the Thomas Abell Reference Library Foundation from the illustrations collection of his son, George Abell (?)
Goodrich, J. B. active 1861–1884, *View of Estuary and Beacon from a Field, Devon*, purchased with the assistance of the Thomas Abell Reference Library Foundation from the illustrations collection of his son, George Abell (?)
Green, Dorrie *Holy Trinity Church and Bicton Place, Exmouth, Devon*, presented by the Exmouth Choral and Orchestral Society as a memorial to Donald White, their Chairman and Conductor (1947–1983), 1983
Hullmandel, Charles Joseph (attributed to) 1789–1850, *Combeinteignhead, View on the River Teign, Combe Cellars, Devon*, purchased with the assistance of the Thomas Abell Reference Library Foundation from the illustrations collection of his son, George Abell (?)
Hullmandel, Charles Joseph (attributed to) 1789–1850, *Starcross, View of Starcorss on the River Exe, Devon*, purchased with the assistance of the Thomas Abell Reference Library Foundation from the illustrations collection of his son, George Abell (?)
Hynard, H. *Thomas Abel (1848–1943), MBE, JP*, purchased with the assistance of the Thomas Abell Reference Library Foundation from the illustrations collection of his son, George Abell (?)
Lloyd, Julia *'Louisa Cottage', Exmouth, Devon*, purchased with the assistance of the Thomas Abell

Reference Library Foundation from the illustrations collection of his son, George Abell (?)
Sharp, Miles Balmford 1897–1973, *Portrait of an Exmouth Lifeboatman*, unknown acquisition method
Sharp, Miles Balmford 1897–1973, *Portrait of an Exmouth Lifeboatman*, unknown acquisition method
Sharp, Miles Balmford 1897–1973, *View of the Strand Gardens, Exmouth, Devon*, unknown acquisition method
Strong, Charles Edward active 1851–1884, *Ships in the Exe Estuary, Devon*, gift from Mr K. G. Utting, 1960
unknown artist *View from the Maer, Devon, out to Sea*, unknown acquisition method

Exmouth Museum

Cole, William d.late 1990s, *Clock Tower, Exmouth, Devon*, gift from the artist
Cole, William d.late 1990s, *Holy Trinity Church, Exmouth, Devon*, gift from the artist; accessioned, 2006
Cole, William d.late 1990s, *Lane to Littleham, Exmouth, Devon*, gift from the artist
Cole, William d.late 1990s, *Prattshayes, Maer Lane, Littleham, Exmouth, Devon*, gift from the artist; accessioned, 2006
Driver, Charles Percy 1911–1988, *Chapel Street, Exmouth, Devon*, gift from the artist
Mair, Thomas active 1901–1924, *Orcombe Point, Exmouth, Devon*, gift from Mrs J. Basgleoppo; accessioned, 1986
Maylor, D. *Lifeboat 'Carolyne Finch' on Call*, gift from Mrs D. Maylor; accessioned, 1988
Mordinoff, R. A. *Robert R. A. Tucker Pain*, gift from Mrs Hilda Vansittart Moorehouse; accessioned, 1985
Morgan, Trevor b.1929, *Chapel Street, Exmouth, Devon*, gift from the artist
Morgan, Trevor b.1929, *Mr Turnip*, gift from the artist; accessioned; 1987
Morley, H. F. *Memories of a Happy Holiday: Exmouth Docks, Devon*, gift from Mrs E. Freeman; accessioned, 2002
Mortimore, A. *Dead Calm sunset in the Bight at Exmouth, Devon (copy after James Francis Danby)*, gift from Mrs Mortimore; accessioned, 1996
Pethybridge, D. C. *Annie Rowsell*, gift from the artist; accessioned, 1987
Stokes, Sybil *The Lane at Littleham Cross, Exmouth, Devon*, bequeathed by G. Elaine Walker, 1994; accessioned, 1995
Tods *The Docks, Exmouth, Devon*, gift from Miss G. W. B. Clarke;

accessioned, 1995
unknown artist *Colonel Thorneycroft*, gift from Mr G. Hill; accessioned, 1985
unknown artist *D'Arcy W. A. Hughes, First Headmaster of Exmouth Grammar School (1929–c.1957)*, gift from Mr. G. Hill; accessioned 1985
Whateley, John *Fireside Domestic Scene*, gift from Rosemary Cook, 2006
Whateley, John *Six Gypsy Children*, unknown acquisition method

Exmouth Town Council

Cotton, Alan b.1938, *Exmouth, Devon, from the Estuary*, presented by the friends and organisations of Exmouth to commemorate the honour of DBE bestowed on Dame Mary Bridges, 1981, © the artist
Penn, William Charles 1877–1968, *Portrait of a Gentleman*, unknown acquisition method, © the artist's estate
Reeves, Tom b.1925, *Chapel Street, Exmouth, Devon (now Magnolia Centre)*, presented to the Town Council to commemorate the artist's 10th year as town councillor, © the artist
Strong, C. P. *Exmouth Estuary with Custom House and Shipyard from Manchester Quay, Devon*, presented by T. Abell and G. J. Abell, 1939

Great Torrington Almshouse, Town Lands and Poors Charities

British (English) School *Captain Thomas Colby (1782–1864)*, unknown acquisition method
British (English) School *Sir James Frederick Palmer (1804–1871)*, presented by Sir Robert Edgecombe
Brooks, Henry Jamyn 1839–1925, *Alderman Nathaniel Chapple, Mayor of Torrington (1871, 1879 and 1889)*, unknown acquisition method
Brooks, Henry Jamyn 1839–1925, *Alderman William Vaughan (1804–1871)*, unknown acquisition method
Collier, John 1850–1934, *The Honourable Mark George Kerr Rolle (1835–1907)*, gift from the Lord Clinton
Cosway, Richard 1742–1821, *John Rolle, Lord Rolle (1750–1842)*, gift from the Lord Clinton
Doe (Miss) *The Bellman*, gift by the Lord Clinton
Doe (Miss) *The Bellman*, gift from the Lord Clinton
Hudson, Thomas 1701–1779, *Anne Rolle (1722–1781)*, gift by the Lord Clinton
Hudson, Thomas 1701–1779, *Christiana Maria Rolle*

(1710–1780), gift from the Lord Clinton
Hudson, Thomas 1701–1779, *Denys Rolle (1720–1797)*, gift from the Lord Clinton
Kerseboom, Johann d.1708, *William Rolle*, gift from the Lord Clinton
Kneller, Godfrey (attributed to) 1646–1723, *Lady Ranleigh*, gift from the Lord Clinton
Kneller, Godfrey (school of) 1646–1723, *James II of England (1633–1701), King of England, Scotland and Ireland (1685–1688)*, gift from the Lord Clinton
Kneller, Godfrey (school of) 1646–1723, *Mary of Modena, Queen Mary II (1659–1718), Queen Consort of King James II of England*, gift from the Lord Clinton
Lawrence, Thomas 1769–1830, *John Rolle (1750–1842), Lord Rolle*, gift from the Lord Clinton
Lawrence, Thomas 1769–1830 & **Robertson, Christina** active 1823–1850 **(attributed to)** *Lady Louisa Barbara Rolle (1796–1885)*, gift from the Lord Clinton
Lely, Peter (studio of) 1618–1680, *Catherine Noel (1657–1733), Duchess of Rutland*, gift by the Lord Clinton

Great Torrington Heritage Museum and Archive

Barber, Judy d.2003, *German Bomber over Torrington, Devon*, commissioned for World War II display, 2001
Gay, Alfred 'Humpy' 1870–1916, *Rothern Bridge, Devon*, presented by Desmond Crees in memory of his parents Florence and Robert Crees, 1998
Gay, Alfred 'Humpy' 1870–1916, *Viaduct for the Marland Railway, Devon*, presented by Desmond Crees in memory of his parents Florence and Robert Crees, 1998
Klingenberg, I. *Breaking Waves*, unknown acquisition method
unknown artist *Torrington 'May Fair', Devon*, gift
Whitfield, W. (attributed to) *Castle Hill, Torrington, Devon*, gift

Holsworthy Museum

Bassett, William active 1850–1890, *Elizabeth Fry, Aged 90*, gift from Mr Ben Oke
unknown artist *Derriton Viaduct, Holsworthy, Devon*, gift
unknown artist *Dunsland House, Holsworthy, Devon*, gift

Allhallows Museum

Barton, Bernard Pawley 1912–1992, *Joe Lake (1926–1998), Town Crier*, gift from Mrs Betty Lake, 2002
Hayes-Valentine, Mary *George Blagdon Westcott (1753–1798)*, gift

from Guy Westcott, 2001
Leyman, Alfred 1856–1933, *Tracey Bridge, Honiton, Devon*, gift from E. Gullifer, 2008
unknown artist *Bishop Edward Copleston (1776–1864)*, gift from John Copleston, before 2001
unknown artist *John Gaius Copleston (1749–1831)*, gift from John Copleston, before 2001

Honiton Hospital

Taylor, Jane R. b.1924, *Stream*, unknown acquisition method, © the artist
Thorne, Sheila J. b.1938, *Festival 1*, presented by the artist in fond memory of her sister Angela Martin who nursed at this hospital from 1963–1979, © the artist
Thorne, Sheila J. b.1938, *Festival 2*, presented by the artist in fond memory of her sister Angela Martin who nursed at this hospital from 1963–1979, © the artist
Thorne, Sheila J. b.1938, *Wetlands*, presented by the artist in fond memory of her sister Angela Martin who nursed at this hospital from 1963–1979, © the artist
Williams, Avril b.1935, *Portugese Fishermen*, unknown acquisition method, © the artist

Honiton Library

Batten, Jean *River Otter, Devon*, purchased in memory of our dear friend and colleague Val Dimond Community Information Assistant (1985–1993), 1993

Honiton Town Council

Gisol *Mézidon-Canon, France*, gift from the town of Mézidon-Canon in commemoration of 20 years of town twinning, 1993
Salter, William 1804–1875, *The Entombment of Christ*, gift
unknown artist *Juanita Maxwell Phillips (1880–1966)*, presented, 1940?

Ilfracombe Museum

Bolton, Don *HMS 'Ilfracombe'*, acquired, c.1986
Darton, J. *Lantern Hill, Ilfracombe, Devon*, unknown acquisition method
Hoare, C. T. *Ilfracombe (The Cove)*, unknown acquisition method
Rudd, B. *The 'Waverley' Coming under the Clifton Suspsension Bridge*, unknown acquisition method
unknown artist *Ilfracombe, Devon, Viewed from Above*, unknown acquisition method
unknown artist *Ilfracombe Harbour, Devon*, unknown acquisition method

Ilfracombe Town Council

Jenkins, George Henry 1843–1914, *Lantern Hill, Ilfracombe, Devon*, unknown acquisition method
Jenkins, George Henry 1843–1914, *Lantern Hill, Ilfracombe, Devon*, unknown acquisition method
Jenkins, George Henry 1843–1914, *The Quay, Ilfracombe, Devon*, unknown acquisition method
Naish, John George 1824–1905, *Ilfracombe, Devon*, presented by F. J. Brown to Ilfracombe Urban District Council, 1939
Sims, Thomas *Dr John Jones, Chairman of Ilfracombe Council (1859–1865)*, unknown acquisition method
unknown artist *Major F. H. Thomas, Chairman of Ilfracombe Council (1936–1938)*, unknown acquisition method

Cookworthy Museum

Crowdey (Miss) *Steve Hurrell (d. after 1915)*, bequeathed by William Hurrell, sitter's nephew, 2006
Gay, W. R. *Burgh Island and Bantham Bar*, gift from Hubert Snowdon
Gay, W. R. *Thurlestone Rock, Devon*, gift from Hubert Snowdon
Lidstone, W. *Hallsands, Devon*, gift from Mrs Nita Foale, 1977
Newman, Tom, *Ella Trout Launching Out from Hallsands: The Men Said, 'Too rough to go out'*, gift from Mr N. Newman, 1980
Newman, Tom, *Ella Trout Said, 'I picked him out of the sea like bass!'*, gift from Mr N. Newman, 1980
Newman, Tom, *Ella Trout and the Boy Willie Trout, Age 10, in the 'Long Seas' Start Bay with the Rescued Man*, gift from Mr N. Newman, 1980
Newman, Tom, *Ella Trout Transferring the Negro Fireman to ML49 off Start Point*, gift from Mr N. Newman, 1980
Pearce, Roger *The Fair on Kingsbridge Quay, Devon*, gift from Roger Pearce, 1980
unknown artist *Bantham Bay, a View of Burgh Island and the River Avon from the Village of Bantham, Devon*, gift from Mrs Nita Foale, 1977
unknown artist *Kingsbridge Rea at High Tide, Devon*, gift from Captain Beer, 1984
unknown artist *Thomas Crispin (1607–1690)*

Kingsbridge Town Council

Bisgood, D. *Return from Alamein No.2*, unknown acquisition method
Saunders, George active 1906–1918, *J. S. Hurrell, JP, CC, Chairman of Kingsbridge Urban District Council*, unknown acquisition method
Saunders, George active 1906–1918, *J. S. Hurrell, JP, CC, Chairman of Kingsbridge Urban District Council*, unknown acquisition method
Williams-Lyouns, Herbert Francis 1863–1933, *Devon Cliffs*, gift, 1934
Williams-Lyouns, Herbert Francis 1863–1933, *Watercress Seller*, gift, 1934

The Fairground Heritage Trust

Barnes and Son Belper (Barrett) *Proctor's Hoopla: Landscape Scene, Dovedale, Derbyshire* (rounding board), on loan from Richard Sandercock
Barnes and Son Belper (Barrett) *Proctor's Hoopla: Landscape Scene, Doveholes, Dovedale, Derbyshire* (rounding board), on loan from Richard Sandercock
Barnes and Son Belper (Barrett) *Proctor's Hoopla: Landscape Scene, Monsal Dale, Buxton, Derbyshire* (rounding board), on loan from Richard Sandercock
Barnes and Son Belper (Barrett) *Proctor's Hoopla: Landscape Scene, Pickering Tors, Derbyshire* (rounding board), on loan from Richard Sandercock
Barnes and Son Belper (Barrett) *Proctor's Hoopla: Landscape Scene, Pickering Tors, Dovedale, Derbyshire* (rounding board), on loan from Richard Sandercock
Barnes and Son Belper (Barrett) *Proctor's Hoopla:Lion's Head Rock, Dovedale, Derbyshire* (rounding board), on loan from Richard Sandercock
Barnes and Son Belper (Barrett) (attributed to) *Landscape Scene* (hoopla shutter), on loan from Pete Tei
Barnes and Son Belper (Barrett) (attributed to) *Landscape Scene* (hoopla shutter), on loan from Pete Tei
Barnes and Son Belper (Barrett) (attributed to) *Street Scene* (hoopla shutter), on loan from Pete Tei
Barnes and Son Belper (Barrett) (attributed to) *Townscape* (hoopla shutter), on loan from Pete Tei
Carter, Richard *Ghost Train, Monsters* (paybox, front panel), on loan from Kate Gamlen
Carter, Richard *Ghost Train, Monsters* (paybox, side panel), on loan from Kevin Gamlen
Carter, Richard *Ghost Train, Monsters* (paybox, side panel), on loan from Kevin Gamlen
Carter, Richard *Ghost Train, Monsters* (paybox, back panel), on loan from Kevin Gamlen
Deacon, E. *Country Garden Scene* (hoopla, rounding board), on loan from Graham Downie

Deacon, E. *Harbour Scene* (hoopla, rounding board), on loan from Graham Downie
Deacon, E. *Landscape and Herons* (hoopla, rounding board), on loan from Graham Downie
Deacon, E. *Landscape and Sailboats* (hoopla, rounding board), on loan from Graham Downie
Deacon, E. *Landscape and Swans* (hoopla, rounding board), on loan from Graham Downie
Deacon, E. *Landscape and Windmills* (hoopla, rounding board), on loan from Graham Downie
Deacon, E. *Landscape in Autumn* (hoopla, rounding board), on loan from Graham Downie
Deacon, E. *Landscape in Spring* (hoopla, rounding board), on loan from Graham Downie
Farmer, Sid *Scott's 'Wonder Walters': Cellist and Mandolin* (shutter, two panels), on loan from Michael Smith
Farmer, Sid *Scott's 'Wonder Walters': Concertina Player and Mandolin* (shutter, two panels), on loan from Michael Smith
Farmer, Sid *Scott's 'Wonder Walters': Conductor and Mandolin* (shutter, two panels), on loan from Michael Smith
Farmer, Sid *Scott's 'Wonder Walters': Drummer and Mandolin* (shutter, two panels), on loan from Michael Smith
Farmer, Sid *Scott's 'Wonder Walters': Flute Player and Mandolin* (shutter, two panels), on loan from Michael Smith
Farmer, Sid *Scott's 'Wonder Walters': Saxophone Player and Mandolin* (shutter, two panels), on loan from Michael Smith
Farmer, Sid *Scott's 'Wonder Walters': Triangle Player and Mandolin* (shutter, two panels), on loan from Michael Smith
Farmer, Sid *Scott's 'Wonder Walters': Trumpeter and Mandolin* (shutter, two panels), on loan from Michael Smith
Farmer, Sid *Scott's 'Wonder Walters': Kentucky Waltz* (shutter), on loan from Pete Tei
Farmer, Sid *Scott's 'Wonder Walters': Young Man Dancing* (false pillar), on loan from Pete Tei
Fowle, Frederick George 1914–1983, *Yogi Bear* (centre panel from a juvenile ride), on loan from Pete Tei
Fowle, Frederick George 1914–1983, *Pixie* (centre panel from a juvenile ride), on loan from Pete Tei
Fowle, Frederick George 1914–1983, *David Wallis's 'Super Walzer'* (front), on loan from Pete Tei
Fowle, Frederick George 1914–1983, *Lion*, on loan from Michael Smith
Fowle, Frederick George 1914–1983, *Mercury Speed*, on loan from Geoff Weedon

Fowle, Frederick George 1914–1983, *Spaceship*, on loan from Geoff Weedon
Gaze, Charles (Swindon) *R. Edwards' 'Galloping Horses': Jungle Animals, Bear and a Boa* (centre shutter), purchased from R. Edwards & Sons, 1986
Gaze, Charles (Swindon) *R. Edwards' 'Galloping Horses': Jungle Animals, Cheetah* (centre shutter), purchased from R. Edwards & Sons, 1986
Gaze, Charles (Swindon) *R. Edwards' 'Galloping Horses': Jungle Animals, Giraffe* (centre shutter), purchased from R. Edwards & Sons, 1986
Gaze, Charles (Swindon) *R. Edwards' 'Galloping Horses': Jungle Animals, Lion* (centre shutter), purchased from R. Edwards & Sons, 1986
Gaze, Charles (Swindon) *R. Edwards' 'Galloping Horses': Jungle Animals, Lion* (centre shutter), purchased from R. Edwards & Sons, 1986
Gaze, Charles (Swindon) *R. Edwards' 'Galloping Horses': Jungle Animals, Polar Bear* (centre shutter), purchased from R. Edwards & Sons, 1986
Gaze, Charles (Swindon) *R. Edwards' 'Galloping Horses': Jungle Animals, Red Deer* (centre shutter), purchased from R. Edwards & Sons, 1986
George Orton, Sons and Spooner Ltd *John Powell's 'Motorcyle Speedway': Motorcyclists* (rounding board), on loan from Powell family
George Orton, Sons and Spooner Ltd *John Powell's 'Monte Carlo Speedway': Winged Wheel* (rounding board), on loan from Pete Tei
George Orton, Sons and Spooner Ltd *R. Edwards' 'Super Chariot Racer': Floral Scene* (top centre), purchased from Frank Edwards with grant aid from the National Heritage Memorial Fund, the Fund for the Preservation of Industrial and Scientific Material and others, c.1996
George Orton, Sons and Spooner Ltd *R. Edwards' 'Super Chariot Racer': Floral Scene* (top centre), purchased from Frank Edwards with grant aid from the National Heritage Memorial Fund, the Fund for the Preservation of Industrial and Scientific Material and others, c.1996
George Orton, Sons and Spooner Ltd *R. Edwards' 'Super Chariot Racer': Floral Scene* (top centre),

purchased from Frank Edwards with grant aid from the National Heritage Memorial Fund, the Fund for the Preservation of Industrial and Scientific Material and others, c.1996
George Orton, Sons and Spooner Ltd *R. Edwards' 'Super Chariot Racer': Floral Scene* (top centre), purchased from Frank Edwards with grant aid from the National Heritage Memorial Fund, the Fund for the Preservation of Industrial and Scientific Material and others, c.1996
George Orton, Sons and Spooner Ltd *R. Edwards' 'Super Chariot Racer': Floral Scene* (top centre), purchased from Frank Edwards with grant aid from the National Heritage Memorial Fund, the Fund for the Preservation of Industrial and Scientific Material and others, c.1996
George Orton, Sons and Spooner Ltd *R. Edwards' 'Super Chariot Racer': Floweral Scene* (top centre), purchased from Frank Edwards with grant aid from the National Heritage Memorial Fund, the Fund for the Preservation of Industrial and Scientific Material and others, c.1996
George Orton, Sons and Spooner Ltd *R. Edwards' Orton & Spooner 'Monte Carlo Speedway': Winged Wheel* (rounding board), purchased from R. Edwards & Sons with grant aid from the National Heritage Memorial Fund, the Fund for the Preservation of Industrial and Scientific Material and others, 1993
George Orton, Sons and Spooner Ltd, Howell, A. 1877–1959 & **Howell, A. S.** 1906–1966, *R. Edwards' 'Super Chariot Racer': Jungle Scene* (rounding board panel in the in the shape of a crown) (detail) (polyptych, panel 1 of 14), purchased from Frank Edwards with grant aid from the National Heritage Memorial Fund, the Fund for the Preservation of Industrial and Scientific Material and others, c.1996
George Orton, Sons and Spooner Ltd, Howell, A. 1877–1959 & **Howell, A. S.** 1906–1966, *R. Edwards' 'Super Chariot Racer': Jungle Scene* (rounding board panel in the in the shape of a crown) (detail) (polyptych, panel 2 of 14), purchased from Frank Edwards with grant aid from the National Heritage Memorial Fund, the Fund for the Preservation of Industrial and Scientific Material

and others, c.1996

George Orton, Sons and Spooner Ltd, Howell, A. 1877–1959 & **Howell, A. S.** 1906–1966, *R. Edwards' 'Super Chariot Racer': Jungle Scene* (rounding panel in the in the shape of a crown) (detail) (polyptych, panel 3 of 14), purchased from Frank Edwards with grant aid from the National Heritage Memorial Fund, the Fund for the Preservation of Industrial and Scientific Material and others, c.1996

George Orton, Sons and Spooner Ltd, Howell, A. 1877–1959 & **Howell, A. S.** 1906–1966, *R. Edwards' 'Super Chariot Racer': Jungle Scene* (rounding board panel in the in the shape of a crown) (detail) (polyptych, panel 4 of 14), purchased from Frank Edwards with grant aid from the National Heritage Memorial Fund, the Fund for the Preservation of Industrial and Scientific Material and others, c.1996

George Orton, Sons and Spooner Ltd, Howell, A. 1877–1959 & **Howell, A. S.** 1906–1966, *R. Edwards' 'Super Chariot Racer': Jungle Scene* (rounding board panel in the in the shape of a crown) (detail) (polyptych, panel 8 of 14), purchased from Frank Edwards with grant aid from the National Heritage Memorial Fund, the Fund for the Preservation of Industrial and Scientific Material and others, c.1996

George Orton, Sons and Spooner Ltd, Howell, A. 1877–1959 & **Howell, A. S.** 1906–1966, *R. Edwards' 'Super Chariot Racer': Jungle Scene* (rounding board panel in the in the shape of a crown) (detail) (polyptych, panel 9 of 14), purchased from Frank Edwards with grant aid from the National Heritage Memorial Fund, the Fund for the Preservation of Industrial and Scientific Material and others, c.1996

George Orton, Sons and Spooner Ltd, Howell, A. 1877–1959 & **Howell, A. S.** 1906–1966, *R. Edwards' 'Super Chariot Racer': Jungle Scene* (panel in the in the shape of a crown) (detail) (polyptych, panel 10 of 14), purchased from Frank Edwards with grant aid from the National Heritage Memorial Fund, the Fund for the Preservation of Industrial and Scientific Material and others, c.1996

George Orton, Sons and Spooner Ltd, Howell, A. 1877–1959 & **Howell, A. S.** 1906–1966, *R. Edwards' 'Super Chariot Racer': Jungle Scene* (rounding board panel in the shape of a crown) (detail) (polyptych, panel 11 of 14), purchased from Frank Edwards with grant aid from the National Heritage Memorial Fund, the Fund for the Preservation of

Industrial and Scientific Material and others, c.1996

George Orton, Sons and Spooner Ltd, Howell, A. 1877–1959 & **Howell, A. S.** 1906–1966, *R. Edwards' 'Super Chariot Racer': Jungle Scene* (panel in the shape of a crown) (detail) (polyptych, panel 12 of 14), purchased from Frank Edwards with grant aid from the National Heritage Memorial Fund, the Fund for the Preservation of Industrial and Scientific Material and others, c.1996

George Orton, Sons and Spooner Ltd, Howell, A. 1877–1959 & **Howell, A. S.** 1906–1966, *R. Edwards' 'Super Chariot Racer': Jungle Scene* (panel in the shape of a crown) (detail) (polyptych, panel 13 of 14), purchased from Frank Edwards with grant aid from the National Heritage Memorial Fund, the Fund for the Preservation of Industrial and Scientific Material and others, c.1996

George Orton, Sons and Spooner Ltd, Howell, A. 1877–1959 & **Howell, A. S.** 1906–1966, *R. Edwards' 'Super Chariot Racer': Jungle Scene* (panel in the shape of a crown) (detail) (polyptych, panel 14 of 14), purchased from Frank Edwards with grant aid from the National Heritage Memorial Fund, the Fund for the Preservation of Industrial and Scientific Material and others, c.1996

George Orton, Sons and Spooner Ltd, Howell, A. 1877–1959 & **Howell, A. S.** 1906–1966, *R. Edwards and Sons' 'Super Chariot Racer': Chariot Scene* (front boards), purchased from Frank Edwards with grant aid from the National Heritage Memorial Fund, the Fund for the Preservation of Industrial and Scientific Material and others, c.1996

Hall, Edwin *John Holland's 'Super Dodgems'* (rounding board), on loan from Pete Tei

Hall and Fowle *Brett's 'Ghost Train'* (backdrop), on loan from Kevin Gamlen

Hall and Fowle *Brett's 'Ghost Train'* (backdrop), on loan from Kevin Gamlen

Hall and Fowle *Brett's 'Ghost Train'* (backdrop), on loan from Kevin Gamlen

Hall and Fowle *Brett's 'Ghost Train'* (backdrop), on loan from Kevin Gamlen

Hall and Fowle *Brett's 'Ghost Train'* (backdrop), on loan from Kevin Gamlen

Hall and Fowle *Brett's 'Ghost Train'* (showfront) (from a design by Edwin Hall), on loan from Kevin Gamlen

Hall and Fowle *Brett's 'Ghost Train'* (showfront), on loan from Kevin Gamlen

Hall and Fowle *Brett's 'Ghost Train'* (showfront), on loan from Kevin Gamlen

Hall and Fowle *Brett's 'Ghost Train'* (showfront), on loan from Kevin Gamlen

Hall and Fowle *Culine's Dodgems: Winged Wheel* (rounding board), on loan from Pete Tei

Hall and Fowle *Victor Hart's Hoopla: Mercury* (rounding board), unknown acquisition method

Hall and Fowle *Victor Hart's Hoopla: Mercury* (shutter), on loan from Michael Smith

Hall and Fowle *Andrew Simon's 'Juvenile': Monogramme 'AS'* (rounding board), on loan from Pete Tei

Hall and Fowle *Mrs Holland's 'Dogdems': Lion* (rounding board), on loan from Pete Tei

Howell, A. S. 1906–1966, *R. Edwards' 'Super Chariot Racer': Jungle Scene* (shutter), purchased from Frank Edwards with grant aid from the National Heritage Memorial Fund, the Fund for the Preservation of Industrial and Scientific Material and others, c.1996

Howell, A. S. 1906–1966, *R. Edwards' 'Super Chariot Racer': Jungle Scene* (shutter), purchased from Frank Edwards with grant aid from the National Heritage Memorial Fund, the Fund for the Preservation of Industrial and Scientific Material and others, c.1996

Howell, A. S. 1906–1966, *R. Edwards' 'Super Chariot Racer': Jungle Scene* (shutter), purchased from Frank Edwards with grant aid from the National Heritage Memorial Fund, the Fund for the Preservation of Industrial and Scientific Material and others, c.1996

Howell, A. S. 1906–1966, *R. Edwards' 'Super Chariot Racer': Jungle Scene* (shutter), purchased from Frank Edwards with grant aid from the National Heritage Memorial Fund, the Fund for the Preservation of Industrial and Scientific Material and others, c.1996

Howell, A. S. 1906–1966, *R. Edwards' 'Super Chariot Racer': Jungle Scene* (shutter), purchased from Frank Edwards with grant aid from the National Heritage Memorial Fund, the Fund for the Preservation of Industrial and Scientific Material and others, c.1996

Howell, A. S. 1906–1966, *R. Edwards' 'Super Chariot Racer': Jungle Scene* (shutter), purchased from Frank Edwards with grant aid from the National Heritage Memorial Fund, the Fund for the Preservation of Industrial and Scientific Material and others, c.1996

Howell, A. S. 1906–1966, *R. Edwards' 'Super Chariot Racer': Jungle Scene* (shutter), purchased from Frank Edwards with grant aid from the National Heritage Memorial Fund, the Fund for the Preservation of Industrial and Scientific Material and others, c.1996

Howell, A. S. 1906–1966, *R. Edwards' 'Super Chariot Racer': Jungle Scene* (shutter), purchased from Frank Edwards with grant aid from the National Heritage Memorial Fund, the Fund for the Preservation of Industrial and Scientific Material and others, c.1996

Howell, A. S. 1906–1966, *R. Edwards' 'Super Chariot Racer': Jungle Scene* (shutter), purchased from Frank Edwards with grant aid from the National Heritage Memorial Fund, the Fund for the Preservation of Industrial and Scientific Material and others, c.1996

Howell, A. S. 1906–1966, *R. Edwards' 'Super Chariot Racer': Jungle Scene* (shutter), purchased from Frank Edwards with grant aid from the National Heritage Memorial Fund, the Fund for the Preservation of Industrial and Scientific Material and others, c.1996

Howell, A. S. 1906–1966, *R. Edwards' 'Super Chariot Racer': Jungle Scene* (shutter), purchased from Frank Edwards with grant aid from the National Heritage Memorial Fund, the Fund for the Preservation of Industrial and Scientific Material and others, c.1996

Howell, A. S. 1906–1966, *R. Edwards' 'Super Chariot Racer': Jungle Scene* (shutter), purchased from Frank Edwards with grant aid from the National Heritage Memorial Fund, the Fund for the Preservation of Industrial and Scientific Material and others, c.1996

Lakin & Co., R. J. (Edwin Hall) *Ashley Brothers' 'Jungle Thriller'* (rounding board), on loan from Lawrence Harper

Lakin & Co., R. J. (Edwin Hall) *Ashley Brothers' 'Jungle Thriller': Jungle Scene* (rounding board), on loan from Lawrence Harper

Lakin & Co., R. J. (Edwin Hall) *Bull Fighting Scene* (front proscenium), on loan from Lawrence Harper

Lakin & Co., R. J. (Edwin Hall) *Jungle Scene with a Baboon* (rounding board), on loan from Lawrence Harper

Lakin & Co., R. J. (Edwin Hall) *Jungle Scene with a Bear* (rounding board), on loan from Lawrence Harper

Lakin & Co., R. J. (Edwin Hall) *Jungle Scene with a Leopard* (rounding board), on loan from Lawrence Harper

Lakin & Co., R. J. (Edwin Hall) *Jungle Scene with a Lynx* (rounding board), on loan from Lawrence Harper

Lakin & Co., R. J. (Edwin Hall) *Jungle Scene with a McCaw* (rounding board), on loan from Lawrence Harper

Lakin & Co., R. J. (Edwin Hall) *Jungle Scene with a Monkey* (rounding board), on loan from Lawrence Harper

Lakin & Co., R. J. (Edwin Hall) *Jungle Scene with a Monkey* (rounding board), on loan from Lawrence Harper

Lakin & Co., R. J. (Edwin Hall) *Jungle Scene with a Wild Cat and Its Kill* (rounding board), on loan from Lawrence Harper

Lakin & Co., R. J. (Edwin Hall) *Parrots* (top centre panel from Wroot's Ben Hur), on loan from Geoff Weedon

Lakin & Co., R. J. (Edwin Hall) *Sam Crow's 'Dodgem Track': Racecars* (front proscenium), on loan from Michael Smith

Lakin & Co., R. J. (Edwin Hall) *Sam Crow's 'Dodgem Track': Racing Car No.2*, on loan from Michael Smith

Lakin & Co., R. J. (Edwin Hall) *Sam Crow's 'Dodgem Track': Racing Car No.3*, on loan from Michael Smith

Lakin & Co., R. J. (Edwin Hall) *Sam Crow's 'Dodgem Track': Racing Car No.8*, on loan from Michael Smith

Lakin & Co., R. J. (Edwin Hall) *Front Proscenium with Ben Hur* (G. Heath & Sons), on loan from Richard Sandercock

Lakin & Co., R. J. (Edwin Hall) *T. Whitelegg's 'No.2 Dodgems': Pegasus* (rounding board), on loan from Pete Tei

Lakin & Co., R. J. *Brett's 'Skid': Mercury* (figure from a handrail), on loan from Pete Tei

Lakin & Co., R. J. *Hummingbird* (top centre panel from Wroot's Ben Hur), on loan from Geoff Weedon

Lakin & Co., R. J. *Silcock's 'Skid': Trumpeting Girl* (top centre), on loan from Pete Tei

Postlethwaite, Victoria *William Wilson's 'Rodeo Switchback': Cowboy Scene* (shutter), purchased from Switchback Ventures, 1993

Postlethwaite, Victoria *William Wilson's 'Rodeo Switchback': Cowboy Scene* (shutter), purchased from Switchback Ventures, 1993

Postlethwaite, Victoria *William Wilson's 'Rodeo Switchback': Cowboy Scene* (shutter), purchased from Swtichback Ventures, 1993

Pratt, Albert *The Gee Gees, Girl Riding on a Merry-Go-Round (shutter from Saunt's Hoopla)*, on loan from Geoff Weedon

Pratt, Albert *The Rotor, Girl on a Spinning Fairground Ride (shutter from Saunt's Hoopla)*, on loan from Geoff Weedon

Sconce, Walter & Sons 1855–1925, *Bioscope Show Banner with a Theatre Stage Scene*, on loan from Richard Sandercock

Sconce, Walter & Sons 1855–1925, *Bioscope Show Banner with a Theatre Stage Scene*, on loan from Richard Sandercock

Sconce, Walter & Sons 1855–1925, *Landscape with a Lake* (banner), on loan from Richard Sandercock

Smith, A. V. (Camberwell) active late 19th C, *Wild Boy* (banner), on loan from Geoff Weedon and Richard Ward

Smith, Alfred (Junior) active late 19th C, *Salome* (banner), on loan from Geoff Weedon

Tei, Peter *Mercury*, on loan from Michael Smith

unknown artist late 19th C, *French Beauty Show* (banner), on loan from Stephen Smith

unknown artist *Billy Wood and Son 'Boxing Booth': Boxer Lee Savold*, on loan from Richard Sandercock

unknown artist *Billy Wood and Son 'Boxing Booth': Boxers Joe Louis and Joe Walcott*, on loan from Richard Sandercock

unknown artist *Billy Wood and Son 'Boxing Booth'* (believed to be of Billy Wood) (showfront) (polyptych, panel 1 of 5), on loan from Richard Sandercock

unknown artist *Billy Wood and Son 'Boxing Booth': Fight between Phil Scott and Larry Gains, 1931* (showfront) (polyptych, panel 2 of 5), on loan from Richard Sandercock

unknown artist *Billy Wood and Son 'Boxing Booth': Fight between Dave Shade and Len Harvey, 1930* (showfront) (polyptych, panel 3 of 5), on loan from Richard Sandercock

unknown artist *Billy Wood and Son 'Boxing Booth': Fight between Billy Wood and Arnold 'Kid' Shepherd* (showfront) (polyptych, panel 4 of 5), on loan from Richard Sandercock

unknown artist *Billy Wood and Son 'Boxing Booth': Unnamed Boxer* (showfront) (polyptych, panel 5 of 5), on loan from Richard Sandercock

unknown artist *Donald Ive's 'Ark': Lion Leaping through a Burning Hoop* (dragon chariot rear panel), on loan from Michael Smith

unknown artist *John Liny's Hoopla (Chicken Joe): Art Deco Sun* (shutter), on loan from Stephen Smith

unknown artist *Barney and Fred* (coconut shy, two panels), on loan from Chris Davies

unknown artist *Flo and Tom Cat* (coconut shy, two panels), on loan from Chris Davies

unknown artist *Huckleberry Hound and Yogi Bear* (coconut shy, two panels), on loan from Chris Davies

unknown artist *Officer Dibble and Tom Cat* (coconut shy, two panels), on loan from Chris Davies

unknown artist *Humphries' 'Shooting Gallery: Lion* (shutter), on loan from Richard Sandercock

unknown artist *Humphries' 'Shooting Gallery': Tiger* (shutter), on loan from Richard Sandercock

unknown artist *Landscape Scene* (hoopla upright), on loan from E. and J. Harrison

unknown artist *Landscape Scene* (hoopla upright), on loan from E. and J. Harrison

unknown artist *Landscape Scene* (hoopla upright), on loan from E. and J. Harrison

unknown artist *Landscape Scene* (hoopla upright), on loan from E. and J. Harrison

unknown artist *Landscape Scene* (hoopla upright), on loan from E. and J. Harrison

unknown artist *Landscape Scene* (hoopla upright), on loan from E. and J. Harrison

unknown artist *Landscape Scene* (hoopla upright), on loan from E. and J. Harrison

unknown artist *Landscape Scene* (rounding board), on loan from E. and J. Harrison

unknown artist *Noyce's Shooting Gallery, Gorilla*, on loan from Richard Sandercock

unknown artist *Noyce's 'Shooting Gallery': Walrus*, on loan from Richard Sandercock

unknown artist *Psychedelic Face*, on loan from Guy Belshaw

unknown artist *R. Edwards' 'Galloping Horses': Birds* (organ panel), purchased from R. Edwards & Sons, 1986

unknown artist *R. Edwards' 'Galloping Horses': Birds* (organ panel), purchased from R. Edwards & Sons, 1986

unknown artist *R. Edwards' 'Galloping Horses': Chariot Race with Cherubs* (organ panel), purchased from R. Edwards & Sons, 1986

unknown artist *R. Edwards' 'Galloping Horses': Mythological Scene* (organ panel), purchased from R. Edwards & Sons, 1986

unknown artist *Spinner Figure, Butterfly*, on loan from Geoff Weedon

Whiting, Henry 1839–1931, *Hatwell's 'Gallopers': Woman Seated in a Tree* (centre panel in the shape of a crown), purchased with the assistance of the National Art Collections Fund and the Victoria and Albert Museum Purchase Grant Fund, 1986

Whiting, Henry 1839–1931, *Hatwell's 'Gallopers': Cowboy Chased by Indians* (bottom centre panel), on loan from Geoff Weedon

Whiting, Henry 1839–1931, *Hatwell's 'Gallopers': Fox Hunt* (bottom centre panel), on loan from Geoff Weedon

Whiting, Henry 1839–1931, *Hatwell's 'Gallopers': Hippopotamus Hunt* (bottom centre panel), purchased with the assistance of the National Art Collections Fund and the Victoria and Albert Museum Purchase Grant Fund, 1986

Whiting, Henry 1839–1931, *Hatwell's 'Gallopers': Horse and a Cyclist* (bottom centre panel), purchased with the assistance of the National Art Collections Fund and the Victoria and Albert Museum Purchase Grant Fund

Whiting, Henry 1839–1931, *Hatwell's 'Gallopers': Man Wrestling an Alligator* (bottom centre panel), purchased with the assistance of the National Art Collections Fund and the Victoria and Albert Museum Purchase Grant Fund, 1986

Whiting, Henry 1839–1931, *Hatwell's 'Gallopers': Tiger Hunt* (bottom centre panel), purchased with the assistance of the National Art Collections Fund and the Victoria and Albert Museum Purchase Grant Fund, 1986

Whiting, Henry 1839–1931, *Hatwell's 'Gallopers': Wild Dogs Attacking Antelope* (bottom centre panel), purchased with the assistance of the National Art Collections Fund and the Victoria and Albert Museum Purchase Grant Fund, 1986

Whiting, Henry 1839–1931, *Hatwell's 'Gallopers': Wolves Hunting Deer* (bottom centre panel), purchased with the assistance of the National Art Collections Fund and the Victoria and Albert Museum Purchase Grant Fund, 1986

Whiting, Henry (attributed to) 1839–1931, *Hatwell's 'Gallopers': Seated Woman with a Cherub* (centre panel in the shape of a crown), purchased with the assistance of the National Art Collections Fund and the Victoria and Albert Museum Purchase Grant Fund, 1986

Whiting, Henry (attributed to) 1839–1931, *Hatwell's 'Gallopers': Woman and an Eagle* (centre panel in the shape of a crown), purchased with the assistance of the National Art Collections Fund and the Victoria and Albert Museum Purchase Grant Fund, 1986

Whiting, Henry (attributed to) 1839–1931, *Hatwell's 'Gallopers': Woman and Two Cherubs* (centre panel in the shape of a crown), purchased with the assistance of the National Art Collections Fund and the Victoria and Albert Museum Purchase Grant Fund, 1986

Whiting, Henry (attributed to) 1839–1931, *Hatwell's 'Gallopers': Woman Holding a Cupid's Arrow* (centre panel in the shape of a crown), purchased with the

assistance of the National Art Collections Fund and the Victoria and Albert Museum Purchase Grant Fund, 1986

Whiting, Henry (attributed to) 1839–1931, *Hatwell's 'Gallopers': Woman Holding a Fan* (centre panel in the shape of a crown), purchased with the assistance of the National Art Collections Fund and the Victoria and Albert Museum Purchase Grant Fund, 1986

Whiting, Henry (attributed to) 1839–1931, *Hatwell's 'Gallopers': Woman Holding a Scythe and a Sheaf of Wheat* (centre panel in the shape of a crown), purchased with the assistance of the National Art Collections Fund and the Victoria and Albert Museum Purchase Grant Fund, 1986

Whiting, Henry (attributed to) 1839–1931, *Hatwell's 'Gallopers': Woman in a Green Dress* (centre panel in the shape of a crown), purchased with the assistance of the National Art Collections Fund and the Victoria and Albert Museum Purchase Grant Fund, 1986

Whiting, Henry (attributed to) 1839–1931, *Hatwell's 'Gallopers': Woman Playing the Violin* (centre panel in the shape of a crown), purchased with the assistance of the National Art Collections Fund and the Victoria and Albert Museum Purchase Grant Fund, 1986

Whiting, Henry (attributed to) 1839–1931, *Hatwell's 'Gallopers': Woman with Cherubs and a Cornucopia* (centre panel in the shape of a crown), purchased with the assistance of the National Art Collections Fund and the Victoria and Albert Museum Purchase Grant Fund, 1986

Wilson, George (Wrexham) 1874–1944, *Tiger and Panther* (banner), on loan from Geoff Weedon

Wilson, George (Wrexham) 1874–1944, *Tiger and Snake* (banner), on loan from Geoff Weedon

Wright, Paul b.1954, *John Walter Shaw's 'Easyrider': Elvis* (centre shutter, recto), on loan from Pete Tei, © the artist

Wright, Paul b.1954, *John Walter Shaw's 'Easyrider': George Michael* (centre shutter, verso), on loan from Pete Tei, © the artist

Wright, Paul b.1954, *John Walter Shaw's 'Easyrider': Madonna* (centre shutter, recto), on loan from Pete Tei, © the artist

Wright, Paul b.1954, *John Walter Shaw's 'Easyrider': Tina Turner* (centre shutter, verso), on loan from Pete Tei, © the artist

Wright, Paul b.1954, *Brett's Ghost Train': Skeleton* (false pillar), on loan from Kevin Gamlen, © the artist

Wright, Paul b.1954, *Brett's 'Ghost Train': Skeleton* (false pillar), on loan from Kevin Gamlen, © the artist

Wright, Paul b.1954, *Brett's Ghost Train': Skeleton in Shackles* (false pillar), on loan from Kevin Gamlen, © the artist

Wright, Paul b.1954, *Brett's Ghost Train': Skeleton in Shackles* (false pillar), on loan from Kevin Gamlen, © the artist

Wright, Paul b.1954, *Brett's Ghost Train': Vampire* (false pillar), on loan from Kevin Gamlen, © the artist

Wright, Paul b.1954, *Showman's Guild Showfront* (detail), donated by the Showmen's Guild, 1994, © the artist

Wright, Paul b.1954, *Caryatid* (false pillar), on loan from Neil Calladine, © the artist

Wright, Paul b.1954, *Thor Holding Lightning Rods*, unknown acquisition method, © the artist

Wright, Paul b.1954, *Thor Power Lightning*, unknown acquisition method, © the artist

Lynton and Lynmouth Town Council

Calvert, Samuel 1828–1913, *Rhenish Tower, Lynmouth, Devon*, purchased with a donation from the estate of Whitman-Pearson of America

Ethelston, Ellen *The Bridge and Part of the Village of Lynmouth, North Devon*, unknown acquisition method

Eves, Reginald Grenville 1876–1941, *John Ward Holman, Esq., OBE*, presented by public subscription in recognition of the sitter's generosity to the twin villages, 1933

Gilson, Marjorie *Queen Elizabeth II (b.1926), Jubilee Year, 1977*, gift

Lee, Arthur active mid-19th C, *Rhenish Tower, Lynmouth, Devon*, unknown acquisition method

Schofield, John William 1865–1944, *Lieutenant Colonel W. W. Lean, Fifth Bengal Cavalry*, presented by his daughter in memory of his lifelong interest in Lynton and Lynmouth, in which parishes he and his forefathers have been landowners for some 200 years, 1922

unknown artist *Stag*, unknown acquisition method

unknown artist *Castle Rock, Lynton, Devon*, unknown acquisition method

unknown artist *Lady Fanny Hewitt*, on loan from a private lender

unknown artist *Lynmouth Harbour, Devon*, unknown acquisition method

unknown artist *Lynmouth Harbour, Devon*, presented in memory of Edwin Edwards

unknown artist *Sir Thomas*

Hewitt, on loan from a private lender

unknown artist *Vellacott Pool on the East Lyn*, donated by F. J. Peddar, c.2005

Moretonhampstead Hospital

Wiley, R. D. *Summer Flowers*, unknown acquisition method

Moretonhampstead Library

Dover, J. *George Parker Bidder (1806–1878)*, unknown acquisition method

unknown artist *Sir Thomas B. Bowring (1847–1915)*, bequeathed by Lady Ann Kinsman How Bowring

Ball Clay Heritage Society

Cox, Frederick C. B. b.1939, *Inclined Shaft, Ball Clay Mining, Peters Marland, North Devon*, gift from the artist, 2001, © the artist

Cox, Frederick C. B. b.1939, *Ball Clay Mining, Kingsteignton, Devon*, gift from the artist, 2001, © the artist

Cox, Frederick C. B. b.1939, *Ball Clay Mining, Kingsteignton, Devon*, gift from the artist, 2001, © the artist

Ilford Park Polish Home

Cymbrykiewicz, Maria 1910–2005, *The Blessed Sacrament*, donated by the artist

Cymbrykiewicz, Maria 1910–2005, *The Immaculate Conception of the Blessed Virgin Mary*, donated by the artist

Dobrawolska *Icon of the Blessed Virgin*, unknown acquisition method

Sobkowiak-Mozdzer, Emilia *The Deposition of Christ*, unknown acquisition method

unknown artist *Christ Blessing*, unknown acquisition method

unknown artist *Christ Preaching*, unknown acquisition method

unknown artist *Polish Man in Traditional Highland Dress*, unknown acquisition method

unknown artist *Polish Woman in Traditional Highland Dress*, unknown acquisition method

Newton Abbot Town & GWR Museum

Armfield, George 1810–1893, *A Spaniel and a Terrier*, bequeathed by Alfred Mills to Newton Abbot Urban District Council; donated to the Museum, c.1988

Armfield, George 1810–1893, *Terriers Ratting*, bequeathed by

Alfred Mills to Newton Abbot Urban District Council; donated to the Museum, c.1988

Cox, Frederick C. B. b.1939, *Departure to Plymouth, Devon*, gift, © the artist

Gaunt, Ray *Supermarine Spitfire P8655 'Newtonia'*, gift

Hacker, Arthur 1858–1919, *The Hours*, gift from Sydney Hacker, Chairman of Newton Abbot Urban District Council and brother of the artist, to NAUDC for the Town, 1928; donated to the Museum, c.1988

Hall, Gordon *Dartmoor Granite Railway at Haytor, Devon*, gift

Houghton, Ruth *Familiar Ways, Newton Abbot, Devon*, gift from Mr John Wright, nephew of the artist

Price, C. *Great Western 1, The Early Years (1840–1902)*, gift, painted to commemorate the anniversary of the GWR, 1985

Price, C. *Great Western 2, Churchward (1902–1921)*, gift, painted to commemorate the anniversary of the GWR, 1985

Price, C. *Great Western 3, Zenith (1921–1949)*, gift, painted to commemorate the anniversary of the GWR, 1985

Price, C. *Great Western 4, Modern Times (1950–1985)*, gift, painted to commemorate the anniversary of the GWR, 1985

Rhys, Oliver b.c.1858, *A Cavalry Camp*, bequeathed by Alfred Mills to Newton Abbot Urban District Council, early 1900s–1920s; donated to the Museum, c.1988

Stacey, Walter Sydney 1846–1929, *St Peter's Church, Tiverton, Devon*, bequeathed by Thomas Shilston, early 1900s

Tyler, L. M. *St Mary's Parish Church, Wolborough, Devon*, gift

Newton Abbot Town Council

Lawrence, David *Synchro Pain and Caterpillar Loop*, presented by the Buckland Amenities Committee

Members of the Newton Abbot Women's Institute *Parish Map*, gift

Smith, Keith A. *The Clock Tower, Newton Abbot, Devon*, presented by the artist

Stacey, Walter Sydney 1846–1929, *Rough Courting*, presented by Burleigh Bruhl to Newton Abbot Urban District Council, early 1900s

Whitehead, Frederick William Newton 1853–1938, *Cattle in a Country Lane at Kenilworth, Warwickshire*, bequeathed by Thomas Shilston to Newton Abbot Urban District Council, early 1900s

Teignbridge District Council

Carter, Ken active 1986–1987, *Estuary View*, commissioned

Carter, Ken active 1986–1987, *Exe Scene I*, commissioned

Carter, Ken active 1986–1987, *Exe Scene III*, commissioned

Carter, Ken active 1986–1987, *Haldon Moor, Teignmouth, Devon*, commissioned

Carter, Ken active 1986–1987, *Exe Scene II Sunset*, commissioned

Cotton, Alan b.1938, *Golden Harvest Landscape, near Gordes, Provence, France*, commissioned, © the artist

Green, John *Charles I (1600–1649) (after Gerrit van Honthorst)*, commissioned and presented to Teignbridge District Council by Councillor Reg Astbury and Mrs Astbury

Holden, M. G. *Forde House, Newton Abbot, Devon*, unknown acquisition method

Holden, M. G. *Charles I (1600–1649)*, unknown acquisition method

Jansch, Heather b.1948, *Out of a Winter Sea*, purchased

Lloyd, Reginald James b.1926, *Dawlish Warren I, Devon*, commissioned by Teignbridge District Council for new council offices in Newton Abbot, © the artist

Lloyd, Reginald James b.1926, *Dawlish Warren II, Devon*, commissioned by Teignbridge District Council for new council offices in Newton Abbot, © the artist

Lloyd, Reginald James b.1926, *Haytor Quarry, Dartmoor, Devon*, commissioned by Teignbridge District Council for new council offices in Newton Abbot, © the artist

Salisbury, Frank O. 1874–1962, *Lady Gertrude E. Smith (Lady Ben), Member of Newton Abbot Rural District Council (1965–1975)*, presented by A. J. Knightley, 1992, © estate of Frank O. Salisbury. All rights reserved, DACS 2012

unknown artist *Portrait of a Gentleman*, unknown acquisition method

Museum of Dartmoor Life, Okehampton

Holding, Emmanuel (attributed to) *Okehampton with a View of the Parish Church of All Saints'*, gift, 1994

Widgery, Frederick John 1861–1942, *In the Gorge, Lydford, Devon*, on loan from Mrs Sarah Farmer

Okehampton Town Council

Ash, Thomas Morris 1851–1935, *From Box Hill, Surrey*, unknown acquisition method

Barrett, John 1822–1893, *Wooded Vale*, unknown acquisition method

Crayer, Gaspar de (attributed to) 1584–1669, *Memento mori*, unknown acquisition method

Heem, Cornelis de 1631–1695, *Still Life with Grapes, Peaches and a Bohemian Glass Goblet*, unknown acquisition method

Herring, John Frederick I (style of) 1795–1865, *Farmyard*, unknown acquisition method

Kurzweil, T. *Good Morning*, unknown acquisition method

Leader, Benjamin Williams 1831–1923, *Riverside Cottages at Dusk*, gift from Arthur Tooth

Linnell, James Thomas 1826–1905, *Thro' the Fields , a Landscape at Harvest Time*, unknown acquisition method

Russ II, Franz 1844–1906, *Young Girl Holding a Spray of Jasmine*, unknown acquisition method

Sinoir, M. *Bridge Scene*, unknown acquisition method

Widgery, Frederick John 1861–1942, *Okehampton Castle, Devon*, unknown acquisition method

Widgery, William 1822–1893, *A Boy by a Rocky Wooded Stream*, unknown acquisition method

Widgery, William 1822–1893, *A Bridge over a Dartmoor Stream*, unknown acquisition method

Woodville, Richard Caton 1856–1927, *A Cavalry Charge*, unknown acquisition method

Woodville, Richard Caton 1856–1927, *Napolean and His Marshals Watching a Battle*, unknown acquisition method

Woodville, Richard Caton 1856–1927, *Saladin's Cavalry Charging the Crusaders*, unknown acquisition method

Ottery St Mary Hospital

Entwistle, Tom *Boats on a Beach*, unknown acquisition method

Wilkins, Julie *West Hill from East Hill Garden*, unknown acquisition method

Dartmoor Prison Museum

L. B. *Windmill*, unknown acquisition method

Coles, E. P. active 1969–1970, *French Prisoners of War Being Transported across the Moors on the 24 May, 1809*, unknown acquisition method

Coles, E. P. active 1969–1970, *The Prison Hulks, Devonport, Devon*, unknown acquisition method

Coles, E. P. active 1969–1970, *Market Square, Dartmoor Prisoner of War Depot*, unknown acquisition method

Duckett, Lewis 1892–1977, *Mounted Prison Patrol Officer on Dartmoor*, unknown acquisition method

unknown artist *Dartmoor Prison*, unknown acquisition method

Wanmantle, James *My Lord and My God*, unknown acquisition method

Wanmantle, James *The Last Supper*, unknown acquisition method

Wanmantle, James *Thou Art the Christ, the Son of the Living God*, unknown acquisition method

Seaton Hospital

Fletcher, Mollie *Gladioli*, gift from the artist

Knightly, L. M. (Mrs) *Farningham Mill, Kent*, unknown acquisition method

Knightly, L. M. (Mrs) *St Michael's Mount, Cornwall*, unknown acquisition method

Neale, George Hall 1863–1940, *Portrait of a Doctor's Wife*, gift from Dora Roberts

Page, Will *Devon Coast*, gift from the artist

Robertson, Kit b.1915, *In the Hedgerow*, unknown acquisition method, © the artist

unknown artist *Stream*, unknown acquisition method

Wilde, Ron *Rain Approaching Axmouth*, gift from the artist, 1988

Sidmouth Museum

Adams, Margaret *That Was the Coastal Path!*, purchased from the artist by the Trustees of Sidmouth Museum, 2005

Allinson, Adrian Paul 1890–1959, *Geranium Plant (Painted from the Ground Floor of No.9 Fortfield Terrace)*, gift from Mrs Phillip Haynes and Miss R. G. Powell, 1984

Antony *Looking over High Peak, Sidmouth, Devon*, purchased by the Trustees of Sidmouth Museum

Dorrington, Edna b.1934, *Monmouth Beach, Lyme Regis*, purchased from Axminster Artists' Society Exhibition, 2007

Dunning, John Thomson 1851–1931, *Clifton Place Cottages, Sidmouth, Devon*, unknown acquisition method

Horsley, Hopkins Horsley Hobday 1807–1890, *Sidmouth Beach and Cliffs, Devon*, purchased

Horsley, Hopkins Horsley Hobday 1807–1890, *The Belmont, Sidmouth Seafront, Devon*, purchased

Horsley, Hopkins Horsley Hobday 1807–1890, *Sidmouth from Salcombe Hill, Devon*, purchased

Leask, William 1892–1977, *Fisherman's Beacon, Sidmouth, Devon*, gift from Mr Laurie Leask, 1993

Moysey, Kathleen *Jim Smith*, unknown acquisition method

Sweetapple, E. F. *The 'Duchess of Devonshire'*, unknown acquisition method

Tucker, John Wallace 1808–1869,

Sidmouth Harbour, Devon (Clifton Beach), purchased from Lowe Books, Landreyne Manor, Cornwall, 2005

unknown artist *Bob Wooley, a Sidmouth Fisherman*, unknown acquisition method

unknown artist *Mouth of the Sid, Devon*, unknown acquisition method

unknown artist *Toll Gate, Sidmouth, Devon*, unknown acquisition method

White, Gerald Ewart b.1932, *Standing Stones on Mutter's Moor, Sidmouth, Devon*, gift from the artist, 2009, © the artist

Woodley, Maureen *Hope Cottage, Sidmouth, Devon (Sidmouth Museum)*, unknown acquisition method

Sidmouth Victoria Hospital

Firth, Irene *Sidmouth Cliffs Looking East, Devon*, unknown acquisition method

Macfadyan, Evan *Still Life with Flowers*, unknown acquisition method

Tavistock Subscription Library

unknown artist *John Commins (1776–1859)*, presented by Allenby John Commins

unknown artist *John Russell (1766–1839), 6th Duke of Bedford*, gift from the sitter, c.1810

unknown artist *The Original Tavistock Subscription Library, Devon (also known as 'The Propylaeum')*, unknown acquisition method

Tavistock Town Hall

Croft, M. D. *Town Criers*, unknown acquisition method

Hawkins, Jane *Lady Laura Russell (c.1850–1910)*, unknown acquisition method

Lane, F. *Hugh Fownes-Luttrell (1857–1918), MP for Tavistock (1892–1900 & 1906–1910)*, unknown acquisition method

Lane, F. *John Hornbrook Gill (1787–1874)*, unknown acquisition method

Prynne, Edward A. Fellowes 1854–1921, *John Ward Spear (1848–1921), MP for Tavistock (1900–1906 & 1910–1918)*, presented by the Duke of Bedford, 1906

Read, Arthur James 1932–2006, *Tavistock Town Hall, Devon*, unknown acquisition method, © Tavistock Town Council

Russell, Laura c.1850–1910, *John Pym (1584–1643), MP for Tavistock (1624–1643) (after Cornelis Janssens van Ceulen)*, unknown acquisition method

Russell, Laura c.1850–1910, *Sir*

Francis Drake (1540–1596), unknown acquisition method

Russell, Laura c.1850–1910, *Colonel John Russell (1618–1687)*, unknown acquisition method

Russell, Laura c.1850–1910, *Elizabeth Keppell (1739–1768), Marchioness of Tavistock (copy of Thomas Gainsborough)*, unknown acquisition method

Russell, Laura c.1850–1910, *Francis Russell (1788–1861), 7th Duke of Bedford*, unknown acquisition method

Russell, Laura c.1850–1910, *George Byng (1830–1898), Viscount Enfield, MP for Tavistock (1852–1857)*, unknown acquisition method

Russell, Laura c.1850–1910, *John Russell (1710–1771), 4th Duke of Bedford*, unknown acquisition method

Russell, Laura c.1850–1910, *John Russell (1766–1839), 6th Duke of Bedford*, unknown acquisition method

Russell, Laura c.1850–1910, *Sir John Trelaway (1816–1885), MP for Tavistock (1843–1852 & 1857–1865)*, unknown acquisition method

Russell, Laura c.1850–1910, *William Lord Russell (1639–1683)*

unknown artist *John Rundle (1791–1864), MP for Tavistock (1835–1843)*, by public subcription, 1856

unknown artist *Alfred Rooker (1814–1875)*, unknown acquisition method

unknown artist *Portrait of a Gentleman*, unknown acquisition method

unknown artist *Portrait of a Gentleman*, unknown acquisition method

unknown artist *Sir Richard Edgcumbe (1440–1489)*, unknown acquisition method

Teignmouth & Shaldon Museum: Teign Heritage

Armstrong, Thomas 1832–1911, *The Ness, Teignmouth, Devon*, gift from Torre Abbey, 2002

Chatfield, Donald Graham 1933–2007, *Fokke Wulfe German Aircraft Approaching Teignmouth*, purchased, 1999, © the artist's estate

Francis, B. *The Newquay Inn*, unknown acquistion method

Lawrence, Thomas 1769–1830, *The Right Honourable Edward Pellew (1757–1833), 1st Viscount Exmouth, Vice-Admiral of England*, on loan from Mark Pellew

Luny, Thomas 1759–1837, *Teignmouth Beach and Ness Point, Devon*, purchased with the assistance of the National Art Collection Fund, the Victoria and Albert Museum Purchase Grant Fund, donations from the Museum and Historical Society

members, and residents of Teignmouth, 1998

Luny, Thomas (circle of) 1759–1837, *Teignmouth Regatta, Devon*, purchased, 2001

Teignmouth Town Council

Egginton, Wycliffe 1875–1951, *Autumn Splendour*, unknown acquisition method

Haywood, Michael Graham b.1950, *Admiral Sir Edward Pellew (1757–1833), 1st Viscount Exmouth (after Samuel Drummond)*, presented by the artist, © the artist

Huggins, William John 1781–1845, *HMS 'Indefatigable' Accompanied by HM 'Amazon' Attacking the French Ship 'Les droits des hommes'*, unknown acquisition method

Loos, John Frederick active 1861–1902, *The Barque 'Eldra'*, unknown acquisition method

Luny, Thomas 1759–1837, *Off Dartmouth, Devon*, unknown acquisition method

Luny, Thomas 1759–1837, *Shipwreck at Teignmouth, Devon*, unknown acquisition method

Luny, Thomas 1759–1837, *Figures on a Beach Unloading Barrels from a Small Boat*, unknown acquisition method

Luny, Thomas 1759–1837, *Fishing Boats in Teignmouth Harbour, Devon*, unknown acquisition method

Luny, Thomas (attributed to) 1759–1837, *Self Portrait*, presented to Teignmouth Town Council by the daughters of Frederick Robert Haswell

Moyle, J. Alfred active late 19th C, *Tol-Pedn-Penwith, Porthgwarra, Cornwall*, unknown acquisition method

Walter, Joseph (style of) 1783–1856, *The 'Eliza' of Teignmouth in an Open Sea*, unknown acquisition method

Anglo-Polish Organisation

K., D. active 2005, *Krakow Market, Poland*, gift, 2009

unknown artist *Folk Painting with Birds*, gift from Gilpin Demolition, 2009

unknown artist *Folk Painting with Cockerels*, gift from Gilpin Demolition, 2009

unknown artist *Folk Painting with Deer*, gift from Gilpin Demolition, 2009

unknown artist *Folk Painting with Flowers*, gift from Gilpin Demolition, 2009

unknown artist *Folk Painting with Flowers*, gift from Gilpin Demolition, 2009

unknown artist *Folk Painting with Flowers*, gift from Gilpin Demolition, 2009

unknown artist *Folk Painting with*

Flowers, gift from Gilpin Demolition, 2009

unknown artist *Folk Painting with Sunflowers*, gift from Gilpin Demolition, 2009

Tiverton Museum of Mid Devon Life

Armstrong, Gordon *The Angel Hotel, the Square, Witheridge, Devon (painted in Starkey, Knight and Ford colours)*, gift from Eileen Voce, 2006

Day, George *Thomas Gamlen, Esq. (1759–1835), of Hayne (copy of an original painting by Ayerst)*, gift from Reverend P. E. Blagdon-Gamlen, 1987

Greenhalgh, Stephanie *Mr James Mclachlan, Former Honorary President of Tiverton Museum (d.1998)*, gift from the artist, 1999

Hudson (Mrs) *G. C. Greenway*, gift from Lady Sheelagh Greenway

Palce, John *Portrait of a Man (said to be the last of the woolen weavers of Tiverton)*, gift from E. B. Hamlin

Pembrey, R. G. *View of Collipriest Walk and a Bridge over a River, Tiverton, Devon*, unknown acquisition method

unknown artist *'Glory', Devon Longwool Ram*, unknown acquisition method

unknown artist *'Matchless'*, unknown acquisition method

unknown artist *15lb Pike Caught in Tiverton Canal in 1905*, gift from Arthur Morton Moncrieff

unknown artist *22lb Pike Caught in Tiverton Canal in 1906*, gift from Arthur Morton Moncrieff

Wannell, F. *Tiverton Railway Station, Devon*, gift from the artist

Weatherley, Dudley Graham 1912–2004, *The Grand Western Canal at Snake Wood*, gift from Mrs Winter, 1999, © the artist's estate

Weatherley, Dudley Graham 1912–2004, *Panoramic View of Tiverton, Devon, Seen from the High Ground at Ashley, Showing the River Exe and Local Landmarks*, on loan from C. J. Weatherley, © the artist's estate

Wickham, Peter 1934–2009, *Tiverton Townscape, Devon*, purchased, 1998

Woolnar, John *Derick Heathcoat-Amory (1899–1981), 1st Viscount Amory*, gift from Lowman Enterprises

Woolnar, John *John Heathcoat-Amory (1829–1914), 1st Bt*, gift from Lowman Enterprises

Tiverton Town Hall

Eastman, Mary b.1921, *Sir Derick Heathcoat-Amory (1899–1981), 4th Bt, Viscount Amory*, unknown acquisition method

Eastman, Mary b.1921, *Sir John Heathcoat-Amory (1894–1972), 3rd*

Bt, unknown acquisition method

Kneller, Godfrey (after) 1646–1723, *George I (1720–1727)*, unknown acquisition method

Mercier, Charles 1834–1909, *Right Honourable W. N. Massey, MP for Tiverton (1872–1880)*, unknown acquisition method

Ramsay, Allan 1713–1784, *George III (1738–1820) (when Prince Regent)*, unknown acquisition method

Reynolds, Joshua 1723–1792, *George III (1738–1820)*, unknown acquisition method

Roden, William Thomas 1817–1892, *Henry John Temple (1784–1865), 3rd Viscount Palmerston, KG, GCB, PC, Prime Minister (1835–1865)*, unknown acquisition method

unknown artist *Portrait of a Gentleman*, unknown acquisition method

unknown artist *Portrait of a Gentleman*, unknown acquisition method

unknown artist *Francis Hole, Esq., JP, Mayor of Tiverton*, presented by Lord Palmerston

unknown artist *George II (1727–1760)*, unknown acquisition method

unknown artist *George W. Cockram, JP, Mayor of Tiverton (1875–1877)*, unknown acquisition method

unknown artist *Sir John Heathcoat, Esq., JP, MP for Tiverton (1832–1959)*, gift from the inhabitants of Tiverton

unknown artist *Sir John Heathcoat-Amory (1829–1914), Bt, MP for Tiverton (1868–1885)*, gift from John Cray, 1907

unknown artist *Thomas Ford, JP, Mayor of Tiverton (1881–1883)*, unknown acquisition method

unknown artist *William Hornsey Gamlen, Esq., of Hayne Aged 29, Mayor of Tiverton (1843–1844)*, unknown acquisition method

Webster, John b.1932, *HMS 'Hermes' after Conversion to a Commando Carrier and an Anti-Submarine Helicopter Ship*, unknown acquisition method, © the artist

Topsham Museum

Boyle, Geraldine Lilian (attributed to) 1899–1992, *Portrait of a Man in a Green Jacket over a Pullover*, part of Miss Holman's Museum Collection, bequeathed by Dorothy Holman to Exeter City Council, 1983

Brice, Henry c.1831–1903, *Jane Bramah Popham (1841–1874)*, gift from John Popham, the sitter's great grandson, 1998

Croos, Pieter van der (school of) 1609–1701, *River Landscape with Travellers near a Wood*, presented by Lutece Foundation through the Art Fund, 1986

Cullin, E. M. *George Henry Voysey (1902–1975), a Topsham Fisherman*, gift from the Estuary League of Friends, 1996

Elliott, Robinson 1814–1894, *Francis Robert Newton Haswell (1834–1912) and Eleanor Mary Haswell (1837–1917), later Holman*, bequeathed by Dorothy Holman to the Friends of Exeter Museums and Art Gallery, 1983; transferred to Exeter City Council, 1993

Harding, Sophie 1902–1995, *Dorothy Holman (1888–1983), Founder of Topsham Museum*, gift from Caroline Oboussier, the artist's daughter, 1994

Harding, Sophie 1902–1995, *Morice Parsons (1913–1998)*, gift from Philip G. Parsons, the sitter's son, 1998

Hiscocks, John *Tom Putt Apples*

Holman, Dorothy A. 1888–1983, *Mrs Sophia Hawkes Holman, née Andrew (1863–1928), Lady in an Armchair*, bequeathed by Dorothy Holman to the Friends of Exeter Museums and Art Gallery, 1983; transferred to Exeter City Council, 1993

Holman, Dorothy A. 1888–1983, *Welsh Pony 'Bessie'*, bequeathed by Dorothy Holman to the Friends of Exeter Museums and Art Gallery, 1983; transferred to Exeter City Council, 1993

Hughes, Nathaniel John Baird 1865–1936, *Mrs Sophia Hawkes Holman, née Andrew (1863–1928), Lady in a Red Dress*, bequeathed by Dorothy Holman to the Friends of Exeter Museums and Art Gallery, 1983; transferred to Exeter City Council, 1993

King, Christopher active 1987, *Three Tom Putt Apples*, gift from the artist, 1987

Reynolds, Joshua (copy after) 1723–1792, *Nativity Scene*, bequeathed by Dorothy Holman to the Friends of Exeter Museums and Art Gallery, 1983; transferred to Exeter City Council, 1993

Simmonds-Roads, Juliette 1900–1995, *Roofs of Topsham, Devon*, part of Miss Holman's Museum Collection, bequeathed by Dorothy Holman to Exeter City Council, 1983

unknown artist *Barque 'Hugh Fortescue', Built in Topsham in 1865 by John Holman & Sons for the China Trade*, part of Miss Holman's Museum Collection, bequeathed by Dorothy Holman to Exeter City Council, 1983

unknown artist *Steamship 'Sam Handford'*, gift from Teignmouth Museum, 1996

unknown artist mid 19th C, *John Westcott (c.1794–1878), Shapter St Gardens, Grower of Excelsior Strawberry*, gift from Gerald May to the Holman Collection, 1977; bequeathed by Dorothy Holman to Exeter City Council, 1983

unknown artist *Screw-Powered Schooner 'City of Exeter', Built in 1870 for John Holman and Sons*, gift from Violet Johnson to the Holman Collection, 1970; bequeathed by Dorothy Holman to Exeter City Council, 1983

unknown artist *Thomas Andrew (1831–1902), Maternal Grandfather of Dorothy Holman*, bequeathed by Dorothy Holman to the Friends of Exeter Museums and Art Gallery, 1983; transferred to Exeter City Council, 1993

Voysey, Eric b.1930, *Fast and Free*, gift from the artist to the Holman Collection, 1972; bequeathed by Dorothy Holman to Exeter City Council, 1983

Totnes Elizabethan House Museum

Barker, Benjamin II 1776–1838, *Town Mills, Totnes, Devon*, unknown acquisition method

Clark, A. *'Phantom'*, gift from Mr Hayford-Irish

Hendry, William Leslie 1891–1981, *Totnes, Devon, Goes Elizabethan*, unknown acquisition method

Hilliard, Nicholas 1537–1619, *Christopher Wise (c.1566–1628), Mayor of Totnes (1605 & 1621)*, gift from Mrs Milner

King, Edward R. 1863–after 1924, *River Dart*, unknown acquisition method

Maclagan, Philip Douglas 1901–1972, *View from Shell Field, Totnes, Devon*, unknown acquisition method, © the artist's estate

Morgan, T. *Rosina, Mrs W. Cole*, unknown acquisition method

Morgan, T. C. *Totnes House, Devon*, gift from Mrs Yvonne Fryer

Pitman, William *Ruined Gate*, unknown acquisition method

Pitman, William *The Walk, Totnes, Devon*, unknown acquisition method

Snowden, Hilda Mary 1910–1997, *Beachy Head, East Sussex*, unknown acquisition method

Sulway, Joy *Two Owls*, unknown acquisition method

unknown artist *The Town Mill*, gift from Mrs Yvonne Fryer

unknown artist *John Trist of Hannaford*, on loan from John Peirson

unknown artist *Reverend John Trist (1718–1781), MA, Vicar of Veryan*, on loan from John Peirson

unknown artist *Totnes Town Mill, Devon*, gift from Mrs Yvonne Fryer

Totnes Guildhall

Brockedon, William 1787–1854, *Ossian Relating the Fate of Oscar to Malvina (from 'The Poems of Ossian' by James Macpherson)*, unknown acquisition method

Brockedon, William 1787–1854, *Self Portrait*, presented to the Corporation of Totnes by Edward Windeatt, 1897

Ford, E. C. *Charles Stanley Jacka (1893–1970), Mayor of Totnes (1950–1951)*, unknown acquisition method

Honeywill, Paul Douglas 1949–2002, *Councillor Rendle Crang (1933–2005), Town Mayor (1986–1988) and Mrs Eileen Crang (b.1935), Mayoress (1997–1999)*, unknown acquisition method

Norman, A. *Councillor Bill Bennett (1927–2004), MBE*, unknown acquisition method

Simpson, Doris *The Butterwalk, Totnes, Devon*, unknown acquisition method

unknown artist *Captain William Short (1762–1825)*, presented by James Gill, Mayor of Totnes, 1857

unknown artist *Christopher Maynard (1577–1635), Mayor of the Borough of Totnes (1632) or Christopher Maynard (d.1669), Mayor of the Borough of Totnes (1648, 1658 & 1665)*, presented to the Corporation of Totnes by F. B. Mildway, 1889

unknown artist *Frederick Bowden (1819–1903), Mayor of Totnes (1883)*, unknown acquisition method

unknown artist *Portrait of a Man*, unknown acquisition method

unknown artist *Portrait of a Woman*, unknown acquisition method

Totnes Hospital

Carter, Peter J. *Architectural Abstract*, presented by Joanna Carter in memory of her husband, 1997

Carter, Peter J. *Steamer Quay, Totnes, Devon*, presented by Mr George and Mrs Ruth Reeves, 1997

Kirk, R. *Totnes, Devon*, donated by Rendells Auctioneers to improve the environment for patients and staff alike

Collection Addresses

Appledore

Appledore Library
The Quay, Appledore EX39 1QS
Telephone 01237 477442

North Devon Maritime Museum
Odun House, Odun Road, Appledore EX39 1PT
Telephone 01237 422064

Ashburton

Ashburton & Buckfastleigh Community Hospital
Eastern Road, Ashburton TQ13 7AP
Telephone 01364 652203

Axminster

Axminster Guildhall
West Street, Axminster EX13 5NX
Telephone 01297 32088

Axminster Heritage
Thomas Whitty House, Silver Street
Axminster EX13 5AH
Telephone 01297 32417

Axminster Hospital
Chard Road, Axminster EX13 5DU
Telephone 01392 356900

Axminster Museum
The Old Courthouse, Church Street
Axminster EX13 5AQ

Barnstaple

Barnstaple Town Council:

Barnstaple Guildhall
The Square, Barnstaple EX32 8LS
Telephone 01271 373311

Museum of Barnstaple and North Devon
The Square, Barnstaple EX32 8LN
Telephone 01271 346747

North Devon Athenaeum
Tuly Street, Barnstaple EX31 1EL
Telephone 01271 342174

North Devon Council:

Barnstaple, Civic Centre
North Walk, Barnstaple EX31 1EA
Telephone 01271 327711

Penrose Almshouses
Barnstaple Municipal Charities, 15 Penrose Square,
Barnstaple EX32 8NH
Telephone 01271 329879

Bideford

Bideford Library
New Road, Bideford EX39 2HR
Telephone 01237 476075

Bideford Town Council:

Bideford Town Hall
Bridge Street, Bideford EX39 2HS
Telephone 01237 428817

Burton Art Gallery and Museum
Kingsley Road, Bideford EX39 2QQ
Telephone 01237 471455

Bovey Tracey

Bovey Tracey Heritage Trust:

Bovey Tracey Heritage Centre
The Old Railway Station, St John's Lane,
Bovey Tracey TQ13 9GP
Telephone 01626 835078

Braunton

Braunton & District Museum
The Bakehouse Centre, Caen Street, Braunton
EX33 1AA
Telephone 01271 816688

Buckfastleigh

Buckfastleigh Town Hall
Bossell Road, Buckfastleigh TQ11 0DD
Telephone 01364 642576

Budleigh Salterton

Budleigh Salterton Town Council
Council Offices, Station Road, Budleigh Salterton EX9 6RJ
Telephone 01395 442245

Fairlynch Museum
27 Fore Street, Budleigh Salterton EX9 6NP
Telephone 01395 442666

Crediton

Crediton Area History and Museum Society
Downes House, Crediton EX17 3PL
Telephone 01363 774441

Dartmouth

Britannia Royal Naval College
Dartmouth TQ6 0HJ
Telephone 01803 677233

Dartmouth and Kingswear Hospital
Mansion House Street, South Embankment
Dartmouth TQ6 9BD
Telephone 01803 832255

Dartmouth Guildhall
Victoria Road, Dartmouth TQ6 9RY
Telephone 01803 832281

Dartmouth Museum
6 The Butterwalk, Duke Street, Dartmouth TQ6 9PZ
Telephone 01803 832923

Dawlish

Dawlish Community Hospital
Dawlish EX7 9DH
Telephone 01626 868500

Dawlish Museum Society:

> Dawlish Museum
> The Knowle, Barton Terrace, Dawlish EX7 9QH
> Telephone 01626 888557

Dawlish Town Council:
Manor House, Old Town Street, Dawlish EX7 9AP
Telephone 01626 863388

East Budleigh

Bicton College
East Budleigh, Budleigh Salterton EX9 7BY
Telephone 01395 562300

Exeter

Dean and Chapter, Exeter Cathedral
The Deanery, 10 Cathedral Close, Exeter EX1 1EZ
Telephone 01392 273509

Devon & Somerset Fire & Rescue Service
Service Headquarters, The Knowle, Clyst St George
Exeter EX3 0NW
Telephone 01392 872200

Devon County Council:

> Devon County Hall
> Topsham Road, Exeter EX2 4QD
> Telephone 01392 382504

Devon Record Office
Great Moor House, Bittern Road, Sowton
Exeter EX2 7NL
Telephone 01392 384253

Exeter Guildhall
The Guildhall, High Street, Exeter EX4 3EB
Telephone 01392 665500

Exeter Royal Academy for Deaf Education
50 Topsham Road, Exeter EX2 4NF
Telephone 01392 267023

Larkbeare House
Topsham Road, Exeter EX2 4NG
Telephone 01392 382517

Royal Albert Memorial Museum
Queen Street, Exeter EX4 3RX
Telephone 01392 665858

Royal Devon and Exeter Hospital
Barrack Road, Exeter EX2 5DW
Telephone 01392 411611

The Devonshire and Dorset Regimental Charitable Trust:

> The Rifles Exeter Office
> Wyvern Barracks, Exeter
> EX2 6AR
> Telephone 01392 492436

The Met Office
FitzRoy Road, Exeter EX1 3PB
Telephone 01392 885680

The Palace, Exeter
The Palace, Exeter EX1 1HY
Telephone 01392 272362

University of Exeter, Fine Art Collection
Queen's Building, The Queen's Drive, Exeter EX4 4QH
Telephone 01392 661000

Wonford House Hospital
Dryden Road, Exeter EX2 5AF
Telephone 01392 403433

Exmouth

Exmouth Library
40 Exeter Road, Exmouth EX8 1PS
Telephone 01395 272677

Exmouth Museum
Sheppards Row, Exmouth EX8 1PW
Telephone 07768 184127

Exmouth Town Council:

> Exmouth Town Hall
> St Andrews Road, Exmouth EX8 1AW
> Telephone 01395 276167

Great Torrington

Great Torrington Almshouse, Town Lands and Poors Charities:

> Torrington Town Hall Office
> High Street, Torrington EX38 8HN
> Telephone 01805 623517

Great Torrington Heritage Museum and Archive
c/o The Post Office, Fore Street
Great Torrington EX38 8HJ

Holsworthy

Holsworthy Museum
Manor Offices, Holsworthy EX22 6DJ
Telephone 01409 259337

Honiton

Allhallows Museum
High Street, Honiton EX14 1PG
Telephone 01404 44966

Honiton Hospital
Marlpit Road, Honiton EX14 2DD
Telephone 01404 540540

Honiton Library
48–50 New Street, Honiton EX14 1BS
Telephone 01404 42818

Honiton Town Council
New Street, Honiton EX14 1EY
Telephone 01404 42957

Ilfracombe

Ilfracombe Museum
Wilder Road, Ilfracombe EX34 8AF
Telephone 01271 863541

Ilfracombe Town Council:

> The Ilfracombe Centre
> High Street, Ilfracombe EX34 8AL
> Telephone 01271 855300

Kingsbridge

Cookworthy Museum
The Old Grammar School, 108 Fore Street
Kingsbridge TQ7 1AW
Telephone 01548 853235

Kingsbridge Town Council:

> Quay House
> Ilbert Road, Kingsbridge TQ7 1DZ
> Telephone 01548 853296

Lifton

The Fairground Heritage Trust:

> The Dingles Fairground Heritage Centre
> Milford, Lifton PL16 0AT
> Telephone 01566 783425

Lynton

Lynton and Lynmouth Town Council:

> Lynton Town Hall
> Lee Road, Lynton EX35 6HT
> Telephone 01598 752384

Moretonhampstead

Moretonhampstead Hospital
Ford Street, Moretonhampstead TQ13 8LN
Telephone 01647 440217

Moretonhampstead Library
Fore Street, Moretonhampstead TQ13 8LL
Telephone 01647 440523

Newton Abbot

Ball Clay Heritage Society
Dunderdale Lawn, Penshurst Road
Newton Abbot TQ12 1EN
Telephone 01626 354404

Ilford Park Polish Home
Stover, Newton Abbot TQ12 6QH
Telephone 01626 353961

Newton Abbot Town & GWR Museum
2a St Paul's Road, Newton Abbot TQ12 2HP
Telephone 01626 201121

Newton Abbot Town Council:

> Great Western House
> 9 Devon Square, Newton Abbot TQ12 2HN
> Telephone 01626 201120

Teignbridge District Council:

> Forde House
> Brunel Road, Newton Abbot TQ12 4XX
> Telephone 01626 361101

> Old Forde House
> Brunel Road, Newton Abbot TQ12 4XX
> Telephone 01626 215747

Okehampton

Museum of Dartmoor Life, Okehampton
3 West Street, Okehampton EX20 1HQ
Telephone 01837 52295

Okehampton Town Council:

> Okehampton Town Hall
> Fore Street, Okehampton EX20 1AA
> Telephone 01837 53179

Ottery St Mary

Ottery St Mary Hospital
Keegan Close, Ottery St Mary EX11 1DN
Telephone 01404 816000

Princetown

Dartmoor Prison Museum
HMP Dartmoor, Princetown PL20 6RR
Telephone 01822 322130

Seaton

Seaton Hospital
Valley View, Scalwell Lane, Seaton EX12 2UU
Telephone 01392 356900

Sidmouth

Sidmouth Museum
Church Street, Sidmouth EX10 8LY
Telephone 01395 516139

Sidmouth Victoria Hospital
All Saints Road, Sidmouth EX10 8EW
Telephone 01395 512482

Tavistock

Tavistock Subscription Library
Court Gate, Guildhall Square, Tavistock PL19 0AE
Telephone 01822 612546

Tavistock Town Hall
Drake Road, Tavistock PL19 0AU
Telephone 01822 613529

Teignmouth

Teignmouth & Shaldon Museum: Teign Heritage
29 French Street, Teignmouth TQ14 8ST
Telephone 01626 777041

Teignmouth Town Council:

> Bitton House
> Teignmouth TQ14 9DF
> Telephone 01626 775030

Tiverton

Anglo-Polish Organisation
Grosvenor House, 25 St Peter Street, Tiverton EX16 6NW
Telephone 07891 239997

Tiverton Museum of Mid Devon Life
Beck's Square, Tiverton EX16 6PJ
Telephone 01884 256295

Tiverton Town Hall
St Andrews Street, Tiverton EX16 6PG
Telephone 01884 253404

Topsham

Topsham Museum
25 The Strand, Topsham, EX3 0AX
Telephone 01392 873244

Totnes

Totnes Elizabethan House Museum
70 Fore Street, Totnes TQ9 5RU
Telephone 01803 863821

Totnes Guildhall
Ramparts Walk, Totnes TQ9 5QH
Telephone 01803 862003

Totnes Hospital
Coronation Road, Totnes TQ9 5GH
Telephone 01803 862622

Index of Artists

In this catalogue, artists' names and the spelling of their names follow the preferred presentation of the name in the Getty Union List of Artist Names (ULAN) as of February 2004, if the artist is listed in ULAN.

The page numbers next to each artist's name below direct readers to paintings that are by the artist; are attributed to the artist; or, in a few cases, are more loosely related to the artist being, for example, 'after', 'the circle of' or copies of a painting by the artist. The precise relationship between the artist and the painting is listed in the catalogue.

Harris, L. (?) 4
Hart, F. (active 19th C) 135
Hart, Solomon Alexander (1806–1881) 135
Harvey, Harold C. (1874–1941) 184, 196
Hasler, F. 35
Hawker, Thomas (c.1640–c.1725) 135
Hawkins, Jane 282
Haydon, Benjamin Robert (1786–1846) 135, 137
Hayes-Valentine, Mary 227
Hayman, Francis (1708–1776) 137, 138
Hayman, John 138
Hayter, Stanley William (1901–1988) 138
Hayward, Alfred Frederick William (1856–1939) 45, 91
Haywood, Michael Graham (b.1950) 286
Heard, Hugh Percy (1866–1940) 45
Heard, Joseph (1799–1859) 5
Heem, Cornelis de (1631–1695) 272
Hendry, William Leslie (1891–1981) 299
Herkomer, Herman (1863–1935) 69
Heron, Patrick (1920–1999) 138, 196
Herring I, John Frederick (1795–1865) 272
Higson, Max 69
Hilliard, John Michael (b.1945) 197
Hilliard, Nicholas (1547–1619) 299
Hillier, Tristram Paul (1905–1983) 304
Hinds, Thorie Catherine (b.1958) 167, 168
Hiscocks, John 297
Hoare, C. T. 231
Hoare, William (1706–1792) 39, 168
Holden, M. G. 270, 271
Holder, Edward Henry (1847–1922) 138
Holding, Emmanuel 272
Holl, Frank (1845–1888) 139
Holman, Dorothy A. (1888–1983) 297
Holwill, Fred Cyril (1887–1980) 81
Honeywill, Paul Douglas (1949–2002) 302
Hoppner, John (1758–1810) 139
Hopwood 26
Horsley, Hopkins Horsley Hobday (1807–1890) 279
Houghton, Ruth 268
Howard-Jones, Ray (1903–1996) 139
Howell, A. (1877–1959) 244, 245
Howell, A. S. (1906–1966) 244, 245, 248, 249
Howell, June 197
Huckvale, Karen 213
Hudson, Esdaile (active 2004–2005) 8
Hudson, Thomas (1701–1779) 15, 16–18, 20, 64, 104, 105, 139, 168, 224, 225
Hudson (Mrs) 290
Huggins, William John (1781–1845) 287
Hughes, Arthur (1805–1838) 139
Hughes, Nathaniel John Baird (1865–1936) 297
Hughes, Robert Morson (1873–1953) 140
Hughes-Stanton, Herbert Edwin Pelham (1870–1937) 140
Hulbert, Thelma (1913–1995) 140, 141
Hullmandel, Charles Joseph (1789–1850) 216
Humphries, Amelia 9
Humphry, Ozias (1742–1810) 141
Hunt, Edgar (1876–1953) 45

Hunt, Edmund Aubrey (1855–1922) 45, 47, 48
Hunt (Miss), C. B. 81
Hunter, Colin (1841–1904) 48, 141
Hutchings, E. A. 87
Hynard, H. 216
Illsley, Bryan (b.1937) 141
Ing, Harold Vivian (1900–1973) 81
Ipsen, Ernest Ludwig (1869–1951) 141
Italian (Venetian) School 131
Jack, Richard (1866–1952) 27
Jackson, Kurt (b.1961) 177, 197
James, Clifford Boucher (d.1913) 48
Jamieson, A. 5
Jansch, Heather (b.1948) 271
Janssens van Ceulen, Cornelis (1593–1661) 20, 35
Jay, Peter 177, 178
Jeany, M. J. 197
Jenkins, Charles (c.1675–1739) 141
Jenkins, George Henry (1843–1914) 107, 232
Jenkins, Thomas (1722–1798) 141
Jennison, Robert (b.1933) 168, 197
Jewell, Catherine (active 1978–2003) 197, 198
Johns, Ambrose Bowden (1776–1858) 142
Johns, Ewart (b.1923) 198
Johnson, Colin Trevor (b.1942) 198
Johnson, Desmond (b.1922) 69
Jones, Patrick (b.1948) 48
K., D. (active 2005) 289
Keenan, John (active 1780–1819) 168
Kemp-Welch, Lucy (1869–1958) 142
Kennedy, Joseph (c.1838–1893) 20, 27, 29, 34
Kerseboom, Johann (d.1708) 225
Kieling, M. 99
King, Charles (b.1912) 39
King, Christopher (active 1987) 297
King, Edward R. (1863–after 1924) 299
Kinsella, Katherine 198
Kirk, R. 303
Kite, Joseph Milner (1862–1946) 142
Klingenberg, I. 226
Knapton, George (1698–1778) 93
Kneale, Bryan (b.1930) 142
Kneller, Godfrey (1646–1723) 142, 181, 225, 294
Knight, Harold (1874–1961) 93
Knight, John Prescott (1803–1881) 142, 169
Knight, John William Buxton (1842/1843–1908) 48
Knightly (Mrs), L. M. 277
Knowles, Gwen 213
Knox, Jack (b.1936) 142, 163
Konkell, E. 173
Kurzweil, T. 273
Ladell, Edward (1821–1886) 142
Lady Abercromby 69
Lakin & Co., R. J. 252
Lakin & Co. (Edwin Hall), R. J. 250–251
Lamb, Henry (1883–1960) 142
Lane, F. 282
Langhorne, Mary (1909–1984) 143

Acknowledgements

The Public Catalogue Foundation would like to thank the individual artists and copyright holders for their permission to reproduce for free the paintings in this catalogue. Exhaustive efforts have been made to locate the copyright owners of all the images included within this catalogue and to meet their requirements. Copyright credit lines for copyright owners who have been traced are listed in the Further Information section.

The Public Catalogue Foundation would like to express its great appreciation to the following organisations for their kind assistance in the preparation of this catalogue:

Bridgeman Art Library
Flowers East
Marlborough Fine Art
National Association of Decorative & Fine Arts Societies (NADFAS)
National Gallery, London
National Portrait Gallery, London
Royal Academy of Arts, London
Tate

The participating collections included in this catalogue would like to express their thanks to the following organisations and individuals who have so generously enabled them to acquire paintings featured in this catalogue:

Buckfastleigh Town Hall Trust
Mary Chugg
Mrs Maria Cymbrykiewicz (deceased)
The People of Dawlish
Devon Libraries
Devon County Council
Devon Community Foundation
Community Council of Devon
Mid Devon District Council
Exeter City Council
Sir David Hoare
Holsworthy Museum Society
Ilford Park Polish Home
National Art Collections Fund (The Art Fund)
Sid Vale Trust
Totnes Town Council
Totnes Museum Trust
The Victoria and Albert Museum Purchase Grant Fund

The Public Catalogue Foundation

The Public Catalogue Foundation is a registered charity. It was launched in 2003 to create a photographic record of the entire national collection of oil, tempera and acrylic paintings in public ownership in the United Kingdom.

Whilst our public galleries and civic buildings hold arguably the greatest collection of oil paintings in the world, over 80 per cent of these are not on view. Few collections have a complete photographic record of their paintings let alone a comprehensive illustrated catalogue. What is publicly owned is not publicly accessible.

The Foundation is publishing a series of fully illustrated, county-by-county catalogues that will cover, eventually, the entire national UK collection. To date, it has published over 30 volumes, presenting over 72,000 paintings.

In partnership with the BBC, the Foundation will make its database of the entire UK collection of 200,000 oil paintings available online through a new website called *Your Paintings*. The website was launched in the summer of 2011.

Your Paintings (*www.bbc.co.uk/arts/yourpaintings*) offers a variety of ways of searching for paintings as well as further information about the paintings and artists, including links to the participating collections' websites. For those interested in paintings and the subjects they portray *Your Paintings* is an unparalleled learning resource.

Collections benefit substantially from the work of the Foundation, not least from the digital images that are given to them for free following photography, and from the increased recognition that the project brings. These substantial benefits come at no financial cost to the collections.

The Foundation is funded by a combination of support from individuals, charitable trusts, companies and the public sector although the latter provides less than 20 per cent of the Foundation's financial support.

Supporters

Master Patrons

The Public Catalogue Foundation is greatly indebted to the following Master Patrons who have helped it in the past or are currently working with it to raise funds for the publication of their county catalogues. All of them have given freely of their time and have made an enormous contribution to the work of the Foundation.

Peter Andreae (*Hampshire*)
Sir Henry Aubrey-Fletcher, Bt, Lord Lieutenant of Buckinghamshire (*Buckinghamshire*)
Sir Nicholas Bacon, DL, High Sheriff of Norfolk (*Norfolk*)
Sir John Bather, Lord Lieutenant of Derbyshire (*Derbyshire*)
The Hon. Mrs Bayliss, JP, Lord Lieutenant of Berkshire (*Berkshire*)
Ian Bonas (*County Durham*)

Peter Bretherton (*West Yorkshire: Leeds*)
Michael Brinton, Lord Lieutenant of Worcestershire (*Worcestershire*)
Sir Hugo Brunner, KCVO, JP (*Oxfordshire*)
Mr John Bush, OBE, Lord-Lieutenant of Wiltshire (*Wiltshire*)
Lady Butler (*Warwickshire*)
Richard Compton (*North Yorkshire*)
George Courtauld, DL, Vice Lord Lieutenant of Essex (*Essex*)

Financial support

The Public Catalogue Foundation is particularly grateful to the following organisations and individuals who have given it generous financial support since the project started in 2003.

National Sponsor

Christie's

Benefactors (£10,000–£50,000)

The 29th May 1961 Charitable Trust
Arts Council England
The Barbour Trust
Binks Trust
City of Bradford Metropolitan District Council
Deborah Loeb Brice Foundation
The Bulldog Trust
A. & S. Burton 1960 Charitable Trust
Christie's
City of London Corporation
The John S. Cohen Foundation
Covent Garden London
Creative Scotland
Department for Culture, Media and Sport

Sir Harry Djanogly, CBE
Mr Lloyd Dorfman
Dunard Fund
The Elmley Foundation
Fenwick Ltd
Fidelity UK Foundation
Marc Fitch Fund
The Foyle Foundation
J. Paul Getty Jr Trust
Hampshire County Council
The Charles Hayward Foundation
Peter Harrison Foundation
Mr Robert Hiscox
Hiscox plc
David Hockney, CH, RA
ICAP plc

Sir Idris Pearce
Roger Neville Russ Peers
The Pennycress Trust
Perkins Family
The Lord & Lady Phillimore
Mrs Margaret Pollett
Simon & Ursula Pomeroy
The Portland Family
Portsmouth City Council
George Pragnell Ltd
The Prince Philip Trust Fund for the
    Royal Borough of Windsor and
    Maidenhead
Provident Financial plc
Mr John Rank
Rathbone Investment Management
    Ltd
The Hans and Märit Rausing
    Charitable Trust
Roger & Jane Reed
Renaissance North East
Renaissance South East
Renaissance South West
Michael Renshall, CBE, MA, FCA
Sir John Riddell
Sir Miles & Lady Rivett-Carnac
Rockley Charitable Trust
Rolls-Royce plc
The Roper Family Charitable Trust
Rothschild Foundation
Royal Cornwall Museum
Graham & Ann Rudd
Sir Nigel Rudd
Russell New
The J. S. & E. C. Rymer Charitable
    Trust
The Earl St Aldwyn
The Sammermar Trust
Scarfe Charitable Trust
Andrew & Belinda Scott
The Trustees of the Finnis Scott
    Foundation
Shaftesbury PLC
Mr W. Sharpe
The Shears Foundation
Robert Shields, DL
Smith & Williamson

South West of England Regional
    Development Agency
Caroline M. Southall
Stuart M. Southall
Southampton City Council
The Jessie Spencer Trust
Hugh & Catherine Stevenson
Mrs Andrew Stewart-Roberts, OBE
Mr Michael Stone
Mr Peter Stormonth Darling
The Stratford-upon-Avon Town
    Trust
Strutt and Parker
Suffolk County Council, through the
    Association for Suffolk Museums
Surrey County Council
The John Swire 1989 Charitable
    Trust
The Tanner Trust
Tennants Auctioneers
Tesco Charity Trust
The Thistle Trust
Prof. Caroline Tisdall
Trusthouse Charitable Foundation
Gladwyn Turbutt
TWM Business Partners
Tyne & Wear Museums
University College Falmouth
University of Derby
University of Essex
David & Grizelda Vermont
Wakefield Metropolitan District
    Council
Robert & Felicity Waley-Cohen
The Peggy Walker Charitable Trust
The Walland Trust Fund
John Wates Charitable Trust
Leslie Weller, DL
The Welton Foundation
West Sussex County Council
Mr & Mrs David Wigglesworth
Wilkin & Sons Ltd
Mr & Mrs Jo Windsor
Peter Wolton Charitable Trust
Michael J. Woodhall, FRICS
Sir Philip Wroughton
Mrs Angela Yeoman

First published in 2012 by The Public Catalogue
Foundation, Printed Catalogue Division,
8 Frederick's Place, London, EC2R 8AB

Devon photography:
Ian Wilkinson

Printed in Hong Kong by Paramount Printing
Company Limited